MIRACLES

PAST AND PRESENT

BY

WILLIAM MOUNTFORD

BOSTON
FIELDS, OSGOOD, & CO.
1870

Entered according to Act of Congress, in the year 1870, by
WILLIAM MOUNTFORD,
in the Clerk's Office of the District Court of the District of Massachusetts.

UNIVERSITY PRESS: WELCH, BIGELOW, & CO.,
CAMBRIDGE.

PREFACE.

THE subject of the Supernatural has engaged my attention, as a student, during many years. It grew upon me as to importance, and deepened as to interest, while I was at Rome, where, like St. Paul, I dwelt two years in my own hired house. This book, which I offer to the public, was written simply because the times seemed to be asking for some such work. And, as nobody else was answering to the call of the times, it occurred to me suddenly, one morning, some sixteen months ago, that perhaps I might myself be not quite clear of the summons. Doubtless a better man than I am was called upon, and a better book was asked for than what I have to offer. I confess that I feel so. And let this acknowledgment be accepted as an apology for such a venture as this is upon such a theme.

Some persons have wondered that I should have attempted to strengthen my argument by availing myself of the phenomena of Spiritualism as evidence of there being about us a sphere of life altogether different from this of nature, and for which science has no methods nor instruments, and for which, therefore, it should not have even one word of denial, or even of doubt. Those phenomena may be called ridiculous, or they may be called demoniac;

but at least and certainly they are cosmical. And, indeed, if I had ignored the subject of Spiritualism because of its being unpopular, how could I ever have borne afterwards to think of Henry More, or of Richard Baxter, or of John Wesley, or his dear brother Charles? Or how could I ever again have consulted Ralph Cudworth, as to the Intellectual System of the Universe? Or how could I have remembered, thenceforth, without shame, the Christian writers from Hermas to Augustine? Or how could I have endured a life among books, when all those, with the greater names, would have seemed to be saying, with one voice, "Thou shalt not bear false witness."

Perhaps I ought to say that I sympathize with the early Christians and their faith as to the Spirit, rather than with anything which I may have seen or heard in Rome, at Whitsuntide. St. Chrysostom says, in one of his homilies, delivered at Constantinople, probably towards the end of the fourth century, that there had been used to be a pause, during the service in the church, wherein for persons to rise, who were moved by the Spirit, and that that space had been closed, almost within his own time. Also after saying that many of the miraculous gifts of the early Church had been withdrawn, he says: "And among the rest, the gift of prayer, which was then distinguished by the name of the Spirit. And he that had this gift prayed for the whole congregation. Upon which account the apostle gives the name of the Spirit, both to this gift and to the soul that was endowed with it, who made intercession with groanings unto God, asking of God such things as were of general use and advantage to the whole congregation; the image and symbol of which now is the deacon, who offers up prayer for the people." Into that customary ancient place in the service, that deacon ought never perhaps to have been intruded. For even when there was in it nothing but silence, it was a place wherein for people to wonder, and to feel conscious of there having been something lost or suspended, as between the Church and its invisible Head.

However, that solemn significant pause, which anciently there was in the public services of the Church, would not have been endured in this present century. Of a certain period in the history of the Israelites, it is written that, in those days, "There was no open vision." But than the frankness of such a statement as that, spiritually, there is nothing which is more foreign to the world as it now is; for the world to-day thinks that, on account of its high civilization, the universe must surely be pledged to its support, in every way which is possible. And it thinks, also, that never could any age previously have been as open to light from every quarter as this present time is. However, the way, according to Chrysostom, in which the Church was closed against the Spirit, during the services on the Lord's day, should hint for us that there may have been also many other ways, by which Christians may have been discouraged from waiting on God, for the Spirit.

Earlier in the Church than Chrysostom, by some four or five generations, was Origen, and he wrote that "all who can say truly that they have risen with Christ, and been seated with him in the kingdom of heaven, live always in Pentecostal days." And as to public worship, very noteworthy is his opinion; for he says that the special advantage of public worship is, that individuals are thereby in communion with those who worship in the Spirit, and in the presence of the Lord and the holy angels; and he adds, "and as I think also of the spirits of the departed." That is a thought akin to the age, wherein originated the phrase of "the communion of saints."

The Church of the Future will be, of course, in some degree, a continuation of the Past; but it will specially be, earlier or later, a revival of the early Church, at its best. And this book has been written and is published under the persuasion that the voice of the early Church is as distinctly audible to-day as it ever was; and that, as far merely as the miraculous is concerned, the Scriptures, when fairly considered, at this present time, are as credible as ever they were.

W. M.

BOSTON, February 22, 1870.

CONTENTS.

MIRACLES PAST AND PRESENT.

THE ANTI-SUPERNATURALISM OF THE PRESENT AGE.

IT is proposed to consider the subject of miracles as connected with Christianity. And perhaps than this there is no religious topic which has been more variously and strangely treated, during the last century. And this is saying a great deal. For how has it fared with Christianity, and even at the hands of those, sometimes, by whom it has been accounted as the Tree of Life? Often, among other anomalous doings, it has been treated as though a gardener should take up a tree and turn it about, to humor every change of wind upon it; and as though, to prove it to be a living thing, he should lay bare its roots for every questioner, and even paint them, to make them more seemly.

Miracles are the possibilities of a miracle-bearing tree; but commonly they are regarded as though they were some arbitrary manufacture. In the New Testament they are simply called "signs and wonders"; but in this age, among both believers and unbelievers, it is agreed that they are suspensions of the laws of nature, or else are nothing. Miracles presuppose the existence of a spiritual world containing spiritual agents and spiritual forces; with laws peculiar to it, and with some laws also capable of intertwining and inosculating with some of the laws of man's nature and of the material world. And yet often, by even the advocates of their reality, miracles are argued wholly and simply as material occurrences, and quite apart from the philosophy of their nature, and, indeed, as though there were really no such philosophy known. And this is because of the spirit of the age, which is so strong in us all. For it is no matter what a man may be, whether philosopher, theologian, or anything else, almost inevitably in some way or other, the spirit of the age will have its say through him, and pervert, if not quench, his meaning.

No doubt, things have often been credited as miraculous which were no miracles at all. But the precise opposite of credulity is not wisdom, always. And if it be said that it is only at Naples that the blood of St. Januarius will liquefy, it may be answered that there has also been such a place as that in it, neither would "they be persuaded, though one rose from the dead." And to-day there are eminent places, where men hold that neither their own eyes, nor the eyes of all other persons, are to be trusted for a miracle, or, as they would say, for anything different from the laws of nature. But, with all their scepticism, these sceptics do not remember that a law of nature may be one thing, and their notion of that law be something else, or something a little different. But, indeed, when incredulity becomes as intense as that, it is self-confounded, self-confuted, even though it should be in regard to such a miracle as that which happened, when the axe-head fell into the water, and Elisha "cut down a stick and cast it in thither, and the iron did swim." For, if a man cannot trust his eyes and ears, how can he rely on his doubts? And how does he know but doubting his senses may be an unworthy, untrustworthy act, and even may, perhaps, be a mere nervous boggling? And how should even a materialist trust the wisdom which has been filtered for him, as he thinks, from outside, through his eyes and ears, if he cannot trust his eyes and ears themselves? But, in the spirit of his times or neighborhood, a man will think and hold what, under other influences, would have been for him only a speculative, tentative position. And because of its being in us and of us, the spirit of the age is the last thing to be suspected, as vitiating sound judgment.

It is in this spirit of the time to judge of everything by uniformity, whether as regards the world or mankind. And so, from what he understands to be the uniformity of the laws of nature, a man of the time thinks himself competent to check the report of the past, and decide that there never could have been water changed into wine, or a demon exorcised, because at this present time water is never seen changing into wine, nor a demon known to be dispossessed of his corporal lodgings. And because of what he fancies must be the uniformity of human nature, this man of the time thinks, too, that from himself he knows of everybody else, as to what they can have seen or cannot have seen; can have heard or cannot have heard; can have felt or cannot have felt; and in the same way, as differing from himself, he is certain that in the past they must all have been loose thinkers; and not the

Jews only, but the Greeks and Romans too, and even Socrates and Plato, because of their having reasoned about things which he himself has never met with, and which, if he did meet, he would never believe his own eyes about.

It is by availing himself of this temper of the times that largely Ernest Renan gets his strength as a controversialist; for what he has to say on the subject of miracles would have been but feeble talk anywhere, one or two hundred years ago, and would sound but inanely even to-day, in such regions as are clear away from the influence of Paris and London. "A miracle is not to be regarded, because it never could have happened; and because even if, perchance, it had happened, there never could have been any people who could have been believed about it." This, in form, is the argument of Renan. But, of course, it is good only for people of that way of thinking, only for persons sensitive to the spirit of the age, and who are ready to add, without another word, "And so I think, because so I am sure."

The following quotation is from the introductory chapter to "The Apostles," by Ernest Renan: "The first twelve chapters of the Acts are a tissue of miracles. It is an absolute rule in criticism to deny a place in history to narratives of miraculous circumstances; nor is this owing to a metaphysical system, for it is simply the dictation of observation. Such facts have never been really proved. All the pretended miracles near enough to be examined are referable to illusion or imposture. If a single miracle had ever been proved, we could not reject in a mass all those of ancient history; for, admitting that very many of these last were false, we might still believe that some of them were true. But it is not so. Discussion and examination are fatal to miracles. Are we not, then, authorized in believing that those miracles which date many centuries back, and regarding which there are no means of forming a contradictory debate, are also without reality? In other words, miracles only exist when people believe in them. The supernatural is but another word for faith. Catholicism, in maintaining that it yet possesses miraculous power, subjects itself to the influence of this law. The miracles of which it boasts never occur where they would be most effective. Why should not such a convincing proof be brought more prominently forward? A miracle at Paris, for instance, before experienced *savans*, would put an end to all doubt. But, alas! such a thing never happens." But, now, oracular though this might be, judged by the manner in which it has been bowed to, what is there in it all more than the mere sceptical spirit of the age? What does it do more than simply tickle the humor of the time? Psychologically, it is a curious passage, because the sweep of its intention is so wide; while the wording of it is so like the unconscious, innocent expression of a child. It is as though a boy, as the easier way of settling with a problem in mathematics, should say: "There is nothing in it. There never was anything learned from that direction. O my master, all the best boys have looked at it, and say that there is nothing in it, — nothing at all. And so, now, how can there be? And, please, even if it be true, it cannot really be unless we let it be." But here it may be asked, whether it is likely that Ernest Renan, as a boy, ever talked in that manner; and to this it may be answered, that it is very unlikely, considering that he was born in Brittany. And it is just as unlikely, too, that he could ever have written the preceding quotation from one of his works, but for his education, direct and indirect. For he was born in Brittany, a country of simple, fervent, unquestioning faith as to the Church. Thence he was carried to Paris, and placed in a primary theological school, whence he was passed on to a similar school elsewhere. Having finished with the latter school, he became a resident in the Seminary of St. Sulpice, which, indeed, inside, is wholly ordered by members of the Society of Jesus, but on the outside is pressed upon by the light, sceptical, and anti-Christian air of Paris. Ernest Renan had been brought up like a child of the Middle Ages, and then found himself, as a young man, where, with a few steps out of doors, he was in the atmosphere of Paris and under the influence of the Sorbonne. And now, with all this, was it not natural that Renan should have become a Rationalistic author instead of a Catholic priest? And because of his being a simple, earnest, intellectual man, was it not all the more natural still, that, by contrast with the air of St. Sulpice, he should mistake for the spirit of truth itself what was but the spirit of the age manifesting itself through a highly educated class, in a city singularly self-centred and self-sufficient?

But, says the critic here criticised, "A miracle at Paris before experienced *savans!*" Elsewhere, too, he explains more exactly what would suit him as to a miracle; that it should be wrought under conditions as to time and place, in a hall, and before a commission of physiologists, chemists, physicians, and critics; and that when it had been done once, it should, on request, be repeated. And no doubt, to the writer, this appeared to be a very fair way of dealing with miraculous pretensions; and no doubt, too, of his most emphatic opponents, there are many to whom, in their secret thought, it would be a puzzle, if such a proposition had been made to Jesus at Jerusalem, why it should not have been accepted at once for the market-place, or the court of the temple. For Renan is simply strong in that way of looking at things, which is characteristic of this present age, and which commonly is called sceptical, but which, also, sometimes is called practical and even business-like. Not jocosely, but in all seriousness, every now and then are put forth and read invitations to the miraculous such as that which Ernest Renan makes. One man writes in abstract, scientific terms, and another in plain English; but both one and the other mean the same thing. "Let miracles come to me in my study, and show themselves inside of my crucible, while my friends are all standing round, and at the moment exactly when it shall be said that we are all ready, and then I will believe; though of course, even then, I should not be absolutely forced to, but still I should, I think. And now what do you say to that?" And there really is nothing to say to it. Martin Luther, indeed, said once what probably he would have remarked again, if he had heard this scientific, common-sense proposal, that for certain, sometimes, over some of his creatures God Almighty must laugh.

But now, as to miracles, it is not pretended that they are absolutely at the ordering of any man as to time and place. But, indeed, is it so that science treats a subject, even less foreign to its own domain than miracles ?

Are earthquakes, as reports, accounted incredible, as not occurring at a time and a place known beforehand, and submissive to the directions of men with clocks and spirit-levels, and with magnetic and other machines all ready for use? And, indeed, a miracle coming to order would scarcely be a miracle. For, coming to order patiently, punctually, and as a scientific certainty, it would by that very fact have parted probably with something essential to its nature as commonly understood.

But really a Kamtschatkan, unmitigated and simple, arguing with Ernest Renan on Sanscrit, could not show himself more insensible as to the laws of philology than Renan shows himself on the subject of miracles; for he is utterly unconscious, apparently, of there being any philosophy connected with them, and of there being laws as to miracles, known more or less by some men in all ages, and as certain as gravitation.

But it may be asked how this can be, Renan being a very sensible writer. And so a man may write well on geometry, and yet show himself to be very stolid as to poetry, and even also as to those thoughts akin to the spiritual universe, which are suggested by the strange properties of numbers, or which come in upon the mind, like corollaries on the demonstration of certain problems. Thus, even by his constitution, Renan may have a strong, keen, serviceable, excellent sense of the life which Jesus lived as other men live, and yet be utterly insensible to the life of Jesus the Christ, as fed by the Spirit, and going forth in miracles, and incapable of seeing corruption. But, indeed, for his manner of writing the spirit of his age abundantly accounts, just as it accounts for some of the more fervent of his admirers, who like in his writings what is weakest, as much as they do what is best.

Of what use, it is asked, can miracles ever have been among people not fit to be believed about them, such as were the people of old time and the people of the Middle Ages, and such as are all the people of the provinces of France, and men of the people and men of the world everywhere? For, as Renan says, neither men of the world nor men of the people are "capable of establishing the miraculous character of an act." An act is what he says, any act, any miraculous act, and not merely some very recondite thing hard to notice. This is one of those general statements which often pass unchallenged, because nobody thinks that they can mean him; but it is not, therefore, the less mischievous. Perhaps there is not a man of the world who allows this opinion, as he reads it, but thinks, though he is no physician and has never been publicly recognized as critic, chemist, or physiologist, that somehow, certainly, he himself must have science and art enough, for being one of Renan's judges of the miraculous, and must have been intended, indeed, to be included amongst them. Physicians, physiologists, men of criticism and chemistry, men of science, the only competent judges as to miracles! For some conceivable miracles they might be; but for some others detective policemen would be far better witnesses. And, for still some other miracles, that men of the world, as judges, are inferior to chemists, —this is a sentiment which can come only from scientific folly, or from much learning gone mad. As to whether the true magnetic pole could be made to swerve for a moment in the heavens, professional men would be the better and perhaps the only proper judges. But men of the people and men of the world are as good judges as men of science on a miracle like this, which occurred in the wilderness: "His disciples say unto him, Whence should we have so much bread in the wilderness as to fill so great a multitude? And Jesus saith unto them, How many loaves have ye? And they said, Seven, and a few little fishes. And he commanded the multitude to sit down on the ground. And he took the seven loaves and the fishes, and gave thanks and break them, and gave to his disciples, and the disciples to the multitude. And they did all eat and were filled; and they took up of the broken meat that was left seven baskets full. And they that did eat were five thousand men, beside women and children."

But now what a want of taste and feeling it seems not to pause here for a little while, after such a glimpse into Galilee at that wonderful time. But it is not permitted, as the world now is, to those who know it theologically. For in comes, on the mind, the recollection of David F. Strauss, the famous writer on the Gospels, who says that he himself cannot believe in a miracle until he has had a solution of the philosophical views which he entertains against the possibility of such a thing. So that with him, even seeing would not be believing, unless, by good luck, there were some sophist standing by, more cunning than himself, who could unloose for him, in his mind, the knots of his own tying. Any man, down in the depths of learning, or up on the heights of science, in a difficulty of that kind, is to be pitied, because of the pains which he must have taken before he could have got there in his senses. But now for David F. Strauss himself pity is not the word, but sympathy. And the sympathy to be felt for him is profound, and as though for a pioneer in the grand advance of civilization, who had got bewildered in a thicket, and at whose position only they can laugh who cannot even faintly conjecture what it is to try a step forwards in theology under religious responsibility. Still, however, it is a certainty that such an avowal as that which Strauss makes of himself, is the self-exposure of "philosophy falsely so called."

And now let us consider the arguments against the supernatural from the uniformity of human nature. At present almost everybody feels the force of it more or less, and not the less unduly often because unconsciously. But, as a dogmatic position, it is commonly assumed by persons belonging to two very different classes, — by studious, scholarly men, and by people who call themselves self-made men, and who boast themselves of having been sharpened by collisions with their fellows. Human nature, it is supposed, is everywhere and always the same, and as uniform as a law of nature; so as that everybody knows of himself whether a spirit has ever been seen anywhere, or a vision ever been had, or a miraculous cure ever been experienced. Now certainly human nature is everywhere human. But then what is this humanity? For, before beginning to deny from it as a ground, it should be absolutely certain how far the ground reaches. Plainly, we are not all the equals of Plato, or Solomon, or Newton. And if, now and then, individuals have proclaimed themselves sensitive to a world of spirit, it would hardly seem to be a greater variation in human nature than what is common in every city, where one man wallows in the mire of sensuality, while another feeds on fruits ripened on the topmost boughs of the tree of knowledge. And certainly a seer does not vary from a Troglodyte more than Plato does; and so why should he not be believed in, on good evidence as to his character?

But, indeed, for those who hold that man is body and spirit, why should it be incredible that there should be varieties of spiritual experience among men, considering that some men do nothing but live to the body, while others live earnestly to the spirit?

If there be a spirit in man, and a spirit with the powers of a spirit, why should it be reckoned a thing impossible, that it should make itself more distinctly felt in one man than another? And why should it be beyond belief or expectation even that, now and then, there might be a person with whom some faculty of the spirit should be more than dormantly alive? — the eye for spirits even, if any should be near; the ear for more than mortal sounds; and the spiritual understanding for a prompting other than that of flesh and blood? But the fact is that the anti-supernaturalism of our times is the result of thought akin to materialism; and from this effect of materialism very few persons are wholly exempt. For even the partisans of a spiritual theology argue it commonly like materialists, — argue it as though it were some field of nature, reaching out of sight, indeed, but to be pronounced upon, from familiar analogies. Even those who rank themselves farthest from the professors of materialism, show themselves to be inwardly affected by it, by their unwillingness to have spirit defined in any other way than negatively. They say that spirit is not substance because matter is substantial; that spirit cannot be known of by men because, though they may be spirits themselves, they can learn only through the five senses; and that spirit cannot act upon matter because it cannot touch it, from the want of some property in common with it. So that, for some fervent disciples of a spiritual philosophy, spirit is not much more than the indefinable. The universality of the materialism of the age is illustrated by the manner in which even immaterialists agree with their opposites on some most important points of denial and disbelief. Some of them talk reverentially of George Fox and his doctrine and experience of the Spirit; but they resolutely ignore all the signs and wonders in his history, which by Fox himself are ascribed to the Spirit. Others of them hold the writings of Jacob Boehme like oracles of spirituality, while they treat like an idle, unmeaning preface, the assertion prefixed to one of them, that it was not written out of his mind, but from thoughts which forced an utterance through him from the Spirit. And still others of them affect Plotinus as a great spiritual teacher; but they shut their eyes on the intercourse with spirits which he held, and on his experiences of the ecstatic state.

A man may hold the creed of his sect or party ever so firmly, but yet largely his thought will be governed by what he can never quite escape from, — the spirit of his age. And narratives or doctrines of the supernatural, in a time like this, can be, at the best, only just not rejected. At present, in meditative stillness, spiritual perception may be attained; but out in the world, almost it quite fails at once, from being stifled by the atmosphere of the world's common thought.

True, thousands and tens of thousands of clergymen preach the supernatural, and millions of persons, week by week, sit and hear them. But this is not evidence of faith any more than the discords, deceits, and discontent, the treacheries, sensualities, and blasphemies of Monday are proofs of what was preached and acquiesced in on Sunday. Perhaps nearly every learned and thoughtful clergyman might express himself in something like this manner: "I am one of His witnesses for these things. I see that they were so and are so. And yet, strange to say, I cannot preach as I feel; or rather I cannot make my hearers feel what I wish to preach. And the sermon which I thought was full of the arrows of the Lord hits no one where I aim, and is indeed no more than the 'lovely song of one that hath a pleasant voice, and can play well on an instrument.'" And, more than that, the sermon does not sound like the same thing, even to himself. And the words which, while they were meditated in secret, were fraught with the Spirit, being uttered in public, do not reach the spiritual man, but only the ear of the natural man, and are powerless except as they may chance to be approved by the intellect testing them by logic, rhetoric, history, and some of the natural sensibilities. And the reason is very simple, for the atmosphere of the world and of a worldly church is not that of a Christian study, with its windows opening towards Jerusalem. And even a preacher may be really "in the Spirit on the Lord's day"; but he must be very happily constituted if he does not find that, with crossing the street, on his way to the pulpit, the Spirit has been more or less quenched in him. And, from exchanging looks with his hearers, he is conscious that he is not quite what he was while in the presence of the fathers, and in sympathy with Jeremy Taylor, and in fellowship with Baxter and Doddridge, and in the communion of the saints. Partly his rationalistic dogmas and forms of speech do not admit fully of either the doctrines or the utterance of the Spirit; and partly, what utterance of the Spirit his words suffice for, often his hearers are not capable of receiving, because in them the sense of the supernatural is very commonly almost quite suspended; and so "they seeing, see not; and hearing, they hear not; neither do they understand." And with the people as well as the preacher this is not so much their fault as their misfortune,— the tendency of the time which they belong to, and which it is not possible to quite escape. And this tendency, this spirit of the age, is not of yesterday merely, but of previous ages. It is an effect of the manner, in which the souls of men have been stupefied by the astounding disclosures of science. It results, also, from the fact that the ordinary modes of religious administration are what have been persisted in, without the slightest modification, since the days when they were the agony of George Fox's soul, and the scorn of Robert Barclay's logic ; and in part, also, it is a consequence of altered ways of life, the growth of luxury, the increasing subordination of the individual to the body politic, and the predominance of the peculiar influences of the city over those of the country.

Perhaps never before has there been as much unbelief, innocent in its origin, as there is at present. In former ages widely prevalent unbelief was caused by moral corruption. But the peculiar scepticism of the present age is not as desperate as that. It is not mainly of the heart, and thus the issues of life are not thereby corrupted, as they otherwise might be. And so at present, in their inmost hearts, men have really more faith than they themselves know of. And often it is observed that, apparently, while sickness thins away the body, there is also a mental incrustation which gives way too, and through which the soul seems to look out with a sweet surprise, and a glad sense of the God who is nearer than was thought. If it may be so expressed, it is for the comfort of the strong more than even of the dying that faith at the present day needs to be strengthened. What general uneasiness there is theologically! Every church is opposed to every other church, and yet also is divided against itself. And the same want of faith, or satisfying conviction, is largely evident in individuals. Vast numbers simply acquiesce in their creeds, and timidly recoil from even learning about them. And how often it is to be seen, that if an individual tries to think for himself, he is at one time zealous for ceremonies, and at another time resolute against them, as embarrassing crutches; and is a believer in mainly one article of his creed one year, and in another article another year. And from those hearts which best know themselves, what an unceasing prayer must be rising from closet to closet, from church to church, from town to town, all round the world, "Lord, I believe; help thou mine unbelief"! The unbelief which is specially of this age is so far from being atheistic that it even prays; for such atheism as is possible now, is what really may be confuted within the range of the mind of a child. Indeed, the unbelief of our time is mainly anti-supernaturalism, or more precisely, perhaps, anti-spiritualism. It is not, however, a denial of the angels any more than of God. But exactly it denies that man, as a class of creatures occupying that particular place in the universe which is the kingdom of nature, is liable to be visited by any other creatures, whether higher or lower, not also denizens of nature. It denies, too, that there are any other avenues to the human mind than what the anatomist can indicate with his scalpel; and, therefore, it denies that the human spirit is open to be acted upon by the Holy Ghost as in the early days of Christianity; and denies, also, that men are ever approachable in any way, or for any purpose whatever, or ever so slightly by angel, spirit, or devil. The denial runs thus: "As to spirit, I have never seen it, and I will believe it when I have. And, what is more, I never have heard of any one worthy of belief who ever did see a spirit. When I am told about my head or my hand I know what is talked about; but about spirit I know nothing, nor anybody else either; and my common sense tells me the same thing. And that God has given me common sense I do know. I do not mean to say that we shall not live again; but I mean to say that at present spirit is what my common sense knows nothing about; and I am for common sense." True; but uncommon things may require an uncommon sense, or rather a sense which is too commonly fast asleep. For the purposes of the natural man which are common sense, the faculties of the natural man suffice; but things which are of God, or which look towards him, are not so discerned. Says St. Paul, "Now we have received not the spirit of the world, but the Spirit which is of God, that we might know the things which are freely given to us of God."

Often, in the very arguments which they employ, persons writing in defence of the Christian miracles, evince their own latent anti-supernaturalism. Continually, in theological works, miracles are defended as realities by those who have no perception whatever of spiritual laws, and no sense whatever of the miraculous. How much infected by materialism persons may be who fancy themselves to be very spiritual in their views, is shown in the attempt which frequently is made, to render miracles credible by analogy with Babbage's Calculating Machine. This wonderful machine is said to work accurately through a long series of figures, till suddenly it throws up a number which is out of order, and which cannot be accounted for, but which, it is supposed, may possibly result from some undiscovered law of mathematics. And it is gravely suggested that, in obedience to some occult property, the great machine of nature has here and there, and especially about Palestine, stopped its regularity for an instant, and thrown out a miracle, at a time foreordained in the making of the clockwork. Anything, rather than suppose the intervention of God, or angel, or spirit! Anything rather than a miracle, as being out of the order of nature, even though really it should be in the order of Heaven! A thousand miracles of the strangest origin may be brought in at the back-gate, if only they can be used for barring the front-door of the intellect, against admitting the possibility of signs and wonders having ever been fresh from Heaven, ever having been supernatural; willed, that is to say, in the spiritual world, outside of nature, and at the very seasons respectively of their being shown.

By certain professors of theology there has been lately published an explanation of the day of Pentecost, as having been a day of misunderstanding among the frightened apostles, in consequence of there having been an earthquake, which they thought was a mighty rushing wind, in the house where they were sitting. And the speaking with other tongues, at which the foreigners were amazed, is argued to have been altogether a mistake, and in keeping with the impenetrable darkness plainly discernible in the ingenious but excusable manner in which the Acts of the Apostles are narrated, up to the day of Pentecost, from the resuscitation of Christianity, whenever and whatever that may have been.

The operation of the Spirit by its gifts, as described by St. Paul, tests scriptural expositors very curiously. One says, virtually, that it means what it means, without attempting to realize it in any way. Another sees into not only the credibility, but also the philosophy, of the various gifts, and yet, as even Neander does, finds the gift of tongues to be unintelligible and improbable. And a third expositor teaches that the gifts of the Spirit are simply natural endowments; that coveting earnestly the best gifts is merely attempting self-culture; and that by the gift of tongues is to be understood not a power for speaking languages, foreign or unknown, but the interjectional, broken utterance of a man choking with emotion. The spiritual blindness of the age is such, that often there is not much more light to be perceived in the Church than there is out of it. And everywhere, too, and in every section of the Church, are to be seen blind leaders of the blind; and continually one or other of them looks up, and with authority says some such thing as that the gift of tongues means broken utterance, an inability to speak.

The anti-supernaturalism of our time is shown, again, in the state of feeling which generally exists on prayer, the Holy Spirit, and everything else which supposes either that the spiritual world can open in upon the soul, or the soul open out on that. Of modern treatises on the nature, operation, and effects of the Holy Ghost, the best which can be said is, as Coleridge expresses it, that they believe that they believe. They believe, indeed, but with a faith which has never realized itself. Why is it, that so rarely the scriptural doctrine of prayer is enforced, except by such men as preach everything which is written, and everything alike? Why is it, that so commonly men pray by the way of duty merely, and with no sense of the Divine bosom to lean against? Why is it, that so many good men pray only the prayer of self-recollection before

God, and never the prayer of faith? Why is it, that they go through their daily supplications as a spiritual exercise, but never both delighted and trembling at once, feel their souls in that state when they not only speak, but are spoken to, when they not only humble themselves, but are consciously lifted up? And in almost any church, anywhere, why is it that it feels as though the heavens overhead were like brass, but that men's hearts fail them for fear, lest praying with the apostles, they should be really hoping against the laws of nature? There is hardly anything which is more foreign to our modern ways of thinking than that a sensible sick man should ever have thought to be the better for calling the elders to pray over him. Says the Apostle, "The prayer of faith shall save the sick." But to-day, faith feels itself powerless for such a prayer, being benumbed by the phrase "laws of disease." And yet the very same persons, who would scout a miraculous cure of the Middle Ages, because of the laws of disease being as inviolable as the bands of Orion or the law of gravitation, these same persons continually forget themselves, and allow or assert that the will of a patient helps on a cure. But, in doing this, they indicate the way in which exactly a miracle is to them incredible. For, precisely their objection to believing in a miracle is because it implies a hand thrust into nature from outside of it; is because it implies the will and action of some one not of this world, God, angel, or spirit.

It is an old proverb, "Like people, like priest." Of course, instances to the contrary must be allowed for; and then it may be said that the spirit of the age preaches from every pulpit. Nor can this be reasonably expected to be otherwise, unless the preachers should be at least all men of rare genius, or have been educated in some other earth than this. The spirit of the age is like the atmosphere; it reaches men everywhere, as they sit at the fireside or in the lecture-room, and as they wander in solitude or kneel in the closet. And with breathing it, when baleful at all, there are very few persons, if any, who can resist being injured by it. And, notwithstanding creeds and articles of admission, it is yet no more to be shut out of a church than air is. And if it could be so excluded, then the remedy of intellectual suffocation would itself be worse than the disease. And thus everywhere among the clergy, when they utter themselves, is manifested something of the same anti-supernatural, anti-spiritual state of mind as what plagues other people. It is true, that the doctrines of supernaturalism are almost universally preached; but a discerner of spirits judges not only from doctrine, but from the manner also in which it is developed. And a preacher may set forth doctrines of a supernatural character, and support them by arguments from history and logic, and he may grace them, too, with rhetoric, and lend them also a sincere utterance, and yet have no lively sense of the miraculous, nor much perception of the spiritual, of which miracles are a manifestation. Miracles are for signs; but they are no proper signs, unless there be in us some faculty or mental state to which they signify. A miracle, believed merely from the force of testimony, and from simply the same state of mind as what believes in the reports of the diving-bell, is not rightly believed, is not believed in the right way, is not believed from that spiritual state from which it ought to be believed, and through which only is it of any good. And that state of feeling is conscious of susceptibilities of its own, and of an order higher than that of nature, and of relations to high answering purposes in God, through which there is not a soul but may possibly be vouchsafed a miracle, and not a neighborhood but may perhaps have the Spirit poured out upon it.

In order to have the miracles of the Bible answer better the purpose of doctrinal proofs, the theologians of this century have often largely availed themselves of the spirit of the times for the prejudices which it prompts against the possibility of the supernatural in any other locality or age than the scriptural. But now Chubb, Toland, and Anthony Collins were unbelievers; and yet they were harmless men, compared with the hapless clergyman who thinks to uphold the miracles of the Holy Scriptures by denying the possibility of any others. He may not know the mischief of his course, but his successor will inevitably develop it.

On the evidences of Christianity there is an argument often made, according to which one well-attested ghost-story would countervail all the angels who have ever visited this earth, whether singly or in hosts, and all the words of the Lord which have ever come to prophets, and all the miracles of Jesus and his apostles, and all the visions of John the Divine. But Richard Baxter knew better what he was arguing about than perhaps any English controversialist of this day: and his manner of arguing was the very opposite of that. For he published a collection of narratives of supernatural occurrences in his own time, which had been attested to him as being true, by the persons to whom they happened, or else had been vouched for, as well authenticated, by friends whose judgment he thought he could trust. Such histories were becoming unfashionable in his day, but Baxter saw clearly and published, that to yield the credibility of such things to the sceptics was blindly to betray Christ to the Sadducees.

Let facts be facts, and good evidence be evidence everywhere, or truth can never be itself. Christianity will never be itself while disciples fear for its fate, or feel it necessary to argue among themselves as to its essence. As an inheritance from the past, the gospel is defensible easily and perfectly; but when it is itself, it is its own sufficient evidence. But even as Jesus in his own country had to marvel at unbelief, and "could there do no mighty work," so might Christianity now, in its own country, complain of unbelief, not as directed upon itself, but, worse than that, as general anti-spiritual sentiment, weakening the air; so as that the soul of man can get no breath nor strength, nor can think freely, nor look clearly into the past, nor hope for what is offered it from above, nor trust even its own faculty for receiving.

In those in whom it is strongest, the spirit of the age boasts itself against all the ages of the past, and denounces them as being unworthy of credit on the greatest things which they have to tell about, and as being incapable, incompetent witnesses on even some very simple subjects of observation. And this it does, notwithstanding that, though calling itself the spirit of this enlightened age, it is the avowed spirit of perhaps not one person in a hundred. Every now and then comes forth some one, who says aloud, after this manner, "I know it, and also every man living, knows by his own eyes and ears, that there has nothing ever been known of the spiritual world, not a word from it even, not a miracle. That there is a state, a region, a fountain-head, a something of spirit, it is now agreed shall be considered as certain. But that anybody knows or ever has known more about it than anybody else, is nonsense. I am myself the standard by which you may measure Abraham the patriarch; and as to his visions, they were merely dreams, such as I have myself. I am the measure of the man Paul. And, you may believe me, as to voice or light from heaven ever having come to him at the time of his conversion, that it was not so. Simply, at that time, he had an attack of vertigo, such as we all know something about. O, the glorious freedom of the spirit, by which I am free to ignore the weary past, so hard to understand, with its miracles and histories! O, this glorious clearing of the mind, by which now, in my view, there is nothing higher anywhere than the level of my own experience! O, what a comfort it is to have miracles shrink into common earthly things, and to know that nobody has ever seen them, any more than I have!" This would seem to be odd comfort; but there are persons who think that they feel it.

The spirit of the age! Just as it is of this age precisely, so certainly is it but a bubble on that stream of spirit which comes down through all the ages of the past, and which will run on for men and through them, till they all on earth shall be no more. Soon, of the self-gratulation and self-glorification of the spirit of the time, all that will remain as palpable effect will be a few very curious lines in the History of Man.

As certainly as the pendulum swings from side to side, as certainly as feeling is subject to revulsion, as certainly as man walks by one step to the right and another step to the left, so surely in the next generation will men of science generally believe in the miracles of the Scriptures, and be curious students also in the idolatries of Egypt, Greece, and Rome, and be interested even in the superstitions of the tribes of Africa, as seeming to suggest the possibility of some singular variations from the commonly received opinion as to spiritual influx.

This world of ours, — this world of our eyes, and of the optical, electric, and other instruments, with which our eyes are helped, — this world of our bodily senses has circumfused about it and permeating it a world of spirit, as to which philosophy conjectures confidently, and which faith is sure of, and as effects resulting from which experience tells of miracles. It may be that in some, perhaps even in many respects, this world may be the antitype of that world invisible; and it may be, as Plotinus has said, that we human beings are the dregs of the universe; but even if it should be so, between us dregs and the good wine above there may be a great difference by inferiority, but there must also be a great likeness. To that spiritual world and this world of ours at least there is one thing in common, a great thing, — the company of vanished friends we have had, who know of our wants and ways and wishes, and, at least, who wonder about us. Between us here and them over there, on some points there must be affinity. And it may be, as sometimes philosophy has taught, that the atmosphere of that world, or rather, perhaps, an effluent, diffusive effect from it, may be necessary to our consciousness as thinking beings, just as the atmosphere of this earth is the breath which we draw in common with other earthly creatures, such as cats, dogs, and horses. But should there be anything like such an atmosphere surrounding us, it would not probably be to be known of very often; and indeed, it might never be distinctly perceptible, except on some occasions of a miraculous kind. But, whatever may be the philosophy of the connection between the world invisible of spirit and this visible world of us people in the flesh, that connection does exist.

It is true, that, above and beyond the ordinary experience of mankind, there is an influence sometimes felt, of which the effects are what is called miraculous, or wonder-causing; and, in the strength of which, it is possible that a common man might show himself like an angel, for wisdom; and, with stretching out his hand, have it answer like the finger of God for miracles; and have, indeed, the inborn, latent faculties of his spirit so quickened, as that both his words and deeds together would be like signs and wonders from Heaven. And, it is true, that the ongoings of this world are capable of being quickened by power from the world invisible, so as that a man might be converted from sin to holiness in a moment; and a man that is a leper be restored in an instant; and even in such a manner, as that a dead man in the tomb might hear and come forth; and so as that in a vessel, water might be so affected, as that upon it might occur, instantaneously, what could otherwise only be the result of slow processes in the earth, on the vine, and at the winepress, and afterwards. It is true, also, that now and then in the process of the ages there have been seasons in which, from the outpouring of the Spirit, young men have seen visions, and old men have dreamed dreams, which were signs and wonders, and proofs of that higher order of things which mortals belong to.

It is true that, from outside of the circle of human nature, there are influences for human spirits, such as those which once, for a simple maiden, quickened forethought into the power of prophecy, and made strong feeling be the outgoing of angelic power, and caused the life of a peasant-girl of Domremy to become the career of Joan Darc; and such as those, with the experience of which George Fox grew to be a prophet and the mouthpiece of power from above; and under the sense of which John Wesley was wrought up to the recognition of spiritual marvels, which the multitude could not believe, and at which still the majority can only laugh,—influences by which every now and then persons are able to affirm, some that they have felt themselves called, warned, or comforted; others that they have been inspired for work, such as otherwise they could only have wondered at and never have done; and others, that they have been conscious of having been guarded in times of exposure, sometimes by angels in person, and sometimes by tendencies started upon them, angelic as to their ends,—influences from above, by which there have been in every age, since the time of Paul, persons who have known what it is to be lifted up, above the beggarly element of mere law, into that liberty with which Christ has made men free, which, however, as to the ends of service, is stricter than even the letter of the law, and concurrently with which often the Spirit will work on a man simultaneously as conviction for sin, as absolution by grace, as inspiration from above, and as acceptance with God.

It is true, that the Waldenses are worthy of belief, and that they hold that among them, at certain periods in their history, there have been events sensibly pointed by the finger of God on their behalf It is true that in the Cevennes, when the Huguenots were nearly in the last agony from persecution, there opened among them a power, by which the machinations of their enemies afar off were sometimes disclosed to them, as though by sudden revelation to one or other of their members, — a power which clothed them with such terror, as that, almost in the manner of the old promise, one of them could chase a thousand; and so as that, indeed, a mere handful of men, as they were, they resisted for long years and successfully the concentrated armies of France, — a power which, going out from a speaker, made even Catholic enemies succumb and confess themselves, — a power which often uttered itself from the mouths of little children, — a power through which they believed many times, and where it is impossible to think that there could have been mistakes, that there was let in upon their mortal ears the songs of the hosts of heaven. It is true, that men worthy of all credence have testified of experiences by which the early history of the Church of Scotland is not unlike a continuation of the Book of Acts. And it is true, that by what the Spirit has been and has done amongst them, the Friends have been justified in trusting to it. It is true that, even in these latter centuries, there have been branches of the Church which have blossomed with the marvels of ancient times, because of the Spirit which has been in them. And it is true, that still and now, there are good reasons for trusting and expecting the Spirit.

The Spirit! The saints of all ages cannot have been deceived, or been self-deceived, as to what they felt and trusted; the martyrs who, one after another, laid down their lives for Christ, until they became a great army; the fervent spirits, like Augustine, who tried one way of life and another, till at last, with turning about, their souls caught the light, at which they rejoiced with trembling; the scholars, like Thomas Aquinas, who, with studying themselves as to the natural, became but the more persuaded as to a something that touched, or held, or drew, or whispered them that was supernatural; and students like Cudworth, who gathered up the experiences of the ages and the thoughts of all great writers, as to what of a spiritual nature had ever been known, or felt, and who gazed upon it, till they saw the Intellectual System of the Universe take shape in it; and hosts after hosts of gentle souls, such as Madame Guion and the poet Cowper, who tasted, as they thought, of the powers of the world to come. It is true, that, except when it gets impeded and disbelieved, there is an opening between this world and the next, as it is called, by which comes the Holy Ghost, and through which it may be that sometimes we some of us are approachable by various occult influences, some of a high origin, and others of a nature not so good. And it is true, that there are good reasons for believing that when Christians can pray again as Christians used to do, and have fitted themselves by acts of faith for seeing it, that there will be felt the approach of a day which, with its coming, will assimilate, still more nearly than at present, the lives of modern disciples to the experiences of the saints of all ages.

One swallow does not make a summer, nor does one Christian make a church. A believer separated from his fellow-creatures by convictions which they do not share; a man living apart from the sin about him in loneliness; a woman shrinking from unsympathetic contact, and dwelling in seclusion with her own heart, — for these all there is communion with God by the Spirit. But there is an answer from above, which is specially for the prayer of two or three. And on an age of controversy separating believers from one another, even though through it there should be higher and better ground to be reached, there is an irremediable, unavoidable drawback attendant, and that is the loss of the unity of the Spirit. The joy which a man has in common with a multitude, is not the same joy which he has all to himself in his closet. And however a man may be sanctified by the Holy Spirit, through religious experiences apart from his neighbors, yet should he ever become one with a great body, wherein by that same Spirit all the members are harmonized together, he would feel a triumphant joy quite new to him ; and he would have such a sweet confidence of God's love to men everywhere and in every state, as would be for him like a new sense of salvation.

Fearful is the penalty which the holiest of dissenters incur, and sometimes without knowing it, and even while, perhaps, it is the voice of Christ from Heaven which they obey, though they do not go without compensation from the grace of God, nor yet without that crown which is specially vouchsafed for martyrs. But yet, so it is, that, in the Church of Christ, with losing the unity of the Spirit, or the Holy Spirit in common, there is a great, grievous loss.

The Spirit may be quenched in the present age from one cause and another, as so largely it is ; but it can re-assert itself. If to-day be clouded by scepticism, to-morrow may be broad daylight from a " sun with healing on its wings." And if in this age, because of sectarianism, Christians can hardly be what they ought to be, as to faith, hope, and charity, perhaps in the next age divisions will have ceased altogether. It may be asked, perhaps, how such a thing as that can ever be hoped for. And certainly it cannot be expected humanly, as though from controversies having been argued out. But even as Jesus Christ, after his resurrection, appeared among his disciples suddenly, while the doors were shut, so perhaps he may again ; and thus it may happen that the various churches of Christendom, which to-day have their doors shut against one another, will some time find themselves all included in one great fold, by the manner in which, through the Spirit, Christ will manifest himself, so as to be recognized of all, in one church and another, irrespectively of walls of separation.

And at that time,—O, dear anticipation, sure though as the heavens themselves, however far off,—at that time Christians will know one another, almost without a word, because of the Spirit; and with assembling together, they will feel joy in the Holy Ghost, such as at present public worship stirs but rarely. In meditation, also, because of the ease with which men will apprehend spiritual things, it will be as though they "were all taught of God." And while inquiring in some particular direction, where there is no seeing for the eye, and no hearing for the ear,—strange and holy experience, which only the holiest hearts are fit for!—while so inquiring, often for the natural man, the darkness will yield to a light not of this world, nor of mere reason, but of the Spirit quickening him from within, by which man sees what he could not otherwise have seen, and understands what is only to be spiritually apprehended; "for the Spirit searcheth all things, yea, the deep things of God."

Strange and incomprehensible language this is for many persons. But yet it means what is the same thing as the text: "Draw nigh to God, and he will draw nigh to you"; it means that it is of the nature of Deity, to gravitate towards souls in earnest. Men, too are encouraged to hope even more than that, and to believe that God will help our helplessness, and inform our ignorant prayers, if we will let him. "Likewise the Spirit also helpeth our infirmities; for we know not what we should pray for as we ought; but the Spirit itself maketh intercession for us with groanings which cannot be uttered." And now again, because of this age which we live in, does this text seem to need still further translation? It means that there is direct action of God upon the soul, and which a man may yield to or resist; and that that operation is not merely such force as that by which the eagle lives, or the pulse beats, but rather is like the presence of a dear father with his son, in a time of trouble, by which the child feels himself fill with courage, and grow strangely quick of apprehension.

In the next age, when men shall have learned how and where to find themselves; when they shall have escaped from the bewildering effects of human science imperfectly mastered, and disproportionately esteemed; when they shall have come to see how this earth revolves, and may yet, very well, have been visited by angels at times; when science, in some great professor, shall have been baptized by the Spirit, then will begin great and multitudinous effects to ensue. And because of the spirit of the times, science then will grow poetic with rainbow beauties, and poetry will grow towards prophecy, from the deeper strain which will be in it of spiritual and eternal truth. It will sing familiarly in a style which Milton reached only a few times, and which Æschylus just knew of, but which more exactly, will be as though King David should return to chant, from his heavenly experience, fresh psalms for his friends on earth.

Also, under the influence of the Spirit from on high, social problems, which now seem to be hopeless, will become very easy of solution. For, when people shall wish to stand right before God, when they shall be willing to let their hearts be drawn and draw them, it will be wonderful, in all righteousness, how soon and naturally and easily they will find themselves standing towards one another as they ought to do. With a general experience of the Spirit, yet no greater than there is to-day of scepticism, but with such an experience of the Spirit, what is there socially which might not be hoped for? Since, because of the Spirit in common, there will be a feeling, — of exactly the opposite origin, however, from communism, — there will be a feeling with the rich for letting their wealth run to common uses, as far as prudence, and political economy, and the state of the world will allow; like the impulse for having all things in common, which was felt by the first Christians, during the first few days after Pentecost. And things which at present are continually being reformed, and always to no purpose; things invincible to reason, and incapable of being corrected by utilitarian philanthropy, will yield at once to the sweet, subtle effects of that Spirit, by which believers will feel themselves to be all "baptized into one body," and by which they will know themselves, for glory and shame, for joy and sorrow, to be really and vitally "members one of another."

There are some special causes of scepticism to-day, which in perhaps the next age will have ceased almost altogether. And, in that better temper of the times, Christianity, as the work of Christ through the Spirit, will manifest itself still móre distinctly than it does to-day. It is oddly characteristic of these times, that as regards the gospel, men are more dutiful than believing. They act out of a higher spirit than they are quite sure of. "Lord, I believe; help thou mine unbelief," — this precisely is their state of mind. With their hearts they believe, but not quite, not altogether with their minds. They would believe wholly but for an accident in social progress, and which indeed is a temporary humor, the mere spirit of the age.

But already signs are visible of a new period, and with its arrival, fresh impulse will be felt from "the powers of the world to come"; and God will be known more dearly, as a mighty fatherly presence about us and awaiting us; and by every believing heart Christ will be more tenderly felt as its personal friend; and by every bereaved and suffering spirit, more vividly still than now, the communion of saints will be felt across the grave.

And because there have been wonders in the past, they will not, perhaps, be wanting to the glory of the future. And again, it may be, will the gifts of the Spirit subserve the work of the Spirit in the Church; and one man find himself preternaturally quickened in wisdom, for the benefit of his fellows; and another, by the way of prophecy, become like the mouthpiece of thought from outside of this world; and another, by reason, perhaps, of some personal and fitting peculiarity, be known as a channel of healing power for the afflicted; and still another, from perhaps some special susceptibility, be remarkable for the faith that will possess him, and through him that will strengthen the brethren.

These are things which we may never see, perhaps, but yet as mere possibilities, they have some meaning for us. It is for human beings that the order of nature is orderly, and not for any other creatures. And when signs and wonders are vouchsafed on earth, it is only to men that they are significant, at all. And no doubt, if men could be the better for it, the heavens themselves would be bowed and brought down. The Lord is willing to meet man as far as possibly he can, consistently with allowing man himself to stir at all.

We men are but like creatures, which have just struggled into life, from out of the dust; and therefore it is no great wonder if we should, some of us, be tempted to think too highly of mere dust.

But beyond the realm of the natural is the region of the supernatural, which we know of, and to which, as knowing of it, we must certainly belong. And reasonably and rightly may we trust those glimpses of it, which have been caught and reported by previous voyagers across the sea of time, even though they may have been but as momentary as the observations at noon, which sometimes have to suffice the sailor for a stormy passage across the Atlantic; for, even of ourselves, we can judge as to whither the current sets which carries us. And, for our comfort, we have faith, which has been wrought into our nature, like an instinct, by our Creator; and therefore it is what may be trusted like God himself. And faith points for us, like the magnetic needle, in a starless night, and is, exactly and truly, "the evidence of things not seen."

SCIENCE AND THE SUPERNATURAL.

AS to spirit, and its laws and likelihoods, a man is prepared for judging by zoölogy, chemistry, and star-gazing, no better at all than he would be by accuracy as to the Greek particle, or by a good instinct for Hebrew roots. Every man to his trade. *Ne sutor ultra crepidam!* We will listen respectfully to the man of science for what he has to say as to the operations and limitations of the laws of nature, within that circle of the sphere of nature which has been explored; but when he would dogmatize on the supernatural,— when he would arrogate the right to deny the possibility of effects which claim to originate with a cause outside of what himself he calls the bounds of nature,— then we would remind him that he ought to keep within his jurisdiction, and not pronounce on matters altogether foreign to him, and which, perhaps, belong to the province of another man. But, the higher the order of mind which they are of, the further are scientific men from the danger of falling into a mistake like that. Many trades and professions have diseases peculiar to them. For the painter there is colic, for the clergyman, sore throat; for the workers in fine steel, consumption; and for the shoemaker, hepatitis. And in the middle ages physicians used to be suspected of the *morbus medicorum,* or a peculiar tendency to unbelief, as the result of their special studies. And, indeed, from a special study of the laws of nature there is of course the danger of making too much of them; an undue tendency towards judging other things by analogy with them; an inclination to deny miracles merely because of their not being uniform with common life and surrounding nature.

There have been persons who have accepted some of the miracles, and denied others, by a curious eclecticism resulting from their special studies or individual characters. One theologian has thought that there may have been some misunderstanding as to the cure of diseases by the laying-on of hands; while he had no doubt at all about the miraculous draught of fishes. And another has believed implicitly in the miraculous multiplication of the twelve loaves and a few fishes, because of there having been three thousand fainting persons to be fed; while he has confessed himself doubtful about the first miracle at Cana in Galilee, because of its having turned water into wine at a festival. And a third theologian has accepted all the miracles of the Gospels but one, but has doubted of one, because of his being unable to see that any good purpose could have been answered, by the withering of the fig-tree. And there have been those who have been unable to believe in miracles affecting matter, but who have been enthusiastic believers in prophecy, and in the spiritual miracle of our Lord's character. But of judgments on this subject, affected by personal peculiarities, perhaps the most curious is that of Lord Herbert of Cherbury, who prayed to God for a sign, which he believed was given to him, to direct him as to publishing a volume, which he had written against the probability of revelations being given from heaven, to individual men, or to particular places.

By a man of the same order of mind, perhaps, with Lord Herbert, though perhaps more ingenious, a theory was invented eighty years ago, and which is still advocated, for maintaining the reality of miracle concurrently with the unchangeableness of the Order of Nature. Thus, it is said that miracles were inserted in nature at the creation, to be developed in order, in its course, just as there is a striking of the clock at certain points foreordained by the maker. On this theory, Christ, by a prophetic impulse, called into the tomb to Lazarus to come forth, just at the moment when the buried man was already waking up from death by a foreordained irregularity, inserted in the Order of Nature. Curious believing this is, even though according to the order of nature! Predispositions of thought, caused by peculiar studies, very easily become prejudices; and they are none the less bigoted and blinding, if they result from science.

This is a common argument. God made the world perfect; and if it be perfect, its laws must be unalterable; and if its laws are unalterable, they have therefore never been suspended; and if they have never been suspended, then there has never been a miracle. But now this is absurd, even in its own way of reasoning. For, indeed, the more absolutely perfect the world is reckoned, precisely the more significant does any variation become in the uniform working of its laws.

But probably a miracle never was a suspension of the laws of nature. The Scriptures do not so define it. And, indeed, about the laws of nature they never say anything at all. And it is very likely that what in our blindness, we should call a suspension of the laws of nature, or a momentary stoppage of nature's clock-work, is really more than that, and is, indeed, matter pliant to spirit; and has occasionally been something more important still than that, and has been really the finger of God in the laws of nature, pointing them to a special purpose of his own; and been, indeed, the showing from heaven of a sign and wonder.

It is true, that, from studying the laws of matter, a man may be indisposed for believing in spirit. Not, however, that the laws of nature have anything to suggest against the existence of spirit; for they have not. But it is an effect of our human weakness, that if habitually we look intently in one direction, we find ourselves disinclined from the opposite. And so it may sometimes be, that the farther a man sees into nature, the blinder he may grow as to what is above it, or to the supernatural. But Bacon and Newton were not sceptical as to miracles. Philosophers, such as they were, have eyes not merely for details, but for the universe as a whole. They are more than the owners of lamps, to grope with, as being themselves illuminated from within; and under their analyzing eyes even solid matter itself seems but like the mist which just holds the beauty of the rainbow; while also to them the laws of nature are not mere enactments, but are qualities of that creative power which is everywhere present, and which everywhere is undivided and uncompounded, simple in essence but various in manifestation; a power which is attraction and repulsion, both in one, and life and death on the same impulse.

The truths which flash like lightning in the soul of the prophet, are not without corroboration from the long processes, by which philosophy investigates. And when he attends reverently to the experiments of science, often the true philosopher testifies that to his feeling there are reported, not only forces pervading matter, but also from outside of nature and above it; and from the place of spirit also, the living eye and the working will, and the existence incorruptible, from which those forces begin.

In the long, early morning of creation, after the world had been without form and void, everything everywhere was a miracle, — the first fern, however it may have been produced, with its leaves heavy with moisture and sparkling in the sun; the first oak, long afterwards, in an atmosphere grown cooler and drier; the last ichthyosaurus, as it died of an altered world; the first horse, proud of his speed on the green turf; the lion, as he first roared after his prey, by an instinct which had not yet learned its own meaning; and the lark, as it first went up into the sky, and filled the air with its song. And so, by the true philosopher remembering this, miracles are not thought of as being antecedently impossible. Nor to him, either, is it an impossible thing, that a disembodied spirit should be able to act on matter move a table, throw stones, make noises; for he remembers that there is no real knowledge of the manner by which even the living man has his limbs actuated by his spirit. A belief in the possibility of miracles is not, then, barred by science.

That God, as being perfect, must have made a world perfect in itself, and with perfect laws, and therefore with laws which never can need to be meddled with, is the great argument against the possibility of miracles. It is of the same kind with that, which the heathen Celsus urged against the probability of redemption through Christ, which indeed was a miracle at the beginning, — "That God has made his work perfect once for all, and does not need, like a man, to mend it afterwards." But perhaps it is exactly because God is not like a man, that he does not make his work perfect once for all, is not obliged to complete it absolutely and at once, and to get it off his hands. Perhaps the world is perfect, not in time, but in eternity. It was not absolutely perfect when it was merely crept upon by the Saurians, nor was it perfect as surveyed by the childlike eyes of Adam; nor is it perfect now, being as it were a creature, groaning and travailing in pain along with man, as St. Paul would say. But perhaps it is really perfect, only as it looks to the angels; only as seen from the beginning all through to the end, with its uses all plain, and its susceptibilities of divine agency all manifest, whether for uniform law, or for signs and wonders from heaven; whether as a school for the education of the human intellect, or as a land, where what is natural, at first, grows to be spiritual; and where man arrives at, and tastes of the powers of the world to come.

Also, there is no analogy between God and man as to their works, whence to argue against miracles. Man, of himself and by himself, can do nothing whatever, absolutely nothing, whether perfect or imperfect. For he cannot stir himself, cannot even lift his hand, but by the help of powers, about which he knows almost nothing whatever, — vital force, the will, the contractility of the muscles. Also, when it is to be reasoned from, the word "perfect" means finished, done with. Now this is a very good word, for the good work of a mortal. But it would seem that sometimes the work of God, who is a spirit, eternal, immortal, might rather be expected to be perfect, by being in a way comparatively imperfect; that is, by being filled with a spirit of growth, and, therefore, of improving change, and by continuing forever in connection with that sustaining power, through which things change "from glory to glory." For the children of the Highest then, as growing more and more receptive, it might be expected that there should be "times of refreshing" to come "from the presence of the Lord"; that it should be in the order of Providence to "put a new spirit within" men from time to time, and subserving the same purpose as creation itself, also to "show wonders in the heavens and in the earth."

And now these wonders do not derogate from the wondrousness of the universe, but really they enhance it. For, as a fact, would the laws of nature be less reliable for a philosopher, because of his believing in the possibility of exceptional occurrences like miracles? And the answer is, No; emphatically, No. Sir Isaac Newton was not a matter-of-course Christian; indeed, he was a Christian scholar. But, from believing in miracles, he does not appear to have been weakened or confused, as a believer in the Order of Nature. And actually it was by him, that the law of gravitation was discovered. It is a legal maxim, that "exceptions prove the rule"; and some day or other, it will commonly be held, that, by their nature and manner, miracles make more plain the very laws against which they would seem to except.

A perfect God can only have made a world perfect, of its kind; and a perfect world must be made of perfect laws; and perfect laws can never need to be suspended or supplemented; and so there is no possible room in nature for a miracle. It is ludicrous, how this argument has been iterated and reiterated, as though logic were just as good against facts as against doctrines. In the last century, by men of science and others who never saw one fall, it was proved to a demonstration, that meteoric stones were vulgar errors. To-day, however, science is sublimely persuaded of them, notwithstanding their having once been natural and scientific impossibilities. And hereafter miracles will be believed, for reasons of various kinds, and for twenty thousand analogies, by the successors of the very men who to-day argue that there is logically no room for a miracle in the world.

The perfect world of a perfect maker excludes miracles! But now, perhaps, the world is not as perfect as it seems, or as some people fancy themselves bound to affirm it. Perhaps, too, it is absolutely perfect only in logic. And perhaps in this case, as is often done, the form of logic has been borrowed by arrant nonsense.

A perfect world, in perfect order from the beginning, and that will keep perfect to the end; and which, therefore, will admit of nothing new in it, not a single miracle, — why, what an assumption this is! For, when the argument takes this turn, there are some questions to be asked. What is this world? What is perfect order? Whereabouts, even, is this world we talk about? Whereabouts is it in those fields of space, which are crossed one way and another, and up and down, by those infinite lines, measured by which from here to the sun is as nothing, and in the course of which, earth and suns and planetary systems are passed by, like moths on a sunbeam? The perfect Order of Nature pleaded against the possibility of a miracle; while nobody knows, or is ever likely to know, in the full sense, what that order is! Perhaps, after all, miracles were in order always, in perfect order, in the order of the universe: as of course they must have been. Perfect order may be one thing, as viewed in the system of the universe; and may be the same thing, with a difference apparent or real, as discernible in some little dim corner in creation, or as manifested in a load of matter whirling on its way, a quaking earth with a magnetic affinity for the north pole, and with other affinities quite as important as that, perhaps, although at present quite unsuspected.

Miracles, or many things in the Bible which commonly are so denominated, may be exceptions to what are called the laws of nature, as at present understood by the best student; but, as witnessed by a seraph, they may have been but the effect of laws more in number than we know of, and some of which acted marvellously, by being in connection with a mind as peculiarly organized as a prophet's is, at a moment of faith in the head of the universe, as almighty and good. And some other miracles may have been momentary effects from this cause, — "There is a spiritual body." Every mortal is both body and spirit; or, as it would be better to say, he is and has what St. Paul means when he says, "There is a natural body, and there is a spiritual body." By death, the natural body is loosened from the spiritual body, and drops and begins to decay, like an old cloak; while the spiritual body has its senses slowly open to the world, in which it finds itself. But, even while cased in flesh, it is possible that some of the faculties of the spiritual body, either by accident or by the grace of God, may be so quickened as to act independently of the flesh. The eye, with which I am to see hereafter, might be opened for a moment, so as that I should get a glimpse of spiritual marvels; and that opening of my eye would be a miracle, like what happened when the prophet Elisha, with his servant, was beleaguered by the army of Syrians. "And Elisha prayed, and said, Lord, I pray thee open his eyes, that he may see. And the Lord opened the eyes of the young man, and he saw; and, behold, the mountain was full of horses and chariots of fire round about Elisha." And in the same manner might the dormant ear also of my spiritual body be momentarily quickened, so as to catch just a word or two, a sound, an alarm, a message, from the spiritual world; which indeed is intimately near, and yet also infinitely far off. And this would be a miracle, like what Paul experienced at his conversion. Also, if by some chance, through some inward predisposition, a man should catch a breath from the air of that world, where the Great First Cause is first felt, where spirits are made messengers, and where ministration looks like flaming fire, the effect on him would be a miracle like what the last words of David tell of,—"The spirit of the Lord spake by me, and his word was in my tongue." These illustrations may be enough for hinting that there is a philosophy of religion, in which faith and science are to be reconciled, and in which the natural and the supernatural may be of one accord. But let now one other illustration be taken. It is conceivable, what in many ages has been generally believed, under the best philosophy of the time, that between us and God, neighbors of ours almost, far below the region of seraphs, not nearly as high up as where angels, with their archangels, congregate, and indeed near upon and sometimes fairly withinside of the realm of nature, are beings who could, for momentary effect, and as though from a long distance, play upon the laws of nature, so as to work what Hugh Farmer and Baden Powell would even call miracles, as being in their estimation acts suspending the laws of nature. Philosophy had very close blinders on, when it decided, with Farmer, that for the elevation of a man in the air, without human assistance, there must be a suspension of the laws of nature. A law of nature suspended for that! It was no more necessary for that, than it is for a man's lifting his hand in the air. Something additional to the laws of nature, as catalogued by philosophers, may have been necessary, some occult law it may be, in unusual strength, or perhaps an agent from a foreign world. But a suspension of the law of gravitation it certainly is not necessary to suppose. As Jesus with the law of

Moses, so miracles with the laws of nature, do not destroy, but fulfil.

Also, in view of an argument, it is always to be remembered that the phrase "laws of nature" is a figure of speech, good enough for ordinary purposes, but liable to be deceptive at a critical point. Law is what has been written for the purpose of being read; and also it is what has been written for the purpose of being read, on the supposition of there being a joint understanding between the writer and the reader. That is law; and it is because of that sense of the word "law," that the phrase "laws of nature" is used against miracles. But now, has ever the God of nature been pledged to any text-book of natural philosophy, so as that Science, or any son of hers, should be able to say, "Because of this book of mine I know all about God, as to what either he will do or what he can allow in this earth"?

Also, it is of the nature of "law," in its primitive meaning, that it should need, and from time to time should admit of adaptation, and amendment by interpretation. But that exactly is what is forgotten, when the majesty of the word "law" is adduced in a controversy on the subject of miracles. And thus it is that against the possibility of miracles, a phrase of fallible origin is urged as an infallible argument.

Laws of nature working together, and yet distinguishable from one another, like powers harnessed in machinery, — of the on-going of nature, this may be a good definition for most purposes; but when by this definition it is proposed to falsify the truthfulness of our Lord Jesus Christ, as to his miracles, then, in the sense intended and for the purpose in view, let it never be forgotten that really there are no laws of nature, and that there never were any. Men talk of forces centripetal and centrifugal, and as though one might have been enacted first, and then the other: but the truth probably is, that the two are but diverse manifestations of a common cause; or, rather, that the two are one, while seeming diverse. Also this common cause seems to man like two different forces or laws, only because of the peculiar and limited manner in which he can apprehend. What poor creatures really men are, as they look about them, with no very wide or keen gaze, as even telescopes and microscopes might remind them! For, with far better instruments than have ever yet been made, and with better eyes than children have ever yet been born with, what marvels might not men see, to their amazement! And yet these men, or some of them; dwellers, too, in a little earth surrounded by infinity; born also in time, as they know they are, yet having also some sense of eternity; these men of a day, and creatures of God, — Feuerbach, the German, and Strauss, a German too, and Renan of France, and Buckle, who was English, with others like-minded, too numerous to count, — these all have proclaimed aloud, that, because of what they know, there cannot have been anywhere, at any time, anything but what they might have expected, and precisely that there never has been a miracle. But for all that, and in spite of their logic, "the Lord knoweth the thoughts of the wise, that they are vain." This sentiment a Psalmist uttered once among the Hebrews, and long afterwards it was quoted by Paul in a letter to Corinth;

but it was never more pertinent than it is to-day. Arago said that outside of mathematics the word "impossible" for anything was rash. Perhaps he said it out of what may be called the common sense of science; which common sense, however, is as rare in connection with science as with anything else. Or it may be that he said it, because of his having studied the case of Angelique Cottin, a girl who was attended by some curious phenomena. But any way, he was very unlike Michael Faraday and some others. "Possible and impossible pronounced upon, by the last edition published of the laws of nature!" This is what is continually being proclaimed by one man and another. It would make people all laugh or else pity, but for the spirit of the age; for, indeed, we are all of us much inclined to the same thing. But it is no matter for these philosophers and their followers, as to who they are or where,—the wise men. For certainly somewhere there is wisdom higher than their wisdom, and from the height of which their self-complacency must be something very curious to witness. But, above and beyond all, there is the truth of the text that "the Lord knoweth the thoughts of the wise, that they are vain."

Laws of nature arrayed against miracles! For an argument in that direction, there are no such things as laws of nature. Or if the phrase "laws of nature" should be allowed to stand, on its being made right by accompanying explanation, it would be found then to be the same thing as the spirit of God, which, like "the wind bloweth where it listeth," and not merely for human creatures on their way from the cradle to the grave, but for worlds, also, while slowly growing into form, and while lengthening out, with change and time, the fulfilment of their respective purposes. It is that spirit which is the transient life of the butterfly, and the inspiration which "giveth man understanding"; that spirit which holds the earth to its time and place, and which yet also strives with men through the conscience; that spirit which is the life of all lives, from the worm to the seraph, and of which the Spirit of Nature, as it is called, is but one of many manifestations.

On arriving at the point of view which we have now reached, there have been persons who have felt the atmosphere about them grow more favorable to faith, and who have exclaimed, "Now I hear them more plainly, those witnesses of old, chosen beforehand. Now I am less at variance with some of the possibilities of faith. Now some things which were hard to be understood are easier. O holy prophets and apostles! forgive me, in these times when the pathway of thought goes winding about, if I have sometimes, with turning, heard you but indistinctly, and fancied that the fault was all with you!"

But there are others, to whom all this would be quite unintelligible, and who simply iterate and reiterate words, outside of the circle of which they cannot see. And now for them, also, let us see if there be anything more to be said, which may avail. It is an eclipse of faith for us all at present: and things which were simple enough formerly, in the broad daylight, now look strangely; and what once would have been comparatively of little significance may now be a great help.

But first let us hear again exactly what Strauss would say. And he says, very emphatically, "There is no right conception of what history is, apart from a conviction that the chain of endless causation can never be broken, and that a miracle is an impossibility." But how, then, has it been with almost every historian, of every age, before David Hume? How was it with Josephus, Herodotus, Thucydides, Plutarch, Tacitus, Diodorus Siculus, Dionysius of Halicarnassus, Pausanias the Topographer, and their company all? According to that little formula by Strauss, they would all be disqualified. Surely, surely, by attempting to prove too much, Professor David F. Strauss has disproved his own position. He is famous for his work on the four Gospels, in which he laboriously eliminated every miracle from the life of Jesus. It was after the publication of this work, that there was offered to him the professorship of theology in the University of Zurich, and which he would have accepted, but for an insurrection of the people of the city. The end of the matter was a letter in which he stated his opinions, and in reference to which it may be said, that he perhaps had more faith even in denying, than possibly some others had even in the heat of dogmatizing, and that not improbably Jesus Christ would sooner have accepted even his unbelief than the unmitigated virtues of some of his opponents. But still, in his attempt to go to Zurich as Professor of Theology, he was in the curious position of proposing to lecture on Christianity, without believing in a single miracle; and of attempting it, too, by the help of historians, not one of whom, as he thought, had any right conception of history. Alas, alas! but so it is, that every step forward intellectually costs a hundred failures first; and it is because of the tears and misery of adventurers on the road to knowledge, that the flints of difficulty are found smooth, by the multitude as they advance from behind.

There has lately been published a volume entitled "Christ the Spirit." It is the serious work of a devout mind struggling with theological difficulty. Says the author, E. A. Hitchcock, in regard to the Scriptures, "If, therefore, we accept these miracles as historical realities, we must refuse the idea of law, and must admit that there is no truth in the doctrine which affirms an order in the course of nature." Perhaps the force of this opinion may have been anticipated, and even perhaps prevented, by some previous remarks. Also it is said, that, if those miracles are to be believed in, there is no such thing possible as science. But that would not appear to have been the opinion of Sir Isaac Newton, the man, of all men, best fitted to judge. And further it is added, that if those miracles are to be believed in, then reasonably Grecian mythology must be believed. Grecian mythology might, for that reason, claim to be examined; but not necessarily claim, therefore, to be believed. And also it is not theology, but sciolism, which would wish to argue Christianity in ignorance of the philosophy and religion of Greece. Light, and still more and more light, let us have, wherever we may be, and even though it should fall on our Bibles, through some crevice in the wall of a Grecian temple!

And now who offers himself next as a witness on this subject? It is Henry T. Buckle, who would tell us, out of his "History of Free Thought," that there is little reason to hope for the enlargement of the ground of the evidences of Natural and Revealed Religion; that the materials already exist from which thoughtful students must make up their minds finally on the questions at issue; that already men are taking up their places, in hostile array, on subjects where no further evidence can be offered, and where there is little reason to hope for the alteration of the state of parties to the end of time; that, as regards Christianity, there never has been an age so hostile to it as the present, and never an age, either, so much actuated by it. Nothing more to be expected on the greatest possible subject of thought! Why, what advanced times we live in! and even without our knowing of it, some of us! The field of thought is cleared by scientific method, and there is no chance of anything to the end of time! This may be true for a near-sighted thinker, but hardly for any one else. Are there, then, experts who can look through the universe as though it were machinery? Electricity, magnetism, and odic force, with which man has affinities, and by which indeed, apparently, he has all manner of possible connections, — have these all been thoroughly explored? And is it so absolutely nothing, as not to be worthy of mention, — the chance of there being a Master for the great Machine, with a will of his own; the possibility of there being a Father in heaven with children on this earth? Man proposes, but God disposes. That is a French proverb, to which every now and then there is a wonderful point, and that point may possibly show itself at any time.

And now next, let what Baden Powell would say be considered. He is Savilian Professor of Geometry at Oxford, and a clergyman, yet he is of opinion that it would be a great good done, if Christianity could be relieved of its responsibility for miracles. Prophecy, however, and some other spiritual marvels, he thinks may rationally be connected with Christianity. This, however, Renan would not agree to; for he holds that miracles are no more possible or credible for the souls, than for the bodies of men. However, Baden Powell is certain that the Order of Nature is the first thing, and everything for belief; and then he argues, very properly, for patience with untoward facts, as likely, some time or other, to get subordinated. He has heard, however, of apparently marvellous occurrences, "such as implied a subversion of gravitation, or of the constitution of matter; descriptions inconceivable to those impressed with the truth of the great first principle of all induction, — the invariable constancy of the order of nature." But then, as about a thing, with which he could have no patience, nor his system either, he cries out that he has "heard it positively affirmed by veracious, educated, and well-informed persons, in perfect good faith, that a solid mahogany table has been seen to rise from the ground and its surface to move in waves." For that, of course, was a thing for which, in his philosophy, there was no hope of a place, any more than for the miracles which he wished Christianity could be freed from. Order of Nature! always only the Order of Nature, — as though there were no such thing conceivable as the Order of the Universe. And yet, by way of analogy with his special studies, it would seem as though he might have thought of it. For problems which are utterly insoluble by arithmetic, and which are outside of its range, are the objects and beauties of algebra, which has been called a diviner arithmetic, and which may well be reckoned by some persons to have wonder-working laws.

And now, on this subject of the Order of Nature, has Baden Powell ever been answered? A table rising in the air, if such a thing might be, would be a sufficient answer for his style of scepticism, according to his own words, apparently. But, apart from that, has any answer been made, by which to justify a belief in the miracles of Christianity, against the Oxford professor with his grand argument against it?

And now, in the sequence of thought, appears James A. Froude, also of Oxford, and late Fellow of Exeter College. And in a recent publication, in a passage which specially refers to the volume of "Essays and Reviews," of all the authors of which Baden Powell was the most notable, J. A. Froude says, that against that style of thought there has nothing been adduced, but "the professional commonplaces of the members of a close guild, men holding high office in the Church, or expecting to hold high office there." Professional commonplaces! Many others besides Froude have found them such, and have thought them to be insufficient answers for the new scepticism. But now, like Baden Powell, J. A. Froude, by implication at least, distinctly acknowledges that the miracles of the Scriptures would be credible, if some of the phenomena of Spiritualism should be realities. To these things his attention had been drawn; and to his knowledge, he avers that they have been vouched for by persons, who would be good witnesses on a criminal trial. But yet he says, "Our experience of the regularity of nature on one side is so uniform, and our experience of the capacities of human folly on the other is so large, that, when people tell us these wonderful stories, most of us are content to smile: we do not care so much as to turn out of our way to examine them. The Bible is equally a record of miracles." The Bible! But, indeed, of what use is it to mind anything, which he may say about the miracles of the Bible, when, according to his own showing, he would not even go out of his way, to see whether they might not be true? For, things which to his mind,—whether rightly or wrongly is no matter,—things which to his mind were of a piece with the miracles of the Bible, he would not even turn out of his way to examine. But against a belief in miracles he urges not only that they are impossible, but that "the miracles of St. Theresa and St. Francis of Assisi are as well established as those of the New Testament.". And now, even if this should be so, what then? Are we for that to forego our belief in the miracles of the Bible? No: quite otherwise. And, if there be anything to be learned from Assisi, so much the better.

Next in order of time, with an argument upon this subject, appears Dr. Louis Büchner, with his volume on "Force and Matter." Says this author, "We should only waste words in our endeavor to prove the natural impossibility of a miracle. No educated, much less a scientific person, who is convinced of the immutable order of things, can nowadays believe in miracles. We find it rather wonderful that so clear and acute a thinker as Ludwig Feuerbach should have expended so much logic in refuting the Christian miracles. What founder of any religion did not deem it necessary, in order to introduce himself to the world, to perform miracles? The miracle-seeker sees them daily and hourly. Do not the table-spirits belong to the order of miracles? All such miracles are equal in the eye of science: they are the result of a diseased fancy." These are the words of a man very clear in his mind; though his mind is not of the same order with Plato's, certainly. "Do not the table-spirits belong to the order of miracles?" Dr. Büchner himself would seem to think so, by the way in which he asks the question. Baden Powell too, no doubt, would have agreed with him; and so also would Froude, the historian. But Büchner has one other word for us. "Even to this day, there is no deficiency of miracles and powerful spirits among savage and ignorant tribes." Are we, then, to be frightened from believing in miracles, because, if there are any at all, there are some also among savages? Just as well might Dr. Büchner expect a Christian to be ashamed of the sun, because the red Indian hunts in the light of it. "Miracles and powerful spirits among savage and ignorant tribes!" Well, the better we know about that thing, the wiser we shall be, and the better it will be for our theology; and it is not everybody who is afraid of learning.

Baden Powell, James A. Froude, Dr. Büchner, and with these might be joined one or two other leaders in the argument against the credibility of miracles, — these would all apparently be ready to test the reality of the miracles of the Bible by the phenomena of Spiritualism, or perhaps more definitely by the reality of the raps, which are called spirit-rappings. In some sense, they may even be said to dare the experiment; and by many high authorities of the Catholic Church, from early down to more modern times, it would have been deemed a simple and very cheap way of settling such a controversy. This is said, however, not because exactly what is called spirit-rapping to-day was known in the Middle Ages, but because of its being certainly akin to many possibilities, which the Catholic Church has always maintained, and faith in which has been a large part of that Church's vitality. The early Fathers of the Church did not think it to be derogatory to their charge, even as Christian chiefs, to show Pagans how to draw an inference from their own Pagan prodigies. And it would have seemed a grand chance to Henry More and Richard Baxter if the opportunity had been offered of arguing from spirit-raps to the truth of the Scriptures, as is abundantly evident from their many works respectively. It would have been an argument, to the nature of which Ralph Cudworth would have assented, and for which at once he would have found a place in the "Intellectual System of the Universe." And Jeremy Taylor, with eyes glancing from high to low, and from unearthly depths to prophetic heights, and with a power of vision for following the strange lines of similitude which permeate creation, and which make it continually, in one quarter or another, glitter and flash with the light of unexpected analogies; Jeremy Taylor — but indeed, as sanctions for the purpose in view it is superfluous to name any more names than those of Cudworth and More and Baxter; for probably with them would have assented nearly all the great men who were eminent in theology in the days when theology itself was eminent. But now, before attending to an incident of yesterday, let us have in mind what the great Platonist addressed to Lorenzo de Medici on the subject of the Christian religion: "I certainly think that, to us undeserving, certain miraculous signs have been divinely given. But all things are not shown to all: many also are not written down, or, if written, are not credited, in consequence of some wicked and detestable men imitating miracles. I have heard of some miracles in our own time, and in our city of Florence, which are to be believed. Do not be surprised, my Lorenzo, that Marsilius Ficinus, studious of philosophy, should introduce miracles; for the things of which we write are true, and it is the duty of a philosopher to confirm everything by its own proper kind of argument."

A short time since in London, one evening, a gentleman enumerated jocularly what he thought were Yankee notions, and he named spirit-rappings. The speaker was a distinguished man of science, and religiously a man after the manner of Baden Powell, with a truly Christian heart, but on the subject of miracles having, perhaps, the eyes of his understanding somewhat "dazed with excess of light" from the sun of science. Suddenly he was accosted by a stranger present, who said, "I am a denizen of that New World; and it is said that in some places there, with walking briskly over the floor at certain times, a man emits sparks from his fingers, with which even gas can be lighted. What would you say to that?" It was replied, "Nonsense! it is impossible." Then said the American, "It was because I expected that answer that I asked you the question. In a scientific circle, I once knew twenty-eight persons out of thirty assent to that same opinion which you have now expressed; but there is not one of them to-day that would. In New York certainly, and in Boston, and perhaps all over America, on a frosty night, in a house warmed by the best modes, often a person with walking briskly over a carpet, and offering the knuckle of a finger to some metallic object, has it emit a blue, detonating spark. And now, by experience, as common almost as that of those electric sparks, I tell you that what are called spirit-rappings are true; or, rather, that those rappings are real which are called spiritual. And now I will ask you in all honesty to answer me as you would in your place in the Royal Society. And supposing that you heard on a table raps, the origin of which you could not possibly connect with cheating, nor yet with science, as it is understood to-day; and supposing, too, that these raps evinced as much intelligence as a boy of five years old,— what now would you think?" Said the man of science, thoughtfully, and after a long pause, "I should say that, to my present belief, it was the greatest thing which had happened since the creation of the world." To this the American rejoined, "Those raps are of far less peculiarity as to significance than you think. But, like many other persons in pursuit of a special business, you have got lodged in a mere corner of the broad field of knowledge, and where you are capable of being astonished by what would be no absolute novelty to the Esquimaux, or to the Maoris of New Zealand."

What is called "rappings" is the most common of all the spiritualistic manifestations, and, for the purpose for which the thing is referred to in the preceding anecdote, it would no doubt have been agreed to by Baden Powell and his fellow-philosophers as being a sufficient test. But also for that thing precisely which he mentions — of the rising of the table from the floor — there is abundant evidence, and some of which is of the very best kind. Büchner says that because of the laws of nature "there exist no supersensual and supernatural things and capacities, and they never can exist"; and so he denies at once table-spirits and all other spirits, and also the possibility of Revelation; but luckily he does also, with other things, deny that any one can read an opaque sealed letter, or guess the thoughts of another; for, besides being mesmeric experiences, these things are spiritual phenomena connected with the rappings, of the certainty of which whole armies of witnesses could testify.

That these rappings do really exist, and that they are as real as gravitation, or as thunder and lightning, may now be fairly and properly assumed, since about them it is no longer a question of the value of testimony. For persons open to evidence on the subject, one hundredth part of the testimony which now exists would be enough; and, for those who cannot believe the present evidence on the matter, a thousand times more evidence ought to be insufficient, and probably would be. Whatever it may be, whether good or bad, the thing is real. Multitudes may have had no opportunity of personally knowing about it; and many persons may think, very properly, that they would themselves be none the wiser for meddling with it; but still it may now reasonably be assumed as a fact. As a matter of evidence, the thing is not as it was twenty years ago, when it was first known of by rumors from Rochester; nor as it was ten years ago; nor even as it was five years since. And science and people who believe by its permission may as well accept the fact to-day as wait for fifty years. For if those rappings should stop to-morrow as suddenly as they began, which not improbably some day they will, yet certainly in the next century they would be believed in as having been real, because of the testimony and literature and wide belief existing to-day on the subject.

But perhaps it may be said that mere unaccountable rappings, even though somewhat intelligent, are no great matter. And they are not any great thing for a child learning the alphabet, it is true; but they become of infinite importance when, by dominant science, they are pronounced to be impossible. A scientific impossibility proved to be true is a wonderful thing; and so wonderful is it, that under no magnifying-glass can it be made to seem too wonderful. But it is also a wonderful thing, with all manner of wonders behind it, possibly.

And it may be asked whether it is good or devilish. For our argument that does not matter. And besides, that question implies what has not been at all assumed, — that the rappings are connected with the spiritual world. But, with a view to the next question, let it be allowed that they are so connected. And now perhaps it is asked whether they are Christian or Mohammedan. And the answer is, that they are both, just as talking is. They are a way of conversing with spirits who may be good or bad, wise or silly, and through which a man may have some such experience as he might have in his native town, if he should, after a long absence, go into a crowded hall, and from a gallery, in the dark, talk with voices down below.

But an argument on Spiritualism started from "the rappings" would be about the same as though, because of having learned the first letter of the alphabet, a man should think to read Hebrew, and want to argue the value of the Mazoretic points, or the nature of prophecy, or the comparative antiquity, respectively, of the various parts of the Book of Genesis. Spiritualism, as it is called, is a field as broad nearly as the presence of the human race, and as long almost as the ages themselves have been. It illustrates the pneumatology of the Scriptures; it is a key to the innermost rooms of the temples of Greece; and it avails for the better understanding of Plato. It solves enigmas as to Mahomet, and it accounts for the career of Joan Darc. It is the light by which in these days to read intelligently the history of Salem witchcraft, the Journal of George Fox, and the account of Edward Irving and the unknown tongues. It is enriched by the study of the Talmud, and not confused; and it answers for information, when it is tried on the religion of almost any primitive tribe, which has been reported upon, even the very latest.

Spiritualism is of many grades; and it may be connected with every sect in Christendom, and with every sect that follows Mahomet, with Buddhism, and with Brahminism. It is the silliness of silly people to-day, multitudes of them; and it is the wisdom of wise men, not a few. Spiritualism, as intercourse with spirits, has its dangers, and in ancient times was helplessly prone to idolatry; and it was on this account, probably, that it was guarded, limited, and directed for the Jews by severe legislation. But like the circumnavigation of the globe, by which, with sailing straight on, man goes out on one side of the world, and returns on the other, so what was the peril of the ancient Jews religiously seems now to stand opposed to that idolatry of science by which the laws of nature are pleaded against the miracles of God.

A strange land is that of which glimpses are got through Spiritualism; a border-land between this world and the next; a region whence spiritual causes can start material effects, and wherein the laws of Nature are in some degree pliant to spiritual agents, and along the line of which, with strange consequences, spirit and matter interosculate through their respective laws; a region where it is suddenly bright, unearthly light, and then as suddenly darkness, and wherein easily a man gets bewildered and befooled; a realm where flits the will-o'-the-wisp, and where fog-banks roll, where often truth looks like illusion, and where, too, illusions are often taken for truth; a field where light is reflected and refracted in a hundred ways, and so as to confuse sometimes like darkness itself; a land whence voices call, sweet and saintly perhaps, but liable in a moment to be cut short like telegraphic wires, and to be continued perhaps by impostors; a region of marvel, with gazing at which many persons have found themselves actuated as though by enchantment; a realm in creation, which sceptics may ridicule, and which some good Christians may ignorantly deny, but in connection with which exist pathways of thought, and across which are distinctly discernible objects, which theology ought to know of.

There is a proverb, that "any stick is good enough to beat a dog with." And the first stick out of the thicket of Spiritualism silences the argument short and sharp, and as incessant as the barking of a dog, which has been kept up so long, and especially in Germany, about the Order of Nature.

By the rappings which come upon a table in the presence of a medium, the laws of nature call out against the philosophy of Baden Powell; and they protest against the notion of Buckle, as to there being nothing new to be expected; and they deride the contemptuous self-complacency of Froude; and they explode the dreary vantage-ground whence Büchner would deny the immortality of the soul.

And now, perhaps, some one will wonder whether the writer thinks that his argument is a cure for scepticism. For every variety of scepticism, he certainly does not think that it can be. There is scepticism which is a part of good sense. And of scepticism as a mental disease there are degrees, just as there are varioloid, small-pox, and confluent small-pox. There is a mild scepticism, which is simply the spirit of the age, and there is a scepticism which is the result of undue constitutional tendency combined with the temper of the times; and of the same thing, viewed as a disorder, there is an extreme degree, which may be called confluent scepticism, and which mostly is incurable. It is more common in Paris than in this neighborhood. It is the state of a person with whom everything runs to doubt. It is a mental state in which a man might see a miracle, only to wonder whether it could be done again; and who would not believe either, though one rose from the dead; and who, if he saw nine men out of ten raised from the dead, would only doubt nine times the more, as to whether the remaining tenth man could possibly be raised. This is confluent scepticism; and it is what converts even remedies themselves into disease.

There have certainly, however, been intellectual Christians, who had been caught at their studies by the spirit of scepticism and been manacled by the logic of science, and who had been unable to get themselves exorcised or liberated by the greatest divines of Protestantism, who yet have felt themselves freed by the first sound of those unaccountable rappings, and able to enter "into the temple walking and leaping, and praising God"; being enabled to pray and trust and hope, by having learned that the Order of Nature is not everything, and that their souls may perhaps be free of it, and free for something higher. And these persons have continued in the same state of joy and freedom and holy hope, comparatively careless as to whether the rappings had been spiritual or demoniac; being only too happy with simply believing them to be something supernatural, something towards a proof, that perhaps the heavens are not brass against us, and that the Order of Nature does not close about our souls like a living tomb.

That the writer hereof should ever have had this to say, of his own knowledge, would have seemed to him in those days, when his faith was according to Mill's Analysis of the Human Mind, to be just as unlikely as his becoming a dancing dervish; or a silent, barefooted Trappist; or a turbaned hadji, squatting on the ground, and intent on the Koran, all day long, at Mecca; or a missionary to the ten lost tribes of Israel; or a Roman prelate pleading with cardinals, against the Devil's advocate, and for the canonization of monks and nuns. But the world is wide, and the world of thought is wider still. And wider and wider still it grows, and at an ever-growing pace, in these days, when with many running to and fro, knowledge is increased; when every ancient history is being drawn forth, to be perused afresh by every light which can be got to bear upon it; when every savage tribe is being respectfully solicited for its traditions; when the monasteries of Mount Sinai and along the frontier of Christendom are yielding up their ancient parchments to enthusiastic scholars; when the King of Siam suddenly stands forth, an eminent astronomer, as the shadow of a great eclipse comes along to cross his kingdom; when, too, the old foundations of Jerusalem are being carefully explored by an English Commission; and when, also, the Great Pyramid is being questioned, stone by stone, as to those singular secrets of which it is believed to be the depository.

How much of what is knowledge to-day will be ignorance to-morrow! And how certainly truths, which in this age are taken for errors, will subserve the pioneers of thought in the age to come! But in this world, where light leads up to a wall of darkness, and where darkness yields indeed, but only recedes, scarcely could man dare to advise with man, but that certainly all things human must be rounded by the infinite mercy of God.

MIRACLES AND DOCTRINE.

OFTEN a painful calculation of the orbit of a comet has been falsified, because of some heavenly bodies which had not been taken into the account, and therefore because of disturbing forces which had not been allowed for. And often an inquiry in philosophy has been futile, because of disturbing forces, which had not been allowed for from theology or history. On the subject of supernaturalism, many persons are prejudiced by what they suppose to be their position as Christians. They lean on faith, as they think; and lean so, as they think, on certain ancient facts of which Palestine was the scene. But there are other persons who not only have faith, but who are themselves, as it were, possessed by it. They say for themselves, like Peter, "Thou art the Christ, the Son of the living God"; and to them this revelation has been made, not indeed apart from all agencies of flesh and blood, but yet from the Father which is in heaven. And these believers find themselves upon a rock, joyful and curious spectators, who know, as they look around, that whatsoever things are true are really in their favor; and that the gates of hell can never prevail against their standing-place, whatever hosts or forms or blasts may be let out. And certainly before all things, men have to be true; for never can the whole body be full of light, Christian or any other, unless the eye be single.

How often has there been willingness to have the subject of miracles grievously misunderstood rather than have it scrutinized! But now, there is no really wise man but will say, "On any book which is worth reading, let us have all the light which we can. And if the Bible be, in any way, the word of God, and it be allowed us to read it, then let all the light of God's world come in upon it, and it will only be the plainer and the clearer. Truth forever, — 'the glorious gospel of the blessed God!'"

And there are theological zealots, who think that they can help a sacred cause by means, which one side of the mind does not wish the other side to know of, by such means as the understanding would keep secret from the conscience. As connected with the Scriptures, how much has been said and done which was not candid! But whether statesmen or cardinals, or preachers to the heathen, — no matter who they are, or under what pretext, — no man can sow the wind, and not leave the whirlwind to be reaped. Help out the cause of God, help it by any other means than the fairest, help it by the wisdom of this world! Remember what happened to Uzza for putting forth his hand to support the ark of God, when that seat of miraculous power seemed to shake upon the cart. If a cause be of God, it will not bear to be propped by the hand of a little faith. And for its support finally, no means will avail but what are holy.

And now let the modern stumbling-block as to miracles, be still further considered than it was in the preceding chapter. The common presentation as to miracles is, that they are acts suspending the laws of nature; that suspensions of the laws of nature are impossible, except by the direct permission of God; that God never would suspend his laws, except for a purpose greater than the laws themselves, — the revelation, that is to say, of himself; and thus that all miracles reported outside of the Bible may be instantly denied. This is the argument of the best book of its kind, — that of Hugh Farmer on Miracles. But at the very beginning it begs the question, in its way of defining a miracle, as being a suspension of the laws of nature. When the apostles and prophets showed signs and wonders, or wrote about them, they never talked about suspending the laws of nature. And really, ourselves, we do not know but what we should call a miracle might be, not an act suspending some one law of nature, but simply an act using, in some new way, another law very familiar perhaps, or very occult. The laws of nature, — this is a convenient phrase for ordinary use. And for the purposes of natural science, and restricted to such ends as those of geology, chemistry, and astronomy, investigation may properly proceed, on the supposition of the laws of nature. But when the suspension of the laws of nature is argued about, for purposes not geological or chemical, but divine, then it behooves us to think more exactly what it is which is talked of.

A certain manifestation in nature is called a law; but it is so called by simply a figure of speech, derived from the manner in which men mutually arrange their affairs. And yet often there is great stress laid on the phrase "laws of nature" for just that very purpose, in regard to which chiefly it is objectionable. And this is done as though it were supposed that, as the commandments were written in Horeb, one, two, three, ten commandments, on tables of stone, so laws of nature were devised and instituted by God, for shaping the void and formless world, — first, the law of attraction, and then that of gravitation; and next one chemical affinity, and then another. For many and most purposes, we do well to speak of the laws of nature; but there are some purposes, in view of which we are to remember that we talk about the laws of nature only by a figure of speech, and when indeed it would be better that we should be speaking of the properties of nature, the qualities of nature, or the spirit of nature.

Suspension of the laws of nature! The force of the phrase, as an objection to the possibility of a miracle, vanishes as soon as ever it is remembered that by the laws of nature, we do not really mean what can be broken one by one, or what can be broken at all; do not at all mean enactments of God, but simply the spirit of nature. To define a miracle, then, as being an act by which a law of nature is suspended, is not according to true philosophy. Also, it is being wise beyond what is written; or, rather, it is very unwise, and especially on the part of the advocates of Scriptural narratives; for the time when the miracles of the Bible were wrought, and when they were written of, was many hundreds of years before what is called the discovery of the laws of nature, and longer still, perhaps, before the invention of the phrase, "Suspension of the laws of nature."

One of the early miracles of Christianity was on a man "which sat for alms at the Beautiful Gate of the temple." Peter, having been entreated for something, did not say, "I hereby suspend, over thee and in thee, laws of nature, by number, one, nine, and thirteen; and now thou art well." And it has been very incautious work in controversy to commit Peter as though he had said such a thing, or anything at all like it. What Peter actually did say was, "Silver and gold have I none; but such as I have give I thee: in the name of Jesus Christ of Nazareth, rise up and walk." As a preliminary to this, however, is written what may have been directly connected with the miracle, that "Peter, fastening his eyes upon him with John, said, Look on us." There is no man but, as to quality, is more than all the laws of nature put together. And so it may well be that the name of Jesus Christ of Nazareth may have been a symbol, an invocation, a channel of power which may have been natural indeed as to its ultimate effect in healing, but supernatural as to origin and intensity.

The Jews and all the disciples of Christ regarded miracles as being of various degrees, and as differing in magnitude and decisiveness. And, in their definition of miracles, Catholic theologians have degrees of greater and less, and always have had. In this manner of estimating miracles, there would seem to be involved another apprehension of them, than as though they must necessarily all of them argue equally the divine will, be all of them the pronunciation of God, and each one of them just as emphatic and distinct and peremptory as another.

It is often argued as though miracles were credible only as happening among persons in covenant with God, through Abraham or through Christ. Yet the fullest account of prophetic vision in the Scriptures is connected with Balaam, a resident of Moab. And, of all the prophetic dreams in the Old Testament, the most wonderful was that with which the Egyptian Pharaoh was inspired, and which Joseph interpreted; and those with which Nebuchadnezzar had his spirit troubled, and which were connected by Daniel with "a God in heaven that revealeth secrets." And at the birth of the Saviour, if wise men arrived at Jerusalem from the East, guided by a star spiritually discerned, it was because, apart from the stock of Israel, there were persons susceptible of miraculous instruction, and favored with it. Dean Stanley says truly, in his work on the Jewish Church, that, unlike the temper of the present age, the Scriptures are always ready to acknowledge divine inspiration outside of the chosen people, and so to admit the higher spirits of every age and every nation among the teachers of the Universal Church.

It will help us to understand better the significance of a miracle among the Jews, if we remember that they were instructed not to follow always even an acknowledged miracle. "If there arise among you a prophet or a dreamer of dreams, and giveth thee a sign or a wonder, and the sign or wonder come to pass whereof he spake unto thee, saying, Let us go after other gods which thou hast not known, and let us serve them; thou shalt not hearken unto the words of that prophet or that dreamer of dreams; for the Lord your God proveth you, to know whether you love the Lord your God with all your heart and with all your soul. Ye shall walk after the Lord your God, and fear him, and keep his commandments, and obey his voice, and ye shall serve him, and cleave unto him. And that prophet or that dreamer of dreams shall be put to death, because he hath spoken to turn you away from the Lord your God, which brought you out of the land of Egypt." A miracle might, then, be acknowledged, and yet its cogency be denied. And even an acknowledged prophet was not to be followed in every direction. In the Book of Exodus, we read that one miracle after another, which Moses showed to Pharaoh, the magicians repeated by their enchantments; and that it was only when their power was surpassed by the fourth miracle of Moses that "the magicians said unto Pharaoh, This is the finger of God." And, as we learn from what happened to Ahab, even four hundred prophets might conjointly prophecy untruly, and that through a lying spirit in the mouth of them all, and of the Lord's direct permission. It would seem, too, that, simultaneously with the mission of Jesus, a miracle might be wrought, to which the apostles could demur. "And John answered him, saying, Master, we saw one casting out devils in thy name, and he followeth not us; and we forbade him because he followeth not us. But Jesus said, Forbid him not; for there is no man which shall do a miracle in my name that can lightly speak evil of me. For he that is not against us is on our part."

It is to be noticed that a miracle, simply as a miracle, Jesus probably never wrought; and Lightfoot, indeed, says so absolutely, and perhaps correctly. Jesus works miracles out of pity, for love, as illustrations or corroborations of doctrine, but not for the sake of the marvellous merely. And further it would seem that when he was sometimes invited and sometimes challenged to evince his Mesiahship by showing a sign, he never consented, but called that manner of testing him the craving of an evil and adulterous generation. His words, when trusted by a sick man, became a miracle of health; when uttered in prayer at the tomb, quickened the dead with life; and when breathed in blessing over five loaves, multiplied them into food for five thousand persons and twelve baskets full of fragments. Even the hem of his garment, a widow could touch in a crowd, and find herself healed with so doing. Signs and wonders went out from him as fast as words, and as easily, too, sometimes. From side to side of the sea of Galilee, and from Capernaum to Jerusalem, he was to be tracked by his miracles. There was a miracle for the Roman centurion, and a miracle for the poor Syrophenician woman; but a miracle never for those who demanded it as such, for Pharisees and Sadducees tempting him, for Jews demanding of him, "What sign showest thou unto us?" Once, in the midst of a great crowd, he was asked, "What sign showest thou, then, that we may see and believe thee? what dost thou work?" But, for answer, he asserted that his doctrine was greater than the miracle of manna in the wilderness; that persons to be converted would follow laws of the spirit, rather than the attraction of a sign; and that himself he was a sign and was also bread, and that more wonderful than the manna of the wilderness. It is consonant with what precedes that St. Paul classes miracles below teaching; though of course it was not ordinary instruction, for which teachers were ranked next after prophets,—"And God hath set some in the church; first, apostles; secondarily, prophets; thirdly, teachers; after that, miracles; then gifts of healing, helps, governments, diversities of tongues."

A miracle may be convincing; but evidently, at the best, it is not the best occasion of conversion. There is a happier, better reason for conviction about Christ than even seeing the greatest miracle with one's own eyes, or our Saviour would never have said to Thomas, as he felt of his hands and side, after his crucifixion and resurrection, "Thomas, because thou hast seen me, thou hast believed: blessed are they that have not seen, and yet have believed." And just as Moses forewarned the Jews against following the lead of every sign or wonder, so does Jesus Christ forewarn the Church: "There shall arise false Christs and false prophets, and shall show great signs and wonders; insomuch, that, if it were possible, they shall deceive the very elect." The thoughts of St. Paul were familiar with Providence as manifesting itself among Jews and Gentiles, as evincing itself in the world's conflicts, as summoning its subjects to put on the whole armor of God, for a fight of a wider meaning than they would perhaps well perceive, as being not against flesh and blood merely, furious Jews, tyrannical magistrates, or Cæsars calling themselves gods; but as being "against principalities, against powers, against the rulers of the darkness of this world, against spiritual wickedness in high places."

And so, writing to the Thessalonians in the spirit of prophecy, he warns them of that wicked one to be revealed, "whose coming is after the working of Satan, with all power and signs and lying wonders." And St. John writes on the same understanding and to the same purpose: "Beloved, believe not every spirit, but try the spirits whether they are of God; because many false prophets are gone out into the world." In the Book of Revelation, we have the visions of one in the Spirit, of one who not merely saw further on than common eyes, but who discerned also the essential characters of coming powers and ages. And listening to the Apocalypse, as it is disclosed, we hear of how "the beast was taken, and with him the false prophet, that wrought miracles before him." And more distinctly, too, we are told that there were to be expected "the spirits of devils working miracles, which go forth unto the kings of the earth and of the whole world." Miracles actually to be looked for from the spirits of demons! Let that be remembered.

But here some persons may ask anxiously, "Can it be that there should be a miracle, any kind of miracle, and the worker of it not be approved of God? Can there be a prophet ever, once in even a thousand or two thousand years, and he be a false man? How shall we know the false prophet?" To this it may be answered, that for all the ends of holiness and faith we may know them by the words of Christ, "Ye shall know them by their fruits." There is, too, a capability in man, which, with the quickening of the Holy Ghost, becomes discerning of spirits; ability, that is, for judging of what spirit a prophet's inspiration is. Lightfoot supposes that in the first age of the Church it was almost impossible to distinguish between magical, diabolical spirits and their operations and the operations and utterances of the Holy Ghost; but that the difficulty was remedied by there having been among the early disciples, a gift for the "discerning of spirits." It may have been that that gift was specially imparted and specially effective for times, when almost it was possible for the very elect to be deceived. But now and always with Christians, for discerning false prophets, seducing spirits, and false teachers, the words of Christ — uttered, too, for this very purpose — are enough: "Ye shall know them by their fruits. Do men gather grapes of thorns, or figs of thistles?"

It would be well for us, no doubt, to get back into the primitive feeling about the miracles of the Bible. It may be that really ourselves we falsify the miracles, by making them more peculiar than they are. It may be that we miss the meaning of a miracle, by thinking that miracles are not only improbable at present, but impossible, and one just as much so as another, the healing of the sick as the raising of the dead. And it is perhaps only with knowing how a false prophet might possibly have a miracle work its way through his nature, that we can even recognize the channel by which the Spirit flowed in upon Christ, not by measure, but as a stream of truth and miracles. In the Scriptures, then, we find that by our position as Christians we are not committed to a denial of the miraculous in any age; and we also find that, indeed, the early Christians were taught to expect it, even aside from Christian uses. What, then, is the proof of Christianity? and what are the miracles as evidences? The answers to these questions shall be in the words of others; and they are all the better for the purpose, that they were not written for an exigency, or to meet any modern difficulty on the subject of miracles: and so there shall be no quotation here of the opinions of Arnold, Newman, and others of the present age.

John Owen of the seventeenth century, in a manly tone, which gladdens the reader, says, if one would begin with the miracles as the foundations of Christianity, that he can get no tolerable assurance that any such miracles were ever wrought. Does he doubt them then? Owen doubt them! No more than any person doubts the sun because he cannot touch it. Hear what he says further: "Many writers of the Scriptures wrought no miracles. And by this rule their writings are left to shift for themselves. Miracles, indeed, were necessary to take off all prejudices from the person that brought any new doctrine from God; but the doctrine still evidenced itself. The apostles converted many where they wrought no miracle; and, where they did so work, yet they for their doctrine, and not the doctrine on their account, was received. And the Scripture now hath no less evidence and demonstration in itself of its divinity than it had when by them it was preached." He adds, that they who do not receive the Bible on this ground will never receive it on any ground as they ought. Says his contemporary, Richard Baxter: "I more sensibly perceive that the Spirit is the great witness of Christ and Christianity to the world. And though the folly of fanatics tempted me long to overlook the strength of this testimony of the Spirit, while they placed it in a certain internal assertion or enthusiastic inspiration, yet now I see that the Holy Ghost, in another manner, is the witness of Christ, and his agent in the world. The Spirit in the prophets was his first witness; and the Spirit by miracles was the second; and the Spirit by renovation, sanctification, illumination, and consolation assimilating the soul to Christ and heaven, is the continued witness to all true believers. "And if any man have not the spirit of Christ, the same is none of his." Even as the rational soul in the child is the inherent witness or evidence that he is the child of rational parents."

Baxter and Owen were men of other days than these, and ministers of another training than the ten thousand clergymen in England, who were lately made to tremble and petition their bishops, in consequence of a volume of "Essays and Reviews," to which four or five of their fellows had been accessory. All this modern talk, about miracles being the foundation of Christianity, by one party, and about their being impossible to be proved, by another party, — it would all have been but as the idle wind to Baxter and Owen. Ministers who knew of the rock on which the Church is founded, — they would have looked round them, on one side and on the other; and they would have said together, "Christianity based on miracles! O you unspiritual brethren! The miracles of the New Testament impossible to be proved in a court of law! So they are; and we acknowledge it willingly. But they are true nevertheless, a thousand times true." But Baxter and Owen were theologians, eminent and acknowledged, in an age when it was not strange to remember that the word theology means the science of God. They were men for whom there was a world of spirit just as surely as a world of matter. They were men of learning, and also they were men of wide and various experience in the world. And they were men, too, of a rarer wisdom than is ever caught from either books or fellow-creatures, men of spiritual insight, and men who knew, or thought that they could know, "the things of God by the Spirit of God."

Baden Powell regards miracles as hard to be believed by the scientific mind, and as becoming more and more incredible to the world at large. And he says expressly: "If miracles were in the estimation of a former age among the chief supports of Christianity, they are at present among the main difficulties and hindrances to its acceptance"; and Renan and others say so too. To this Baxter and Owen, only that their time of speaking in this world is over, might be supposed to answer: "To the scientific mind miracles are incredible. Nor is this to be wondered at, since the natural man receiveth not the things of the Spirit of God; for unto him they are foolishness. But, to him that is spiritual, they are the wisdom of God and the power of God; for they are not only reported to the world by history, but also by Christians they are susceptible of being spiritually discerned." And such a statement would be legitimate and sound; for what cannot be quite proved in one court by direct testimony may be abundantly demonstrable in another court, by circumstantial and presumptive evidence.

And what can never be proved to a scientific demonstration, a man may yet be insane if he does not believe. And things which would be utterly impossible to a man of the earth, earthy, even though his earthiness were of the very finest kind, and energetic as a tiger's, and sagacious as an elephant's, — these same things might become abundantly credible to him, as soon as ever his earthiness had been touched by "the second Adam," the "quickening spirit," "the Lord from heaven." And about God, though viewed, as often he is, as being a mighty machinist, heartless really, though delighting in work, there are things which would seem to be very unlikely, but which are easily credited by a man, who, because of his having been reached by the Spirit, has felt himself "in subjection unto the Father of spirits." For, whatever the eternal necessity of things may be, it can never be supposed, before the throne of grace, if there be one, that necessarily men and butterflies must be alike.

But now, because the thing has got to be done, it must be done, but yet it is not without reluctance and even some pain; for Renan is a man of some fine characteristics, though not perhaps, in all respects, of the very happiest schooling in life. Referring to the earlier chapters of the Book of Acts, in his volume on the Apostles, he says, "It would be unjust to dwell on anything we may see to be shocked at, in this sad page of the origin of Christianity. For vulgar hearers, the miracle proves the doctrine; for us, the miracle causes the doctrine to be forgotten. When a belief has consoled and ameliorated humanity, it is excusable for having employed proofs proportioned to the weakness of the public, whom it addressed." There are persons who would call this French sentiment. There are others who would utter words about it, keen enough and true, but words also of crimination and condemnation. But that shall not be done here. Christianity is an excusable imposture, according to Renan. That Christianity is an imposture, possibly a man may believe honestly; but that, as an imposture, it is excusable because of what has happened with it,—for the supposition of such a thing as this, there are no easy words to comment with which are strong enough. Let the reader peruse again the words of Baxter and Owen, and thank God that he can so readily sweeten his mind, after such a sentiment as has been submitted to him.

Miracles are so intimately connected with the personality of Jesus and with the lives of his apostles, that it would seem as though it might be impossible for a sane man, should he bethink himself, to say that the miracles are false, while Jesus is true; or to say that Paul could write as he did out of a mind either crazy or deceitful. Concurrently with a belief in Christ, as a manifestation of the Highest, a man indeed may say: "Christ Jesus I bow to, as a Revelation started from somewhere between me and the unknown God; and he is the highest, holiest manifestation, amidst primeval darkness which I have to trust to. As to the miracles connected with Christ, it is so that I cannot understand them, that I cannot conscientiously say, in the proper meaning of the word 'belief,' that I do believe them. It may be that constitutionally I am unfitted for a belief in the marvellous, just as many men are disqualified for music and mathematics; and it may be that some time my mind will open to light, which at present it is closed against; and, should that light ever come, it will be welcome and blessed." A man may be in such a position as that mentally, and be a very good Christian perhaps. But there would seem to be a wall of separation between him and the man who denounces the miracles of the New Testament as being impostures. For the latter person really can find in Christianity but very little which is worthy of respect; vitiated to his mind, as it must nearly all of it be, by its connections with what he supposes to be imposture, — that is, if he be a man who can be justified in reasoning at all on such a subject as Christianity.

In illustration of the subject of Christianity, as vouched for by miracles, may be considered the following passage from a homily by St. John Chrysostom, about the beginning of the fifth century: —

"Tell me, if it were at your choice either to raise the dead in the name of Christ, or to die for the sake of his name, which would you wish to do? Would you not certainly prefer the latter? And if there were offered to you either the power of changing fodder into gold, or a will which could despise wealth like fodder, would not you choose the latter of the two? And rightly would you do so, because men would be best persuaded in that manner; for, if they saw you change fodder into gold, like Simon, they would wish to share the miraculous power with you; and so their love of money would grow upon them. But, if ever they could see gold despised like fodder, they would soon be cleansed from their disease. You see, then, that it is a good life which avails most."

And, now, a very different man from the golden-mouthed bishop, an ancient Rabbi, Simeon Ben Lachish, from his point of view would remark: —

"The proselyte is more beloved by the holy, blessed God than the whole crowd that stood before Mount Sinai. For unless they had heard the thunderings, and seen the flames and lightnings, the hills trembling and the trumpets sounding, they had not received the law. But the proselyte hath seen nothing of all this, and yet hath come in, devoting himself to the holy, blessed God, and hath taken upon him the kingdom of heaven."

And here may come in a quotation from the Pneumatology of Heinrich Stilling, as corroborating somewhat indirectly, but from the fact of experience, the position of Baxter and Owen, as to the relative influence of miracle and doctrine. After saying that an apparition may cause a panic, but seldom or never operate a conversion, he adds, "I know instances of professed materialists and freethinkers having positively seen spirits, so that they were convinced that it was the soul of one of their deceased acquaintances; and yet they continued to doubt their own immortality and self-consciousness."

From a very different quarter, very rich, however, in psychological information, may be adduced the following testimony of Emmanuel Swedenborg: "A sixth law of the Divine Providence is that man should not be reformed by external mediums, but by internal mediums; by external mediums means by miracles and visions, also by fears and punishment; by internal mediums means by truths and goods from the word, and from the doctrine of the Church, and by looking to the Lord; for these mediums enter by an internal way, and cast out the evils and falses which reside within: but external mediums enter by an external way, and do not cast out evils and falses, but shut them in. Nevertheless, man is further reformed by external mediums, provided he has been before reformed by internal mediums."

Not in controversy about miracles, as disconnected, isolated facts, can there ever be found the truth about them. But let the denier of miracles study pneumatics, and learn the marvels which will be disclosed to him: and let the mere dogmatic asserter of miracles explore the philosophy to which they belong; and then the two will find themselves meeting on peaceful ground, amazed, indeed, but not lost in amazement.

MIRACLES AND THE BELIEVING SPIRIT.

AND with the event just now supposed a new era would probably begin for the Church. There is nobody living who can read the Bible as he ought to do. If he be not a Christian, he reads it with at least some small remains of the hostility, which was wakened in his predecessors by the hatred with which they were once pursued. And if he be a Christian, he reads it as though it were a book by itself; as though there had been no time anywhere else, while the ages of Jewish history were slowly passing; as though, body and soul, the ancient inhabitants of Palestine had been such a peculiar people as that poetry, with them, had been altogether another thing from poetry in Greece; and as though the prophets of Homer, Plato, and Pausanias were so utterly different in constitution and purpose from the prophets of the Scriptures as that even the false prophets of the Bible could not possibly be likened, in any way, to the prophets of the Iliad, or of the Travels in Greece. Even the heathenism denounced in the Scriptures is held, not in veneration certainly, but yet in such a reserved, conservative temper as that hardly ever does any one think to illustrate it by the heathenism of Hindostan or Africa. Analogy is rarely thought of as being possible between the demoniacs of the New Testament and "the sufferers" in Salem, some two hundred years ago, or the people of strange experiences lately, at Chambery in Savoy, and more recently at Morzine. And notwithstanding the little philosophy which is accessible on the subject of prophecy, never perhaps to any formal commentator on the Scriptures has it occurred to illustrate the manner in which, characteristically, as it would appear, often the prophets of the Old Testament were convulsed, by any reference to the peculiarity which caused the society of Friends to be called Quakers. It is as though it were thought that even the devils, mentioned in the New Testament, would be profaned by having anything modern likened to them.

More and more the tendency has been to read the Scriptures by the least light possible of a spiritual character; but sea and land, the while, have been compassed to learn about the mustard-tree, or as to leprosy, or as to how wine was made, and cakes were baked, anciently, or as to the niceties of the old law on polygamy and divorce. And it seems like a daring statement, when one reads, in the grave work of an English dignitary, that prophetic power has existed outside of the churches, both Jewish and Christian. And it has seemed to be very anomalous, when it has been hinted, by the way of comparing small things with great, that there may possibly be some analogy between the ancient "laying-on of hands" and the processes which were stumbled upon by Mesmer.

And yet to demur to illustrations of the Scriptures from psychological experiences, modern or mediæval, is really about the same thing as though one should hold that Miriam's triumphal ode, on the shore of the

Red Sea, could never have been made audible by such breath as mortals draw; or as though one should deny that the harp to which David sang from inspiration could possibly have been such an instrument as might have been bought in a market-place. Such confusion often do men seriously and solemnly, — and all the more readily because of the solemnity which they are under, — such confusion do men make between a mere channel and the water in it, which really constitutes the stream. As Jesus ascended from Jericho to Jerusalem, a whole multitude accompanied him, with their hosannas "for all the mighty works which they had seen." This action of theirs the Pharisees would have had Jesus rebuke. "And he answered and said unto them, I tell you that if these should hold their peace the stones would immediately cry out." And if this had happened, as it might have done, it would not have been that the stones would have become adorable, or that they would have remained anything else than common stones; but simply it would have been made plain and memorable that the Holy Spirit which was shed abroad there, can make anything vocal, though perhaps the stubborn heart of a man may be almost the last thing to be pliant to its promptings.

On the subject of miracles it is very curious how men dogmatize sometimes; for a man will argue on behalf of the miracles of the Bible as though they were simply things of history, and almost of yesterday, in a neighboring city, having no eye for the long perspective of history, and having also no more idea of the history of the Bible, and the books which compose it, than the wicked Ahab had of geology and the formation of mica slate; while another man in attacking the credibility of miracles does it as though, "by the grace of God," he were a king of thought, with a right to legislate for his own wants in argument, and to raise up and put down witnesses at will. This man, however, is essentially of the same character with his humbler brother, who holds simply, "Everybody is as good as any other body, and is just as much entitled to an opinion; and let him have it and say it."

A man must have some sense of the miraculous before miracles can be to him what they ought to be. He must believe them himself aright before he is fit to convince others. And to argue them simply by the way of testimony and history, as is commonly done, does more mischief than good, and has often, with pressure, roused a conscientious antagonism of unbelief. Now and then a man is to be heard who takes credit to himself for believing in the miracles of the Scriptures, while actually his belief is just what he might have for the measurement of Nineveh, should it ever be published, or for the locality of the pool of Siloam. "Believing in miracles, is believing in history," says the confident man, "and when I say history, I mean the Bible." But now history is not exactly the same thing to one man as it is to another, nor to the same man is it the same thing at all times. And miracles, as a subject, need for their appreciation, not the temper of the market-place, nor the tone of the council-chamber, but the spirit of a worshipper, who has been admitted further into the temple than the fore-court, and who, if he has never seen inside of the holy of holies, has yet distinctly recognized the veil of separation, which hangs before it.

What constitutes a prophet? How did the word of the Lord come? and by what faculty was it received? How did the Spirit rest upon a man? What exactly was the state of a man when he saw visions? And what precisely was it which happened when a man had a revelation in a dream? Surely, these are questions which theology ought to be ready to answer anywhere, in a moment; and especially, as at least, the answers have always been latent in the Scriptures themselves. And yet there are theologians by profession, who are very impatient of such inquiries as these, who yet would be scandalized at being thought to be impatient Christians. The pneumatology of the Scriptures, from one cause and another, is utterly unknown, and even unsuspected by many persons, who perhaps would be ardent students in it, but for the spiritual twilight of our day, occasioned by the long, low, dense cloud of anti-supernaturalism, which has been passing over us. Often in controversies about miracles it would be ludicrous, only that it is sad, to see and know that on neither side have the opponents a right to any opinion whatever, any more than if they were two unlettered Celts arguing about the binomial theorem.

And among even the assailants of miracles as being credible, there is that difference of opinion which argues that it is not because of broad daylight that they act, but really because, being intellectually active, they have been unable to sleep through this long "eclipse of faith." Renan thinks that visions and prophecies are as much exceptional to order, and as incredible as material miracles. But Baden Powell does not think so. He would have been perplexed and almost shocked by a miracle involving atoms of dirt, or which might have seemed to compromise chemistry, as in the healing of a sick man, or the multiplication of loaves and fishes by Jesus; but readily he would have credited visions and prophecies, as the result of spiritual interference with the spirits of men.

In the immortality of the soul a man may believe for fifty years, and in the fifty-first year, with "newness of life" may find that for the half of a century he had been believing with his fancy only, and not his heart. And after illness or great trouble often a man finds that, in some way or other, he has become "a new creature," because of the new book into which, for him, the old Bible would seem to have changed. And in this world's darkness there have been leaders of the people religiously, who, because of their having been enlightened from above, have been ready to humble themselves in the dust, not only before the Lord, but in the congregation of their fellow-creatures, because of their having spoken of "the things of the Spirit," without having personally known of the Spirit, and who would have wished to have said with Isaiah, "Woe is me! for I am undone; because I am a man of unclean lips, and I dwell in the midst of a people of unclean lips: for mine eyes have seen the King, the Lord of hosts."

Miracles presuppose a miraculous world, a world of spirit, from which, now and then, may be manifested "signs." But if that world be itself denied, or if the means or channels for any effect from it be disbelieved, or if the sense for it be asleep, men may talk about miracles, and may believe them, as they believe in the ring of Scipio Barbatus, which is said to have been found in his tomb. But believing in that manner, they do not believe miracles aright, do not believe them, as being what exactly they call themselves, which is "signs." Miracles are "signs." And signs presuppose a quarter whence they are made, and a mind which makes them. In the New Testament, at least, miracles are "signs," — signs of a presence which could not itself be borne perhaps, — signs of a something which of itself would be too vast for human comprehension.

But the significance of miracles in this manner, is exactly what has been generally surrendered to the assaults of science. Theology grown timid from many causes, and feeble too, has allowed young audacious science to strip it, almost without resistance. And outside of the Catholic Church, the utmost which it attempts to-day is to entreat scientific men, for the love of God, to spare some of the miracles of the Bible, and to let believers believe them, because of various ingenious theories, by which miracles may conceivably be true. And this it does very often, without remembering that these various and ingenious theories are opposed to one another, and do not need the unbelief of an enemy to expose and quash them.

Angel or vision, spirit or demon, dream or impulse, — none of these things ever come into this world, to anybody, from out of another world: that is what the common philosophy of the day says; and it is what generally, among Protestants, theology agrees to, though with many curious make-shifts for saving its dignity, and with one reservation. And the reservation which theology makes for itself, before succumbing to the imperious scepticism of science, is merely this: that in a certain country, at certain times there may have been miracles, though provided for, perhaps, from the beginning of the world in some curious way, by which science need not feel itself compromised, except very slightly or almost not at all. And this is theology, is it? Modern theology, it may be, but it is wofully weak. And it is no wonder that the miracles of the Bible are regarded as untenable accounts, and as scarcely worthy of an argument, by young students, in whose eyes they can be, at the best, but like relics descended from a mighty past, dead now and over; and vouched for also in merely the same traditional way as the holy curiosities in the treasury of some Catholic church in France or Italy, — a skull perhaps, a piece of a cloak, an old shoe, a little finger, a lock of hair, and other things, for which, living connection and vital significance have long since ceased.

During the last three or four generations, the miracles narrated in the Holy Scriptures have been defended, variously defended, ingeniously defended, hotly defended, defended with lofty scorn, and defended with erudite contempt; but they have not proportionately been preached upon, or expounded, or gloried in. And it is a very singular, significant fact, that latterly the subject of miracles has been avoided by genius as something unattractive, and by holy meditation as something uncongenial. The defence of miracles has been free and multitudinous; but then it has been made much in the same way as the doors of a church might be barred against a mob, and in much the same temper. Miracles have been defended against the spirit of the times, by men of the same spirit themselves. And by the very way and tone in which miracles have been defended, there has been drawn upon them a keener and more concentrated attack.

The arms with which Christianity is assailed to-day on account of the miracles connected with the gospel, the ingenious arguments against them, have nearly all been got out of Protestant armories, and are actually the same weapons which Protestants, during two or three centuries, have devised and welded, and used against the credibility of the miracles of the Catholic Church. "Anything outside of the order of Nature, must be a miracle inside of the Church, or else it must be the work of the old enemy of the Church, and therefore, in a way, is still a testimonial to the Church." And not a little of the controversy between the Catholic Church and Protestants, has presupposed this false issue. And always it has been done to the detriment of Protestantism; for a man cannot fight, any more than he can sleep in a cramped attitude, without being the worse for it. Perverted by philosophy sometimes, and heated by controversy, it has often happened that Protestantism has defined miracles not quite rightly, as to both their nature and significance; and thus it has chanced that while combating the credibility of the mediæval and modern miracles of the Catholic Church, the leaders of Protestantism have actually exposed their own position, as Christian believers. And all the while really, in one place or another, age after age, have been occurring, among Protestants themselves things of the same nature as have sufficed at Rome for the canonization of saints, or for evidence of close communion with the spiritual world.

In the seventeenth century lived an Irish gentleman of the name of Greatrex, who healed diseases in a manner which would be commonly understood as being miraculous. The evidence about him is what would be supported by Evelyn and Jeremy Taylor. But now, what that man did would suffice in the Congregation on Rites at Rome for the canonization of fifty saints. And in the life of the Seeress of Prevorst, within the present century, were instances of intercourse with spirits, so many and of such a nature as would have made her the glory of any Order of Nuns for ages. It is not in the Catholic Church only that people sometimes are pious and clairvoyant both; and there have been many Protestants, and especially while in suffering, who have had spiritual experiences which, in the life of St. Philip Neri, would have counted for additional graces. There is a book entitled, "Devotional Somnium, or a Collection of Prayers and Exhortations, uttered by Miss Rachel Baker, in the City of New York, in the winter of eighteen hundred and fifteen, during her abstracted, unconscious state." The account of this Presbyterian girl presupposes a spiritual peculiarity like what constituted, not indeed the saintship, but the marvellousness of St. Bridget, in relation to whom there is a folio volume, in Latin, printed at Munich, in the seventeenth century, edited by a Cardinal, and enriched by various historical, literary, and philosophical illustrations, — "Celestial Revelations of the Seraphic Mother, St. Bridget, of Sweden, the Foreordained Bride of Christ, and the Foundress of the Order of her Bridegroom, the most Holy Saviour."

It has been the misfortune of Protestantism in its controversy with the Catholic Church, that it has had to argue the subject of miracles, as authorization of doctrine, while itself suffering, by way of circumscription, from "philosophy falsely so called," or only in part ascertained. Twelve years ago, there was published in Paris, a Life of St. Joseph of Cupertino. It was preceded and accompanied by a loud challenge to Protestants, on account of certain marvels which had happened in connection with the saint. The Protestant notice of the work was simply a jeering, flat denial of the marvels which seemed, however, to be well fortified by documents as to their credibility. And yet actually to that Catholic challenge it might have been answered, that, apart from goodness, the marvels for which St. Joseph of Cupertino was canonized are not peculiar to the Catholic Church, but are incidental to human nature, as is the truth to the knowledge of the writer hereof, and of perhaps a whole host of other Protestants. Dreams, visions, and impulses, of an extraordinary character, are of infinite interest to Catholics, religiously; but during the last hundred years or more, to nearly all enlightened Protestants, they have been, at best, but the halves of "singular coincidences," or they have been "queer things," and things not to be named or even thought of respectfully, for fear of science and public opinion.

On this subject of miracles, through controversy with the Catholic Church, there is another way in which Protestantism has suffered. Any statement as to miracles by a Catholic is what has been prepared and indorsed for him by the concentrated authority, learning, experience, and wisdom of his Church. Whereas, any statement by a Protestant is merely what an individual can best make. And thus it happens that Protestants argue about miracles in different ways, and in ways which are destructive one of another; and by the conflict of which, generally, faith is weakened and bewildered. But perhaps, any time, if the average sentiment of Protestants on the subject of miracles and the Catholic Church could have got embodied and expressed, it would have been something very different from that of their foremost controversialists. But such an expression of opinion, of course, could have been only conglomerate and not homogeneous. For Protestants are people of varieties and characteristics known, all of them, to no man living, perhaps. They are Lutherans, Calvinists, Episcopalians, and Presbyterians; Unitarians, Moravians, Quakers, Baptists, Methodists; people who eat, and drink, and work, and go to church, but who never think seriously; people who never go to church, except now and then in some regions, to assure themselves that they are Protestants; and people who go to church for duty, and who, at home, think so differently and so sweetly otherwise from what they have been taught, that they are an astonishment to themselves; Fellows of the Royal Society of London; English peasants, who have never been outside of their native counties; occupants of Swiss valleys, like the Bàn de la Roche; and suffering, sorrowing pietists, in such spots of dense heathenism as exist in London. And out of all these classes, the aggregate expression would probably have been, "You Catholics are not afraid of science, for inside of your countries it can only speak by permission of the Church. But with us Protestants, it is different. And somehow, our scholars can neither think, nor speak, nor feel, nor see, except with a twist, which they got in college. About science we generally know nothing, but we hope the best. However, we do know about facts. And your miracles, if that be what you call them, — things like some of your miracles, — have always been as common among us as they are with you; only that we do not think as much about them; nor have we either any authority among us to interpret, and magnify, and publish them."

Much of the salt of the Church has been what never was dropped from the pulpit. And there have been quiet, reverential, God-fearing peasants, believing in ghost-stories, who, simply because of their sense of the supernatural, have done more for Christianity, without one word for it intentionally, than many a doctor of divinity with even a quarto volume.

Of all the mistakes committed by scholarship, there is none worse than to forego sympathy with the ways of unlettered thought, and to feel contempt for the multitude. The primitive instincts are the best part of our lives; and household phraseology is the better part of our speech. A philosopher cannot deliberately and contemptuously forego communion with the poor, without being liable to drift away into vagaries and ineptitudes of thought; and especially and manifestly has this been the case on the subject of the Supernatural.

There is in existence a hymn-book, and of no obscure use either, in its day, in the preface to which it is said, that the hymns have been made to conform to modern philosophy, by the words, soul, and spirit in them having been changed into mind, reason, and understanding. Philosophy to-day is not so widely different from that modern philosophy as it might seem to be, by its affecting strongly the words "soul" and "spirit," and even making them fashionable; for always that philosophy will have us understand by spirit a something largely void of spiritual characteristics, as known alike to both Jews and Greeks. This emptying the word "spirit" of its meaning is in accordance with the anti-supernaturalism of our times. And, in the same manner, the Scriptures have been discharged of much which would imply preternatural connections for man. This, however, is a subject for further and fuller consideration.

Very largely a man can find in the Scriptures only what he is prepared to see. This is true of any book. But over and above those reasons which rule for a legal document, there are others which specially govern as to such subjects as are involved in an earnest study of the Scriptures. Before a man can be open to the full meaning of words which were written by persons within the sphere of the Holy Spirit, he himself must have been touched by that Spirit. That touch is what is said sometimes to throw an ignorant, disorderly backwoodsman into convulsions, because of the manner in which body and spirit are laced together. But it is different with a quiet, orderly person, studious of truth, and seeking for light. And when the Spirit reaches such a person it affects him like a great thought, like a flash of light in his soul, from above, and with the coming of which he feels at once humiliated and exalted, and as being what truly he is, — a creature in affinity with the Creator, and a child on earth suddenly found, and touched, and drawn by the Father in heaven.

By argument merely an anti-supernaturalist may be convinced that he is not justified in denying the miracles of the Scriptures. And by argument, perhaps, he may be made even to believe them historically. But for making him believe them aright, believe them to the best purpose, argument is not enough. To believe miracles with the intellect is one thing, and to believe them with the heart is another. A true believer believes them with both head and heart. In these times to propose converting an unbeliever to Christianity, as is often attempted, by simply historical argument, long drawn out, as to the reality and authority of miracles, is about the same thing as though, in the case of a priest losing his faith, it should be proposed to revive him spiritually by clothing him with surplice, bands, and beretta, and reading to him a lecture on apostolic succession.

According to the Psalmist, "The fool hath said in his heart, There is no God." His atheistic folly may be corrected, to a certain extent, by a good theologian. And the fool may be made logically to see and know that there must be a God. But he can have his heart revive from its atheistic numbness only with waiting and humility, and by the healing influence of that Spirit which indeed is the God "in whom we live and move and have our being," which makes ministers out of angels, and which perfects praise out of the mouth of babes; which gets itself glorified as to its purposes, by even the wrath of man; and which, reaching us as Christians is the Spirit which bears witness with our spirits that we are the children of God; and which, blending with our spirits, helps our infirmities, and prays in our prayers; and which manifests its strength in man the most, when man himself is at his weakest.

A Christian believer being of bad habits may be persuaded to reform his manners; but it is not at the will of either himself or his advisers, that he shall have what, however, will surely come, with perseverance,—joy in the Holy Ghost.

A philosophical materialist may have been convinced of the system, which is the opposite of what he had held; but yet, not at all as a sequence to his reasoning, and altogether really apart from his logic, it may flash upon him that he is not only a spirit clothed in matter, but that also he is a spirit in a spiritual world, a spirit open to he knows not what; but certainly, if anything be certain, open to the Holy Ghost; open to the gentle approach of the God under whose supremacy he came into being, and began to know of hope and fear, and of the struggle between virtue and vice.

If a creature of yesterday be to meet what is from all eternity, if what at its very best is folly is to be noticed, however distantly, by infinite wisdom, it can only be because wisdom from all eternity must be of infinite condescension, and willing even to "bow the heavens and come down"; and because, now and always, as to true worshippers, "the Father seeketh such to worship him."

And on the subject of miracles, argument, however acute it may be, is not everything. A man may be convinced of a mistake without therefore being filled with wisdom. And a man, by argument, may be made to feel that he has no right to deny the reality of the miracles of the Scriptures. But before they can become to him signs as well as wonders, there must be open in him an apprehension to which they signify; and there must be waiting in him a state comingled of expectation, awe, and faith, to which they answer.

After Thomas the apostle, who could not believe on testimony, had been satisfied, by the details of a personal interview, that his Lord was alive again, after his crucifixion, death, and burial, "Jesus saith unto him, Thomas, because thou hast seen me, thou hast believed: blessed are they that have not seen and yet have believed." By this text, not a little witticism and worldly wise remark has been started, as though it had been a sentiment devised for proselytizing purposes. Whereas, simply it would mean that blessed were they who could believe in his resurrection, on good testimony; because of their having souls larger than what might suffice for a detective policeman; because of their being of a temper which could possibly believe in a miracle, without seeing it; because of their not being too hard of heart; because of their knowing that the world is governed not only by magistrates like Caiaphas and Pilate, but by authorities and powers, invisible indeed, but higher still than they, by the ministration of angels, and by God Most High; and because of their being of a spirit, informed by the experiences of their people;—hopeful on account of their having Abraham to their father, and from the expectations, with which prophetically they had been inspired as to a Messiah; and ready, in an hour of darkness to trust the future, because of what Elijah had been, and Daniel had been proved. And perhaps, also, this further thought may have been involved in those words of the Lord,—that blessed were they who, because of what they knew of Jesus, and because of what they had felt of his transcendent spirit, and because of their sense of him as the Holy One, could readily believe that his soul was not to be left among souls below, and that indeed by death "it was not possible that he should be holden."

But there are persons who say, with many airs and much emphasis, "What have I to do with the past? Let the dead past be buried with the dead. I am a child of the present." And anything more derogatory to his manhood could anybody well say? A child of the present! That is exactly what a monkey is. But all the more that a man is a man, the more truly is he not only the child of the present time, but the grandchild of the last century; and also a descendant of the ages which were before Luther and Cranmer, and before William the Conqueror, and before Justinian with his Pandects, and before Plato and Homer, and before Christ, and before the captivity of the Jews, and before Moses, and before Abraham was. A monkey may chatter to-day, and does, as monkeys chattered thousands of years ago. But no man to-day speaks exactly as anybody did a hundred years ago. There is no man but speaks by his connections with almost every decade of every century of recorded time. And the better he speaks, the more widely does the man evince what his connections are, with Saxons, Normans, Danes, Britons, Romans, Greeks, with France and Spain, with Arabia and Persia. A man cannot well even order his dinner, but in words which connect him not only with the cooks of to-day, but with the ancient Germans in their forests, with the Normans of a thousand years ago, and with Britons, ages before Julius Cæsar. By almost every word he uses, by almost every inflection in his speech, by almost every thought he has, and by almost every shade of every thought, the man of to-day is the child of the past, a thousand times more than he is a child of the present. But the monkey is really the child of the present, and of it only, and always is so. Monkeyhood is exactly the same, to-day, which it was a hundred, a thousand years ago, or when Aristotle was alive.

Man is a child of the past, and ever more and more anciently descended. But concurrently with the mental wealth which is derived to him from the scholars and institutions and nations of the past, there are obligations and fealties to the past, which get fastened upon him.

By courts, and lawyers, and judges, and great reverence, do men endeavor to perpetuate among themselves, and to get expounded and made intelligible, the principles of law, which are the essences of the accumulated experiences of many men, in many ways, in many ages, and in many lands.

And a man has no right to denounce or discard, or even to suspect, the miracles of the Scriptures, merely because they are not in keeping with his own notions, or, as he says, because of his being himself a child of to-day, and free of the past. For free of the past, whether for knowledge, or obligation, or fealty, is what a man can be, only just as he nears the irresponsible, disconnected, untaught, playsome individuality of the monkey in the woods.

THE SCRIPTURES AND PNEUMATOLOGY.

THE Bible is a book which "he who runs may read." But if a man will read it, as a critic, he is bound to read it by all the light which he can get; and to remember also, that even so he may be but in a dim twilight. "Rise, take up thy bed and walk," were words which turned to a miracle of healing for a poor man, so as that he could roll up his bit of carpet and walk away. But for want of that information, with which always the background of Scriptural scenes ought to be filled up, in an old Dutch engraving, the sufferer of thirty-eight years is pictured as walking away with a four-post bedstead, curtains, and bedding on his shoulders. And often on the miracles of the Scriptures there are comments made which, philosophically, are just as unwitting as that Dutch picture. For indeed miracles presuppose some kind of pneumatology. But this is a thing which is hardly ever thought of, because of the anti-supernaturalism of the times, which latterly men have been living through. "Pneumatology, — what is that, and what can that have to do with the Scriptures?" These are questions, which have been asked in all seriousness, by persons, like whom there are thousands of others, both among those who attack and those who defend the Scriptures.

Pneumatology is the science, or rather is the best understanding of men as to the spiritual universe, as to the ranks of spiritual beings, from the highest to the lowest, and especially of men as spiritual beings, and of the ways in which spiritually they may affect one another; of their connections also with the spiritual world, and of the modes by which men may be affected, while yet in the flesh, by the influences and occupants of that world to which they belong spiritually, and also for eternity; and of the liabilities, too, and possibilities incidental to human nature, because of man's mixed constitution, as to body and spirit. This is pneumatology. And the pneumatology of the Scriptures, is that understanding of the spiritual universe which the sacred writers had, when they wrote their respective books, psalms, and epistles. A matter this of infinite importance! And it never could have been so commonly lost sight of, as it has been, but for the anti-supernaturalism of these latter times, and but that the best belief of the best believer to-day is not much better than the glimmering perceptions of some materialist philosopher, when first the eyes of his understanding begin to open spiritually. Deny the miracles of the Scriptures, without ever having known of the pneumatology involved in them! A man might as well denounce the calculations and predictions of astronomy, because they are not of a piece with his pocket arithmetic.

And the defence of the Scriptures, in ignorance of the pneumatology pervading them, is, of course, but blundering work. And with a pneumatology of his own, however imperfectly understood, the ordinary

Jew, of ancient times may have been a much better witness as to miracles than many a modern critic, in his place, would have been, who, however scientific he may be as to matter, has no science of spirit whatever. From the want of a Scriptural pneumatology, some things in the Bible are almost unintelligible, which would otherwise be very simple. Also the necessities of theologians in controversy have betrayed them into some false positions on Scriptural subjects, which they would never have occupied, if they had known the lay of the land on which they were contending, as through a pneumatology properly ascertained they would have done.

It has been widely held as a truism, that there never have been any other miracles than what are recorded in the Bible, or than certainly what happened in Biblical ages, or than what were seals of the Almighty set upon doctrines. This, however, is not Scriptural, and though it is intended as a defence of the Scriptures, it is ruinous to the philosophy of miracles.

That the gods of the heathen were stocks and stones, or, at best, fine statues, is become even a truism. And yet, notwithstanding what two or three passages in the Old Testament may seem to say differently, it is as certain, apparently, as the reality of the first commandment, that besides Jehovah there were other gods of some kind to be had.

And similarly, at present, the prophets denounced in the Old Testament are commonly supposed, all of them, to have been persons who pretended to prophesy, while they knew themselves that they were only impostors. Whereas commonly, the false prophet was a man of prophetic nature, who was false to the Lord, and who allowed himself to be used as a mouthpiece or other agency, by some false god, some demon or human spirit, who had got lodged, it may have been, in a temple, and by some such means, probably, as are used now for enticing martins to build in a garden.

And because magic might seem to render miracles less miraculous, it has been fancied, that there may have been anciently, a curious modification of language taken for granted, occasionally, by which, when a thing was said to have been done, it was understood as having simply been pretended to have been done. And thus in Exodus, in rivalry with Moses, when "the magicians did so with their enchantments," it has been held that the proper understanding is, that merely the magicians seemed or pretended to do so.

It has been supposed absolutely, that before Christ, there was no belief in another life among the Jews. And on this account, the revelation of a future life by Jesus Christ is thought to have been the more peculiar and wonderful. What, then, does all the legislation by Moses mean, as to "familiar spirits," if such a thing as a familiar spirit had never been conceived of? And if it should be said that one might have believed in a spirit, without necessarily having conceived that that spirit was a man with prolonged existence, then let the account of the woman of Endor be considered, — a woman that had a familiar spirit. Through her, says the narrative, she having seen "gods ascending from the earth," Saul talked with Samuel, much to his distress. The ordinary comment on this interview says that it was all imposture. But the

Bible itself does not say so. But even supposing that one might contradict the history, in that flat manner, there still would remain all for which it is here cited, that among the Hebrews, at that early time, there was such a belief, in a disembodied existence of the human soul, as that Saul the king thought that the prophet Samuel, though dead and buried, might yet have a word for him in his sore extremity. No belief, among the ancient Jews, in another life, even though it were only before Malachi, the last of the prophets! It would seem as though it might have been common even as "a familiar spirit." Certainly Jesus fully presumed on such a belief amongst them, when he said, "As touching the resurrection of the dead, have ye not read that which was spoken unto you by God, saying, I am the God of Abraham, and the God of Isaac, and the God of Jacob? God is not the God of the dead, but of the living." And surely this is a plain statement of doctrine. But it may be asked, what, then, was meant by St. Paul when he wrote that our Saviour Jesus Christ "hath abolished death, and hath brought life and immortality to light, through the gospel".? Perhaps this may mean something far in advance, doctrinally, of what is commonly thought. As a matter of fact and history, it is certain that, at the appearing of our Saviour, the Jews did all believe in a life to come, with the exception of the small sect of Sadducees. But by those words of his, what, then, did St. Paul mean, over and above the general belief of the time? He says that life and immortality were brought to light; he does not say that they were brought out of utter darkness; but he adds, that it was by the gospel. By the visible resurrection of Christ, it was evident that there was a way by which men might live again. But besides that, though simultaneously with that knowledge, by the spirit of Christ, the connections between this world and the next were made manifest, and especially as regards faith and righteousness. Because of the spirit which they had got from him, all the early Christians felt themselves as though raised from the dead in Christ. In Greece and Rome, a life after death was as distinctly believed in by the Pagans as it is to-day at Rome or Athens. But why, then, was not ancient literature more tinged by some coloring reflected from the world believed in? Precisely because the Pagans were without Christ. Life and immortality were believed to exist, but they were not brought to light as they are by the gospel; were not felt as familiarly as Christians feel them; were not believed in, because of the indwelling Spirit, which teaches, but were credited mainly because of ghost-stories, which were true enough, perhaps, in themselves, but which could affect only the externality of a man's nature, and not his inmost heart, out of which are the issues of life for this world and the world which is to come, — thought, speech, and holiness, literature and righteous action.

In the Hebrew Scriptures there is a word which is commonly translated "grave," but sometimes when that could not possibly be the rendering, it is translated "hell." But it means neither; and it means simply and exactly the place of souls. The word is "sheol." "The place of ghosts" is the meaning of the word, according to the Hebrew and Chaldee Lexicon of Dr. G. B. Winer, published in Leipsic. But how, then, does it happen that a mistranslation of the word into "grave," or "hell," should run throughout the Old Testament? It has been for the same reason, for which that mistranslation has been recently perpetuated in a late Cyclopædia, published in England. It was done originally, because the early English translators of the Bible could not think that any word therein could possibly lend any countenance to the Catholic doctrine of purgatory, or ought to. The place of souls might have been understood as purgatory possibly, and so it was translated either into hell outright, or else into the grave. And the consequence of this is to the English reader, that the ancient Hebrews, from their Scriptures, would seem to have been a people who almost never had a thought of another life, except now and then of hell, topographically. The word "hades" is mistranslated in the New Testament in much the same way. This all, at present, would be a great disgrace to the quarter where any authority or responsibility on the matter may belong, only that every Protestant living, perhaps, by his own mental condition, is more or less accessory to it. The Rabbi Ben Levi assured Dr. Priestley in a printed letter, that through Moses there was known to the Jews the certainty of a life hereafter. And no doubt this was much to the philosophic doctor's amazement and amusement, both. For on this subject, about every good Protestant, the words are true which Paul wrote to the Corinthians in regard to a kindred subject of ignorance. "But even unto this day, when Moses is read, the veil is upon their heart."

The demoniacs are another illustration of the anti-supernatural understanding, with which the Scriptures are read by many implicit believers of the New Testament, both scholars and pietists. "The demoniacs were merely epileptic patients," say certain ponderous theologians. And in this opinion certain other theologians acquiesce, belonging to two or three different schools, and they say, "We do not see what else they could have been." And so the demoniacs of the New Testament are to be accounted epileptics, mainly because modern theology cannot conceive of a demoniac. And why cannot modern theology conceive of a demoniac? Because it can hardly even conceive of a prophet; because of the nature of prophecy it has scarcely a word to say; and because, though intensely spiritual with some professors, it is yet almost as destitute of pneumatology as materialism itself. And yet in the Gospels, if there be any one thing which would seem to be plainer than another, because of the many times when it is mentioned, and the various ways in which it is presented, and the solemn manner also in which it is complicated with the highest claims of Jesus as the Christ, — that one thing would seem to be the reality of spiritual possession, the certainty that there have been demoniacs. Possession by intruding unclean spirits, is a liability to which human beings are subject by nature. It is a human trouble, as rare, perhaps, as the plague or the black death, but historically just as certain. Nor has it been an abnormal thing, probably. But whenever it has happened, no doubt, it has been as the result of laws as definite as those which used to conduce to leprosy, or as those which are now concerned with cholera. But now if really devils, demons, unclean spirits, or intruding spirits of any degree of unworthiness, were ever cast out of men by Jesus Christ or his apostles, then is this world a very different place from the world which Buckle knew all about.

When the Reformers broke away from the Catholic Church, they did leave, probably, much bad practice behind them, but they abandoned also some good theology, as well perhaps as much that was bad, and also a great deal of useful pneumatology, besides probably information, which was of an esoteric, oral character, though not the less important on that account. And besides this, they wrenched themselves from Catholicism so violently as to twist themselves, and distort their judgments. But indeed that wrench away could not well have been different from what it was, when an argument, whether good or poor, was foredoomed to conclude with a death at the stake. However, Protestants complain, and not unfairly, of the vulgate version of the Bible, as being Roman Catholic. But certainly the mistranslation of the word "sheol" into "hell" or "grave" makes the authorized version of England be essentially Protestant.

In the Bible, managed as it has been by prejudiced translators and sectarian commentators, the miracles narrated are more miraculous, that is, they are primarily less credible, than they ought to be; because the general narrative and doctrine are not in as good keeping with them as they ought to be, in some respects. The prophet Samuel, emerging from a state of corruption in a hole in the ground, would be one thing; but a very different thing indeed, as to conceivableness and credibility, would be the prophet Samuel emerging on mortal vision, like "gods ascending from the earth," for people who believed that there was a "sheol," a region of departed spirits. When the patriarch Jacob was at the end of his life, he said, "I am to be gathered unto my people: bury me with my fathers, in the cave that is in the field of Ephron the Hittite." It was the death of a man who had no knowledge of a hereafter, many theologians have said. But now how differently these words sound, if it be supposed, on perhaps a good translation of his words, that in his grief for his son Joseph, "He refused to be comforted, and he said, 'For I will go down to the assembled spirits, unto my son mourning.'"

Miracles for people, whose fathers and forefathers were living souls, angel-visits to people who believed in a disembodied life, would seem to have been more probable in themselves, and more credible, than as though they had happened among persons who were without any knowledge of another world, and who were also without any of the ways of feeling which are akin to that knowledge. The Catholic Church may perhaps formerly have made too much of the Supernatural; but through recoil and accidentally, Protestantism from its very beginning would seem to have had something of an undue tendency towards anti-supernaturalism. The effect of this inherited prejudice, a student has got to allow for, if he would find his right place on the field of thought.

MIRACLES AND SCIENCE.

MULTITUDES who read the Scriptures have quick eyes for the texts which seem to concern the doctrine of the Trinity, or the nature of baptism, or the manner of church-government. But they are very few indeed who have an eye for the supernatural. Long ago, even Richard Baxter, towards even the end of his life, ingenuously confessed how much he had been astonished, on counting up, at the number of occasions on which angels are mentioned in the Bible. As to there being a science of spirit involved in the Scriptures, how very few people ever think of such a thing! And of those who attack the credibility of the Scriptures, as compromising the dignity of Jehovah by making him appear to men and talk with them, and give them visions, how very few remember that already and a very long time ago it had been said, "No man hath seen God at any time"! And of these inconsiderate critics, how much fewer still are they who have tried what Maimonides — good old Rabbi — could do for them, even though indisposed to follow him entirely! Thus writes Maimonides in his book "Gad": "Know also that all the prophets who mention prophecy as coming to them ascribe it either to an angel or to the blessed God, although it was by means of an angel, without doubt. On this point, our rabbies of blessed memory long ago delivered their opinion in explaining, 'And the Lord said to her' thus, — by means of an angel. And know further, that whenever it is written that an angel spake with one, or that the word of the Lord came to him, this has not taken place in any other way than in a dream, or in a prophetic vision. There is an ancient agada respecting communications made to the prophets, as they are recounted in the prophetic books, which states that they were made in four ways. First, the prophet makes known that the communication was made by an angel in a dream or vision. Secondly, he merely mentions the communication of the angel to him, without explaining that it was made in a dream or vision, because of the well-established principle that prophecy is confined to one or other of these two methods, 'I will make myself known to him in a vision, I will speak unto him in a dream.' Thirdly, the angel is not mentioned at all; but the communication is ascribed to God, the Blessed One, who speaks it to him, but who makes known that it comes to him in a vision or dream. Fourthly, the prophet simply declares that God spoke to him, or said to him, do this, or say this, without explaining, either by mentioning an angel, or by mentioning a dream, on account of the well-established, fundamental principle, that prophecy or prophetic revelation comes only in dream or in vision, and through the agency of an angel." And in explanation of another point, Maimonides adds, "Furthermore it ought to be known that the expression 'And the Lord said to such an one' is used when, strictly speaking, he has no prophetic vision, but the communication was made to him by means of a prophet." It will be remembered, of course, that by vision is meant what is experienced in a preternatural, trance-like state. Thus, at Joppa, the Apostle Peter "fell into a trance, and saw heaven opened, and a certain vessel descending unto him." But at Jerusalem, giving an account of this experience, he said, "I was in the city of Joppa, praying; and, in a trance, I saw a vision, a certain vessel descend." This is the meaning of the word "vision," as it is used by Maimonides; it is a vision during a trance.

Does all this seem strange? Yet it is all, or very nearly all in the Old Testament itself, and not very hard to find; only that we are "slow of heart to believe all that the prophets have spoken," and need for our enlightenment almost a miracle, like that with which Christ favored the two disciples, on their walk from Jerusalem to Emmaus, when he expounded the Scriptures, beginning at Moses and all the prophets. Christian divines of all ages, and some of the greatest, have agreed with the statement just quoted from Maimonides. But indeed, a thousand years before the Rabbi, one of the earliest of the Christian fathers, Justin Martyr, had written, "He, whom we call the Creator of all things, has never been seen by anybody; nor has he ever of himself spoken to any man." Philip à Limborch, explaining in what sense Moses saw God face to face, on a comparison of texts, says, "Hence it results that the whole revelation made to Moses was by the instrumentality of an angel, who represented God, and who was therefore exactly like God himself speaking." It was to that abbreviated way of describing revelation that Jesus perhaps referred when, in argument with the readers of the Old Testament, he said, "If he called them gods, unto whom the word of God came, and the Scripture cannot be broken." Soon after the resurrection of Jesus Christ, the Jews were addressed by Stephen as having "received the law by the disposition of angels." This view of the Jewish revelation is evidently taken for granted in the Epistle to the Galatians. And in the Epistle to the Hebrews Judaism is described as "the word spoken by angels." And writing to Timothy, Paul said that the appearing of our Lord Jesus Christ was what "in his times he shall show, who is the blessed and only Potentate, the King of kings, and Lord of lords; who only hath immortality, dwelling in the light which no man can approach unto; whom no man hath seen, nor can see: to whom be honor and power everlasting." This is not quite the state of things spiritually, which some people would seem to suppose. And there must be agencies active in this universe, and after a manner which would surprise not materialists only, but some very good Christians also.

After what has preceded, it will strike the reader more; but otherwise how few people are ever properly impressed by the commencement of the Book of Revelation! "The Revelation of Jesus Christ, which God gave unto him, to show unto his servants things which must shortly come to pass; and he sent and signified it by his angel unto his servant John: who bare record of the word of God, and of the testimony of Jesus Christ, and of all things that he saw."

The Revelation was given by God to Jesus Christ; and by Jesus Christ it was communicated to an angel; and by the angel it was delivered to John: and by John it was published in the Church, — a revelation from the Father of Lights, that came down from above, and, as it were, through one world and another, till it reached this earth, to show unto his servants things which must shortly come to pass.

Many a Christian divine would be astonished at the position with which he would have to take up, if he were asked by a Jew to tell him, out of the Book of Acts precisely and exactly, how it was that Christian Jews felt themselves authorized to baptize and accept Gentiles as Christians. And many a good Christian, who thinks that he knows all about Providence, would feel himself, as it were, called away into a strange region, if he were asked to explain why God communicated with the Jews through angels, while all the while not a sparrow fell to the ground without his knowledge, nor was there a man even but on his head the hairs were all numbered.

If the miracles of the Bible seem incredible to any one, let him bethink himself that he perhaps has never read the Scriptures; for passing the eye over the words is certainly not the same as catching the sense. Many a man has defended the reality of miracles, out of a Bible which was blinded against him by his own unconscious anti-supernaturalism. And many a disbeliever, if he knew the spiritual philosophy involved in the Scriptures, would accept both miracles and doctrine alike, and at once.

When the words are read in church, "The word of

the Lord came," how few people have ever wondered as to how it came, or as to how Isaiah or Hosea received it! And worse still than this, there are persons who deride the prophets, who yet have never thought, nor inquired, nor even suspected, whether possibly a prophet might not have been an honest man, with some constitutional peculiarity, fitting him for prophecy. "And he said, Hear now my words: if there be a prophet among you, I the Lord will make myself known unto him in a vision, and will speak unto him in a dream." There are many scientific men who would not doubt, for a moment, but that they know proportionately as much about Christianity as they do about science. And yet, out of all their multitude, for one man who could define the nature of prophecy, there must be a thousand utterly ignorant about it, though they know well about chemical affinities as operative on the floor of the ocean, and have curious information as to bivalves, and as to the manner in which flat fish are acted upon by light reflected from below.

Miracles incredible as narrated in the Scriptures,— it is no wonder that they should have become so, to some persons; because so many connections of probability and credibility have been stripped away from them, or have been at least forgotten. And now for this state of things what is the remedy? It will come not with argument at all, perhaps; nor will it probably result much from any forthcoming information; but it will come with time and the grace of God; and for some persons it may be that it will come in a way not altogether alien to that by which the earliest Christians, on the reappearance of their crucified Lord, were mentally reinstated after their bewilderment. "Then opened he their understanding, that they might understand the Scriptures."

And indeed not the Bible only, but even the globe itself, is to a man what simply himself he is ready to have it be. To one man this earth is a heap of dirt in which to worm his way; and to the red Indian, uncorrupted, it was a broad hunting-field, on which the Great Spirit showed him favors. To one man it is chiefly of interest as having been once the plaything of natural forces, geologically, the ways of whose gambolling he delights to trace and classify. While in the eyes of another it is like a great egg, with vital powers operative in it and about it, which are instructive to watch. And for still another man, scientifically, it is like a book of common understanding between himself and the Creator. And for still another student of science the earth, with all its fulness of laws chemical, dynamic, and vital, is as towards God but "the hiding of his power." And another rarer person still, feels as though continually a voice were calling to him, "The place whereon thou standest is holy ground," because of the heavenly affinities with which the world is wrapped about for believing souls; because of what prayer effects all round the earth; and because of the manner in which the forces of nature concur with spirit for spiritual ends. And to spirits of different orders, it is conceivable that our earth varies still more than it does to the feelings respectively of its own inhabitants. And even of spirits, who have departed from the life of this earth, there is an old philosophy, according to which, for various reasons, one spirit might for a while keep a clear view of the earth and its inhabitants, while another might have lost all sight of it, with his last mortal breath. And it is conceivable, too, that the most familiar spot in this world is what we should not know, if we could look at it through the eyes of a seraph.

And what happened for his servant at the instance of the prophet Elisha, "Lord, I pray thee, open his eyes that he may see," — were this done for any man to-day, what a change, in a moment, there would be in everything about him! The solid earth, perhaps, would have become but as a vapor, just dense enough to hold the spirit of nature and manifest its play and glow; while distances above, around, and below would be felt to be at once infinitely great and curiously small, changing, so to say, with the spectator's changing mind. Also, for that man, the clouds and atmosphere would have disappeared, while the invisible ether perhaps would have become visible, and alive with currents of fluid more subtile than electricity, and with angels passing in glory like shooting stars, and with resemblances of auroras and seas of gold, and also with threads of sympathy between souls on earth and souls departed, and which may be none the less real or useful, for not being known of, on either side. Also with some appearance, not far from him, some silvery, golden sheen, which he might notice, he might have an experience like that of St. John the Divine, and see the smoke of incense, with prayers of saints, ascending up before God, from a golden censer in an angel's hand. And after this in a moment, with merely remembering his dead father, he might find himself, face to face with him. And then, as this opening of his eyes was closing, and while his sight was becoming again that simply of "the natural man," he might retain perhaps, out of all that he had seen, only some few incongruous reminiscences, and a sense that the great glory itself of the vision was what it is not possible for a man to utter.

World beyond world! World within world! Not only are the miracles of the Scriptures credible, but because of what information now faith can extract from science, more and more natural does the supernatural seem to become, and more and more supernatural, because of its susceptibilities, does the kingdom of nature seem to grow.

A glimpse about us with those eyes, which will open for us first probably only after death, — a glimpse with those eyes, with which we are to see to all eternity, — just a glimpse of the spiritual world, which indeed already we are living in, though we are cased against it by the flesh, — with just one glimpse we should feel, that in such a world as there is about us, and that with such worlds within worlds, as there are which probably concern us, that the promises of Christ may yet perhaps be to be fulfilled, and that greater works than have yet been done, Christians may yet do by invoking, in faith, Him of that name, which is above every name, and unto whom morals, politics, and science, rule, authority, and power, and all things, are to be subdued. And with that one glimpse, too, what impossibilities as to belief would vanish!

For in that widened sphere, vitally connected with humanity, that the spirit of demons might be competent to add confusion to human affairs, by working miracles, in some way or other, on the road, and at the time contemplated in the book of Revelation, — this all would seem to be not much more improbable than that wicked rulers should ever be backed by genius. And between the highest and the lowest sources of miracles, foretold in the New Testament, there would seem to be place for those spirits, about whom there is a forewarning by St. John, that they ought not to be believed as spirits simply, but that they should be tried as to their being of God, because that actually and already, and to John's own knowledge, and as though by inspiration from spirits, there were many false prophets "gone out into the world."

Miracles impossible because of science! They are impossible to the belief of a man, simply because of the conceit which comes of learning, but in no other way. For really the powers of nature, as they are discovered by science, would seem to be the ready, pliant agencies of supernatural purposes. Why should not the demons of Plato's theology be as much at home on magnetic currents as men are in steamboats? Why should not an angel be able to approach this earth, by subordinating electricity to his use, as well as Benjamin Franklin have been able to draw, and concentrate, and enslave it for human purposes? Science! what has science, in the court of common sense, to say against the miracles of healing, by a word or a touch, which are told of in the Scriptures? It has nothing, absolutely nothing whatever to say, except that it has not heard of such things of late centuries, and that they do not appear ever to have been very common. But that is nothing for science to tell. To an angel of wisdom, or to the eyes of the best inhabitant of the star Sirius, imported into this earth, as a judge, belladonna would not seem to be any more likely, as a curative agent, than a man's hand. And when it is remembered what a man's hand may be as a channel,—how it is connected with his brain, and through his brain with a wide universe of forces known and occult, and with God, the fountain-head of all power; and when, by Christians, not as necessary to the argument but additionally, it is remembered that through the Spirit, God was in Christ, and Christ in his apostles and others, it does not then seem to be incredible, even in itself, that the human hand, stretched forth in faith, may have been as efficient for healing as dried herbs at their best, and quicker than they as to operation. In the Gospel of Luke it is written that "it came to pass, when he was in a certain city, behold a man full of leprosy, who, seeing Jesus, fell on his face and besought him, saying, Lord, if thou wilt, thou canst make me clean. And he put forth his hand, and touched him, saying, I will: be thou clean. And immediately the leprosy departed from him."

THE SPIRIT AND THE PROPHETS THEREOF.

AND now let miracles be considered in connection with persons. There is a restricted use of the word "miracle," as what might concern only material substances. But it is not Scriptural. And there is a restricted use of the word "prophet," by which it means simply a foreteller. But neither is this Scriptural. In the Scriptures themselves, prophets are not all of one class. Also in the times of the Scriptures, a man was specially a prophet who filled officially and by public recognition the place of a prophet. Daniel was a prophet, but he was also an exile in Babylon; and it may be for this reason that, in a Hebrew Bible, the book of Daniel is not printed along with the books of the prophets, but elsewhere. Then again, however, Abraham is styled a prophet. But some little variation in the use of words during two thousand years is of course to be expected. And so, in the account of Saul's first visit to Samuel, it is written "he that is now called a prophet was beforetime called a Seer."

What, then, was a prophet? He was a channel for spirit, — for the Spirit of God, or for the inspiration of an "evil spirit"; he may have been, according to Jeremiah, one of "the prophets that prophesy lies," or one of "the prophets of the deceit of their own heart," or he may have been according to what is perhaps the better understanding of a text in Zechariah, the prophet of "an unclean spirit"; he may have "prophesied in the name of the Lord," or he may have "prophesied by Baal." He was a man through whom incorporeal, intelligent power expressed itself, by thoughts foreign to the man's mind, or by actions passing human ability, as to quality or intensity. In this definition, the word "through" is used in its broader signification, and as meaning sometimes "concurrently with," and thereby as embracing some miracles, which were begun and finished outside of the person of the prophet, but yet withinside of a sphere, wherein was available that peculiarity of his constitution whereby he was prophetic. Though also it would seem as though some few of the miracles narrated in the Bible, and especially in the earlier ages, may perhaps have been independent of the person of a prophet, and connected with him simply as an associate assistance.

But there are yet two or three other things to be noticed. Balaam is not called a prophet, notwithstanding that wonderful history, in which he was concerned: and notwithstanding that "the Spirit of God came upon him"; and notwithstanding that he was Balaam, the son of Beor, "which heard the words of God, and knew the knowledge of the Most High, which saw the vision of the Almighty, falling into a trance, but having his eyes open." This is an exact description of the prophetic state. Nor yet was Gideon called a prophet, notwithstanding his having been addressed by an angel, and been favored with miracles, and notwithstanding that "the Spirit of the Lord came upon Gideon." But this may have been because of his never having had any experience like the special characteristic of a prophet, because he never "saw the vision of the Almighty, falling into a trance, but having his eyes open." Also as used by St. Paul, prophecy is simply speaking from the Spirit, and might seem to be of no kinship with miracles. But then there are those famous words addressed to the Corinthians, in which miracles and prophecy are said to be of the same origin, and to be indeed one and the same thing, at their coming forth from spirit into nature. "There are diversities of operations, but it is the same God which worketh all in all," quickening, illuminating, and endowing men, according as they are susceptible and willing. "The manifestation of the Spirit is given to every man to profit withal. For to one is given by the Spirit the word of wisdom; to another the word of knowledge by the same Spirit; to another faith by the same Spirit; to another the gifts of healing by the same Spirit; to another the working of miracles; to another prophecy; to another discerning of spirits; to another divers kinds of tongues; to another the interpretation of tongues; but all these worketh that one and the selfsame Spirit, dividing to every man severally as he will."

Also, says St. Paul, "He that is joined unto the Lord is one spirit"; and so, necessarily, he is become a man of infinite and innumerable possibilities for this world or the next, being united with the fountainhead of all goodness and truth and power, even though for the present it be only by a channel coming down from above, and along the far-away course of which angel calls to angel, up the heights of heaven. By the Spirit of God, all men are not affected exactly alike, because with it men are still men, and of their respective nationalities, generations, and individualities. Samson was a man of rude strength, and in a rude age, and with Philistines to think of. "And behold a young lion roared against him. And the Spirit of the Lord came mightily upon him, and he rent him, as he would have rent a kid, and he had nothing in his hand." But Paul in Samson's place, probably, could never have done the same thing, or have been so strengthened perhaps, any more than the hand of Samson would have availed for Paul's epistles. And so differently indeed, by the same Spirit, was Paul affected from Samson, that he wrote, "When I am weak, then am I strong."

And Gideon, — "The angel of the Lord appeared unto him, and said unto him, The Lord is with thee, thou mighty man of valor." And how was the Lord with him? It was through the channel of the valiant man's valor. For "the Spirit of the Lord came upon Gideon," and it blew through his trumpet, and it clenched for him his right hand upon his sword; and that sword was "the sword of the Lord and of Gideon." Azariah and Zechariah being prophets, the Spirit of God with them became messages, beginning with "Thus saith the Lord." Says David, "The Spirit of the Lord spake by me"; and the historian adds, "Sweet psalmist of Israel." And his psalms are the psalms of the Spirit and of David. And now how was it with Simeon of Jerusalem, when "the Holy Ghost was upon him"? It was according to his condition, which was that of a devout old man, hopeful and expectant, at a time of extremity, because of what his nation was historically. "And it was revealed unto him by the Holy Ghost that he should not see death before he had seen the Lord's Christ. And he came by the Spirit into the temple, and when the parents brought in the child Jesus, to do for him after the custom of the law, then took he him up in his arms, and blessed God, and said, Lord, now lettest thou thy servant depart in peace, according to thy word: for mine eyes have seen thy salvation."

The protomartyr Stephen probably knew of the council, as to taking no thought beforehand for magistrates, for what he should say. And how was it with him, "full of faith and power," when he was confronted by enemies? "They were not able to resist the wisdom and the spirit by which he spake." And more than that, "all that sat in the council looking steadfastly on him, saw his face as it had been the face of an angel." Altogether different from that of any of the personages before mentioned was the experience of the Spirit by St. John the Divine: and very widely different it certainly was from what Gideon or Samson knew of. Says John of himself, being in Patmos, long enough after the death of his Lord, to date by the Lord's Day, and with a mind in all probability anxious about the future of the church, "I was in the Spirit on the Lord's day, and heard behind me a great voice as of a trumpet, saying, I am Alpha and Omega, the first and the last: and what thou seest write in a book."

Before one can estimate fairly the significance of a

miracle, he must know how the worker of the miracles was estimated. Commonly every prophet is supposed to have been "a man of God" even through the name of prophet merely; and every word which he may have uttered, it is often supposed, must have been holy. And yet there is an account, under the reign of Jeroboam, of the misdeed and capital punishment of "the man of God, who was disobedient unto the word of the Lord."

The history of King Saul is very instructive as to the faculty of prophecy in connection with character. After he had been anointed by the prophet Samuel, and just as had been predicted for him, "Behold, a company of prophets met him; and the Spirit of God came upon him, and he prophesied among them." Awhile after that, because of an atrocious proposal of the Ammonites, "the Spirit of God came upon Saul, when he heard those tidings, and his anger was kindled greatly." After this, there are accounts of the untoward ways of Saul: and then it is to be read that "the Spirit of the Lord departed from Saul, and an evil spirit from the Lord troubled him." Soon after this "the evil spirit from God came upon Saul, and he prophesied in the midst of the house"; and directly afterwards "Saul was afraid of David, because the Lord was with him, and was departed from Saul." And then a little later, because of the Spirit of God, which mastered all his messengers, and made them prophesy, as they approached Samuel, instead of discharging their errand, himself, "he went thither to Naioth in Ramah: and the Spirit of God was upon him also, and he went on and prophesied until he came to Naioth in Ramah. And he stripped off his clothes also, and prophesied before Samuel in like manner, and lay down naked all that day and all that night. Wherefore they say, Is Saul also among the prophets?" According to this history, then, Saul prophesied at one time from the Spirit of God, and at another time from an evil spirit, and then again from the Spirit of God. With Saul, then, the faculty of prophecy was independent of its use; just as poetry may sing to the glory of God, or may be a ribald jester in the household of Satan.

There is a curious history in the thirteenth chapter of the First Book of the Kings. A prophet had been on a wonderful errand to Bethel, and by the word of the Lord, had been ordered not to eat or drink there. But he was accosted by an old prophet, who "said unto him, I am a prophet also as thou art: and an angel spake unto me, by the word of the Lord, saying, Bring him back with thee unto thine house, that he may eat bread and drink water. But he lied unto him. So he went back with him, and did eat bread in his house, and drank water. And it came to pass, as they sat at the table, that the word of the Lord came unto the prophet that brought him back. And he cried unto the man of God that came from Judah, saying, Thus saith the Lord, Forasmuch as thou hast disobeyed the mouth of the Lord, and hast not kept the commandments which the Lord thy God commanded thee, but camest back, and hast eaten bread and drunk water in the place of the which the Lord did say to thee, Eat no bread and drink no water; thy carcass shall not come unto the sepulchre of thy fathers." Here a man known as an old prophet, immediately after hearing of a series of striking miracles, lies fearfully in pretending a message from an angel, by the word of the Lord. And yet quickly afterwards to that same old prophet "the word of the Lord came" with a prophecy against the prophet who had been deluded by him, and which was almost instantly fulfilled.

Moses and Aaron and Miriam were brothers and sister, and had been witnesses together of great miracles in Egypt, at the Red Sea, at Mount Sinai, and at Taberah. Yet Miriam and Aaron spake against Moses: and they said, "Hath the Lord indeed spoken only by Moses? hath he not spoken also by us? And the Lord heard it." And although she was a prophetess, and even perhaps all the more readily, because of that psychical channel or condition through which she was capable of being made prophetic, she found induced on her suddenly a miraculous leprosy. And of Moses himself, there is to be read what is very striking. He had gone up with miraculous attendance, and at the call of the Lord, on to Mount Sinai, where he remained forty days. And the Lord "gave unto Moses, when he had made an end of communing with him upon Mount Sinai, two tables of testimony, tables of stone, written with the finger of God. And when the people saw that Moses delayed to come down out of the Mount, the people gathered themselves together unto Aaron, and said unto him, Up, make us gods, which shall go before us; for as for this Moses, the man that brought us up out of the land of Egypt, we wot not what is become of him." Whereupon ensued bestial idolatry, of a piece with what they had known in Egypt. "And it came to pass, as soon as he came nigh unto the camp, that he saw the calf, and the dancing: and Moses' anger waxed hot, and he cast the tables out of his hands, and brake them beneath the Mount." It was in holy indignation that this was done, no doubt, but still it was, as it is written, in anger.

David was a prophet, but yet there was a terrible occasion, on which another prophet, Nathan, was sent to him to say, "Thou art the man." Peter is called at Rome the Prince of the apostles, but yet, it was he who denied three times over that ever he had known his Lord. As St. Jerome remarks, miracles were wrought by Judas the apostle, even when he had in him the mind of a traitor. And even of that high-priest Caiaphas, who was accessory to the crucifixion of Jesus, it is written that just before that event, being in council, he pronounced an opinion. "And this spake he not of himself: but being high-priest that year, he prophesied that Jesus should die for that nation."

Not only do miracles not vouch for character; but even the very agents of miracles could quarrel among themselves, and be doubtful about doctrine. In his epistle to the Galatians, Paul writes, "He that wrought effectually in Peter to the apostleship of the circumcision, the same was mighty in me toward the Gentiles." And then because of the time-serving of Peter, Paul says, "When Peter was come to Antioch, I withstood him to the face, because he was to be blamed." On one occasion Barnabas and Saul, "being sent forth by the Holy Ghost," journeyed together. And Barnabas saw great miracles wrought through Paul, at

Paphos and at Lystra; but for all that, after a little while, "the contention was so sharp between them that they departed asunder one from the other." That miracles were wrought through Paul, did not make Barnabas think that Paul was a better judge than himself in common things. Nor apparently would he have yielded to Paul, if even he had known already what happened soon afterwards. "And God wrought special miracles by the hands of Paul: so that from his body were brought unto the sick handkerchiefs or aprons, and the diseases departed from them, and the evil spirits went out of them."

And indeed it is one thing for a man to serve as a channel for the Holy Ghost; and it is a very different thing indeed, for that man himself to appropriate that Spirit for his own enlightenment and sanctification. St. Paul himself had a very vivid sense of this. And on this very point, writing to the Corinthians fourteen years after his marvellous experience, he says, "I knew such a man (whether in the body, or out of the body, I cannot tell: God knoweth) how that he was caught up into Paradise, and heard unspeakable words, which it is not lawful for a man to utter. Of such an one will I glory: yet of myself I will not glory, but in mine infirmities." He could glory in the miracle but only as though he himself had had nothing whatever to do with it. A wonderful man! The apostle, too, of everything in the Church which is not Jewish! The great apostle of the Gentiles! But inwardly also he was great. And the greater the insight has been, which the greatest men have attained to, the more wonderfully plain has it become to them, that Paul was a channel for the Holy Spirit, not merely with his lips and the surface of his nature, but through that great heart of his, which for that purpose had ripened, as the tenantless earth did in the broad light of the sun, by inward heat and convulsions from mysterious powers, and by processes which were at once purifying and enriching, and also terrible.

Paul might have been able to withstand harmlessly the bite of a deadly viper, because of the power which was in him; he might have been once and again taken for a god by both Greeks and barbarians; he might at one time, by merely sending his handkerchief have cured disease, or have chased away evil spirits; or he might have been able to say to the Corinthians, "I thank my God, I speak with tongues more than ye all." But it was because of what was more than all that, because of his wonderful self-knowledge, because of his philosophy, because of the quickening which he had had from the Holy Spirit, that he could also say to the Corinthians, "I keep under my body, and bring it into subjection: lest that by any means, when I have preached to others, I myself should be a castaway."

What an autobiography Paul might have written! It would seem as though it might be like a key to endless mysteries, if only we could know the process of his feeling during his time of isolation in Arabia. "When it pleased God, who separated me from my mother's womb, and called me by his grace, to reveal his Son in me, that I might preach him among the heathen; immediately I conferred not with flesh and blood; neither went I up to Jerusalem to them which were apostles before me, but I went into Arabia." After that wondrous conversion of his, and he being the man he was, what was it which went on with him and in him, during that seclusion in Arabia, before he returned again to Damascus, whence, after three years, he went up to Jerusalem to see Peter? Perhaps really he never could have reduced it into words, any more than he was able to tell what it was that he saw when he was "caught up to the third heaven." For, indeed, very often, by persons of marked experience, it has been a confession, that withinside the surface, which had been witnessed by the public, and withinside still of what they themselves could tell of, there was a dim sense of what they had been drawn through, which it was not possible for them to explain, — as being a something concerned with powers outside of the material world, and for which, as to the intercourse, the words of mortals are nothing.

And now, from this chapter what is the inference? For fairly stating it, some accompanying explanations would be necessary; but, in a general way, it may be said to be this: The Spirit of God would keep itself for recognition, as distinct as is possible, and as free as possible from confusion with the human agencies, through which it signifies itself. And, indeed, if it were manifested only through saints, it would be thought to be an attribute of human goodness; whereas, really, it is a manifestation, more or less direct, and more or less imperfect, because of human infirmities, — it is a manifestation of the Spirit of the universe, and of the God, who is that Spirit. And thus it is, — and no thanks to Jonah or any man of his kind,—thus it is, that the Spirit of God, for its purposes, can make use of an unwilling man, and an unmerciful man, like the prophet Jonah.

But, indeed, every gift or grace of any magnitude, is almost instinctively held by the heart, like treasure in an earthen vessel. And with the least glimmer of insight, a man of any greatness sees at once, that the best part of himself is not himself at all, but what is confided to him, like "treasure in earthen vessels." Those words of St. Paul, as to his experience, have been repeated age after age, by the greatest men, sometimes in triumph, and sometimes in tears; by scholars as to their faculty, by poets as to their genius, and by every saint as to his holiness. Those words of Paul are what John would have joined in, and what Peter would have affirmed; they are what David would have gloried in, for singing like a psalm; and also of all "holy apostles and prophets" they are the solemn testimony to the world, and before Heaven,—"But we have this treasure in earthen vessels, that the excellency of the power may be of God, and not of us."

ANTI-SUPERNATURAL MISUNDERSTANDINGS.

NOR is it the Bible only which is wronged by the anti-supernaturalism of the reader, but other ancient writings also suffer from the same cause. And from the same cause also there is sometimes a great misapprehension of certain eras of history. There are some words, frequently quoted from a work by Cicero, which simply are a sentiment which he puts into the mouth of a man in an imaginary conversation. But it is quoted as though it were his own deliberate opinion; and it touches heathenism only on one point, which by its nature was always accounted as being variable; and yet it is often adduced to show that Cicero was estranged from heathenism with his whole mind, and that also every educated person was ready to abandon heathenism, before the birth of Christ. But a Roman might say all that Cicero said on the nature of the gods, and yet continue to be especially heathenish, and might have a soul liable, any day, to flash up and fill out all the old creed with credence. And actually, on the death of his daughter, Cicero built a temple, which he dedicated to her ghost.

It is quite true, that the worship of Jupiter Capitolinus declined very largely during the first century of the present era. Was it, however, because Rome had become less earnestly idolatrous? No; not in the least. It was because Rome had become more idolatrous than when it was founded, and because the idolatries of all nations had been brought and assembled there. And this is certain by legislation on the subject; for age after age, the Senate issued injunctions and complaints as to the manner in which the old gods of the country were being neglected, for the more fashionable deities and services of foreign origin.

It is not true, that Christianity had its way in the world largely facilitated by the decline of heathenism. It is an anti-Christian position which is never challenged, but yet it is not tenable. Heathenism did not die of public indifference, nor of indifference at all. It never was more thoroughly believed than it was by its last professors. And as to favors granted him by his gods, there never was a man more thoroughly persuaded about anything than the Emperor Julian was about that. But that he could have been so persuaded is what is almost impossible for a scholar to think, because of that general anti-supernaturalism, which everybody suffers from, like an influenza. Even a writer like the German Tholuck can instance Pausanias as being sceptical about his religion. But now that writer was of a certain school in Pagan theology; but he was not, therefore, the less thoroughly hearty in his Paganism, if that may be called so, which got the name somewhat later than his time. To suppose that he doubted about Hellenism, for any reason contained in his book, is much about the same thing as though, by way of an incongruous comparison, yet apt enough for the point, one should doubt the Christianity of Izaak Walton, because of his friendship with Bishop Ken.

Pausanias, who writes of the various occasions on which he was warned by visions or dreams sent from the gods, and of his sacred obedience accordingly; who tried, too, some of the marvels connected with Paganism, and who testifies about them as being real; and who, besides, had a most affectionate and tender interest in all the antiquities of Paganism in Greece, — Pausanias, a doubter, and, in the second century of the Christian era, an example of failing faith in his religion! It might as well be said that the Maccabees were doubtful about Moses, or that Alban Butler, in the "Lives of the Saints," was not quite sure about the Church. And there have been persons who have so written about Plato, as though it might have seemed evident that, to their apprehension, there was no demonology of any kind involved in his writings. How has it happened that of what Plato wrote there are things which some of his most fervent disciples would seem never to have noticed? This case may be passed over to Pausanias. And how has it been that Pausanias could ever have been accounted an instance of declining faith in Hellenism? For the whole tone of his book is that of a fervent, unquestioning believer. And there are perhaps ten narratives of what he believed were his own experiences of it, preternaturally. How, then, is it that he should ever have been accounted a doubter, or even a man with misgivings as to his Pagan religion? It could only have been from prejudice, and from thinking him, perhaps, a man too wise to mean exactly what he wrote. Or rather, the writer who first published that impression about him must have been a man whose eye, by anti-supernatural habit in reading, slurred over what really Pausanias had to say about himself.

Paganism growing effete as a power, and thereby yielding the more readily to the preaching of Christianity! It is what never happened. That anti-Christian position has been acquiesced in by some Christian divines, from a mistaken notion as to the law of progress, by which it has been fancied that, as one religion was dying out, it was of the mercy of God that there should be, under Providence, another and better religion to succeed it. The notion of those divines was true; but it was not the whole truth, even on their plane of thought. Heathenism as a social power, yielding easily to the soft coming of Christianity, — is that, or anything like it, corroborated by the history of the Colosseum? No: and there is not a brick there, nor a stone, nor scarcely a grain of dust, but, like blood crying from the ground, protests in every intelligent ear against Gibbon, the historian, for what he has said. And how is it about the other monuments of ancient Rome, as connected with that idolatry which was the soul of it? They nearly all of them witness, in one way or another, to the strength of that heathenism which had to yield to the "foolishness of preaching." The circus of Maxentius was dedicated, and the temple of Romulus, the son of Maxentius, was built only in the very last year of heathenism, the very year before Constantine entered Rome as a Christian emperor. And the grandest monument surviving of ancient Rome, the Pantheon, was but a fresh building at the birth of Christ, having been finished and inscribed less than thirty years before. Of nearly all the temples which remain in Rome, the very dates attest the strength of idolatry there, ages after Paul had looked on, as a prisoner, — the temple of Remus, that of Ceres and Proserpine, that of Vesta, that of Antoninus Pius, that of Venus and Rome, built by Hadrian, and that of Minerva Medica, of the age of Diocletian. And all round the Forum, by the dates at which they were built, all the temples attest that heathenism was never stronger socially than whilst Christianity was preaching against it, — the temple of Concord and that of Vespasian, — the temple of Saturn, between the Forum and the Capitol, and the temple of Antoninus and Faustina, with its startling inscription, alongside of the Via Sacra. And if more testimony were needed, it might be reasoned out from the arch of Constantine, erected in the fourth century of our era, and from that arch of Titus, in the first century, which bears inwrought into it, what is almost a cry from the dead, in the marble form of Simon the son of Gorias, as he was dragged triumphantly into Rome, after the capture of Jerusalem, along with the spoils of the temple, sculptured also on the arch in colored marbles, — the silver trumpets, and the table for the shew-bread, and also the seven-branched candlestick. The history of Christianity in struggle with Paganism has not been written yet; nor can it be written, but under another philosophy of religion than what has prevailed since the archives of the past have begun to be generally accessible. And the persons through whom, by one trial after another, it shall ultimately have been accomplished, will have testified to a very different struggle from what Gibbon ever thought that he was writing about, and will have attested the words of St. Paul, as having been true: "For we wrestle not against flesh and blood, but against principalities, against powers, against the rulers of the darkness of this world, against spiritual wickedness in high places."

How wonderful is that text in Isaiah, new once, but now again almost as fresh for meaning as it ever was: "The vision of all is become unto you as the words of a book that is sealed, which men deliver to one that is learned, saying, Read this, I pray thee; and he saith, I cannot; for it is sealed: and the book is delivered to him that is not learned, saying, Read this, I pray thee: and he saith, I am not learned." A general blindness this, and perhaps without the fault specially of any individuals. And what came from Isaiah in prophecy as to his time and nation is what in modern times people have been undergoing, and especially in Protestant countries. Has this been for any special fault of theirs; or is it to be counted for a disgrace? By no means. It has even become a proverb: "I would rather be wrong with Plato than right with any one else." And the writer hereof would rather be wrong with some anti-supernaturalists than be right with some good people whom he has known at Rome. On a choice between poets and merchants of the same honesty, it would be beyond all comparison better that this world should be managed by men of business than by men of "vision and faculty divine." And if there is to be advance in the world, as the world is, it can only be by steps, for every one of which really there must be some drawback. But the recognition of that drawback is a large part of philosophy at any time.

And in it indeed is involved that philosophy of human nature, never distinctly recognized but under Christ, by which it is plain that human creatures are meant to be mutually helpful, and "members of one another." In a good spirit, the man who contradicts me is one side of my mind. And surely and reasonably, there must always be a private account to be balanced, if only it could be done by any happy mediation, between the man of introspection and old books, and the man of outlook by the telescope and the chemical retort. For neither of them, by his speciality, is likely, as it would seem, to be right on all points absolutely. And even, perhaps, the best application of a spiritual philosophy to human wants may be expected from men who have known to the uttermost, by experience, what Rationalism can do.

At this point, especially, does the writer hereof remember a very dear life-long friend, a native of New York, though a British subject, who has never been long absent from his thought while these papers have been in preparation. At one time it was a sore trouble to him, that he was unable wholly to believe in the miracles of the Scriptures; and all the while his doubts about them were more believing than the certainties of some other persons. But he lived to publish, a little before his sudden death, a work on "Unconscious Prophecies, and their Fulfilment." The miraculousness of human nature, as connected with a world of spirits, and the prophetic susceptibility of human nature,—of these things he had become persuaded by wide observation and wise induction. And by the force simply of wide notice and patient thought, he had attained to a better sense of prophecy than he could ever have got from any theological treatise, of the last hundred years. The public was indebted to him without ever having known of him. Somewhat of a sufferer, but cheerful, hopeful, and almost joyous as to his tone of life, and with an easy, infinite confidence in God, which was a veritable gift of faith, he was a blessing simply to know of. He was always among advanced thinkers on all subjects. And that Arthur Lupton believed in prophecy may be accounted a sign of the times, on account of the scientific manner in which his conviction about it had been wrought out. For his friends, it is still as though he were within and above their horizon, because of the trail of light which survives in the sky, and which he left behind when he vanished like a shooting-star. And, as Jeremy Taylor might have said, there is one who could wish, at the end of the great harvest, that his soul may be found in the same bundle of life with the soul of his friend.

THE LAST ECSTATIC.

AND now let the line of remark be resumed, as to blindness to things immediately under the eye, but of which, every now and then, somebody unexpectedly becomes conscious. Less than a month ago there appeared in the Times newspaper, of London, what has already been republished in this country, an account of an ecstatic in Belgium:—

"A NEW ECSTATIC. — The *Impartial de Soignies* devotes five columns to a description of a new ecstatic named Louise Lateau. It appears from the statement of the Belgian journal that for some months past this young girl presents every Friday the phenomena which are called the stigmata of the Passion. She has on her hands, feet, and over the heart sanguineous blisters, which exude abundantly. The ordinary functions of life are suspended. The eyes open, and, turned obliquely towards heaven, appear to be attentively fixed on some object. The pupils are dilated, the face is pale, the mouth partially opened, and the features express a sentiment of admiration mingled with a sweet sorrow. At times the object she seems to contemplate produces a painful starting. When not in ecstasy, she is in catalepsy. At three o'clock she starts up all at once and suddenly flings herself on the flags, without the least attempt to protect her face with her hands; yet she receives no injury. She remains for an hour in this horizontal position, her arms and feet crossed. About half past four o'clock she raises herself quickly, without any assistance, her arms still in the form of a cross, as if some invisible power had placed her in this vertical position. She then falls on her knees, next sits down, and in about ten minutes the body is subjected to a kind of torsion, and the Ecstatic of Bois d'Haine — for so she is called — throws herself supine on the ground. Then it is that she is waked up; but to accomplish this, the persons about her must belong to the Order of the Passion."

And now what is to be thought of this account? It is an easy thing for blind leaders of the blind to jeer at it, and to get honor of such a kind as their followers have to give. But all that cannot avail long in an era like the present, in which news and opinions are exchanged so fast.

Some twenty-five years ago, tales went through the newspapers in England as to a young Tyrolese girl, who was an ecstatic. At these tales many Protestants thanked God that they were not superstitious Catholics. But at that time, also, the Puseyite movement was gathering strength. A letter was published in The Morning Chronicle by the Earl of Shrewsbury, who had visited the saintly sufferer, or the suffering saint. The letter might have been published in a Catholic newspaper, and never have reached a Protestant. For what is published in a religious newspaper is read by its subscribers only; and if anything extraordinary of any kind happens to appear in such a paper, it is scarcely regarded as credible, even though written, printed, published, and vouched for by some of the best men in the world, unless they should happen also to go to the same church as the reader. The letter, however, of the Earl of Shrewsbury, descriptive of the

Ecstatica of Caldaro, was published in the chief liberal, secular newspaper of the time in London. By that letter there were a few persons, who were made to pause with wonder, like the writer hereof. But there were still more people, through Puseyite preparation, who read the account excited, aghast, and wondering what they should do to be saved. And it was not without assistance from that letter that many Puseyites became Catholics. For the old way of settling such a point, as was involved in that letter, was no longer quite sufficient, although it was very nearly so. But there were Puseyites, who could not feel that a letter like the earl's, was answered by two or three good jokes from Oxford Fellows, or by a running fire of laughter all over the country from comfortable rectors, strong in their legal position as members of the Establishment.

And now, how did that letter of the earl's act? Let us see how it was pointed. This, however, can be done now only from the book into which the letter grew, by additional accounts of other ecstatics. Let it be remembered that the letter was dated from circumstances much the same, and in kind exactly the same, as the phenomena attendant on the Belgian ecstatic, which have just been described. "Are we not safer in believing with Maria Mörl and the two Domenicas, and the great body of the Christian Church, both ancient and modern, than in pinning our faith — if such were possible — upon the dissenting tenets of one solitary fanciful individual, — tenets all of them easily proved to be erroneous?" But becoming still warmer and still more personal with his argument, the earl says: "Putting all other evidences out of the question, can Dr. Pusey give me any one sign and wonder in defence of his doctrines, equal to the assurance I have received in favor of mine, from these simple, humble, but gifted souls ?"

But now, instead of succumbing helplessly to any meaning, which anybody may please to put upon a prodigy, it would seem to be right to ask, what actually the meaning of the prodigy may be. Maria Mörl may have instanced effects resulting from intense devotion of a certain kind, without necessarily having been thereby marked out as a favorite of heaven, or even as an example to be patterned. And unless for persons predisposed to think so, really the state of these Italian ecstatics, entranced at times, but bedridden, and at times cataleptic, clairvoyant often, but very weak, and made still more singular as to their condition by those strange marks on the body, — all this would not necessarily and obviously seem to mean the special favor of Heaven, for a particular mode of worship. No doubt, there was something very extraordinary in their cases. But that the meaning of those extraordinary manifestations bore against Dr. Pusey it is not necessary to suppose, notwithstanding that some of his followers did think so, to the great discomfort of the Church of England.

In view of his book, to doubt either the earl or the witnesses whom he cites as to what was seen, is what the present writer would not think of, for a moment. Also, he would think it to be a great good if certain other people, within a certain sphere, could feel as he does. For, truly it is not for everybody, in every sphere, to get good from everything. And for all persons, outside of what they are ready for, it is better that they should flatly deny than weakly affect to believe. Though yet there are some few better people who, though finite by nature, do yet know and feel themselves to be children of the Infinite, and who therefore do not feel bound to deny and denounce everything, which they may not be ready to understand, at any moment.

Dr. Pusey must have felt himself sorely pushed by the earl at that time, while he was struggling hard to be thought a Catholic, when he found himself contrasted for the worse with Domenica Barbagli, the ecstatic of Monte San Savino, "this pre-sanctified spirit, this chosen soul, undoubtedly favored by seraphic communings with her God." But what he felt has never appeared, nor yet the way by which he avoided the conclusion on to which the earl would have forced him. But on his followers the appeal had great effect. And, at least, the remembrance of it will be revived by the report of the ecstatic in Belgium, so near to England.

Towards the end of his book the earl, a very candid writer, says that his attention had been drawn to mesmerism, as accounting for many of the phenomena which he had witnessed in the ecstatics. He acknowledges the pertinency of the suggestion; but he demurs to it as an explanation, for several reasons, of which the first is the best, although it is worthless. And that reason which the earl alleges, is simply that mesmerism is not known in the Tyrol. But he might as well have said that electricity and thunder-storms are unknown in the Tyrol, because the names of Benjamin Franklin and Joseph Priestley had never been heard there, and because, perhaps, an electrifying machine had never been introduced into Caldaro or Capriana. And really all which the earl witnessed in those ecstatics, about whom he wrote, except as to the stigmata, are things fairly within the circle of mesmerism. Though very curious, and what astound millions of intelligent persons, yet they are some such effects as could be induced and manifested by processes which are called mesmeric. For mesmerism, as it is called, is by thousands of years older than Mesmer, good man. The vital forces of which he availed himself are, of course, as old as Adam: nor was he the first person, by hundreds, perhaps, to systematize as to observation and use in connection with them. And when mesmerism was suggested as accounting for the clairvoyance, catalepsy, and trance of the ecstatics, it was not probably meant that there were persons who mesmerized them knowingly, on purpose, and by art; but that accidentally, so to say, and naturally too, through intense suffering and almost continual fasting, they were in an abnormal condition, through which they were readily susceptible of catalepsy, clairvoyance, and trance, and through which, too, they were liable to be mesmerized by chance. And even in illustration of the stigmata, the records of mesmerism might be found to furnish some curious though distant analogies. And the marks on the body, even though they be like those of a crucifix, would not seem of necessity and exclusively to argue the especial favor of God Most High. Perhaps even they might more properly be regarded as manifesting human nature, and the manner in which the body can be acted upon from the state of the soul; the soul of the ecstatic being full of longings and expectations, and full of sympathy with the sufferings emblemed by a crucifix, and also in affinity, perhaps, at the same time, preternaturally with attendant spirits of the same household of faith as her own.

The utmost, logically, which would seem to follow from the earl's premises would perhaps be, that among sensitive, ascetic, and exhausted persons there may be a rare case, now and then, which may show that a strange marvellous likeness to a crucifix may be induced by a profoundly reverential contemplation thereof. For the mere marvellousness of the thing is not of itself necessarily encouraging. It may have been supernatural and yet not divine. And miracles have sometimes touched where they certainly did not mean to sanction.

Perhaps it ought to be noticed here that ecstatics have been long known, and that the word "ecstasy" was not probably of Christian origin. The experience described by the word was common among the Neo-Platonists in the fourth and fifth centuries. Thus, by his biographer, Plotinus is said "in ecstasy to have seen the supreme god," and also in ecstasy to have been elevated from the ground. The manifestation of the stigmata, was that by which Francis of Assisi became famous in the thirteenth century. Since the days of St. Francis, there have been about sixty similar cases recorded, of which perhaps ten have been within the last thirty years. When the stigmata appeared on the person of Maria Mörl, they had even been anticipated by her confessor for five months. And one of the ecstatics whom the earl saw, he expected would have been favored with the marks, but she was not.

But it is curious, that as to the clairvoyant and cataleptic states, and as to the levitation of the body in the cases of these ecstatics, there was nothing detailed by the earl as heavenly sanction, but something like it, long ago, had been alleged as condemnatory fact, on trials for witchcraft.

Of transference of marks, there have been some curious cases by electricity. Once the exact likeness of a tree was printed on an object near, by a flash of lightning.

These words of the earl are noticeable: "Yes! it is under the very shadow of the large crucifix, which is suspended over her head, that the spirit of ecstasy is infused into her." And now for an incident that stops the earl's argument short, and which would seem to argue the favor of Heaven for Protestants, more distinctly than all those sixty ecstatics argue it for Catholics. In the "Adversaria" of Isaac Casaubon, there is an account of a storm at Wells, in England. The information was given to Casaubon by the Bishop of Ely, who received it from the Bishop of Wells, and other personal witnesses. On a Sunday morning in the year 1596, while the people were in the cathedral, there was such a tremendous burst of thunder, that in their terror the whole congregation knelt together. Though a thunderbolt fell, there was no one hurt. "But a wonderful thing was afterwards discovered by many persons. For images of the cross were found marked on the bodies of those, who had been at the time in the cathedral. And the Bishop of Wells told the Bishop of Ely that his wife (and she was a most honorable woman) came to him and told him, as a great miracle, that there were marks of the cross on her body. But when the Bishop laughed at this, his wife uncovered her person, and proved that what she had said was true. And then he noticed that the same very plain mark of the cross was impressed on himself, and as I think on his arm. While with others it was on the shoulder, the breast, the back, and other parts of the body. And that most illustrious man, the Lord of Ely, narrated this to me, in such a manner, as forbade any doubt about the truth of the history."

In this brief account there is involved probably a grand chapter on psychology, if only one knew how to evolve it. But the philosophy of the matter is akin to the marks of crucifixion on the ecstatics, much more closely than would at first thought seem at all likely. Also, there have been persons, as the writer hereof can testify, as it happens, on his personal knowledge, although they are perhaps more rare than ecstatics, with whom have appeared spontaneously on the skin, and as though very slightly embossed, letters, figures, and flowers. One of these instances was a rose of the breadth of two inches, which appeared in answer to a sudden suggestion, and which was as accurately marked as in a fine etching. The explanation, not of course of the shapes, but of the marks, was that they had been made by the blood having been forced into capillary veins, so as to press them against the cuticle, and thus to redden and slightly raise it. These marks, which had been watched while coming out, vanished without leaving a trace in less than ten minutes. As to how this happened, even though it were, as it might well seem to be, through an inflation of capillary veins, passes conjecture: because a certain belief that it was by the agency of an intervening spirit, if adopted, is not explanation, but only some semblance of information, and is indeed marvel added to mystery.

It is a matter of not unreasonable conjecture, whether Dr. Newman would have entered the Catholic Church in his state of mind, if he had known of the experience of the Bishop of Wells; for, not improbably it would have seemed to counterbalance the argument from the ecstatics, by the Earl of Shrewsbury.

But however that may be, with the preceding comments, the latest account of an ecstatic may be read by some persons with more patience, than it might otherwise have been, and by some others with less bewilderment. For the excitement made by that famous letter of the earl's was not so much because of what it was in itself, as it was through the temper of the people addressed. They were acted upon by that letter as though by an apparition; whereas they would not have been affected by it so strongly, if they had not been men of their time, even while trying hard to belong to the Middle Ages, and if they had not been, so to say, anti-supernaturalists in reading and observation, like almost everybody else.

The account of the Belgian ecstatic has been seen by multitudes of Protestants, but it will have been noticed by very few persons, because generally the eyes of Protestants are proof against reporting such things to their brains. Marvellous occurrences are as common now, perhaps, as ever they were in the Middle Ages; and they are published in the newspapers, to a far greater extent than most readers would easily believe. But even what are read and accepted as facts are seldom or never retained in the mind, but fade from the memory like dreams, as having no hold and no proper place. For indeed by education, and in accordance with the intellectual temper of the age, and as an effect of modern literature, there is an effort, unconscious, but not therefore the less real, in almost every mind to throw off every preternatural recollection as being useless, foreign, uncongenial, and inwardly indigestible. And thus always many good intelligent persons are at the mercy of the first prodigy, which may actually strike them. And if they should show themselves insane with it, it is because really they were already insane, as having been unreasonably sceptical, as having hardened themselves habitually against the facts of the universe, and as having despised the hints which are allowed to transpire from time to time as to a world of spirit, invisible indeed, but interfused among things seen and temporal, and pervading them, though commonly it may be without touching.

And now if any one would ask the writer, as to what then he thinks of the stigmata on the persons of the ecstatics, he would say that they may be preternatural without therefore being divine; and though they may be the effects of a certain kind of intense devotion, that they may still not be distinguishing favors. The case of Louise Lateau, of Belgium, could it be understood as the angels see it, would no doubt be of great use for clearly understanding spiritual laws, which every person is living under, though blindly. Nor does this remark presuppose, that her state must therefore be akin to the angelic; because it is even from the study of disease, that much has been learned as to the laws of health. And it is reverently suggested that Louise Lateau is an ecstatic with the stigmata, not probably because she is more favored of heaven than every other girl in Belgium, nor primarily because even of her being a Catholic, but because of some peculiarity in her constitution, by which anciently perhaps she might have been a prophetess, if the Lord had needed her; and by which, too, if she had been a fervent Friend or an earnest Methodist, she would have been receptive of gifts and graces corresponding perhaps to her faith, and to such hopes and expectations as might have been strong in her, by her religious connections.

By peculiarity of constitution, however, is not meant anything in kind different from human nature, but only something remarkable in degree, — a sensibility in receptiveness common to everybody, though only very feeble perhaps in most persons; and which being great in itself and from birth, may now and then operate wonderfully, from accidental causes such as fasting, or through illness, from some negative and restraining powers in the system having been enfeebled.

A case like this of Louise Lateau ought to be of infinite interest in theology. That there may be no knowing what to make of it is no reason for ignoring it, but is a reason rather for keeping it, in mind, against the coming of light on it from heaven : and which no doubt will arrive as soon as men are willing to receive it. And it will come probably by channels already existent and waiting, psychological, medical, and scientific.

Of course, all facts are not of equal use to everybody, any more than hay is good for chickens as well as horses, although oats may be. And there are large classes of creatures for whom diamonds must ever be valueless, such as bumble-bees, pigs, and the dirt-eating men of South Africa.

And it is not everybody, for whom the case of Louise Lateau can be expected to be interesting; and neither is it likely to be so for all theologians, though it really ought to be. And there may be some who will wish that it had never happened, or had never been published. And what will that wish of theirs be but infidelity to the truth; and what will the state of mind of such persons be, but blasphemy against the manner in which, under God, the world manifests its hidden powers?

As to the story of Louise Lateau, and other such things, there are words of Plato which are worthy of notice by all persons, and especially by some good Christians, although they are older than Christianity by some four hundred years. They are contained in his Second Epistle: "For almost as it seems to me, than such as these, there are no histories, which are more ridiculous to the herd of men, and none either, which to better minds are more wonderful, or more capable of inspiring them with a sense of God."

And now since this last paragraph was written, there has been published a volume entitled "Planchette; or,

The Despair of Science." And if indeed science should despair of the planchette to-day, it ought not to do so long, any more than the left hand should despair of its ability, while there is a good right hand to help it. And through science, when it is informed by psychology, the strangeness of the planchette may develop like the Greek mystery about amber. Amber, with the Greeks, was "electron"; and with rubbing it, was got what was called electricity. It was an unaccountable, useless manifestation. But since the time of Aristotle, and through science, it has developed into speech like lightning, between man and man, and across distances perhaps twenty or thirty times greater than any flash of lightning ever illumined.

In the volume referred to there is quoted a letter written at Rochester, nineteen years ago, and which was published in many newspapers at the time. That letter was by the present writer. It told fairly what was witnessed at a spiritual sitting, and which, as it happened, was nothing satisfactory whatever. And if the writer did not conclude correctly as to the motives of the mediums, it may be some excuse for him that at that time the Rochester knockings were to him an unheard-of novelty, and that the mediums themselves at that time knew nothing of the laws and limitations of the phenomena which were manifested through them.

MATTER AND SPIRIT.

GENERALLY at present the minds of men are very impatient of anything supernatural. It is a result partly of the materialistic philosophy which lately dominated in all things, and partly also of the hard, practical tone of the times, by which everything is judged according as it will work somehow or other, and promptly in a factory or a creed.

Now and then perhaps on a Sunday, or in the evening twilight, a man thinks gently on some strange occurrence, bordering perhaps on the supernatural, which he has heard of, and which perhaps may have been a family tradition. And thus he has his mind filled with thoughts and feelings from his inner spirit. The air about him feels as though almost it were aglow with latent light. In his ears there is an expectant sense, as though of something just ready to speak. And almost it is as though he felt himself, through all his senses, porous and open to a surrounding world of spirit. But with a rap on the door, or a sudden start, the man is himself again, as he thinks: though indeed it is only his inferior self which he thus suddenly becomes. And he is a man of the world again, because some divine affinities of his nature have suddenly shrunk into unconsciousness. And so, in a moment, things have become incredible for him, with which, however, his soul had been delighting herself, as connected with the communion of saints, the significance of miracles, and the nearness of the spiritual world.

There is an inner spirit in us, or rather there is an interior state of the spirit, which sometimes we know of; and when silently and softly we seem to breathe the air of another world than this; and when there comes over us a peace, not as the world gives; and when our thoughts come in upon our minds steadily and grandly, and as though from afar off; and when the heart feels, as it were, the magnitude of some crisis closing round it; and when indeed we are a wonder to ourselves. And under the fresh effect of such an experience the miracles of history seem to be but in fair keeping with human nature, and even with our individual selves, because of "the signs and wonders" which our own souls are capable of giving out. But more quickly than the sensitive plant, at the touch of flesh and blood, does this inner self shrink and contract, and, immortal as it is, yet seem to fade and disappear.

The Book of Revelation is not for reading in any and every mood. And it is not at all possible that a Materialist can understand St. John, as he writes, "I was in the Spirit on the Lord's day, and heard behind me a great voice, as of a trumpet." And a man must be a Spiritualist by philosophy, and at least as intelligently so as George Fox, the Quaker, before he can know what was to be listened to and how, when he reads, "He that hath an ear let him hear what the Spirit saith unto the churches."

And it is because the Book of Revelation, manifestly, is not for every state of mind that we may infer or at least suspect that the Scriptures, generally, may not always be read aright by human eyes, simply as being very sharp. The Bible cannot possibly be a revelation of the Spirit, to the angry minds of textual controversialists. And therein lies indeed the true objection to the use of creeds. For supposing that Christianity, as a whole, were capable of being put into words, an attempt at a creed might be reasonably and fairly made, on every fresh kaleidoscopic combination of texts or doctrines, which a congregation or an individual might believe. But for really Christian effect, it would seem as though every individual spirit ought for itself to find and feel the Spirit in the Scriptures, notwithstanding any intellectual aids, by which reverentially it might be thought desirable that a person should be prepared for that solemn communion of the finite with the infinite.

By the temper of the times it is the last thing to be wished for, or hoped for, and so, of course, it would be the very last thing to be minded, — anything fresh of a spiritual origin. It is a disease of this age, though now rapidly abating, that was just breaking out when the word for it was invented by Ralph Cudworth, which was pneumatophobia, — a shrinking from spirit, as cause, or explanation, or hope, and thereby and therefore, of course, from belief even, as very strongly felt.

There have been ages not barbarous, nor yet besotted, when a variation from the order of nature, or what seemed to be such, was what kingdoms would have consulted about, through eminent men. But to-day, by thousands of the most intelligent persons, variations from the laws of nature might be heard of and even credited, and yet awaken no interest. And now why should this be, or even be possible? Simply it is because it is not in the people to be interested. And that is because they have not such a belief in the spiritual world, as that they can possibly imagine even the possibility of a sign of it near them. The spiritual world about them, and they themselves now in it, and connected with it, and as certainly so as they ever will be, after they have lost or slipped their bodies, and according to philosophy and revelation both! It is a thing to them inconceivable, provoking, and ridiculous, and what they can neither think nor feel. But really, whether it pleases them or not, it is so that they are made; and also the thing which they do not like to think has been the glory of the greatest thinkers, since the world began, and has been the inspiring and informing thought, by which, as by a thermometer, the spiritual height of any age is to be measured, — not its height indeed, as to the externality and fashion of life, nor as to science which is conversant with the externality of the universe, but as to faith and poetry, and those virtues and graces, which in greater or less numbers are their inseparable concomitants.

Often a good Christian will say, " I hope, and for worlds I would not but think, that after I am dead somehow I shall be resuscitated and live in God forever." And then it is a terrible shock to him, should he be reminded that now already in God " we live and move and have our being." And then such a man will look about him in despair, and wish that he were not bound quite to believe it. For he is thinking to himself the while, " What! living in God now, and I what I am?" And the worst of it is what the man himself does not know, that so probably it will have to be with him to all eternity, so long as he himself is what he is, — so long as, somehow or other, the primitive instincts of his spirit are stifled: because an actual spirit, as he is even now, though embodied for a while, the man has no feeling of the spiritual universe surrounding him, no sense of it as power, nor any immediate expectations from it, by the way either of fear or hope.

We are spiritual creatures now, though embodied, and really living in a spiritual world, however much it may be clouded to our perceptions, or it would never have been written for Christians, "Draw nigh to God, and he will draw nigh to you." And that which is written is written, although we are what we are, and notwithstanding however divinely we may walk, that we are not to expect ever to be met by the glories which were witnessed by "the seven angels before the throne of God." But still, just as really as there were unearthly splendors for those heavenly eyes to see, when they looked, so there are experiences of unworldly origin which, with expectation, our spirits are in the way to find, and which serve as assurances of faith and answers to prayer. Speaking like an immortal, but with a sense of our infantile state for fleshliness, says St. John, "Beloved, now are we the sons of God, and it doth not yet appear what we shall be: but we know that when he shall appear, we shall be like him; for we shall see him as he is." Already in us prisoners of nature there are powers, susceptibilities, and rightful expectations which reach beyond the region of nature for their objects. "Our Father which art in heaven" may begin a prayer, which may be heard beyond the sun, and quite apart from the laws of acoustics and gravitation; and perhaps also it may be offered as incense before the throne by angels in whose view, amid wide-spread splendors, all earths and suns are but like thin vapors.

The child unborn has its senses for the world upon which it is to emerge: eyes for the light by which it is to see; ears for those waves of sound through the atmosphere by which it is to hear, and infantile instincts, serving for life and prophetic of it, and which it delights a mother's heart to recognize. And indeed a child in the womb has not only an eye for seeing about the world into which it is to be born, but an eye also which will fit a telescope upwards and a microscope downwards for exploration; and has also congenital faculties, through which it will grow into the ways of the world, and fill a place in society. And just so, in this womb of nature, wherein "the creature waiteth for the manifestation of the sons of God," human beings have all the spiritual faculties which are to fit them for the spiritual world, — eyes of the spirit, a spiritual understanding, ears with which to hear what the Spirit saith, and — O strange, unearthly, but sure experience! — a susceptibility by which "the Spirit also helpeth our infirmities; for we know not what we should pray for as we ought: but the Spirit itself maketh intercession for us with groanings which cannot be uttered."

All that is here attempted to be said, about persons in the flesh being open to effects from the world of spirit, is strong conviction, is inmost knowledge to the man who has ever felt the Spirit praying inside of his spirit, and informing his prayers, with an earnestness, and faith, and wisdom which were a wonder to himself, and an awful mystery, when at the end he said "Amen." And the inference from this is what St. Paul shall declare. And the words are from his grand argument on the struggle of the creature in its earthly environment, and against it, and they are that we mortals are "waiting for the adoption, to wit, the redemption of our body."

"There is a natural body, and there is" — the apostle does not say that there is to be, or shall be, but that there is — "and there is a spiritual body." And the Greek word for renewed life after death recognizes that statement of St. Paul's in a manner which the Latin-English word "resurrection" does not, commonly. By dissolution in the earth, "bare grain, it may chance of wheat, or of some other grain," shows what a body had been latent in it, though invisible, yet alive and wonderful, "first the blade, then the ear, and after that the full corn in the ear." And there is not a man living but has in him latent a spiritual body, endowed already with all those faculties, by which hereafter he may be free of the heavens, and feel himself at home in the house of many mansions, and as St. Paul would say, no stranger or foreigner, but a fellow-citizen with the saints, and of the household of God. The saint on earth has in him already all that he is to be in the great hereafter.

And thus for a human being with a twofold constitution, by which, mentally, he is adapted to this earth, and spiritually also to a new earth, under new heavens, it might seem that not impossibly or incredibly a person might now and then, and through some one or other of the thousand sensibilities by which he is an immortal soul, have experiences outside of the sphere of the natural man. And unless barred from such a supposition by a divine revelation, it might seem reasonable to anticipate that sometimes, with the weakening of "the body of this death," the latent faculties of the immortal spirit might even begin to manifest themselves. And indeed than the preternatural experiences of the dying, there are no phenomena perhaps in mental history which are more common. Said Schiller, for his last words in dying, "So many things are becoming to me so much plainer than they were." And no doubt the light in which he had wished to live was brightening on his soul. But more express even than this is the multitudinous testimony, which might easily be gathered, as to the death-bed experiences of persons within the last few years, and by which it would seem as though the departing spirit were sometimes met, before parting from the body, by some sign of the new world near it, by unearthly music perhaps, or by some spirit who was once an old friend, or by some vision of glory unutterable.

But also, in the same manner, and for analogous reasons, strange preternatural experiences, originating with spiritual causes, may reasonably be credited, for persons of peculiar conditions, whether congenital as to the body, or accidentally incurred by disease, or occasioned perhaps by an unusual sensitiveness, as to some of the forces which are necessary to vitality, electric, magnetic, odic, and others perhaps more occult than they. Thus somnambulism supposes the natural eye to be asleep, while the eye of the spirit sees through it. In clairvoyance there is sight independently of matter, as to the substance of the eye, and whether bandaged or not, and as to walls or long distances; and yet, as an effect of looking through a material eye-ball, the spirit sees material objects. But indeed wonders would seem to be likely enough, as the experiences of spirits in the flesh, and of mortals on their way to immortality. And how, then, might it be proper that such things should be judged of? Just as such things ought to be, by such creatures as men and especially by the enlightened disciples of Christ, — by rules of probability and analogy and good sense, and by the grand ruling test as to what "the Spirit itself beareth witness with our spirits." And indeed St. Paul could imagine the possibility of an angel from heaven preaching what Christian common sense might boldly and at once count accursed.

Always in an emergency of thought, it is well that a man should bethink himself as to where he is, and what he is. Because all things are not uniformly of the same significance everywhere. That may seem to be erroneous which is absolutely correct. And scientifically between navigators and the polar star there are causes of variation, as to guidance, which have to be allowed for, if that guidance is to prove exact. The polar star is polar truly for only the wisest people. And it is not to everybody, idle and studious alike, and not to the prejudiced at all, that even the Scriptures can yield their true meaning. What a man does not want to see, he will be very likely not to recognize. And this may happen about a fact, perhaps of no great importance in itself, but which yet, because of his state of mind, might for him individually be newness of thought, or a clew to some baffling and bewildering mystery.

That method of picking and choosing evidences, that fashion of thinking only alongside of well-trodden roads, that determination which idolizes agreeable facts, and winks hard against what are irreconcilable, which has been so common in theology, and for the sake of it, — of all that, what possible outcome can there be but folly, such as earlier or later must become plain? "Unclean spirits" are not a very pleasant subject of thought to any one, and to theologians in some enlightened regions almost they are inconceivable and incredible. And yet because of the New Testament, it might seem as though a person could not quite well understand what Christ was in the world, without some philosophy or understanding as to those "unclean spirits" whom he commanded, and against whom he gave his apostles power. And in the Old Testament, "familiar spirits" and their kindred are as essential to the action as Moses and Elijah. And for lack of this perception, there are many ingenious and elaborate works on the Old Testament, which could only be equalled by some such work as a history of the battle of Waterloo, wherein the French should be regarded, for some philosophical reasons, as having been only figures of speech. And yet the historical reality of a "familiar spirit" made certain by modern analogies, would probably be but an unwelcome fact, in many theological schools. Yet facts — facts are the words in which the universe reads to man its unending lesson. They may be odious by themselves, sometimes, while yet through their connections, they may be very valuable. But because of human weakness, it is often the alternative about a new fact, that either it is an idol, or else anathema. And truly also a fact is often treated in this manner, when really, except as being novel for a few people, it is nothing more than a pebble, a mere make-weight in the universe, which pebble, however just in its place and office, is of universal concern.

But with anything extraordinary to think of, or phenomenal, a man should remember himself. And then instead of finding himself on a judgment-seat, or rightfully glowing with the consciousness of a seraph, he will feel himself to be but a mortal creature, walking and working about a little spot in a little planet, attendant upon a sun, which sun itself is reasonably suspected of being also only a planet. But "he that humbleth himself shall be exalted." And when a man in that manner has felt his nothingness, he is ready then to appreciate the compliment which science pays him, by her assurance that the weight of his body, his mere fleshly clothing, is what the universe could not spare, without planets and suns and fixed stars running together, and there being an end of all things.

And in this way, even were there no other way, might a man reasonably suspect that perhaps also there are conditions concerning him as a spirit, of which he may not necessarily be aware. But then it is said that between mortal and immortal, and between matter and spirit, that the difference is such that there can be no reasoning with a man from any circumstances of to-day as to his connections with the spiritual and eternal.

And by some, who hold that this earth is isolated from the spiritual universe surrounding it, on the subject of miracles, often axioms are used as authorities, which really have long been anile and effete. That spirit can never impinge upon matter is assumed as an axiom by Thomas Aquinas; and it is pleaded to-day like a text from the gospel. But even supposing that it were true, it would not therefore follow that means might not be found or contrived, by which devils or angels might make themselves sensibly felt, and might act upon matter. It is true that spirit is spirit, and matter is matter. But then what is spirit, and what is matter? Of the difference between the two there are notions of mediæval origin, which are obstinately pleaded to-day, for ends which Thomas Aquinas and the schoolmen would never have sanctioned. Also, what did Thomas Aquinas know of electricity, galvanism, or magnetism? What did he know of the odic force? He knew no more of them than he did of optics, or chemical affinities, or the law of gravitation. Definitions as to spirit and matter, originating ages before Bacon, adduced to-day on the subject of miracles are gross anachronisms.

Matter! what is that as a basis whence to argue psychologically, while even by science it is speculated that all the matter of this earth may perhaps be compressible into a nut-shell? Really science is the young sister of spiritualism, and is of no kin whatever with materialism, to the positive knowledge of those who know them all three. The old mediæval understanding as to spirit and matter is obsolete; for through science matter itself seems semi-spiritualized. And, so to say, rightly understood, matter and spirit, in the common use of the words, are not opposites, except in some such way as that by which the roots of a tree in the ground are opposite to the blossoms high up in the air.

Spirit cannot impinge upon matter, because spirit is spirit; and spirit is impalpable, and therefore it cannot affect what is solid and hard! But when confronted these are but old-world positions, which properly were obsolete long ago. For perhaps the fluids called electric, galvanic, and magnetic are material, or perhaps they are spiritual, or perhaps they traverse fields intermediate between matter and spirit. But on any one of these suppositions, there are one or two old philosophical axioms as to spirit and matter, which are falsified at once, just as owls show themselves to be out of time and place when they attempt to fly in the broad sunshine.

The body of a man is not such matter as might sometimes seem to be supposed by some philosophers, but is really "dust of the earth," porous throughout every particle, to electricity and magnetism, which at least are semblances of spiritual forces. And if Thomas Aquinas had lived in these last days, instead of writing what he did on some points, and getting quoted by people of another dialect in philosophy than his, as having meant what he certainly did not intend, he would probably have held that matter was such a mere nothing, such a mere meeting-place of immaterial forces, as scarcely itself to need notice.

Instead of something like untanned leather, a man has a skin, by which he is open to influences and effects from the ends of the world, from the sun, and from the circumambient atmosphere. And all the more he learns from science, the more wonderfully does he feel this. And spiritually, when he is willing to attend, he finds himself connected in an equally wondrous manner. And many a man who thinks himself to be an Anti-Supernaturalist, with an honest confession of himself, as to some of his private experiences, which, for fear of being nonsensical, he is hardly willing to acknowledge even to himself, and also with fair respect for testimony from friends whom he personally esteems, — many a man, in this way, would find that a field of wonder widened round him, away in the far east of which he would feel that very probably there may indeed have been gates of revelation, and the place of rising of the sun of righteousness.

In Boston an Englishman was staying, who " many lands and many men had seen," and also many years, since the time of his leaving school. He certainly in his life had never dreamed of the school, and for many years had scarcely even had a thought of it. But one night he had a dream of it. Accompanied by his aunt, he walked up the road which led to the school, wondering all the while at the perfectness with which he remembered every little object. He passed in through the gate into the yard, when he noticed heaps of rubbish under the walls ; on which, he turned to his aunt and said, "This stuff ought to be cleared away. It never ought to be allowed here." Then, with the old familiar feeling, he went up the steps, and opened the door of the school, and was surprised at seeing, not boys at their desks, but six or eight workmen busy on the demolition of the building. And at this point he awoke. But in the morning, while he was at the breakfast-table, he received a foreign letter, which proved to be from a trustee of the old grammar school, soliciting a subscription from him towards the rebuilding of the edifice. It was an undertaking in which his aunt was much interested; and she had herself given the address for the letter.

The following narrative is vouched for by the best possible evidence. When the emigration for California had begun, a youth belonging to the town of Lynn embarked for San Francisco. After some months had elapsed, his mother dreamed that she saw him, that he looked wofully wasted, and that he stretched out his arms to her, and cried, "O mother, mother, take me. I am dying of thirst." Early the next day, she went to a very intelligent gentleman, with her heart full of agony: and at her request, he put the history and date of her experience into writing. After many months, eleven perhaps, a letter reached her from the captain of the ship in which her son had sailed. The vessel had suffered much in storms off Cape Horn. Because of the long passage, the supply of water had not lasted. And for want of water, several persons on board of the vessel had died before reaching port; and among them was her son. And the time of his death, as given by the captain, corresponded with that night of the mother's dream.

These two incidents have never been published before; and it is because they are new that they are given; for it would be very easy to cite hundreds, and perhaps thousands, of recorded dreams, which are at least as impressive as the preceding, and some of which are even more striking.

Some six or seven years ago a vessel arrived in Boston with a great number of shipwrecked people on board. The ship in which they had been sailing had foundered at sea, and left them on the water, clinging, most of them, to floating objects. A vessel, bound to Boston, arrived in their midst and picked them up. But how did that ship get amongst them? The captain of it said that he was on deck at night, and a bird flew in his face, and at the same time he was filled with a strong, strange feeling for putting the ship about, and sailing back on the course by which he had been coming. A second time, and a third time, a bird flew in his face. And the feeling with him for putting the ship about became irresistible. And after sailing for three hours in the dark, he found himself to be a savior at a great shipwreck.

In such incidents as the preceding history abounds, whether ancient or modern, classical or profane. And why is it that they are read contemptuously, or heard with impatient pity? Simply it is because of what is ignorantly fancied about the laws of nature, as being exclusive of marvels of unknown origin. And just as though also the laws of nature, to common notion, would not have been against the possibility of submarine whispering, if it had ever been thought of, before electricity had yielded itself to human management! And just as though a thousand and ten thousand similar facts do not imply something in common, some common cause, and it may be probably some common law! And what if that should seem to be a spiritual law? Is that a supposition so improbable as that even Christians cannot think it? Such Christians certainly as many people say they are, cannot think it: and worse than that, they would rather not believe it, as they say; and what is worse still than that, they avow that they would rather not believe what might seem to diminish the peculiarity of the miracles of the Scriptures. "O ye of little faith!" As though God would be less God for any man's knowing something about him of his own knowledge! As though the Bible would be less credible for being confirmed in any way, even the least! As though it had not been a Scriptural promise, as to some spirit-stirring times, both in the Old Testament and in the New: "Your young men shall see visions, and your old men shall dream dreams"! And as though it were not one grand purpose of the Bible to develop the mysteriousness of human nature, and to make men feel, with many other strange things, that whether there be hosts below them or not, or hosts above, that by Jesus Christ they have been made "kings and priests unto God and his Father"!

There is a containing sky about us, in which the aurora flames. There is an air about us, in which it thunders and lightens. And surrounding us there is an atmosphere, through which we are affected for life and for death, in ways which, year by year, are enumerated by science more and more wonderfully.

A spiritual atmosphere about us, or an atmosphere

slightly spiritual, or something which we mortals should call such, — why should it be accounted strange or incredible? Surely not because the knowledge of it was not given by Moses, or through the New Testament. And if such a belief be fairly deducible by observed facts, what is it but a thing for which to thank God, as enabling believers in the Scriptures to conform the better to the rules of what is called modern science, even on its own plane? Revelation! People who believe in it ought to be afraid of nothing, as against it. And no man, with a soul to believe, does believe in it, with earthly misgivings of any kind.

It has been supposed, what is even the besetting difficulty of many earnest persons, that there never can have been a call upon mortals from the world immortal, for want of a way, a channel. Does therefore the significance of that call diminish because there might seem to be a greater possibility for it? Says some one, "Eh, eh! I never believed it. But now I see a quarter, a law, a spiritual connection, whence that old call may have come." But that would not seem to be all that is to be said, unless a man should think more of the importance of his own sense than of what the universe itself may have to say to him. And when such a man finds his own earthiness to be more spiritual than he had thought, it is surely no reason for his beginning afresh to doubt about his spiritual connections.

THE OUTBURST OF SPIRITUALISM.

THIS is a great subject, which can be noticed in this place only just as it illustrates the line of thought in these essays.

The phenomena of Spiritualism, even the simpler, are very curious in themselves, but they are important mainly for the method which is in them, and for the philosophy which they involve. Witchcraft was no good in its day, certainly; "but," said John Wesley, "to give up witchcraft is to give up the Bible." And, similarly, to gainsay the possibility of Spiritualism is to repudiate the spiritual philosophy of the Scriptures. The writer hereof has what is for him an opinion about Spiritualism, but it would need the space of a volume in which to justify as well as unfold it. And therefore any mention of it here should be taken, just as it is made, merely by way of allusion, and for the special points indicated.

How vast and various is the universe, even to human apprehension! The infinity surrounding them, men are ready enough to remember for glory, but not for humility. And so, under the lamp-light of history, merely, some great philosophers show very strangely, as critical occupants of the universe. So, often, on one subject or another, have even great men shown themselves to be as blind as ants in a hillock. What would ants be the wiser, if alongside of their hill there were a highway of commerce reaching to the ends of the world, or an observatory by which, as to view, the heavens are brought down? It is true that emmets are born with the knowledge which they need, and that human beings are born to the knowledge into which they are to grow. Yet still many men are as blind as ants to "the balancings of the clouds"; and many immortal souls have their faculties for understanding and belief fast closed against evidences of the spiritual universe about them. And as to the things of the spirit, and the philosophy of the spiritual world, and the ongoings of the spiritual universe, there are still those even who can "see and not perceive," and who are altogether amenable to the remonstrance, "Having eyes, see ye not? and having ears, hear ye not?"

Is it indeed true philosophy, which thinks that every fresh suggestion from the universe must necessarily be just what might have been looked for? And as to signs and effects from the spiritual world, is mere probability any kind of a rule by which for souls to judge, who themselves are but of yesterday's creation? Yet there are people who are confident as to the possibilities of the universe, merely through their own feel of it. But even though his five senses be sharpened to the utmost, and be helped by every kind of instrument and contrivance, yet what is any man for a judge as to the likelihoods of a universe, which appeals, not to five senses only, but perhaps to five hundred faculties! And the claim of Christianity is that the soul has senses or sensibilities for channels and quarters, outside of the range of what technically is called science.

In the "Recognitions of Clement," that oldest of Christian novels, says Simon Magus, "While all sensations possible belong to one of the five senses, that Power which is superior to all things, cannot add any new one." But to this it is replied by Peter, "That is false; for there is a sixth sense, that of prescience; for the other five senses are capable only of knowledge, but the sixth of foreknowledge; which sense the prophets had." As being a spirit imprisoned in a body, a man has extra-mural relations, and as a living soul he has supersensual susceptibilities. And so it might seem to be, in itself, anything but incredible, if, now and then, some soul should have something to report as to some foregleam of immortality; or as to some glimpse faintly caught of the scenery or the company, to which it is itself predestined; or as to occurrences as fitful as the aurora of the north, and as wayward as the lightning, and which, for earthly effect, start perhaps from the meeting-point between spirit and matter; and which point, it may be, is more mysterious than even spirit itself is.

To what can the outbreak of what is called "Spiritualism" be likened for effect? On the world at large, it has been as though a ghost had appeared at a sitting of the Royal Society, in London. But a thing may seem to be out of place, because really the observer himself is out of his own proper place. And many Christians have been startled, provoked, and confounded by "Spiritualism" because of the extent to which they themselves were out of place, intellectually and religiously. Not improbably, if Christians had been such believers as they ought to have been, the thing which technically is called Spiritualism, might never have been manifested amongst them. Near Jerusalem once, if the multitude of the disciples had not praised God, the stones might immediately have cried out. The testimony of the stones would not, perhaps, have been very edifying, except by being very startling. Even though the various conditions necessary to the phenomena of Spiritualism are not well known, yet it is conceivable and it is highly probable that, if the atmosphere of the Christian Church had been what it ought to have been, instead of there being mediums and their attendant marvels in the world, there would to-day have been in the Church the manifestation of the Spirit, and one good man would have been full of the Holy Ghost, and another man, perhaps, would have seen visions, and still another would have abounded in hope, through the power of the Holy Ghost; while for the public benefit one man would have shown the gift of healing, and another have been endowed with the word of wisdom, as a gift.

As it is, however, some of the more material of the Spiritualistic phenomena, such as noises, are as though the stones cried out, to assure men that really they are not as much at home in the universe as they fancy,—that there may be qualities, and ways, and a soul in the universe, such as they have never thought of,—and that themselves instead of being altogether self-sufficient, actually that they are but like bubbles made of the will of God and spared of his mercy.

There is a philosophy, and that, too, of fervent

Christians, which would have taken up at its very commencement, this portentous subject of Spiritualism as a very little thing, — the philosophy of Henry More and Ralph Cudworth, and a long ascending line of scholars, reaching up to the Fathers, and in amongst the foundations of the Church. From this philosophy, which implies the coexistence of two worlds for man, — one for the body and another for the spirit, — thinkers have been greatly estranged during the last century, because of the inordinate and disproportionate attention which has been drawn to the material world, by the novelty and multitude of its disclosures scientifically. But the more that the range of the five senses is explored, and the more definitely it is ascertained what the properties are of which matter is susceptible, the more certain it becomes that in the universe there is a causative power transcending what the sun and moon have ever felt, and of which man is an object.

Spiritualism ought to be nothing novel or strange to a theologian, and would not be but for the anomalous state of theology itself. Men have been so intent, so long, on splitting hairs metaphysically, for theological use, that almost the breadth itself of theology has been forgotten. By the modes which are called Spiritualistic people are to-day communicating with spirits from a plane which is common to them, with the Chinese, the Esquimaux, and the aborigines of Australia, and probably with the prophets of ancient Greece, and the priests of ancient Rome, and with the last philosophic survivors of Hellenism. And if any Christians think that thereby there is over them the supremacy of heavenly illumination, by that much, at least, they may believe themselves, as before heaven, to be standing apart from where the early Christians stood.

All the preceding remarks will hold true by those laws of evidence by which still higher things than Spiritualism will be judged a hundred years hence. For, what is under our eyes proverbially is the last thing to be noticed. But when, with the recession of time, it has got to be viewed on the plane of history, along with other distant even though more important objects, then it becomes what cannot so easily be overlooked. And it will certainly be well for some persons, if by fairness or spiritual receptiveness they should be enabled to anticipate the use of that information, which is certain to pass on to the next generation, and if possibly in no other way, then certainly as an unopened letter, wonderful in itself, but more wonderful still, perhaps, as having never been minded when it was written.

Rightly considered, though more fully than is possible here, the manner in which the announcement of the phenomena commonly called Spiritualistic, was received is almost as instructive as the manifestations themselves. For it is only by an invincible, inward anti-supernaturalism, which has grown with them from childhood, that commonly men of ordinary sense have been able to withstand the multitudinous testimony, which exists as to some of the simpler phenomena which are called Spiritualistic. Nor is it out of his own strength, nor yet out of his own weakness, that a man is able to contradict, as he sometimes does; but it is from the spirit of his age, from the breath which he draws of public opinion, and from his being one of a banded host. And this remark is made quite independently of what the thing called Spiritualism may be in itself, whether sense or nonsense, and whether good, bad, or indifferent. "Spiritualism is the work of evil spirits," says one who had never in his life before had a word to say about devil or evil spirits, and into whose theological mind never a thought of one could have entered, but as a ready way of answering what he was not prepared to argue. Says another, "It is either the Devil, or else it is imposture, or else it is all a misunderstanding by the people concerned." This might be the judgment of some personage standing aback and above the origin of all philosophy and all action on this earth, but for the comments which are adjoined, and which show that the utterance was simply a superficial view of possible chances on the subject, and made by a man who knew that he did really know nothing at all about it. So again there was once a warning against Spiritualism given from the text: "And when they shall say unto you, seek unto them that have familiar spirits, and unto wizards that peep and that mutter: should not a people seek unto their God?" The warning was well meant, and much of it was good. But in the ear of reason it was all spoiled, when there was added to it, from conscientiousness, that really there never had been any "familiar spirits," and that their mention in the Scriptures was only by way of accommodation to the prejudices of ignorant times. And so it was that a theologian thought he was denouncing from the Scriptures, what all the while was actually corroborating the Scriptures against him.

Often, when overwhelmed by evidence, and unable to deny the reality of the phenomena of Spiritualism, people say, "Well, what of it! what does it all show?" To which the answer is simple enough, though it cannot always be made for fear of discourtesy, that the Spiritualistic phenomena are fairly and properly for intelligent persons, and fully as much so as algebra, or trigonometry, or logarithms. Says one, "I have no doubt that, in the presence of some persons, called mediums, tables dance and are rapped upon, and in fact I know it; and I have no doubt that persons have been raised into the air without any human agency, because of what I have been told. And I will acknowledge that the secret thoughts of my mind have been recognized and published in a way which I could not have believed, and could hardly have wished. And it is all very funny; but what of it?" And this is sometimes said as confidently as though the intellectual system of the universe would echo the words and say, "What of it?"

And what of the theology which talks in that manner, what of that? What else can it be than a mere semblance of something, the mere ghost of a faith, a shell empty alike of learning, sense, and earnestness? The phenomena of Spiritualism acknowledged to be real, and yet scorned as being unimportant, unsuggestive, meaningless, and unworthy of theological notice! What flippancy! What mere blind leadership of the blind such theology must be! What a fantastic trick before high heaven! "Thou hast a name that thou livest, and art dead."

As to the significance of those phenomena, it is enough to say, that by them Bishop Douglass, with his great name in theology, would have been amazed, as though by a latter-day revelation; and that Hugh Farmer, formerly the great authority as to miracles, would have found himself thereby flatly contradicted on important points, though not much to his grief, because of the good, honest man he was.

St. Bonaventura, while writing the life of St. Francis of Assisi, and entranced in thought, was, according to history, seen to rise in the air. And Thomas Aquinas, who happened accidentally to be a witness of the marvel, said, "Let us leave a saint to write for a saint." This anecdote has been much ridiculed, and yet it has a wide kindred in history. Thus it is said that Ignatius Loyola was seen in prayer to be raised more than a foot from the ground, saying, "O my God! O my Lord! O that men knew thee!" But for persons who would wish to belong to the communion of saints, whether with or without a pope, it would seem to be important and interesting, if anything might enable them to believe, instead of harshly denying what implicates such names as Bonaventura and Thomas Aquinas.

According to Farmer, in his Essay on Miracles, a human body raised into the air, without any human agency whatever, would be a real and evident miracle, because contrary to the known course of nature. A man may affirm a thing to be true, and say, "What of it?" But if he affirms that to be true which Hugh Farmer could not imagine as possible, except by the direct intervention of God, the man may be certain that he has done a great thing, whether he knows it or not, or whether he knows or does not know how to make use of his own knowledge. The levitation of the body is affirmed in history, in regard to persons canonized as saints, and also as to people accused of witchcraft, and it has been again and again published as to Pope Pius the Seventh. At present, for almost all Protestant eyes, even when acknowledged as being probably true, it is an incongruous fact, but surely it ought not therefore to be despised as useless; but rather it should be reverentially remembered, as being likely, some day, to flash light on the mystery of the connection between the soul and the body. And indeed it is really anything but ridiculous to think of, by a person of reading, and of good common sense and earnestness. And if it does not immediately teach anything, it may yet draw one up into the mount of contemplation, whence things have a different look to what they have in the common world below, and whence, too, the laws of nature seem but like the surface, and not the soul of things, — a surface, perhaps, of a lake, on which for ripple, and figure, and glancing sheen, it is because "the wind bloweth where it listeth, and thou hearest the sound thereof, but canst not tell whence it cometh, and whither it goeth." And it may be added that also the remaining clause of the text is true, not only as to the conversion of a man morally, which properly it means, but also as to the change which a man may, and often does, experience as to his estimate of nature and science, under a vivid sense of what is omnipotent and omniscient, — "So is every one that is born of the Spirit."

"And what of it?" many good people have said, while acknowledging that, in connection with what is called Spiritualism, their secret thoughts had been recognized and answered through many secret windings; as though such a fact were nothing more than the capricious barking of a dog as to significance. In a recent theological work, Dr. Walter Scott says about some printed account of a boy, who was supposed to be a demoniac, and to have been sensible of an adjuration, even when only addressed to him in the secrecy of the mind, "I would ask, Are we warranted by either Scripture or reason to believe that any evil spirit, even if it had been Satan himself, can know the thoughts, the most secret workings and prayers of the heart in the way in which this is supposed to have been done? I must think that we are not." The theology of Dr. Scott, in the history of opinion, is what dates mainly from St. Augustine. And the writings of Augustine should have instructed him differently from that statement of his, and by the saint's personal experience.

The previous quotation is contained in a work, highly important at least as to the auspices under which it was published, and the man who knows anything differently, and thinks nothing of it, stands opposed simply by information to people whose looks would astonish him, if they were assembled about him in their multitude and respectability. And if such a man should further wish to try out of the present age, and in the last, the importance of what, though real, he accounts as worthless, then let him listen to a remark of Jortin on Ecclesiastical History. "It seems to be beyond the abilities of any created being to know the thoughts of a man, particularly of a man who is agitated by no passion, and gives no indications of his mind by any outward sign." Such a different thing it is, for a man to talk just out of himself, and for a momentary purpose, from being ready to hold his position in full view of history and men of earnest thought!

It may be, that two persons might be found of the same school in philosophy, according at least to the words in which one would claim fellow-belief with the other; and of these two, one would say that the phenomena of Spiritualism are impossible, while the other would say that they are as meaningless as the miracles of the Scriptures, which may or not be true. But now thence it might seem, as though the occurrence of an impossibility might be nothing wonderful.

One man, with the first report of the simpler phenomena of Spiritualism, exclaims; "That is the Devil." And another, with the first certain communication of something which could not be other than preternaturally given, exclaims, "The heavens are open again." And besides these, there are the large classes who say, some in one way and some in another, but all of them conjointly what is tantamount to this,—"Ah, well, very likely, no doubt, but perhaps there is possibly, no knowing truly, so to say, anything about anything."

In such an atmosphere of thought, spiritually, as almost all people would seem to be living in, so thin and hazy and uninspiring, so dead and bewildering, it might seem as though for a theologian, anything spiritual, even though it might really be devilish, ought to be useful, as enabling him perhaps to find his whereabouts, or, as the French say, "to face the East"; though certainly it could not aid him to do so, unless by nature or grace he might happen to be ready for the guidance.

It is sometimes pronounced as though judicially, for a verdict, "By acclamation of the public, Spiritualism is a thing which cannot be entertained for a moment." But now how is this pretended verdict ever supposed to be made up? It is agreed upon by people who do not agree among themselves, even as to the facts concerned. One party says, "By the laws of nature what is called Spiritualism is impossible, and therefore it is not a subject to be entertained for a moment." Another party says, "Spiritualism is true, horribly and fearfully; and, therefore, as a subject of thought cannot be entertained for a moment." And a third party says, "The intuitions of the individual mind are for the individual. And therefore also for the public, as far as the public may be complicated with his individuality, the intuitions of the individual are supreme. And from outside whatever would conflict with the supremacy of intuition, may be accounted extraneous, intrusive, and, like Spiritualism, a thing not to be entertained for a moment." And a fourth party says, "The Bible is enough for us, and as we have not time for everything, Spiritualism cannot by us be entertained for a moment." Strange parties these to a common verdict, — parties who disagree about the facts concerned, and who yet are summed up together for apparently a unanimous opinion.

But whatever Spiritualism may be, it has had a singular, instructive effect, by the remarks which it has elicited from philosophers taken by surprise; from "children tossed to and fro and carried about with every wind of doctrine"; from self-opinionated men, exasperated by the rebelliousness of facts against them;

and by theologians who, with denying the possibility of Spiritualism, have suddenly found themselves flatly opposed to the Bible. For both theology and philosophy have been wofully at fault about Spiritualism; which, however, they never would have been, only that first they had themselves become egregiously faulty by having become too set in doctrine, and by having thereby largely foregone the perception and the love of facts, as evolved by daily experience, or as recorded in history.

While he was a Jew, Neander was turned towards Christianity by the Pedagogue of Plutarch. This incident was a sign of the times, really. For by an old Pagan was done unintentionally, what all the Christian apologists of the day might have attempted in vain. For, by timidity and by the taint of anti-supernaturalism in many places, Christianity has been so weakened and attenuated, as that it cannot be spiritually or intellectually attractive, for persons of intelligence. And indeed by a man of spiritual insight and critical faculty, there is more Christianity to be distilled out of Paganism itself, than some theologians seem able to find in all the New Testament.

Belief in a spiritual world, as the early Christians felt it, has become so much weakened by sickly intellectualisms of materialistic kinship, that really what the earliest disciples eschewed might serve to-day as a first lesson in pneumatology, for many Christian divines. Many believers in Spiritualism are as ignorant as other people, and some of them as ignorant perhaps as even Abyssinian Christians. But the Spiritualism of the most ignorant Spiritualist persuades him, of his personal knowledge, that the demonology of the New Testament was true.

As has been stated before, Spiritualism is not of any particular church or creed, any more than a telescope is, or an electric telegraph, or a badly kept post-office, or a miscellaneous library. But just as Paganism itself might help to make some Christian believers to be better believers than they are, so even Spiritualism might avail theologically for some distinguished divines. And truly such is the spiritual ignorance of this highly scientific age, that "an unclean spirit," fit only for exorcism in ancient times, would to-day, for importance, in almost any theological school, be like a new revelation; because a real, earnest belief in the demoniacs of the New Testament would necessitate the formation of a pneumatology of the Scriptures, for want of which, to nearly all readers, the sentences of the Bible sometimes hold together but like ropes of sand.

"And it came to pass, as we went to prayer, a certain damsel possessed with a spirit of divination met us." If anything to-day might make her seem, by analogy or otherwise, to have been exactly what the writer says, then there would be many an honest doctor of divinity, on that knowledge, who would confess that what little pneumatology he might have was wrong, and also his philosophy of religion, and also that inspiration was a more real thing than he had ever thought. But now the account of that girl, with the spirit of Pytho, is to be believed in, according to Spiritualism, exactly as it is written, and not stupidly, but with a lively, intelligent apprehension. Can it be that anything in the Scriptures should be the plainer for Spiritualism? Certainly, and no great wonder either! How many various understandings there are of the New Testament, — Catholic, Trinitarian, Arian, Unitarian, Calvinistic, Arminian, and five, ten, twenty others! There can only one of them be right absolutely, and probably there is not even one. Such various understandings of the same book argue the obfuscated state of theology, and argue too the probability, that theologians differ from one another so variously, for something else than the letter of the Scriptures; and indeed because of a something which, more or less, they all lack, and which in full strength with them would be "the unity of the Spirit"; and because largely of the general infectiousness of the anti-supernaturalism of the times. But, as has been already remarked, it is such a state of things at present, that even "the unclean spirits" mentioned in the New Testament, if made certain by analogy or any other way, and even though of the same class as the "dumb and deaf spirit," would yet, simply as being known of, be of great use to wanderers in the field of theology, bewildered as it now is.

Spiritual rappings have been derided as mere materialism, but only, however, by persons who must have been intensely materialistic without knowing it; because an intelligent rapping or word by a spirit, suggests to a spiritually-minded man, that there must be channels and conditions through which a spirit can partially return into nature, and also that possibly there may be some human beings, who may be spiritually acted upon, as well as tables. Then, too, it is said that Spiritualism is worthless as a subject of thought, because the spirits never tell what was not known before. But no matter how stupidly it may be done, if a spirit can show himself at all, he does the greatest thing of the age, on this earth; for he returns by a door where theology has said there was no opening.

And now again let it be said that all this, which may seem novel and startling on the first reading, is yet nothing strange, if read in the spirit of the Scriptures, and by the light of history.

Spiritualism, dated even as of Rochester origin, is of infinite importance to the state of mind which denies its possibility. But to the mind which believes it, it may be very mischievous, or at best may minister to a poor, low kind of spirituality, apart from the philosophy connected with it, and which involves in its completeness both modern science and ancient history, and the experiences of almost every primitive tribe; and also which appeals to the New Testament as to the discerning of spirits, and which strengthens itself as to its positions, by the history of the Christian Church, while it was in conflict with heathenism.

In manner there is a great likeness between the mistakes respectively of some men of science and some adepts of Spiritualism, — between philosophers with telescope and microscope, who think that they know all about God, because of their having searched out some of his ways, and Spiritualists who think that they know all about the spiritual universe, from having a few spirits to talk with. And in neither of these classes, do the professors remember the limitations, under which they learn. For through a telescope God is not seen, but only the divine way of handling dirt. And through spiritual mediums there is communication with the spiritual universe, but only as to the first step perhaps on an endless flight, and on which step, also, it is, as Henry More said two hundred years ago, that often, spirits "are very great fools; that there are as great fools in the other world as there are in this."

By the necessity of things, the best effect from the spiritual world cannot ordinarily result from such communications as departed spirits can ever word, though even they may themselves rank with seraphs in wisdom; but it must come from such thought as may be quickened in good minds, well prepared by education, and by faith in the Holy Spirit, with a willingness to wait for it and to trust it. And in the same manner, however mysterious may be the way of it, the first true thought of God in any soul is by revelation; for it is a flash of light in the mind, or it is a sudden terror of the conscience, or it may be that it is an infinite yearning of love. But whatever it may really be, it is a something with very different qualities from anything, which can enter the mind through the tube of a telescope, or be started in the understanding purely by science.

There have been many outbursts on the world, which have been in a general sense like what is now called Spiritualism. Such was the movement which began with George Fox. Such also was the commencement of what is called Shakerism, and such, though in a manner less strongly marked, were the beginnings of the people called Irvingites, of some thirty years ago, and also of the Franciscans, who are an order of friars in the Catholic Church. These, however, are only instances out of a multitude of such things, which might be cited at will, from history, ancient and modern, and from the experiences of the last thirty years.

Through George Fox, "the Spirit" was a rebellion against that formalism of thought, into which Englishmen began to fall soon after the Reformation. And whatever else it may be, the Spiritualism which is commonly supposed to have begun at Rochester is a witness against the materialism to which men were inclining to succumb, under the undue influence of science. And indeed as to these things there actually is a philosophy, and which is none the less sure for being only distantly akin to mineralogy and ichthyology.

There are two sides to a thunder-storm, — what is below and what is above, as to state. And similarly, there are effects to be experienced, and even perhaps to be incurred, by laws which act through human wants, and which may be not unlike perhaps to the demands of a decaying region below, on an atmosphere above, and which get answered by thunder and lightning and sanitary good.

Electricity is generated in more ways than one, as by the spontaneity of nature, by artificial contrivances, and by what may be called accidental causes. And so spiritual fire may flash on a man from above; or it may be caught from another like a flame; or it may burst from some heart, like spontaneous combustion, and like the experience of the Psalmist: "My heart was hot within me; while I was musing, the fire burned: then spake I with my tongue."

The recent revival in the north of Ireland, like

twenty other revivals, was an outburst of spiritual power, by which many hundreds, and even perhaps thousands of souls were acted upon in a way, by which they manifested many things, in curious analogy with the phenomena of Spiritualism. Why was this? And if that revival were a reality, and Spiritualism be not an imposture, why were not the two things exactly alike as to their effect? Simply because the people concerned were not the same people in the two matters, and were not looking in one and the same direction. Pressure on a man bodily may vary in many ways, and so may pressure on a man spiritually. And perhaps the connections and susceptibilities of a man through his spirit may be innumerably more than through his body.

The Spirit, as it came on Samson, was one thing, for result; and as it came upon Paul, it was another; though to both it was from the same God that the visitations were made.

In an age characterized by an infestation of "unclean spirits" exorcism was an appropriate manifestation of power superhuman or extra-natural. And if to-day tables are tipped, or danced about, or made to seem intelligent, contrary to the laws of nature, it may be because of what has seemed right to spirits, perhaps at no great height above this earth, and far below that step on which the seraphs stand in ranks about the throne of God. Or it may be that table-tippings and similar things are even directly concurrent with the designs of Providence, and are to be accounted as means, whereby the minds of men may be exorcised from fascination by the laws of nature, which, though true enough for men as mere mortals, are not the half of the truth for them as immortal souls.

And if through some mediums Spiritualism should seem to stand apart from Christianity, and therefore to be strange and portentous, then let an incident in the Gospels be considered; and let it be noticed how easily the confidence of a Christian ought to transcend even the heroism of mere honesty. "And John answered and said, Master, we saw one casting out devils in thy name; and we forbade him, because he followeth not with us. And Jesus said unto him, Forbid him not; for he that is not against us is for us."

THOUGHTS ON SPIRITUALISM.

SPIRITUALISM is properly the antithesis of materialism, and holds that man is not only an animated, highly organized body, but also a living soul, and from his birth connected with a world spiritual and eternal. And Spiritualism technically so called is simply an affirmation of the foregoing statement, under the interest and conviction produced by certain phenomena of the last few years, and which are very curious, and apparently preternatural.

A medium may be lowly and ignorant, and also laden with every infirmity of the flesh, and yet can be the sudden, utter confutation of materialism, even while it is affecting to lean upon science, and to deck itself with the beauties of poetry. But some persons may think it strange, that instruction is to be got from a lowly, ignorant medium. But surely the loftiest philosophy should be able to condescend to new facts, anywhere, and at any time. Yet often the phenomena of Spiritualism have been despised by persons who yet gloried, under science, in having been instructed, by mere stones and petrified bones, as to the order of creation, and as to the look and habits of creatures, animals, and vegetables, as they appeared and fulfilled their times and uses.

To the writer hereof, the phenomena of Spiritualism

are useful, not so much because of what they are in themselves as incidents, as because they are evidences and illustrations as to pneumatology. Through the persons called mediums is there really communication with the world of spirit? That there is intercourse to be had with that world is certain; but as to the spirit to be talked with, there can be no absolute certainty. Because of some men at least, the minds lie open to the inspection of spirits, like the most compendious and convenient of day-books, so as that, through a medium, a spirit can read to a man out of his own memory things which he had himself forgotten. And for this and other reasons an impostor-spirit can have a mortal at such a disadvantage, as that actually for the present writer, conviction as to the identity of a spirit communicating through a medium, would not be wrought by even fifty times of the amount of evidence, which would suffice for identifying a person in a court of law. How is this then? And what, then, does this mean? It means that mortals must remember at least what they are; and that as clay-clad creatures they are but dull and blind as to the spiritual world and its ways and occupants. Nor should this be any marvel; "for Satan himself is transformed into an angel of light."

And now the way is open by which the writer can express himself still more freely. From his own experience, then, he is satisfied that some spirits have power to come into the realm of nature some little way, and so as to be able to make some signs, such as the moving of objects, the ringing of bells, playing on a harp, and touching a person, and such also as taking possession of the body of some living person, more or less completely, and using the hand for writing, and the voice for speaking, and the eyes for seeing with, after the manner of a mesmeric clairvoyant, only much more successfully. Also he knows that the death of a person can be announced, and that even also minute peculiar circumstances attending it can be detailed, some days before there could be even a possibility of such information being to be given by natural means. Also the writer would tell, in obedience to a sense of duty, of his having seen and examined and seen vanish ghost-hands,—hands of spirit, which had been materialized as to surface, at least, and which had thereby been made capable of looking and doing, for a little while and to some little purpose, like hands of flesh and blood.

There may be, and perhaps, all things considered, there really is, through a medium, sometimes at least, communication between friends in this world and friends departed; though perhaps it may be as rare as the loving appearance of a mother to a distant child, whom she could not but long for as she died. For reliable intercourse between a person in this world and a particular spirit in the world of spirits, there must be a right adjustment of conditions, of which some perhaps are known, but of which many more are not even to be conjectured.

But now really, of my vanished friend, I am sure as to the love, already and out of my heart, beyond all assurance which he could ever possibly give me, by getting his hand inside of the sphere of nature, and making signs to me; just as when he was a mortal

I credited him for affection, beyond what he ever uttered, or what I should have wished to hear him breathe.

What, then, do these phenomena testify? They witness as to human nature what it is in itself, and what it is open to, through exposure or by grace. And they are proofs as to what a world of mystery it is, in which men live. And also they are challenges to inquiring minds.

People are amazed at the phenomena of Spiritualism, and astounded by them, and are sometimes even sceptical as to their possibility; and all the while, really, they are but the accidents of our transcendent connections, of our being immortal though mortal, and spiritual while yet of the earth, earthy. Are they therefore supernal? No. And the proneness which there is to worship prodigies, though they should be only such things as haunted houses or wonderful dreams, begins really in the same state of mind as that in a theologian, which defines a miracle as being a suspension of the laws of nature. By making too much of the supernatural, it may actually be nullified as to usefulness.

And indeed to such a pass had things come, on the subject of miracles, among honest controversialists, that it might seem as though it had been in the order of Providence that the phenomena of Spiritualism should be developed, merely as materials for pneumatology, and for the use of competent observers. And by this, it is not necessary to suppose that Spiritualism is divine, any more than is the cholera which enforces useful lessons. There are diseases of the spirit, which begin with God's mercy, and which end more mercifully still. And it would not be without historical analogies, as strong almost as demonstration, if it should be said that the Spiritualism of to-day, so abundant, familiar, extensive, is a reaction, not of the will of man of course, but of the constitution of the universe, against the materialism, which was beginning to affect Christianity itself as an easy conquest.

Spiritualism is of great interest, as restoring the background of the Scriptures, as a picture, and as thereby also making the foreground more vivid, if not more intelligible. By Spiritualism certainty is restored as to the familiar spirit of the Old Testament, and as to the nature of the unclean spirits mentioned in the New Testament, as to the history of the woman of Endor, as to the seductive nature of the worship of Baal, and as to the actual possession of a certain damsel by a spirit of Pytho. And there is no honest divine, among Protestants, but would say, if those things were made certain, that then the field of theology would widen about him, and have indistinct traces grow into plain paths, and have also certain dark quarters in it illumined with unexpected light. And if Spiritualism can illustrate the manner in which Saul prophesied from an evil spirit, it aids thereby, some little at least, in making intelligible the manner in which "the Spirit of God came upon him; and he prophesied." By Spiritualism, too, for Christian use, is affirmed emphatically and amended as to translation, that text which latterly has been understood distinctly by very few divines. "Now the Spirit speaketh expressly, that in the latter times some shall depart from

N

the faith, giving heed to wandering spirits, and the instructions of demons."

And if Nature for a theologian be suggestive of many contrarieties, so also is that region in the spiritual world which is nearest to the natural, and whence mostly spiritual approaches are made to men. And just as the Christian has a faith, — which through all her regions Nature can only illustrate humbly, and never fully corroborate, — so also the faith of a Christian is what can be curiously indeed, but yet only partially, supported by evidences from the spiritual world, such as can be given through tables, or even by the hands and tongues of men, as mediums.

The reach upwards of the human soul, the yearning affinity of its faith, surmounts the region of nature, and goes up beyond the level of the world of spirits, and aspires after what alone is its proper object, — the Spirit of God Most High.

There are men of intellect at this day, who would readily believe in Moses, if merely they could be satisfied as to the magicians of Egypt, who yielded to him. There have been persons, darkened in their minds by materialism, who, with seeing merely what they thought was an apparition, have had their eyes so thoroughly and effectually opened, as that the spiritual world, and all their relations to it, were credible at once and intelligible. And there have been travellers who have returned from the East, stronger in their faith as Christians, for knowing of the preternatural things, which in some places, the natives sometimes assemble for, at their temples. And there have been persons who have been benefited by the counterpart of what was anciently accounted as dangerous and unworthy, — "the familiar spirit." These and many other such things may, under Heaven, be good, not so much because of what they are in themselves, as because of the lowliness of the persons for whom they can be lessons. Many a man has thought that the heavens were opening above him, because of the spiritual phenomena which he had experienced. Whereas mainly the things were wonderful only to his spiritual ignorance, only to his never having known of matters with which, in one age or another, and in one place or another, the human race have always been familiar. Height above height! There are many steps from an emmet to "a familiar spirit"; but more than they countlessly are the steps between the level of "familiar spirits" and the first even of those spiritual heights, down from which comes "every good gift and every perfect gift."

What are called the Spiritualistic phenomena are never all of them manifested through one medium. Sometimes a person is a channel for one marvel, and sometimes for two, three, four, and five varieties of the marvellous. But of all these marvels, there is scarcely one but reaches out into history in all directions. And there has scarcely ever been an age, but, in one place or another, was familiar with two, three, or more of the prodigies of the present day. Of marvels united to-day in the same medium, some have been evidences on which persons have been canonized as saints in the Church; and others have been proofs on which poor wretches have been executed as witches; and one at least, in the same age, has served as conclusive testimony in Italy as to holiness, and in England as to deviltry. It is so as a fact, and perhaps also, under Providence, it is vouchsafed as a privilege, that by the commonness of these spiritual phenomena, it is as though the past returned upon the present, and offered itself again for study, and the chance of a better understanding.

Sometimes the phenomena of Spiritualism remind one of agencies active in the Scriptures, and sometimes of narratives in the ancient classics; sometimes of Plotinus, the scholarly heathen of fifteen hundred years ago, and sometimes of St. Augustine, the great father and doctor of the Church, and continually also of the lives of saints, and the charges against wizards, and of the records of the Catholic Church. And indeed there is no general reader, with his eyes more than half open, who is acquainted with Spiritualism, but recognizes the existence of the common phenomena of Spiritualism, from north to south, the world round, among all primitive nations and tribes, even though described as ignorantly as things commonly are by mere travellers. The angekok of the Esquimaux is exactly some good American medium. And at the other end of the world, in New Zealand, are phenomena which correspond spiritually with those among the Esquimaux. And Madagascar offers for examination the same state of things spiritually, which obtains among the Maoris, and among their Northern opposites. Through spiritual mediums to-day there are concentrated, within an area of two hundred miles round Boston, phenomena which are akin to the ancient oracles, and to the marvels of Mohammedanism, as attested by Oriental writers and by European travellers, and to the miracles of the Catholic Church, during the last — during indeed all the years since the Catholic Church has been specially Roman Catholic.

The Spiritualism of to-day is nothing new, and might even by the Scriptures, almost, be called as old as Adam. What there is new in it is simply the easiness with which preternatural phenomena are to be got at. But may not this be in accordance with that grand overruling law, by which one change, and another, and another are like successive mile-marks along the earth, while yet also under the arch of the heavens? Under God, the material universe is allowed to disclose its laws astronomically, electrically, chemically, optically, magnetically, dynamically. And so might it not then seem to be by analogy, if concurrently, also the spiritual world should appear to be opening before mortals? As a mortal within a hundred years, how much man has been enlightened as to the earth, which he lives in, and also as to the wide kindred of worlds which sparkle in the sky at night! And proportionately, under Providence, it might seem as though openings and disclosures might be expected as to the position of man as an immortal soul, among the influences, forces, and inhabitants of the spiritual universe.

As has been said already, the Spiritualistic phenomena of to-day are simply easier of approach, and more common perhaps than they have ever been before. And that they are not new, whole volumes of evidence might be adduced to show. In the "Life of a Chinese Traveller in India," the autobiographer exalts China, although Brahma had not been born in it, because there "they know how to make demons and spirits appear." Just about two thousand years ago there is said to have been in the upper classes in China a great panic about death, and for which the writings of Confucius were no comfort. And upon this ensued a great resort to the schools of Tao-tse: the Tao-ists, at this time, having become great theurgists, and even professing to give prescriptions for disease from the prince of demons, in his own handwriting. At this present time a spiritual medium is called in China, "a celestial doctor."

And now let us read evidence from as different a quarter from China as can well be found. In his "Treatise on the Soul," Tertullian gives what probably was one of his Montanist experiences. Nobody could define better than he the difference between body and soul, so that when he speaks of the soul as being corporeal, he is to be understood as meaning that the soul is "a spiritual body." "To the soul also we attribute corporeal outlines, not only from our judgment being persuaded of its corporeal character, but also as decided for us, by grace, through revelation. For because we recognize the gifts of the Spirit, we have been favored with obtaining a prophecy, after the manner of St. John. At this very day there is with us a sister endowed with the gift of revelations, which she receives in spiritual ecstasy, during the services of Sunday. She converses with angels, and sometimes even with the Lord, and both sees and hears holy things. She discerns the heart of some persons, and she prescribes medicines to those who wish. But now according as the Scriptures are read, or Psalms are sung, or addresses are delivered, or prayers are offered, are supplied the subjects of her visions. On one occasion we discussed something or other about the Soul, when as it happened this sister was in the Spirit. The people being dismissed at the conclusion of the services, in accordance with her custom of telling me whatever she sees, — for indeed these things are all most carefully, reported, so as that they may be, tested, — says she, "There is shown to me a human soul. And truly the spirit was seen, but not empty, not destitute of all qualities, but in such a manner as that it would even allow itself to be held. And it was tender, lucid, and of an aerial color. And in all respects it was of the human form." Tertullian then adds that if this corporeality of the soul be not credible from its reasonableness, yet that it ought to be so from this vision, which was not without God as a witness, and not without some concurrence from that apostle, who is the appropriate surety as to future gifts in the Church.

Round Tao-tse and Tertullian, in regard to the supernatural, in their respective eras, might easily be assembled a crowd of witnesses, Socrates and Plato, Plutarch and perhaps more than half the people of whom he was the biographer, Pliny, and it may be almost all the classical authors, nearly every father of the Church, and nearly every historian of the Catholic Church, during the Middle Ages. And if these magnates of intellect could be assembled together, they would be found agreed in a state of mind, to which at once would be credible such works as Baxter's "Certainty of the World of Spirits," and Aubrey's Miscellanies, and Turner's Providences, compiled though these volumes largely are from incidents, such as transpire at present merely to be despised, or at best to be whispered among friends only in moments of confidence. And now of the state of mind of all these great thinkers, and as to the preternatural occurrences which they wrote about, and as to the modern marvels, which they would have been ready to credit, Spiritualism furnishes the explanation, being, as it is, the key which fits an intricate lock, and yielding as it does to intelligent inquirers knowledge as to the laws involved in portents and prodigies.

And now possibly somebody will exclaim, "Then the writer thinks Spiritualism is divine." But now he does not think so, any more than he would think that the dry old bone would be divine, from out of which, as belonging to any creature whatever, it is said that an eminent naturalist could evolve the outline and habits of the animal, when it was alive, and therefore also the general character of the climate and country in which it lived. Learning, to-day, reaches over a wider field than some people would suppose; and even the methods of science are applicable in ways which some persons have never thought of. Earthquakes, the plague, the black death! What is there to be named, as mischief, like what folly, like what even fool-hardiness has been in theology? In manners, there is nobody so insolent as a person of weak pretensions; and in theology there is nobody so bigoted as the clergyman who is too weak inwardly to digest the creed, which outwardly he has had to mark and learn.

Many Christians are provoked by the phenomena of Spiritualism, in just the same way as they have been annoyed sometimes by the marvels which have been reported as attendant on religious revivals. A spiritual novelty troubles them, unsettles them in their minds, and makes them feel as though nothing were certain. And this is because they do not half know themselves. For, man as a spiritual being, whether looking towards heaven or towards hell, or towards some opening between the two, with earnest longing, is thereby in affinity with the powers of a spiritual world, and capable of being quickened by them, as to faculties in him which ordinarily are latent. But truly, if the universe be infinite, it must have myriads of qualities; and if God be the head thereof, and we " heirs of God, and joint heirs with Christ," we must have senses, susceptibilities in us, many more than five. And it would seem as though such a multifarious nature might, now and then, by accident or the favor of Heaven, express itself or be receptive in ways, which are outside of the utilities of ordinary life: just as some common flower with five petals might show ten with cultivation.

If tables, by the presence of a medium, should simply beat time to sacred music, millions of people would believe that the heavens did thereby vouchsafe to show their sympathy with men. But as that tipping of the table is not for sacred music only, but for anything else almost, just as man talks with man, it would seem as though something through it might be inferred, more important still, as information, than even the sympathy of the heavens. For of heavenly sympathy with him, there is no poor wretch but ought to be sure, who has ever been inside of a church. But if, through a table or anything else, there be signified from outside of this visible world, a common understanding with man, and as though of all kinds of persons, good and bad, wise and silly, then is man informed, not so much as to the heavens, about the favor of which he ought already to have been sure, but as to there being spirits and regions, intermediate between earth and heaven. And with knowledge like this, and with even a suspicion of it, there are texts of Scripture, which deepen in meaning, as the eye regards them.

The susceptibility of man as to the spiritual world, — this is what Spiritualism would teach. At a religious revival, the strange things, which sometimes accompany conversion, are akin to the manner in which the prophets were affected; and that this is so is a truth, made sure and evident to a Christian, by the psychical laws, which are involved in the phenomena of Spiritualism. It is an easy thing for a man to say that, as a Christian, he cares only about the temper of the New Testament, and to keep himself in it. But surely the Scriptures do not justify an expositor in that position. Signs and wonders, or rather the possibility and the way of them, are essential to the philosophy of revelation. Miracles may be no more, but at least they are a proclamation of the channel, and proofs as to an openness, by which revelation may be made. They may sometimes in the past have been false cries; and just as a boy might alarm a neighborhood, so miracles, may have startled people in the past, and may again in the future, though starting, as the Scriptures have forewarned, from where there is nothing good to follow, and sounding like " O earth, earth, earth, hear," when really there is no word of the Lord to ensue. There is a channel, by which human beings are open to the spiritual world, and to effects from it. To deny the worth of what comes through it may be sometimes right, and be sometimes, according to the Scriptures, even an imperative duty; but to doubt the reality of the channel itself may be a grievous mistake and be indeed what may vitiate a whole system of theology.

But why should these spiritualistic phenomena be so much more abundant and familiar in this age than apparently at any former period? Why are there so many more mediums to-day than were ever known before? It may be because of an occult something in the air; or it may be because of something, by which the bodies or the souls of this generation are affected unconsciously, and perhaps only for a time, and in a manner which may be disease, or even perhaps improvement. After having agonized in spirit, for some years, George Fox suddenly found himself living in light, and also preternaturally acquainted with the names and properties of all vegetables and minerals. Also he found that he had become a mouthpiece for the Spirit, and a man with attendance on whom people were convulsed in their bodies and quickened in their souls, and often also made into such channels of the Spirit as he himself was. And in the early days of the Shakers and the Irvingites there were many things which were curiously like the marvels which attended on George Fox. And indeed in history are many instances of movements which began from the spiritual world, and which yet were also characterized by the wisdom or ignorance or other peculiarities of the mortals through whom first the impulses were given.

If certain psychical channels were a little enlarged with men generally, and yet not more than they have often been, men to-day would find themselves, as it were, staggering to and fro, under the bewildering intensity of influences, against the coming of which mere schooling in the order of nature would prove to have been no preparation whatever. And judging by the signs of the times, the guides of public opinion for keeping it both sober and enlightened will need to understand well the pneumatology of the Old Testament, and the nature and reasons of the Jewish theocracy, and also the psychology involved in the New Testament, and the nature of the liberty, and thereby also of the responsibility, "wherewith Christ hath made us free."

It is but walking in a vain show, when a man is thoughtless as to the spiritual world, to which already he belongs, and careless as to the channels by which he is himself approachable from it, and heedless as to its atmosphere, which yet he may sometimes be inhaling as breath, without knowing of it.

According to the phenomena of Spiritualism, the constitution of human nature is manifestly still the same, as what the lawgiving of Moses presupposed, and as what the revelation of Jesus Christ was given to meet; and still the same as it was at Athens, Rome, and Antioch, when the gospel began its struggle with idolatry. And it is only with ascertaining the place where the first hearers of the gospel stood mentally, that one can catch with full force the words which were addressed to them. And anything to-day which might, more or less, enable a student to read the

Epistles of Paul, in that state of mind about the universe, which Paul addressed, would be or should be a great blessing. And the Christian expositor, who is regardless of the philosophy which attaches to the case of that "certain damsel who had a spirit of Pytho," and who was exorcised by St. Paul, would seem to be a little out of the light in which the Epistles of Paul ought to be read.

But now a man may live a healthy life and a good life, while ignorant of geography, and of his relative position among a thousand million fellow-creatures on this earth, and while utterly ignorant even of the chemistry of his own bodily economy. And whatever may be our locality in the spiritual universe, and whether we suspect it or not; and whatever may be the channels by which spiritually our lives are sustained; and whatever the mysteries of our spiritual constitution; and whatever also may be the gifts of the Spirit of which we may fail, from causes connected with our individual personalities, or with the era which we belong to, yet there is certain for us, under Christ, a more excellent way than any, which can be accidentally or blindly missed. "For now we see through a glass, darkly; but then face to face: now I know in part; but then shall I know even as also I am known. And now abideth faith, hope, charity, these three; but the greatest of these is charity."

But that charity — what is it? It is not simply giving goods to feed the poor, nor is it even a man's willingness to let himself be burned alive. For it is what is more than that, being, as it is, what is of a man's inmost nature. Because it is that sympathy which rejoices with them that do rejoice, and which weeps with them that weep, which believes all things and hopes all things; and which therefore is that attractiveness in a man's spirit, which silently and imperceptibly procures for him more of the spiritual use of the universe than possibly his intellect could ever search out.

Really to a true Christian, and still more to a Christian as well instructed for his day as Moses was, when he "was learned in all the wisdom of the Egyptians," the phenomena of Spiritualism may be interesting, but they ought not to be amazing. And it is just as far as a man denies their possibility, that he may measure his distance from the pneumatology of the Scriptures; or, more precisely speaking, from that point where the apostles would have had him sit down as a heathen learner, and sit long as a Christian hearer, before they would have had him stand up as a teacher. There are many persons who by birth and happy education are such, that the actualities of Spiritualism have nothing to show them except what they may well believe, on a mere hint almost. But then of these born priests of the church there is never one — blessed man — that "sitteth in the seat of the scornful." Alas! in unsettled, discordant times, like the present, how large a part of our best learning is simply getting to unlearn! And in regard to bad habits to be broken, when life becomes earnest, how much caution there has got to be about that seat of the scorner! So often the fountain-head of wisdom in a man is choked by notions originating with people wise in their own conceit, or perhaps with blameless men helplessly bewildered in intricacies of thought! But when wisdom is not to be got from the outside world, there is still a way through which it is to be gained by simplicity and faith. "I said, Days should speak,"—but then so often they do not! "I said, Days should speak, and multitude of years should teach wisdom. But there is a spirit in man, and the inspiration of the Almighty giveth them understanding."

A MIRACLE DEFINED.

WHAT is a miracle? It is a fearful question to start in a theological library. For at once that library becomes a Babel of angry disputants, scarcely one of whom can understand another or would even wish to. A miracle has been defined in one way, and another way, and in so many ways, that almost, as a word, it has become meaningless. It is plain, that commonly Protestants in defining a miracle, have been actuated by anti-Catholic prejudice, and not simply by that spirit of truth, which would guide into all truth. And this remark is true even of some Protestants, who, for purity of character, might very properly, as Catholics even, have been sainted. And indeed, always, more or less of allowance will have to be made for a writer, as long as he is connected with books, and breathes vital air, and is capable of being provoked by his fellow-creatures.

As to their reality, miracles may be tested by their usefulness as to the gospel: miracles are credible, as good evidence, if accompanied by inspiration: miracles not directly connected with doctrine are not worth thinking of: miracles are of use in founding a faith, but not in preserving it, and therefore can never have happened since the earliest days of Christianity: miracles were acts, by which the laws of nature were suspended, and which acts are made certain through history, because of considerations which are acquiesced in by learned and honorable men.

But now all these definitions of the miraculous were made with a view to the claims, controversially, of the Catholic Church. Catholicism, throughout the wide regions which it covers, appropriates every marvel to itself, and knows how to use itself skilfully. An ecstatic, the report of an apparition, a wonderful dream, healing in the manner which is now called mesmeric, — all such marvels as these the Catholic Church can argue from, in one way or another. "See the marvels which are among us every day, somewhere or other. See how these things are a continuation of the miraculous powers, which witness our special descent from the apostles. Or else, see how they happen in attestation of our doctrines as to the spiritual world."

To all this, practically, Protestants have said: "We cannot look, and we will not look. We should be silly to look at what is impossible. But we will define against you." And so a late English Dean, while attempting to define a miracle, was evidently conscious of his scarlet hood, and of the front which it was desirable to show against the Papists, — mild, firm, and justly dogmatic. And in his definition of the miraculous, the Protestant minister of Paris evidently had in view things among Catholics, the reality of which as facts he was not willing to challenge, but the cogency of which as marvels it was his object to forestall. Miracles are to be tested by their necessity to the gospel, — but this leaves it uncertain what the gospel may be, and what necessity may be; and as coming from Bishop Warburton, it leaves it uncertain also whether those divines of his age might not by him have been accounted right, who argued that miracles ceased in the Church, with the political establishment of Christianity by Constantine; and in whose minds, therefore, Christianity was a gospel, which could spare "the manifestation of the Spirit" as soon as it became strong in armies, old temples, and money. And there is the Scotch bishop, Douglass, who in his time and place defined a miracle as being credible, if accompanied by inspiration. That definition may have seemed good to some people at a particular time: but to-day it appears as though it would say that a miracle by itself is impossible, but that a miracle conjoined with a mystery is fairly credible.

At one time a miracle was defined as against the doctrinal claims of the Catholics, and at another time as against the Catholics and Gibbon, and with an eye also to Hume. And to-day the acute Protestant theologian, who fancies that the Church is a fortress of which he is a defender, would wish to define a miracle so as to stop off Catholics, Spiritualists, and anti-supernaturalists.

And now for intelligent, discriminating, earnest persons, what is the outcome of all the controversies of the last hundred years, as to miracles? It is simply, at the best, the hope that none of the parties concerned may have known what they were talking about; as so few out of the number of mutually contradictory opponents can possibly have been right, even if any were. And thus in these latter times, on the subject of miracles, it would seem as though something had been happening like what Paul was thinking of, when he wrote of how "the world by wisdom knew not God," or like the nullifying effect of that inappropriate learning with which Jesus reproached the Jews, — "Thus have ye made the commandment of God of none effect by your tradition."

Thoroughly persuaded as to the supernatural, and speaking to people who no more doubted about it than he himself did, Luther, in his fearless, unguarded way, once spoke of miracles as playthings, which the Father Almighty in heaven let fall among his children on earth; and Jerome Huss also expressed himself as to miracles in the same way. And they both of them did well enough, thinking, no doubt, while they were speaking, of the priesthood of their time; which commonly was eager to magnify every little marvel of the day or neighborhood, for purposes more exactly ecclesiastical than religious.

In the common version of the Scriptures, the word "miracle" occurs in all the Old Testament but five times; and in the Gospel of Matthew, not once; in that of Luke, but once only; and in the Gospel of Mark, but twice. And of those instances in Mark, one use of the word "miracle" is in a passage, where nothing like the word was written by St. Mark, in Greek; and the other is in a text, where more properly it might be translated as meaning "power" or "enabling faculty." But in the Gospel of John, the word "miracle" occurs eleven times. How then is this? It is because the word which is commonly translated "miracle" means really "a sign." In the three first

Gospels, it is always so translated, except on three occasions; in two of which the original Greek is not concerned, and in the third of which, it is the same word which otherwise is always translated as meaning "a sign." But now, why is there this difference in the rendering of a common and important word from the Greek into English? It is, no doubt, because the Commissioners for translating the Scriptures, under the authority of King James the First, of England, at their separate pieces of work, translated the same Greek term, some of them by one word, and others of them by another.

What a relief it seems to be to learn this! For, about that word "miracle," there has gathered such a darkening of "counsel by words without knowledge"! To theological students the word is like a football, kicked and indented on the field of controversy, amidst the shouts and passions of opposing parties, age after age, till for any exact use it has been kicked out of all shape.

Sometimes in the New Testament "signs and wonders" are mentioned, but this phrase means simply "wonderful signs." Sometimes things of a miraculous character are called in the Greek, and are translated into English, as merely "works." But the original Greek word, whether any dictionary knows it or not, means a peculiar kind of works, with a mighty spirit in them; as is evident by the use of the word among the Neo-Platonists.

About things called miracles, then, the general meaning of the phraseology employed is that of significance. Miracles are signs; or rather "signs" really and exactly are those things, which are commonly called miracles. Indeed, the word "miracle" has been so miserably abused by controversialists, that it would be well if it could be disused for fifty years, and some synonyme be employed in its stead. But as that thing cannot be, then always let it be remembered that in the Scriptures by "miracles" are meant "signs," or manifestations of power originating outside of the sphere of nature.

Of all the passages in the Bible, which implicate the subject of miracles, it is of course impossible, here, to enter into an examination. But there are certain distinct, grand, overruling enunciations as to miracles, to which all other texts must be regarded as subservient, for reasons as to incidental utterance or local connection. And perhaps there is no honest theologian but would acknowledge in a moment, that there are no texts in the Scriptures but actually are congruent with these great direct statements. According to the Gospel of John, Jesus said: "Believe me, that I am in the Father, and the Father in me; or else believe me for the very works' sake. Verily, verily, I say unto you, he that believeth on me, the works that I do shall he do also; and greater works than these shall he do: because I go unto my Father." In this passage are foretold the powers with which the disciples might find themselves invested. And in the following passage from the Gospel of Matthew, it is foretold that miracles may not only be signs of the coming of the kingdom of heaven, but may also herald a movement from the side of the Prince of Darkness. "For there shall arise false Christs, and false prophets, and shall show great signs and wonders; insomuch that, if it were possible, they shall deceive the very elect. Behold I have told you before." Also St. Paul foreshowed to the Thessalonians the working of a mystery of iniquity, through which he would be revealed, "whose coming is after the working of Satan, with all power and signs and lying wonders." Through the Apocalypse, St. John foresaw the struggle between the gospel and hell, typified in various ways. "And every creature which is in heaven, and on the earth, and under the earth, and such as are in the sea, and all that are in them, heard I saying, Blessing, and honor, and glory, and power, be unto him that sitteth upon the throne, and unto the Lamb for ever and ever. And the four beasts said Amen. And the four and twenty elders fell down and worshipped him that liveth for ever and ever." But John saw also something else, as he stood upon the sand of the sea, and beheld a beast come up out of the earth. "And he doeth great wonders, so that he maketh fire come down from heaven on the earth, in the sight of men, and deceiveth them that dwell on the earth by the means of those miracles which he had power to do, in the sight of the beast." The early Christians then expected miracles from more quarters than one, and from elsewhere than heaven; and they were prepared for the coming of false prophets as well as true.

In the Gospel of Mark it is promised, "These signs shall follow them that believe; in my name shall they cast out devils; they shall speak with new tongues; they shall take up serpents; and if they drink any deadly thing, it shall not hurt them: they shall lay hands on the sick, and they shall recover." Signs were to follow them that believed; and also were to be looked for from persons who were worse than unbelievers. For still as written in the Gospel of Mark, and still also as the words of Jesus himself, it was foretold that "false Christs and false prophets shall rise, and shall show signs and wonders, to seduce, if it were possible, even the elect."

That through miracles there is a manifestation of the Spirit St. Paul wrote to the Corinthians. And to the Thessalonians he wrote, that power and signs would some time be, from the working of Satan.

A miracle is a seal beyond a counterfeit, which God sets to his word when he speaks. This is a statement which has been agreed to by theologians of all degrees, by bishops and priests and ministers and laymen, but never by either fact or the Scriptures. The voice of the Scriptures, indeed, on the subject enunciates distinctly its meaning through the texts just cited, which are direct, emphatic, and overruling.

The field of the miraculous is wider and more mysterious, than might seem to be supposed by some people, and even by many divines. According to the Scriptures, miracles, and of more kinds than one, apparently, a man might work, and yet be no Christian. And, as it would seem, a man might even work miracles in the name of Christ, and possibly by even the virtue of that name, and yet truly himself not be a Christian. "Many will say to me in that day, Lord, Lord, have we not prophesied in thy name? and in thy name have cast out devils? and in thy name done many wonderful works? And then will I profess unto them, I never knew you: depart from me, ye that work iniquity." That is a warning for persons about themselves, as channels for the miraculous. And now let a caution be considered, as to the origin and laws of marvellous manifestations. Because there were going about many false prophets, that is, many persons who were liable to be inspired by bad spirits, St. John, in his first Epistle, gives what would be a test, for at least the people individually to whom he wrote. "Beloved, believe not every spirit, but try the spirits whether they are of God; because many false prophets are gone out into the world. Hereby know ye the Spirit of God: every spirit that confesseth that Jesus Christ is come in the flesh is of God; and every spirit that confesseth not that Jesus Christ is come in the flesh is not of God."

And now let it be understood that, no doubt, these false prophets appeared among the Christians as they assembled themselves together, and, so to say, in Church. And as to the opening which was possible for them, let the fourteenth chapter be considered in the first Epistle to the Corinthians. In that chapter is indicated remarkably the attitude which Christianity would have its disciples assume towards spirits who might wish to inspire any of them, and, therefore, also towards the prophets themselves, as to what they might have to say on the prompting or inspiration of those spirits. "The spirits of the prophets are subject to the prophets." The prophets are to exercise their own discretion, as to time at least, towards the spirits, who would wish to make them speak. And with this monition of St. Paul agrees curiously and wonderfully that advice by St. John: "Beloved, believe not every spirit, but try the spirits whether they are of God."

By the foregoing texts, lines are marked on a field of thought, in which possibly some persons may feel as though they could only move blindly. And yet some time, perhaps, it may be to them like a familiar region; after they have been, as St. Paul would say, renewed in the spirit of their minds by, it may be, a new philosophy which they may have taken to, or by internal processes in the spirit which they may have experienced; and as to which, perhaps, there is nothing to be suggested more distinctly than what is to be read in the book of Job: "For God speaketh once, yea twice, yet man perceiveth it not. In a dream, in a vision of the night, when deep sleep falleth upon men, in slumberings upon the bed; then he openeth the ears of men, and sealeth their instruction."

And truly the world intellectual and spiritual must be alive with laws, powers, and agencies, in a thousand ways, as to which we mortals can know nothing whatever, but of which for importance and nearness we may conjecture something, from the manner in which the outer material world has revealed itself to eyes, fitted with telescope and microscope. In the fourteenth chapter of the Epistle to the Corinthians there is a glimpse of what the souls of men are capable of manifesting as to prophecy, and as to the discovery of the secrets of the heart, and as to speech in unknown tongues of men and, it may be, of angels. But it was the doctrine of Paul, that than all such marvels as these, charity is far better evidence as to the operation of the Spirit. By these remarks there is implied another spiritual world, than what some theologians suppose; but it is not, therefore, the less certain or Scriptural.

And now again, what is a miracle? Of all the words then in the Scriptures, so translated, and guided also by the connections in which the words are used, the general sense of "miracle" would seem to be "a sign." And a sign would seem to be of various degrees and even varieties of significance, and even perhaps to be more or less contingent on human or earthly conditions. That wonderful scene of the Transfiguration was not for all Jerusalem, nor even for all the twelve apostles. But it is written: "Jesus taketh Peter, James, and John his brother, and bringeth them up into a high mountain apart, and was transfigured before them; and his face did shine as the sun, and his raiment was white as the light, and behold, there appeared unto them Moses and Elias talking with him." But in his own country, where people asked in reference to his miraculous power, as to how it was, and why it could be, and whether he was not the carpenter? "Jesus said unto them, A prophet is not without honor, but in his own country, and among his own kin, and in his own house. And he could there do no mighty work, save that he laid his hands upon a few sick folk, and healed them. And he marvelled because of their unbelief."

Of there having been a varying estimate as to miracles, among the multitude at least, this text would seem to show, "And many of the people believed on him and said, When Christ cometh, will he do more miracles than these which this man hath done?" And that ultimately miracles, as to significance, have to be understood by doctrine, that is, through the human reason quickened and enlightened by the Holy Spirit, is evident even from the position which Jesus Christ assumed in argument. "Then was brought unto him one possessed with a devil, blind and dumb; and he healed him, insomuch that the blind and dumb both spake and saw. And all the people were amazed, and said, Is not this the son of David? But when the Pharisees heard it, they said, This fellow doth not cast out devils, but by Beelzebub, the prince of the devils. And Jesus knew their thoughts, and said unto them, Every kingdom divided against itself is brought to desolation; and every city or house divided against itself shall not stand: and if Satan cast out Satan, he is divided against himself: how shall then his kingdom stand?"

And so, there is recorded another argument by Jesus, made apparently with reference to what he was himself, and as to what the world about him was, with his being in it, and its being thereby alive with miraculous possibilities: "Ye hypocrites, ye can discern the face of the sky and of the earth; but how is it that ye do not discern this time? Yea, and why even of yourselves judge ye not what is right?" And for the estimate of miracles as connected with the apostles, it would seem as though these words might be fully applicable, as implying that the miracles of the apostles were like those of Jesus as to significance: "The disciple is not above his master, nor the servant above his lord. It is enough for the disciple that he be as his master, and the servant as his lord. If they have called the master of the house Beelzebub, how much more shall they call them of his household?"

As to the significance by authority, which miracles claim in the New Testament, perhaps the preceding texts are sufficient. And as to the authority of miracles in the Old Testament, perhaps Maimonides, the Rabbi, may be a good teacher; and what he says agrees altogether with the Gospels, and with the doctrine of St. Paul. "We do not believe every one who works a sign or a wonder to be a prophet, but only the man whom we have known from the beginning to be fit for prophecy, — to have raised himself, by his wisdom and his works, above all the men of his age, and to have walked in holiness and separation. Afterwards, if he come and do a sign or a wonder, and say that God hath sent him, the command is to hear him, as it is said, 'Unto him shall ye hearken.'"

The general sense, then, of the word "miracle" in the Bible is "a sign"; as in Exodus, where it is said to Moses by the Lord, "And it shall come to pass, if they will not believe thee, neither hearken to the voice of the first sign, that they will believe the voice of the latter sign"; and as in the account of the expulsion of the traders from the court of the temple, when "answered the Jews and said unto him, What sign showest thou unto us, seeing thou doest these things?" and as on other occasion, when "certain of the scribes and of the Pharisees answered, saying, Master, we would see a sign from thee."

The word "sign" is a general word, though more precise than the word "miracle." For a sign of miraculous origin means at least something of an unearthly origin, intended for the notice of earthly people. There is, however, no word in the Bible which distinguishes as to the marvellous, between what might herald an angel, or such a startle as might be given by Satan, or by any one of those spirits or agencies, for which in the aggregate, perhaps, the word "Satan" is a synonyme in the Scriptures. In the Apocalypse were foreseen "the spirits of demons working miracles." But the word which is here translated as "miracle" is the same word "sign" which was used by Jesus when he said, "The powers of the heavens shall be shaken; and then shall appear the sign of the Son of man in heaven." And according to the prediction of Jesus, "signs" were to attend upon those who believed in him, and also "signs" were to be shown by false Christs and false prophets.

And now let us notice the tone, simply, in which miracles or signs are spoken of, and we shall feel perhaps that miracles, or signs and wonders, are signs simply, and not absolute proofs. In the Gospel of Matthew it is written, "Then certain of the scribes and of the Pharisees answered, saying, Master, we would see a sign from thee. But he answered, and said unto them, An evil and adulterous generation seeketh after a sign; and there shall no sign be given to it, but the sign of the prophet Jonas." And so by implication, at least, and actually by the philosophy of the Scriptures as to miracles, the argument of Jesus is, that miracles were not for them — Scribes and Pharisees — because of their souls having been averse to his preaching. "The men of Nineveh shall rise in judgment with this generation, and shall condemn it: because they repented at the preaching of Jonas; and behold a greater than Jonas is here."

In the minds of the Pharisees, the cure of the man born blind scarcely counterbalanced by its miraculousness the prejudice which was created by its having been wrought on the Sabbath. "They brought to the Pharisees him that aforetime was blind. And it was the Sabbath day when Jesus made the clay, and opened his eyes. Then again also the Pharisees asked him how he had received his sight. He said unto them, He put clay upon mine eyes; and I washed and do see. Therefore said some of the Pharisees, This man is not of God, because he keepeth not the Sabbath day. Others said, How can a man that is a sinner do such miracles? And there was a division among them." According to some theologians, every miracle is the direct act of the Most High God. And thus a miracle to-day should be like the sound of a trumpet, in advance of legions of angels and of heavenly hosts, and of power almighty. But it was not so that miracles were regarded at Jerusalem, by the chief people. After Lazarus had been raised from the dead, "Then many of the Jews which came to Mary, and had seen the things which Jesus did, believed on him. But some of them went their way to the Pharisees, and told them what things Jesus had done. Then gathered the chief priests and the Pharisees a council, and said, What do we? for this man doeth many miracles. If we let him thus alone, all men will believe on him; and the Romans shall come and take away both our place and nation."

To the apostles Jesus said, "Believe me that I am in the Father, and the Father in me; or else believe me for the very works' sake." This was as though his own sweet words should have been more persuasive than miracles. In his own country, "When the Sabbath day was come, he began to teach in the synagogue: and many hearing him were astonished, saying, From whence hath this man these things? and what wisdom is this which is given unto him, that even such mighty works are wrought by his hands?" The mighty works, however, even though thoroughly credited, were not supposed to be for significance, what should have stopped the rudeness of the further questioning, "Is not this the carpenter, the son of Mary, the brother of James and John, and of Juda, and of Simon? and are not his sisters here with us? And they were offended at him."

By contrast with the preceding occurs to the mind the account of the poor woman, who said, "If I may touch but his clothes I shall be whole." From her case there is a little more to be learned as to miracles. "She felt in her body that she was healed of that plague"; and she was cured as to her body through her soul, or rather through that state of her soul which was like a sensation of Christ, as "she touched his garment." After this, "the woman fearing and trembling, knowing what was done in her, came and fell down before him, and told him all the truth. And he said unto her, Daughter, thy faith hath made thee whole; go in peace, and be whole of thy plague." At Capernaum, when the heathen centurion told his tale; and "when Jesus heard it, he marvelled, and said to them that followed, Verily, I say unto you, I have not found so great faith, no, not in Israel." And then, as showing that the spiritual state of the "man under authority" was consenting to the miracle or concerned with it, "Jesus said unto the centurion, Go thy way; and as thou hast believed, so be it done unto thee. And his servant was healed in the selfsame hour."

Of the soul there is a state or an attitude, by which it is "right before God." It does not follow, however, even under Christ, that every spirit right before God should be a channel of miracles, whether few or many. For, all the conditions concerned with miracles are not known. As a right state of the body is favorable to right thinking, so there may be some nervous condition or magnetic peculiarity, which may favor the soul's expression of itself by miracles. And with the free manifestation of miracles, it would seem as though not only the spiritual state of individuals might be concerned, but also the state of the community of which they may be members.

Also, religiously all times are not the same. One age is a time of fervor and trust, wherein man can walk with God gladly and joyously, though clouds and darkness be about him. Another age is a season of intellectual curiosity, when men fancy that they can "by searching find out God" and that indeed they ought to learn about him before trusting to him. But really that picture of the Transfiguration by Raphael, at Rome, has never been seen through a microscope, and never will be, even though every bit of the canvas should be passed across the field of the best possible instrument. A believer can walk with God in spirit, but not the man who thinks that before starting he ought to find out God by analysis and logic, even though not unto perfection. And in many other ways, too, may men disqualify themselves spiritually for things which they would attempt. Often in the chambers of his soul a man will deliberately close the skylights and the higher windows, and try to see only by such light as is nearest to the basement; and he thinks, in so doing, that he is keeping close to nature. But he makes the same blunder as that which would search out the beauty and meaning of Raphael's great picture with a microscope. Dogs are excellent within the range of their faculties, — the mastiff, the setter, the Newfoundland; but as something to be judged upon, "Give not that which is holy unto the dogs."

And not only can a man not judge who is no judge; but under no outpouring, whether Pentecostal or any other, can a man receive who has no receptiveness. The Pharisees and Sadducees were not often the people, through whom there was any manifestation of the Spirit. In the time of Jesus it does not appear that ever a Pharisee was healed; or that there was a Pharisee among the seventy sent out by Christ, who found themselves endowed with miraculous power. And commonly the Pharisees would seem to have been spiteful about the miracles, even when they could not but acknowledge them, as being real. The seventy had returned with joy at the effect of their new powers in the places where they had been, saying, "Lord, even the devils are subject unto us through thy name." At this, and thereby also at the state of mind which had been thus found existing abroad, "Jesus rejoiced in spirit, and said, I thank thee, O Father, Lord of heaven and earth, that thou hast hid these things from the wise and prudent, and hast revealed them unto babes: even so, Father; for so it seemed good in thy sight."

It has been quoted already, but it is of that significance that it may well be cited again, that when Jesus was in his own country, "he could there do no mighty work," but only heal a few people, by laying his hands on them. There was then possible a state of feeling in a place, at a certain time, which could hinder the working of miracles even by Jesus Christ.

And as what may result from spiritual recognition between persons, and from trust and faith, the miracle at Lystra is an instance; at which city there was a poor sufferer, who happened to be within the reach of Paul's voice as he preached. "The same heard Paul speak: who steadfastly beholding him, and perceiving that he had faith to be healed, said with a loud voice, Stand upright on thy feet. And he leaped and walked." By this it would seem to be implied that for miracles in curing there was necessary, not only a power ready to heal, but also a state of expectancy, receptiveness, and faith on the side of the sufferers.

"Draw nigh to God, and he will draw nigh to you," says St. James in his Epistle; and if there be an age, by the spirit of which men generally are withdrawn from God, then necessarily the manifestations of the Spirit must become very few, and be what can be credited very faintly by most persons. And this must be, notwithstanding what concurrently may be the experiences of individual Christians, who perhaps may be peculiar as to constitution, or happy in some way, as to education, associates, or neighborhood.

From Jesus, after he had risen, and before he had ascended, the apostles received as an answer to a question, "It is not for you to know the times or the seasons, which the Father hath put in his own power." And that there is a varying distance, in some sense, between mortals and their God, is implied in the words of Peter, in his address at the temple, in Solomon's porch, when he said to the people who had come running together on account of a miracle, "Repent ye therefore and be converted, that your sins may be blotted out," against what is in the future, "when the times of refreshing shall come from the presence of the Lord."

And as showing the manner in which the human spirit may be in connection with powers outside of itself indeed, and which yet are not foreign to its nature, let the words of Jesus, spoken to his immediate disciples, be noticed; for though they were not fulfilled in the age when they were uttered, and are not likely to be at this present time, yet they hold good for all who are, or who ever shall be in him, "that is true, even in his son Jesus Christ." It is the philosophy of faith, which is stated in this merely occasional remark, "Verily I say unto you, if ye have faith as a grain of mustard-seed, ye shall say unto this mountain, Remove hence to yonder place; and it shall remove; and nothing shall be impossible unto you."

And now what is faith? It is the confidence of moral persuasion, — it is the sense of what must be, because of what ought to be: it is the state of a soul which is open towards God, and therefore receptive of the Holy Ghost; and which thereby also is capable of becoming prophetic, and of blossoming with Christian graces, like gifts, and of developing latent powers, in a superhuman way, for teaching and healing, and for spiritual perception, and communion. Faith is the instinct of a soul, as to its affinities; and about which, as to reliability, the blind life of a bee in the hive ought to be hint enough.

There is an instinct of faith in us, or a something, which for want of words, cannot perhaps be better defined, but which men are free to trust or not, because of the manner in which they are created to live, or are let live, or at least are free to feel.

"Faith as a grain of mustard-seed!" There is a whole volume of spiritual philosophy in these words, though only dimly discernible by the writer hereof, and perhaps by most other persons, at present. In a parable Jesus spoke of "a grain of mustard-seed, which, when it is sown in the earth, is less than all the seeds that be in the earth; but when it is sown, it groweth up and becometh greater than all herbs, and shooteth out great branches; so that the fowls of the air may lodge under the shadow of it." And just as in a mustard-seed there is the possibility of a tree, so in every man of faith there is what might remove mountains, not perhaps any day in any century, but in Pentecostal times. That our souls begin from God, and live by him, is Christian doctrine; and it was the belief of the best of the heathen, as St. Paul showed to the men of Athens, when he reminded them of the words of one of their poets, "For we are also his offspring." And if only by faith our souls were as natural as mustard-seeds, or as pliant to super-agency, they would have their various faculties supplied and filled from a fountain-head eternal of wisdom, power, and goodness, and have all such desires, as faithful souls can have, easily and abundantly satisfied.

And now again what is a miracle for us human beings, according to the Scriptures? But as preliminary to the answer, let it be remembered that our souls and all souls are living in God, as indeed, in some way, all things must be; and not merely such intelligences as Moses and Socrates were, but also bees busy in the hive, and devils even while they believe and tremble.

According to the Scriptures, then, miracles are "signs" of activity in a moulding and pervading world of spirit; and which were appealed to, by the Jews, as proofs sometimes of greater and sometimes of less significance, in connection with the persons through whom they were wrought. Also, concurrently with the foregoing statement, and as enlarging it, it is to be remembered, according to the Scriptures, through the world of spirit which is round us, that demons, like any other spirits, may possibly make "signs," and may try even to be taken for angels of light.

And thus, according to a Pindaric phrase, by many windings of thought, or as Swedenborg might say, by a spiral progress, we have arrived at a point, perhaps a little higher on the scale of information, but still with the same view, whence Ralph Cudworth looked out, as a student of the Intellectual System of the Universe, when he wrote, after citing Pagan as well as Christian miracles and prophecies, "All these phenomena of apparitions, witchcraft, possessions, and prophecies, do evince that spirits, angels, or demons, though invisible to us, are no fancies, but real and substantial inhabitants of the world; which favors not the atheistic hypothesis: but some of them, as the higher kinds of miracles and predictions, do also immediately enforce the acknowledgment of a Deity, a Being superior to nature, which therefore can check and control it, and which, comprehending the whole, foreknows the most remote, distant, and contingent event." Also, though it be the same thing in other words, it is yet worthy of being read again, "Though all miracles, promiscuously, do not immediately prove the existence of God, nor confirm a prophet, or whatsoever doctrine; yet do all of them evince that there is a rank of invisible, understanding beings, superior to men, which atheists commonly deny."

Those last words as to an atheist remind one of a fact, which by a late writer was stated very vividly, that in modern times there has nothing been debated or proposed in the realms of thought or imagination, as to theology, or metaphysics, or social organization, but was agitated in England during the times of the Commonwealth. And from that furnace-like condition, in which mind once was in England, no doubt there has resulted in its inhabitants that something, which is a part, at least, of what by foreigners is sometimes called sobriety, and sometimes slowness of thought.

Ralph Cudworth, Richard Baxter, John Owen, Henry More, John Smith and their compeers, may be supposed by some critics to be out of date for citation as authorities on philosophical or religious subjects, as having been persons innocent of a thought of Pantheism, and too simple and professional, ever to have known what hostile scepticism might have had to say for itself, in their time. But than this there is not a greater mistake to be made in literature by anybody. For the foregoing are all men of great names; and the age in which they lived was not a time for cheap reputations. And, indeed, for spiritual insight and learning, and for experience from a wide knowledge of men and collision with them, there are no twelve men, today, to be found in all England, or throughout the United States, who could be fairly compared as a jury on a theological question, with such men as were known to Henry More and Richard Baxter. And truly, at this time, the direct affinities of the best thinkers are with the scholars of two hundred years ago, rather than with those who wrote English under Queen Anne, or who loved to be Addisonian while George the Third was king. By searching upwards and around with the telescope, and downwards with the microscope, into the magnitudes and affinities which are latent in every atom, science confirms the doctrine of the Unity of God. But that doctrine had been a primary truth of revelation for thousands of years before those optical helps were invented. And, indeed, beyond its assent as to the doctrine of the Unity of the Godhead, and those illustrations which it furnishes of truths which are at least as old as the Old Testament, science has yielded nothing new whatever for the uses or the consideration of theology. With the discovery of the law of gravitation Newton did not find himself changed theologically; and to the end of his life he believed profoundly in a world extra-human and spiritual, and in prophecy, as an effect from it.

And now, after having striven to view this subject of miracles, as it exists in the Scriptures, by light from every quarter which is open towards him, the present writer would suggest the following propositions.

I. A miracle is a "sign" that men are vitally connected with a sphere, which is wider than what is commonly called "nature," and which transcends it.

II. A miracle is a "sign" as to individuals and sometimes as to communities, of an increase in sensibility as to influence from the spiritual world.

III. A miracle is a "sign" that in the persons through whom it is wrought, there is a state of openness towards the spiritual world, through which, more or less effectually, they may be receptive of spiritual suggestions, prophetic and doctrinal: which suggestions, however, like the miracle itself, may possibly be not from above.

IV. A miracle of magnitude and beneficence would seem to create a high presumption, and to be a "sign" as to the goodness, and therefore as to the reliability of the person through whom it is wrought.

V. A miracle or sign is a possibility of the present day, and from quarters both good and bad.

VI. As to the significance of miracles, or as to signs given or coming from the spiritual world, men ordinarily may judge of themselves, and always they may learn from the Holy Spirit; the monitions of which will never fail, while there are two or three disciples to gather together truly, in the name of Jesus Christ.

MIRACLES AS SIGNS.

BY anti-supernaturalists it is an argument against the probability of miracles ever having happened, that the force of them as to authority, and therefore also as to credibility, must depend on the mental state of the person witnessing them, or hearing of them. But this is no new discovery; for it is implied in the Scriptures continually. And St. Paul, in his First Epistle to the Corinthians, discriminates thus as to miracles which might even happen together in the church, "Tongues are for a sign, not to them that believe, but to them that believe not: but prophesying serveth not for them that believe not, but for them which believe." And in the first chapter of the same epistle, St. Paul would say that there are conditions as to preaching Christ, under which "signs" are not thought of, and wisdom of the Greek kind is not minded, "For after that in the wisdom of God, the world by wisdom knew not God, it pleased God by the foolishness of preaching to save them that believe. For the Jews require a sign, and the Greeks seek after wisdom: but we preach Christ crucified, unto the Jews a stumbling-block, and unto the Greeks foolishness; but unto them which are called, both Jews and Greeks, Christ the power of God, and the wisdom of God."

Miracles dependent for their meaning on the persons

attending to them, — of course they must be, and always have been. For, outside of what is mathematical, hardly anything can be uttered but varies as to force, with the various minds which receive it, and especially on such subjects as are moral and religious.

It has been said, as though by the complaisance of lofty intellects, and as though by concession to the ways of Providence, that a belief in miracles may have had its use in times of darkness, and so may have served a good end, though itself being utterly baseless. But a sentiment like that, instead of being welcomed, is eschewed by anything like "the truth as it is in Jesus," and by every honest atom in the universe.

It is true that a miracle may be more striking one day than another, and in one age than another, just as it might be with one person more than with another. But what of that? From even the same occurrence do all the spectators receive uniformly the same impression? What sermon ever was exactly the same thing, to even only two persons in a congregation? A miracle might be seen and acknowledged by twenty witnesses; and some of them would thank God for "a sign and wonder"; and some others would say that it was very curious, and worth thinking about: while still more, by their utilitarian remarks, would show themselves to be of the same mind with the people, whom Jesus once answered, when he said, "Verily, verily, I say unto you, ye seek me, not because ye saw the miracles, but because ye did eat of the loaves and were filled."

Never were miracles understood in the Catholic Church, as being of the same significance as in the

Evidences of Religion, by Joseph Priestley. And before Moses addressed Pharoah, it was anticipated that among the Egyptians one sign might be more cogent than another, and two signs be more persuasive than one. "And it shall come to pass, if they will not believe thee, neither hearken to the voice of the first sign, that they will believe the voice of the latter sign." Is a miracle, then, really the less probable as an occurrence, or is its significance the less certain because the minds of men, as to the "sign and wonder" may not be uniform, age after age?

It has been said that the day for miracles is past, and that whatever use there may have been in them is worn out. This, however, is the word of a writer who actually never knew what a miracle was, and who therefore could never have known properly about its significance and use. For really and truly, there never was a time when a miracle was as much itself, as it is today. There never has been a period when a miracle could have been as suggestive and as instructive as it might be at present. There never has been an age when a miracle could have meant as much as it does at this moment. And never, in all time past, could a miracle have been as much of "a sign and wonder" as it might be, and should be, at this present time. For, as is commonly and scientifically supposed, the Order of Nature is clearly and distinctly against anything like a miracle; and those powers of omnipotence and omniscience, by which the realm of nature is pervaded, are rightly regarded as guaranties against the possibility of a miracle by accident. And so, in these enlightened days, the humblest miracle, or work, or sign, on which formerly only a minor stress would have been laid, is arrayed in a portentousness of meaning, with which anciently it was never accredited, even by those who most heartily believed it. And thus, like a remark which has been already made, for such spiritual discernment, as most persons have at present, or are likely to have before they die, "the unclean spirit," so often mentioned in the Bible, would, as to the constitution of the spiritual universe, be as great a sign as they are capable of receiving. And yet from the Spirit of God an abundance of other "signs" are waiting on us all. But as to these invisible signs we experience nothing, and can scarcely even think or feel anything, because of our living, for some reason, in a state as to the miraculous, somewhat like that of those Jews to whom Jesus said, "Perceive ye not yet, neither understand? have ye your heart yet hardened? Having eyes, see ye not? and having ears, hear ye not?"

Certainly a miracle is not of the same meaning in every age: but it is not always because of its seeming to diminish in significance. King Saul believed that Ahimelech the priest had "inquired of God," at the request of David. At this day it seems, that whatever the answer might be, which even an enemy might get as an oracle from God, as though certainly, we all of us could only say, "The Lord's will be done!" But Saul did not feel so: but said, "Thou shalt surely die, Ahimelech, thou and all of thy father's house." This seems to be like insanity; but things have been enacted and done in Europe within the last century, from a state of mind not as intense indeed as that of Saul, but like it. And indeed, history may well make the most intelligent man fear for himself, as to what nonsense or wickedness he may some time find himself committed to, for what may have seemed to him to be good reasons drawn from theology. But in connection with Saul, let us read further. "And the king said to Doeg, Turn thou and fall upon the priests. And Doeg the Edomite turned, and he fell upon the priests, and slew on that day fourscore and five persons that did wear a linen ephod." Kill a man who could "inquire of the Lord," — kill a man who was like the mouthpiece of God! This would seem to be like anything but a belief in miracles. Yet actually, it was because he was believed to be a man of miracle, that Ahimelech the priest was killed.

"A man of God" had wrought great miracles at the altar in Bethel, and an old prophet wished to detain him, notwithstanding that he pleaded "the word of the Lord" to the contrary. "He said unto him, I am a prophet also as thou art; and an angel spake unto me by the word of the Lord, saying, Bring him back with thee into thine house, that he may eat bread and drink water. But he lied unto him." Certainly the force of a miracle varies with different persons, and from one age perhaps to another. But the anti-supernaturalists of this age would probably think much more of a miracle than would seem to have been felt by an ancient Israelite, who not only believed in the possibility of miracles, but who also was himself known as "an old prophet," and who indeed was himself again, just about to be made prophetic. In the book of the Acts of the Apostles, it is to be read, "And when Simon saw that through laying on of the apostles' hands, the Holy Ghost was given, he offered them money, saying, Give me also this power, that on whomsoever I lay hands, he may receive the Holy Ghost. But Peter said unto him, Thy money perish with thee, because thou hast thought that the gift of God may be purchased with money." But here some one may say, "By the manner in which miracles seem to have been regarded anciently, and sometimes perhaps by those even, who knew best about them, they may not really have been what I have thought they were." For which the answer is, "Perhaps not: but they are not therefore the less true, nor the less Scriptural, nor the less significant, nor yet the less reliable as being the spiritual mortar with which are cemented together those human experiences which constitute the Bible, and which make it be like the visible gateway and gate, which open into glory, and into the "house not made with hands, eternal in the heavens."

Miracles not as wonderful to-day as they were before the days of science began,—this is what has been sometimes said, and what has been still oftener felt. It is true, that we are not as the Egyptians were, nor yet as the Jews were, scientifically. But neither yet are we as they were, geographically, or historically; and yet vitally we are very like them. Be it so, that there is knowledge now about what are called the laws of nature; and that even some of the laws can be indicated, through the use of which some miracles may perhaps have been wrought. What then; does that abolish the meaning of a miracle, as a sign? Or does that properly end our human wonder, as to what a miracle may mean, or as to who may be the primary cause of it? It might as well be supposed that with learning the Greek language, as Plato wrote it, that his wisdom would be found to evaporate. The radicals and inflections of a language are not thought, but only a channel for the expression of thought. And for such a "miracle" as is a "sign," the laws of nature, when they are concerned, are but the channels of will, power, and intelligence, combined in an agency which is invisible, and not fleshly, mortal, nor human. When a message reaches a person by telegraph, electricity is not the whole explanation of it; for the significance of the message began actually with the person who from a distance caused the sign, and sent the communication. Science does but make a miracle to be more distinctly "a sign."

It is pleaded as an axiom by some theologians, "If we can prove the miracles, we have proved Christianity." What a sense of pertinency these theologians must have; and what a sense, too, of moral fitness! For almost they might as well say, "Learn well the multiplication-table, and you will certainly feel the genius of Raphael." Before any one can prove the truth of Christianity by the miracles of the Scriptures, he must be able to show the spiritual philosophy of miracles, and thereby be able to make people discern, for themselves, the possibility and probability of miracles having really happened. But this is a thing which is never thought of by the man, who thinks that he can create a belief in Christianity, by an historical argument as to miracles. "The Bible is the word of God, and the miracles in it are the seals of the Almighty; and I can show that always those miracles have been believed; and if we believe them, then we are Christians." A very simple argument this is, certainly; but somehow, the end of it, even when it is best managed, is acquiescence, simply, and not conviction, and of course, not fervent conviction. As indeed how should it be? For actually the argument, as it is usually conducted, presupposes a state of mind, unfortunately not unlike that of the Israelites under Moses. Says Lightfoot in his Horæ Hebraicæ et Talmudicæ, "They went under four or five miracles: as the appearing of the cloud of glory, the raining of manna, the flowing of the rock, or the waters at Horeb, the continual newness of their clothes, and the untiredness of their feet. Yet did they forget and were continually repining against him, that did all these wonders for them."

There is a curious narrative connected with the Jews while in the desert, which shows that miracles may be profoundly believed by some persons, and yet to no good purpose; because of their state of mind, being itself akin to idolatry, as being blind and sensual. For the sins of the people, there was amongst them a plague of fiery serpents. But afterwards, "The Lord said unto Moses, Make thee a fiery serpent, and set it upon a pole: and it shall come to pass that every one that is bitten, when he looketh upon it, shall live." This was a miracle, which was of a kind, by which there was likely to be a deep and permanent impression made. And so in the Second Book of Kings, at a date which would seem to be seven hundred years later than that miracle in the desert, it is to be read that King Hezekiah "removed the high places, and brake the images, and cut down the groves, and brake in pieces the brazen serpent that Moses had made; for unto those days the children of Israel did burn incense to it. And he called it Nehushtan," that is, a piece of brass. And at the present day, there are persons, high and low in intelligence, and some of whom would look grandly, if arrayed in their worldly circumstances, who inwardly are of that old Jewish company in the desert, and who, but for the spirit of the time, could almost more easily worship a "sign" rather than God, who reveals himself through it.

It has been said, rather arrogantly, that with the growth of intellect miracles will cease to interest men. What, then, with the growth of intellect, will men be curious about? Because oysters, intellectually, will not serve forever, nor monads, nor yet gorillas. And it would seem, indeed, as though miracles might serve men as subjects for inquiry, and as suggestions for speculation, even after the earth shall have yielded up every one of its hidden secrets.

With the growth of intellect, some men have fancied that the basis of morals, and also the sanction, is simply utility. And it has happened even that "the world by wisdom knew not God." At present, of that world, to which men are related by bodily organization, the curiosities and laws draw an interest disproportionately great in comparison with what is felt as to those laws and wonders, which are connected with man as "a living soul." This, however, is only by an accident of the moment, and because of the weakness of the human intellect; which, though it be only of yesterday, is yet confronted simultaneously with the necessities of the passing hour, and with problems akin to the infinite and eternal. There may have been times when miracles were senselessly magnified; and it would seem as though there might also be a time when they may be as absurdly neglected.

But yet miracles, and even of the far distant past, will interest man as long as he is a creature of aspiration and hope, because of their being evidences of a spiritual world, and proofs also, that man spiritually is enriched with receptiveness against "when the times of refreshing shall come from the presence of the Lord," whether in this world or the next. For indeed there is not a miracle but is an argument as to our human nature, for what it is in its faculties, and what its connections must be with a world invisible, of angels and agencies, which it is a glory to think of.

Miracles effete as to meaning, — what a strange notion! Because that they never can be, while men can wonder and reverence, and believe in the certainty of what must transcend their own pettiness, and dust, and ignorance.

Miracles effete as to meaning! That they never can become while men are human, mortals who have not yet become immortal, and clear of the fleshly veil, which separates between us newly created spirits, and that world eternal, immortal, invisible, for which we are predestined, but which yet "flesh and blood cannot inherit."

Miracles effete as to meaning! That they can never be; while men can have their thoughts started afresh, from time to time, as to who they themselves may be, or what, relatively, their place in the universe may be, under that Supremacy of Power which is called God, and as among "all things created, that are in heaven, and that are in earth, visible, and invisible, whether they be thrones, or dominions, or principalities, or powers."

Miracles effete as to meaning! That can never be, while the human soul is in its inmost self, prophetic, and capable at times of being "taught of God," and of showing graces, which have been quickened from above.

Miracles effete as to meaning! That can never be, while a man can be a wonder to himself; for, by the mysteriousness of his own nature, when he feels it, a man knows that the surrounding universe must certainly be alive with laws and marvels, against the astounding effects of which his soul is saved, only by the creative arrangements of God, who lets his universe "not speak unto you as unto spiritual, but as unto carnal, even as unto babes in Christ."

Miracles may cease to interest men, as prodigious tales of distant ages, and remote places; or as occurrences, of which there can nothing be made. But "miracles," as "signs," will be significant as long as human nature lasts; which means, so long as men are mortal, and have their daily walk bordered by a world immortal, whence effects are possible, or can even possibly be imagined, as to influence or intervention.

Because, according to the Scriptures, all human beings are more or less susceptible of the miraculous, or of being acted upon, otherwise than through their bodily senses; or, more exactly still, of being influenced from the spiritual world.

It is true, that we live by laws, some of which probably are unknown, and others of which are named respectively as being chemical, dynamic, electric, odic, and vital: but, at the best, this all is but a scientific and incomplete statement of what St. Paul credited even the heathen for knowing as to God, when he said, that, "In him we live, and move, and have our being."

Living and moving in God, and as his offspring! Then the realm of nature does not bound the circumference of our susceptibilities, even at this present time, probably. And then certainly, also, there must be latent in us the germs of new beginnings, which may start with us, as to effects, in one world after another, on our eternal progress; and as to which, for opening and delight, he may well be trusted, to whom we belong, and who is "from everlasting to everlasting."

And now, finally, a "miracle" being a "sign," what is a sign? It may have at the time of its giving, an individual and momentary pertinency; but it has also for everybody, who knows of it, a personal and eternal meaning. In the sense of "miracle," a "sign" is a sign made for mortals, from the world immortal; and it is also a proof that the soul of man is in some kind of affinity with wonder-working powers, which are active outside of that realm of nature, with which we are familiar by our bodily senses or common experience.

When read of in a thoughtless way, miracles in the distance may be but mere marvels; but really when they are "signs" they are signs which have been made for men, from the spiritual world; and they are illustrations of the laws of that world, which we mortals belong to spiritually; and they are evidences of the interest, which is felt there, about us spirits in the flesh. Miracles considered as signs, are flashes of light by which we all of us may discern the grandeur and also the peril of our earthly walk.

It was argued by St. Peter, that prophecy in the Scriptures had never been merely for individuals, because of its having been a movement by the Holy Ghost. And like his argument, is what St. Paul wrote to the Corinthians, as to even the distant miracles of the age of Moses: "Now all these things happened unto them for ensamples; and they are written for our admonition, upon whom the ends of the world are come."

MIRACLES AND THE CREATIVE SPIRIT.

ACCORDING to the book of Genesis, the creation of man was thus, — "The Lord God formed man of the dust of the ground, and breathed into his nostrils the breath of life; and man became a living soul." There may perhaps, at the Creation have been more ways than one, by which man might have grown in knowledge; but that which obtained with him, was what is referred to, in Ecclesiastes, where it is said that "much study is a weariness of the flesh"; and which indeed often ends in self-confusion; and which also, at the best, commonly incurs some loss, as a counterbalance against every gain. And because for us human beings, science, or philosophy, or learning, or all of them combined, are only a lamp of knowledge, it happens that things are out of sight or in it, and seem great or seem small, not because of what they are in themselves, as because of the light, by which they are looked at. And hence partly has resulted the strange variety of opinions, which have been published on the subject of miracles. Man indeed may well be the subject of marvellous experiences: "For we are but of yesterday and know nothing." And yet there is not one of us but might say, "The Spirit of God hath made me, and the breath of the Almighty hath given me life." Images of God as we are, and living souls, we have all of us, been created in the spirit of the universe, and are therefore susceptible of its disclosures. And if we have no great or common experience of them, in these days of dulness and flesh and mortality, we are yet none the less certain of having them hereafter, when seraphs shall be on the wing about us, and we be walking alongside of "a pure river of water of life, clear as crystal, proceeding out of the throne of God and of the Lamb."

In the Scriptures, it is to be read that, more than once, leprosy was caused by a miracle, and that several times, by a miracle, it was cured. And perhaps by the way in which the first man incurred disease, there was something miraculous involved, just as certainly as at Lystra and other places, through Paul by a bodily touch, or by some point in them spiritually being affected, sufferers were strengthened and cured. Finite creatures, surrounded by the infinite, and more or less vitally connected with it, we are wrapped about, and we are pervaded, by possibilities of a miraculous character. "For I am fearfully and wonderfully made: marvellous are thy works; and that my soul knoweth right well."

As to outward appurtenances, and as to those powers of his, which tell instantly on the surrounding world, generally a man is quick enough, but as to his make, it is almost the last thing ever to be thought of. So wonderfully am I made, that I do not know myself, nor understand myself. And the constitution of my body is known to me through discoveries, which are only very recent, notwithstanding that the nature of the human body was a matter of great and vital concern, to millions of men, in many past ages. And the more there is known about it, manifestly the more there is to learn; not perhaps as regards its composition, but as to its relationship by electricity and magnetism to the atmosphere, and it may be to the sun and moon and planets. For indeed we are not simply denizens of this earth, but we are creatures of the universe, borne about by a planet, which is one of many sisters; the whole family of which are related in every direction infinitely.

A man can hear only what his ears will let him hear. Over our heads may be made the music of the spheres, though inaudibly to us; and yet it might be distinctly perceptible perhaps, were our hearing a little quickened, or were the reporting power of the air or the ether a little intensified. This is readily credible. And really, by analogy, which is largely what we all of us think by, the ongoings of the universe hint to all persons, who are not mere arithmeticians or logicians, that we are concerned with laws, which science has never yet detected, and which perhaps, by their nature, transcend its methods. And therefore anything, which might be called a miracle, instead of being treated defiantly, should as perhaps being spiritually "a sign," be as welcome, at least, as the news of another asteroid, or of some affinity among salts, just freshly detected. "Oh," says some one, "but the Bible is enough for me." And so truly it might well be, if only he could read it aright. But apparently it was not meant, that the Scriptures should be a very easy book for everybody, and for all persons alike, the self-conceited and the humble, the worldly-wise and the man "taught of God." Else, how does it happen, among Christians, that there are so many sects, Roman Catholic, Greek Catholic, Episcopalian, Methodist Episcopalian, Presbyterian, Orthodox, Unitarian? The Bible, as a history of the manifestation of the Spirit of God, the writer hereof trusts to, as his highest guidance; but he believes that it was meant to be read as it was given, concurrently with Providence, and by the help of such light therefrom, directly and indirectly, as may fall, from time to time, on such eyes as may be open to receive it. All criticism, historical, dogmatic, chronological, being fairly allowed for, the Bible is manifestly to-day, the greatest treasure which is held in any earthen vessel; and such it will be to the end of time, no doubt, or at least till time shall begin again in some new æon, millennial or other. But though the Bible is always the same, as to what is written, the eyes with which it is read vary at least from one generation to another. By Providence, it is ordained that men shall pass through this life of ours, one generation after another; and through Providence also it is foreordained, that for the people who read it in succession, the Bible shall widen in meaning. For, anything from the Spirit of God, addressed to mere spirits in the flesh, must be found to mean more and more, the longer it is looked at.

No one, with an eye for history, can glance across it, without being struck by the manner in which often beliefs grow and fail, and apparently without sufficient reasons, from among men themselves. A striking remark was made by an awe-struck writer as to the French Revolution, and by De Tocqueville, perhaps; and it was this, that the spirit of that revolution went abroad, touching and transforming persons in a way, which was not to be accounted for humanly, either as to benevolence, religion, or taste; but spreading as though by infection. And no doubt with that strange manifestation, there was more concerned than simply the diffusion of words. Men were men, and tongues were tongues; but there was that in the air, which the men breathed, which perhaps was new. It may have been something of the nature of magnetism, which may possibly have originated altogether with men themselves; or it may have been something of that kind, intensified through spiritual affinities, active in more directions than one. It was a something, so to say, in the air: and as some bodily diseases are infectious, so also, it would seem, are some diseases of the spirit. And in both cases the condition of disease is suggestive of the channels of health, and may illustrate them. And the reverse of panic or of fanaticism by infection is courage or is faith, by the Holy Ghost. And we are Christians fully and joyously, only as far as it has been our personal experience, that "By one Spirit are we all baptized into one body, whether we be Jews or Gentiles, whether we be bond or free; and have been all made to drink into one Spirit." Commonly, logic is but an oar, almost without a blade, by which a thinker fancies that he is making an independent course; while really his soul is afloat upon a stream which is infinitely stronger than his arm: and while he thinks that he is rowing himself independently of all the forces of the universe, he is carried indeed to a port of his willing, but which he would never have aimed at, but for the air upon the water, and which indeed he had to breathe for his life. And at the best, and in order to be at its best, logic is only movement, step after step. It does but work slowly, and as it were on the deck of a ship, which itself may all the while be driven of the winds of heaven, and tossed upon the waves of the deep.

Live believingly by logic alone! That is what a man may do, with only the one half of his nature alive; and that, of course, the half of him, which is only a little more than what does live "by bread alone." But to find the way to the Father in heaven by logic would be such a hard thing for even the greatest intellect that God condescends to us. And at this day, by a miracle, which has never been intermitted since the days of Pentecost, for those of us who are willing, "God hath sent forth the Spirit of his Son into your hearts, crying, Abba, Father."

To live by logic, working merely on earthly information, is what may be done by individuals, and almost even by individual generations; but it is what cannot last, because of its not being human. For we human beings, though native to "the heavens and the earth, which are now," are yet now already living withinside the outskirts of "a city, which hath foundations, whose builder and maker is God." And so, certainly, until the last man shall have been gathered into the bosom of eternity, miracles, marvels, wonders will be dear to the human race as proofs, presumptively, that men are of more than fleshly make, and as "signs," perhaps even vouchsafed to them, of there being another world than this, in which we live, and have to die.

Hard as glass is, yet it is pervious to the impalpable rays of light; and electricity will run along a wire hundreds of miles in length. Well then may the "wonderfully made" body of man be credited for susceptibilities, which though they may commonly be occult, may yet also sometimes be the channels of great wonders. "As thou knowest not what is the way of the spirit, nor how the bones do grow in the womb of her that is with child, even so thou knowest not the works of God who maketh all."

Human beings are spirits held in clay; and though that clay indeed be vitalized by the lungs and the heart, it is yet porous and pervious to forces which sweep round the world, or which stream from pole to pole, such as electricity and magnetism. And there is also the odic force. And concurrently with these forces, only so lately known of, though now so positively ascertained, it would seem as though there might be other powers, higher and still more occult than they. And therefore it might seem as though some doctrines and statements in the Scriptures should reasonably appear to be more credible to such persons as have doubted spiritually, because of their having been infected by materialism. In man there is an eye for seeing, and an ear for hearing; and it is through the air that ear and eye both perceive. And through the air also there is the possibility by which a great thunder-storm at the Cape of Good Hope might be known of almost in a moment, as affecting the atmosphere electrically, at Cape Horn, and on the Himalaya Mountains.

Think of the electric telegraph, as to what it is in itself and as to the way in which it works; and under the best information, consider what man is as to body and spirit; and then many strange marvels will seem indeed to be transcendent, but not therefore unnatural nor incredible, — such as prophetic dreams, sudden persuasions as to far distant occurrences, the experiences of second sight, an occasional apparition even, and deep, true impressions received unaccountably, and as though from some whispering spirit. Electricity seems to be, in common language, more than the half of the distance from matter to spirit. And it is conceivable, and it would seem even to be highly probable, that as electricity coexists with gravitation, so there may also be forces in the universe, transcending electricity, and nearly akin even to spirit itself. And with these powers, probably, we mortals are concerned more or less, as we are with magnetism or with the oxygen of the atmosphere.

But it may be asked, "If there be a spiritual atmosphere, or anything like it, which concerns man, and through which spiritual causes may affect him, why has he never been informed of it, by revelation, just as by revelation he learns that he is spirit as well as body?" To this question the answer is very simple. Man lives by breath; and yet he was not born with an instinctive philosophy as to the properties, uses, and dangers of the common air. And after all these thousands of years, since the first man died, men are but now just beginning to understand the nature of the atmosphere. Even if the science of spirit had been imparted to the first man, it could not have lasted long with men, if it had been widely out of keeping with their science as to nature. And this indeed would seem to be implied by the words of Jesus, "Verily, verily, I say unto thee, we speak that we do know, and testify that we have seen; and ye receive not our witness. If I have told you earthly things, and ye believe not, how shall ye believe, if I tell you of heavenly things?" And thus, indeed, ultimately, instead of there being a domination of Christianity by science, it will result that science will but have predisposed Christians themselves for a better understanding of the Bible. For there are some important verities in the Scriptures, which are almost latent at present. And indeed truths uttered from the Spirit, in human words, or in metaphors derived from nature, must always have to wait long, before they can commonly be well understood, because they are only to be "spiritually discerned."

A thousand years ago, and even almost within the last two hundred years, in the most enlightened spot of Europe, a farmer toiled upon his land, and felt the while as though outside of his township there was nothing but danger and darkness. To-day, however, there is not an American agriculturist but feels that to do well, he must know of the circumference of the world, and also of the natural forces which sweep through the land, and which keep the earth alive; and that indeed for skill, he has got to be one of "the laborers together with God." There has been this great change with "the natural man." And is it not, then, reasonable to expect an extension of that knowledge, which is the field of "the spiritual man"?

Doubt about a miracle, merely as a great surprise! And yet by optics, there have been as great surprises given to men, as any spirit ever gave. And surely, if a man did not study science, and think by it, as a soldier moves, who has been sworn to service, and whose business it is to know no more than what he is put upon, optics alone might well predispose him to believe in marvels, without end.

Look at a tadpole through a microscope, and what a marvel is manifested out of nothing! Yet the microscope is as true, in its way, as the telescope; and probably there are spirits living, in the universe, who belong to a region far below the steps of the throne of God, whose eyes have of themselves the power of both telescope and microscope combined. Also we, human beings, by birth, probably have visual faculties as strong as telescope and microscope, but for the flesh in which we walk about. With a little bodily disorganization, the spirit of a man becomes "clairvoyant," and he can read well, and can even walk and climb more securely with his eyes shut than when wide awake. So, even scientifically, a man should be inclined to believe in miracles, as wonders, or as signs made from steps above him, in intelligence.

By the electric telegraph, we begin to realize certain characteristics of the spiritual world, and, as Swedenborg would say, the comparative unimportance of time and space. At any hour, almost, it is possible for a person to communicate with any city in Europe, though at a distance, perhaps, of three or four thousand miles. But, in comparison with this actuality, it would have seemed, a hundred years ago, that intercourse was just as likely with "Jerusalem, which is from above." And surely, if man be "a living soul," and be, by birth, a native of "the world which now is," and heir to "the world which is to come," it would seem as though the marvels which science discovers might be but the earthly counterpart of miracles or "signs" unearthly, which denote solemnly the opening of the heavens, and that something may be happening, like what was meant when it was said, prophetically, that "times of refreshing shall come from the presence of the Lord."

If the ancients could possibly be confronted with the philosophers of the present time, it might well be proposed for them to compromise as to incredulity, and that the moderns should believe in the spiritual world because of science, and that the ancients should believe in science because of their belief in spirit; for, really, miracles are what signs are possible from an extra-sensual world, while science is largely the report of semi-sensual forces, outside of that solid world in which anciently men thought that they lived.

But, if we are accessible from the spiritual world by influences or visitants, why have we never been told of it? And now, really, what more express telling could there possibly be, on any subject, anywhere, than there is on this, in the Scriptures? And again, if there be an opening between this world and another, it may be asked, why the way of it is not to be read of in the Scriptures. But now, there is a philosophy of this present world, which has only very lately been known of, but yet to the advice of which chemically, as to health, we trust ourselves implicitly. And if it should be objected, "Oh, but the soul! How can a man think to know more about it than his ancestors did?" And to this, answer may be made by another question, and it is this: "What kind of a creature would man have been, if, by his science, he had been a Troglodyte or a dirt-eater, and been also bright the while, with the wisdom of a seraph, and warm with the love of a cherub?" Certainly, it cannot have been otherwise than that at the creation of man, it must have been ordained, that he should have the Intellectual Universe disclose itself to him spiritually, as fast at least, as he of himself should be able to find it out scientifically.

"The heavens declare the glory of God, and the firmament showeth his handiwork." That was David's belief. But then David believed in enlightenment from above; and indeed, among his last words he said, "The Spirit of the Lord spake by me, and his word was in my tongue." The Psalmist said, "The heavens declare the glory of God." But there are persons assuming the attitude of philosophers at this present time, who would say, "There cannot, perhaps, be glory for what has not self-consciousness; but truly and grandly the heavens, on being found out, do declare the glory of astronomers and the human intellect." And there are people who think that this sentiment is something new! And yet their forefathers in intelligence, thought in the same way, perhaps, twenty-five hundred years ago; for, in the book of Habbakuk the prophet, there is to be read of fishermen who worshipped their nets, because of a good catch. "Therefore they sacrifice unto their net, and burn incense unto their drag; because by them their portion is fat, and their meat plenteous." To grow in intellect, or even in the humblest skill, is to grow godless, except as those susceptibilities in a man are kept open which are Godwards. "But," as St. Paul wrote to the Corinthians, "but as it is written, Eye hath not seen, nor ear heard, neither have entered into the heart of man, the things which God hath prepared for them that love him. But God hath revealed them unto us by his Spirit: for the Spirit searcheth all things, yea, the deep things of God. For what man knoweth the things of a man, save the spirit of man, which is in him? even so the things of God knoweth no man, but the Spirit of God." And in the proper sense of the word "miracle," the Spirit of God, as it is experienced by individual Christians, from one generation to another, is itself a continuous, unceasing miracle in the world.

In a right temper, when a man remembers that his life began with his birth, only a very few birthdays back, then no wonder seems to him so great, as even his own ability to ask about a miracle. And no miracle, perhaps, ever was greater than what is implied by the manner, in which a person can be accused by his conscience all through his life. For, what actually would conscience seem to be? It is a faculty of human nature, certainly, and yet, certainly, not in quite the same way as logic is; for, it is a faculty which would seem to be open to re-enforcement, and to have in it the spirit of a higher world, for meaning and strength. Conscience, by its manner of acting, would predispose to a belief in "signs and wonders" and miracles.

It is a common conceit, that between matter and spirit there is such a gulf of separation, as that the possibility of anything spiritual in this world, may rightly be denied at once, whether it be as regards angels or devils or apparitions, or the Holy Spirit, the

Comforter. And this notion is common even with some mere Scripturists. And yet, surely, there is nothing like it in the Scriptures. The laws of the material world act together, like those of the human body: and they connect together in such a way, the lower with the higher, as to suggest spirit itself as the end, if that may be called an end which is a beginning, connected with immortality.

In the human body, what diverse laws do by some means communicate with one another; as the chemical with the dynamic, and these again with other laws, such as those of gravitation and electricity! Spirit unable to touch or affect matter under any conditions — what nonsense! For, in the body of a man, laws, hard to distinguish from spirit, are assembled together, and blend, as it were, into one spirit-like force, which is called vitality.

That a spirit cannot do anything for men to know of, and cannot give "a sign," seems to some persons to be absolutely certain, because, as they think, spirit cannot possibly touch, nor handle, nor know of matter; and yet they believe that they, individually, are body and spirit united. They cannot tell how anger clenches for a man his fist, nor how their own thoughts become words; and yet they are certain that spirit can never affect matter in any way; and they are certain of this, notwithstanding that they do not even know what a spirit may be. And yet, actually, by its immortal nature, a spirit may have endless aptitudes, and appliances, and powers of self-adjustment.

At one time, anciently, it was held in psychology that some demons or wandering spirits were spiritual bodies possessed of absorbent powers, by which they could assimilate some of the finer particles of matter from the air, and so become thinly embodied, and faintly visible. And it would seem as though it probably might have been so; and if so, really it is a very curious fact. But other things like it have been recorded; and of which one or two, by pneumatology, would seem to have analogies in the Scriptures. And on the supposition that they are true, they are more important than they might seem to be at the first sight; because they illustrate the possibilities of the universe, and the manner in which the supernatural may begin from the natural; and even also they may elucidate perhaps Christian doctrine. For, if we are the workmanship of God, and are created in the image of God, it would seem to imply that there must be latent in us many affinities, by which hereafter we shall be connected with the works of God, in many and perhaps infinite directions. For if men be "heirs of God," they would seem to be qualified by their spirituality, and under the Divine permission, to reach and enter upon one world after another, notwithstanding what the constituent arrangements of those worlds, individually, may be. It is to be read in the Book of Revelation, "Write, Blessed are they which are called unto the marriage supper of the Lamb." And blessed are they in the highest; for, by the wedding-garment they are free of every mansion in the Father's house. And, as children of God Most High, it would seem as though there must be the possibility by birth, for all souls to be free of all worlds, not in a moment, of course, but only very slowly. Because human souls are but creations, as it were, of yesterday; and though they are predestined to be eternal, yet, while living by the laws of nature, they might well appear in the eyes of an archangel to be but like phosphorescent particles upon the sea of time, which are bright for a moment, and then vanished forever. "But thanks be to God, which giveth us the victory through our Lord Jesus Christ."

Some persons are utterly disconcerted, when it is urged seriously as to God, that "In him we live and move, and have our being," and that, thence as a fact, there are inferences to be drawn, as to what human beings are, or may hope to be. And yet that text, "Draw nigh to God, and he will draw nigh to you," and that beginning of prayer, "Our Father which art in heaven," — these would seem to teach that, while yet in the flesh, we may be living by the Spirit, and that really "signs" are possible for us, even though there may never be more than one "sign" to be realized by us, while we are earthly. But that one sign, however, should perhaps be the greatest of miracles for those who can apprehend it; and it is this, — that we and God are living together — he "from everlasting to everlasting," and we by "the breath of the Almighty."

Oh that infesting, nonsensical notion of there being a sharp line of demarcation between matter and spirit, in consequence of which, in the universe, somewhere or other, there is non-intercourse! And if really there were such a line, man would not be concerned with it; for, if man be clay, he is also spirit with all its properties, some of which certainly are active with him, though others may be dormant.

Under God, this universe is a living whole, dust and stars alike included, and from coral insects up to "the seven Spirits which are before his throne."

For most persons, the omnipresence of God, notwithstanding its infinite significance, is almost a benumbing phrase, because of the inane manner in which it has been taught as a doctrine. "Fear not them which kill the body, but are not able to kill the soul: but rather fear him which is able to destroy both soul and body in hell. Are not two sparrows sold for a farthing? and one of them shall not fall on the ground without your Father. But the very hairs of your head are all numbered." The full meaning of these sayings of Jesus perhaps the most pious man living has never felt, even while agreeing to it thoroughly as being the truth. And as to miracles, there is more than one way of believing. For, to acquiesce in certain ancient statements, merely because we cannot deny James, and John, and Peter, is not a very quickening faith. And even to trust our own senses, as to marvels, may well be, without our being spiritually minded. Mere assent as to miracles is a very different thing from knowing of them believingly, in the spirit of wonder, and from a sense of our being widely connected with an unknown universe.

Unknown by us, and yet not utterly unknown is this universe, wherein we are dwellers. Our souls, at present, live cased in clay, and according to the laws of this planet, which is called earth; but when our souls, by the death of the body, shall be free of such laws as enchain us through matter, we shall find ourselves as to God, still saying as we do now, that "In him we live and move and have our being." And so shall we have to say to all eternity: because by our living and moving in God, we are now already, living in that Spirit, infinite and eternal, which knows nothing of height or depth, as being itself all which there is of either, — that spirit, without which the lightning cannot flash, nor the glow-worm shine, which lets loose "the sweet influences of the Pleiades," and which strengthens "the bands of Orion," and from the sense of which, once, about this earth, "the morning stars sang together, and all the sons of God shouted for joy," — that spirit, which is nature in those "who, having not the law, are a law unto themselves," and which again as being above the law, can quicken where "the flesh profiteth nothing," — that spirit by which the prophets prophesied, and David as a psalmist was inspired to sing, and which yet is freer than daily bread, for such persons as can really ask for it, — that spirit, which is the consummation of all miracles in one, for the man who has full experience of it, because "Now the Lord is that Spirit," and "He that is joined unto the Lord is one spirit."

That a miracle should be defined or be objected to, as an act suspending the laws of nature, may seem, at this stage in our argument, to be absurd, as perhaps it really is. For a miracle says about itself, only that it is "miraculum," a little wonder, or a "sign and wonder." An angel might give me a sign, at the recollection of which hereafter, I should smile, should I ever become an archangel. But because I can anticipate the possibilities of eternity in this bold manner, it does not follow that a miracle is anything less than miraculous to-day, or less than a precious hint given to me from outside of this world, as to there being more spiritual activities than I know of, and with some of which my own nature may be more or less involved, by affinity.

Miracles are like signs, made from steps above me, on Jacob's ladder. The dream of Jacob, on leaving his father's house, is curiously illustrated by the theory of Plato, as to the spiritual universe and the manner in which men are influenced and taught; and it is wonderfully corroborated by the spirit of the Book of Revelation, and incidentally indeed and often by texts, throughout the New Testament. St. James writes in his Epistle, "Every good gift and every perfect gift is from above, and cometh down from the Father of lights." Most wonderful indeed is that dream, or probably that vision in a dream, which happened to the patriarch Jacob in Syria, some thirteen hundred years before the age of Plato the philosopher of Greece. "And he dreamed, and behold a ladder set up on the earth, and the top of it reached to heaven: and behold the angels of God ascending and descending on it. And behold the Lord stood above it, and said, I am the Lord God of Abraham thy father, and the God of Isaac." And to-day that ladder stands over every one of us, the emblem of revelation, and of the divine government of the world; even though on to the lower steps of it, spirits, who are not angels, may get to stand for a moment, and thence give signs occasionally. It is true, that when my spirit shall be called up the height of that ladder, I shall transcend the greatest of all such miracles as I have ever yet known of; but then, too, I shall have the stars beneath my feet, and science itself also, and I shall have learned perhaps what the song was, which was sung over our newly created earth, when "all the sons of God shouted for joy."

Men are the children of the Father in heaven, and not simply occupants of a planet, and natives of dirty cities or the sweet country. And there is in every one of us, now already, what will correspond with every step on that ladder, which Jacob saw reach up to heaven. And what becomes us, as mortals, is to trust in the certainty of that ladder, and in the reality of those affinities, by which we are connected with spirits and angels, and through which miracles are possible, and signs can be vouchsafed for us.

Said Jesus to his disciples, "Verily, verily, I say unto you, He that believeth on me, the works that I do shall he do also: and greater works than these shall he do, because I go unto my Father." In comparison with greater works miraculously, there must be some which are less. And it would not be altogether apart from the prophecy of Jesus himself, should it be found that in some places, at certain times, miracles of healing, because of their frequency, had been less thought of, than they were among the Jews, in the age of Jesus. And if this were true, what then? For, what is a miracle, but a sign? And what is a sign, in the sense of a miracle, but signification of there being power which concerns us, though outside of our ordinary world. It would seem, then, as though conceivably the miracle of one age, might become so common in another, as to begin even to grow less wonderful. But the more, what had been a miracle, should lose in wonder, the more significant still would it grow in another way, as making more and more certain what at first it had only hinted as to the vital, spiritual, eternal connections between spirits in the flesh and the spiritual universe. Because, indeed, we mortals belong to the world immortal, invisible, through our spiritual nature, by perhaps a thousand powers or susceptibilities, which probably are nearly all of them merely latent in us at present. And of these latent powers, it may be, that the miracles of all ages have been intended to suggest for us the actuality of some five or six.

For the "heirs of the kingdom," doubtless it will prove that all the miracles of the Scriptures will have been but like prophecies of the powers, and the joys, and the company to which they were destined to attain. And this supposition is perhaps by the same line of thought as that along which St. Paul looked, when he foresaw as to Jesus Christ that "when all things shall be subdued unto Him, then shall the Son also himself be subject unto him, that put all things under him that God may be all in all."

There cannot possibly be any power in nature at large, which man can discover, but must have some meaning for him, as to his own nature, and be indeed in some sense, an extension of it. Nor is there anything spiritually, of which man can be persuaded, as having spiritually discerned it, but must prove for him, an introduction to some glory beyond, and which may reach up the heights of heaven to all eternity.

The telescope and the microscope are merely human inventions, but even they report that there are worlds within worlds, and worlds beyond worlds, which concern us. But when these instruments discover wonders, in their way, in the material universe for the material man; they do also, to the man who is spiritually minded, suggest prophetically as to the spiritual world, of there being wonders there, which are only the beginnings of wonders, and of there being one heaven above another heaven.

As binding worlds together, and as holding them in intercourse for some purposes, gravitation and magnetism and electricity may be instanced as powers. And also they may be regarded as gross similitudes as to the ways, by which our spirits will find themselves living hereafter, when possessed by aspirations after the heaven of heavens.

The universe is all alive, and it is alive all throughout it. And miracles are signs made for us mortals by spirits, in different conditions from ours, higher it may be, and perhaps even lower, and perhaps even as high as that of the Seven Spirits.

But when miracles are signs from heaven, there comes with them that Spirit, which is its own evidence for those who can feel it, because of the irresistible manner in which the spiritual man is thereby persuaded. When God Most High touches a man with the finger of miracle, the man feels that touch in his inmost nature, as to holiness and newness of life. But miracles of a lower origin than the highest, may for some persons, excite only the externality of their nature, and make them perhaps merely wonder, and perhaps also grow in self-conceit.

But whatever the constitution of the universe may

be, of worlds within worlds, or of heavens one above another, we mortals are the offspring of the living God, the King Eternal, Immortal, Invisible. And there is that in every one of us, which quickened by his Spirit, would be affinity with all worlds, and with everything which has ever happened under the throne of God. "The Spirit itself beareth witness with our spirit, that we are the children of God; and if children, then heirs, heirs of God, and joint-heirs with Christ."

MIRACLES AND HUMAN NATURE.

AGAINST the probability of miracles, or of "signs and wonders," ever having been vouchsafed, it has been objected that they are such things as could not always and everywhere, and to all men be equally credible and important. And so it is supposed, that the miracles of the Scriptures are inconsistent with the Providence of a just God, unless the impression made by them should have been uniform as to meaning and authority, from the time of the eyewitnesses to the last public professions by Christian converts in Madagascar and China. But otherwise are all men impressible alike, and exactly by the same thing? Is the same sensation received from the sun, by both Lapps and Bengalese? Is there any drug, which is uniform as to strength and effect on persons of every age, tribe, and region? From even a table of logárithms, would a uniform impression be received by everybody, withinside of even the four walls of a market-place? And from any chapter of the Bible, even though read by the best reader, are there two hearers in any church or any street, who would receive a uniform impression? Also, is justice the less certainly just, because of the Dyaks of Borneo? Or is purity the less pure, because the negroes of Bonny are not impressible as to that virtue, equally with the best nuns of Rome, or with Christian matrons radiant with "the beauty of holiness"? The miracles of the Scriptures are for all men, but only just as everything spiritual and intellectual, is for everybody. And indeed the full meaning of miracles can be developed, only as they are differently apprehended by different minds, by Origen and Augustine, by Bossuet, Fenelon and Pascal, by Jeremy Taylor, Robert Barclay, Swedenborg and Neander.

It is even possible, that the resurrection of Jesus, may be more significant to-day, than it was on that "first day of the week," and that it may be better believed at this time, after eighteen hundred years, than it was even by those who "departed quickly from the sepulchre with fear and great joy, and did run to bring his disciples word." And indeed there seems, at this present time, to be forming such a philosophy of the Intellectual Universe, as that in the light of it, the fragmentary account of the resurrection of Jesus will glow with that newness of meaning, which will be its own sufficient evidence as to truth. And already on some minds there dawns a light, in which it seems as though reaffirmed from above, when it is read, "And, behold, there was a great earthquake: for the angel of the Lord descended from heaven, and came and rolled back the stone from the door, and sat upon it. His countenance was like lightning, and his raiment white as snow, and for fear of him the keepers did shake, and became as dead men. And the angel answered and said unto the women, "Fear not ye: for I know that ye seek Jesus, which was crucified. He is not here; for he is risen, as he said. Come, see the place where the

Lord lay and go quickly, and tell his disciples that he is risen from the dead; and, behold, he goeth before you into Galilee: there shall ye see him: lo, I have told you."

In its relation to human nature, what is a miracle? Simply it is an incident which happens to a mortal through his immortal connections. At the mountain, by the Sea of Galilee, when Jesus with handling five barley loaves, fed five thousand men, "those men, when they had seen the miracle that Jesus did, said This is of a truth that prophet that should come into the world." But the next day, in consequence of their behavior, "Jesus answered them and said, Verily, verily, I say unto you, ye seek me, not because ye saw the miracles, but because ye did eat of the loaves, and were filled." But indeed of the apostles themselves, the night after the miracle, it is written, that having seen Jesus walking on the sea, in a storm, and having taken him for a spirit, and having had that storm subside with his mounting their ship, "they were sore amazed in themselves beyond measure, and wondered. For they considered not the miracle of the loaves; for their heart was hardened." The loaves and fishes of the miracle had been wonderful food, but yet what could be swallowed and forgotten; but if the miracle had been understood, and been taken for "a sign and wonder," then Jesus would at once have been known as "the bread which cometh down from heaven, that a man may eat thereof, and not die." According to the Scriptures, then, a miracle might be food for the body, or it might be a cure for it; but when "spiritually discerned," it was also "a sign" as to realms and connections outside of the range of "the natural man."

It is the Scriptural philosophy as to human nature, that man is both body and soul; and that though born into this world, he belongs to a world which is to come; and that he is capable, even on this earth, of being born again. This is man as he is known to "the Shepherd and Bishop of your souls"; and also as he is created by the Father Almighty, who numbers, every moment, everywhere, the hairs of every head, whilst yet, also, he is the circumference of the universe as to power, and is also Providence to "the young ravens when they cry."

Miracles have occurred to men, not unnaturally, but conformably to their nature. A spirit living and moving in a marvellous clothing of flesh, — that is what man is. A man in a diving-suit, weighed down to the floor of the ocean, and exploring it, but endowed with faculties by which he would be more completely at home in the upper air, hints to us the condition of the human being, as he ploughs the earth, and journeys about it, endowed the while with faculties, by which he may be perhaps free of the heavens, and rich in instincts which never here leave him quiet as to his hereafter. "For we know that if our earthly house of this tabernacle were dissolved, we have a building of God, a house not made with hands, eternal in the heavens. For in this we groan, earnestly desiring to be clothed upon with our house which is from heaven: if so be that being clothed, we shall not be found naked."

Instead of aspiring to what is above, and living by aspiration, we may try to accommodate ourselves to our immediate circumstances, and propose to "live by bread alone," and with only such thoughts and feelings, as are akin to daily bread of our own procuring. But in so doing, we can live only, as creatures of the earth, earthy. For, by our better nature, there is always in us a hunger "for that meat which endureth unto everlasting life, which the Son of man shall give unto you." And as to this spiritual meat being within our reach, and as to the "well of water springing up into everlasting life," perhaps miracles, rightly understood, always are suggestions or proofs. This, even the woman of Samaria would seem to have felt, as, humble and ignorant, she talked with Jesus by the well. And indeed always, the more a man has "tasted the good word of God, and the powers of the world to come," the more confident must he be of that world, as being his natural and predestined home. "For the Spirit itself," — and therefore, also, all its gifts, whether prophecy, or the gifts of healing, or faith, or the working of miracles, — "the Spirit itself beareth witness with our spirit, that we are the children of God."

In the book of Deuteronomy there is to be read, what was affirmed anew by Jesus, when he "was led up of the Spirit into the wilderness, to be tempted of the devil"; and when "he answered and said, It is written, man shall not live by bread alone, but by every word that proceedeth out of the mouth of God." And by this text, it would seem to be implied that man lives, at his best, contingently on a dispensing will, which is higher than nature, and not merely by such laws of nature as fulfil upon him the prediction, "In the sweat of thy face shalt thou eat bread, till thou return unto the ground; for out of it wast thou taken.

That there is spiritually any higher source of thought

for us than nature, and any other inspiration for us than from surrounding nature and fellow-creatures, is denied by implication, when the possibility of miracles is denied. And the possibility of miracles is denied, because of what is fancied must be the inviolable uniformity of the laws of nature. And this is said and done, as though all the forces and properties and contingencies and affinities of nature, and the whole broad field of it also, were as familiarly known as what a player relies upon for his game at a billiard-table.

For the universe there are laws, some palpable, and others which are more or less occult, and there are some laws, which, as blood in the veins, are like laws within laws; and of these laws there are some which have affinities for one another, and some which are mutually repellant. And from all the agency and intercommunication of these laws, it results that the material universe is sustained and quickened by laws innumerable, for which as a whole, spirit is the name, and no other word. Spirit, indeed, in the full sense of the word, is all laws in one: and God is spirit.

But God manifests himself through what is beneath him, and yet mostly perhaps through ranges and spheres, far above what men know of. But in our planetary system, and in this earth, his creative power operates through five, ten, fifty, and perhaps hundreds of separable, distinguishable manifestations, which may be called laws. And yet because of their four or five senses, aided one of them by glasses telescopic and microscopic, there are men, who think that from their personal knowledge of the ways of the universe, they can positively deny the possibility of a miracle, or of any opening, by which an angel, or a spirit or a demon might be able to make "a sign."

A man denying the possibility of a miracle, is a creature of yesterday with a little knowledge, and at the best, only a very little, who yet dogmatizes about the possibilities of the infinite, the invisible, and the eternal.

Telescope and microscope being allowed for as to their powers, and anatomy, chemistry, and geology also; and botany and icthyology and palæontology being fully credited for their reports, yet the words of Zophar are no less pertinent to-day than they were of old, though they may sound somewhat more scornfully now than as they were first spoken to Job. "Canst thou by searching find out God? Canst thou find out the Almighty unto perfection? It is as high as heaven; what canst thou do? deeper than hell; what canst thou know?"

High as heaven, deep as hell, — how possibly could it be found out? And miracles are hints, suggestions vouchsafed to mortals, as to the inscrutable.

But how, then, is a man to know a miracle when it occurs? He may know it by his astonishment. For a miracle calls itself simply a wonder. If a miracle called itself, or if the Bible described it, as being a suspension of the laws of nature, it would, of course, be necessary to know altogether about all the laws of nature, before there could be any certainty as to whether one of them were suspended or not. Generally, in the Scriptures, a miracle is a wonder. But "a sign and wonder" would seem to mean something more express than the vaguely wonderful, and to be indeed a significant wonder, "a sign from heaven," or possibly elsewhere, made and given for a particular purpose.

And it is at this point that the subject of miracles becomes serious. For, as to the miracles of the Scriptures, there are persons who say, as they would say also about the marvels of all ages, "It is very likely that they did happen; for all laws have exceptions which are wonderful. Also, strange things certainly do happen, but always, of course, according to the laws of nature. Though we can only seldom know what the strange things were exactly, and still less can we exactly know what the laws of nature were, which may have been concerned." These persons do not object to miracles, as curious, exceptional facts, and especially when ancient. They demur only to the essence of a miracle, its soul, its main reason, to its connection with another order than this of things visible, and especially to its being "a sign" made or given. They would be willing to allow that perhaps "Stephen, full of faith and power, did great wonders and miracles among the people." And miracles in connection with Jesus Christ, they would think, might be credited. But miracles with an earnest meaning, and connected with God, are what they cannot agree to, as being likely. They can get back to the day of Pentecost. They are even ready to believe that miracles may have happened; and they can get within hearing of the appeal of St. Peter, "Ye men of Israel, hear these words; Jesus of Nazareth, a man approved of God among you by miracles, wonders, and signs, which God did by him in the midst of you, as ye also know." But this argument they cannot assent to. They can believe in a miracle as a marvel, but not as "a sign," and especially as vouchsafed by God: because for that belief, as St. Paul would say, they have been spoiled "through philosophy and vain deceit, after the tradition of men, after the rudiments of the world." They can assent as they read, "and fear came upon every soul, and many wonders and signs were done by the apostles." They can believe that miracles and wonderful works may have happened; but that they were started as signs from the spiritual world is what they do not like to have to think. Yet of Paul and Barnabas at Iconium it is written that "Long time abode they speaking boldly in the Lord, which gave testimony unto the word of his grace, and granted signs and wonders to be done by their hands." So, also, they can acquiesce, as they read about Philip in the city of Samaria, "And the people with one accord gave heed unto those things which Philip spake, hearing and seeing the miracles which he did." But the following verse they can assent to, only on the supposition of its being ancient and obsolete phraseology. "For unclean spirits, crying with loud voice, came out of many that were possessed with them." Because that ever the other world was so near to this, as to let out upon it "an unclean spirit," which could enter into a man or haunt among tombs, is what they can think no more than they can heartily believe that God "maketh his angels spirits."

Commonly at this present time, religionists think more of the machinery of the universe than of the universe itself, and more of even the lowest of his laws than they do of even God Most High. Whether of demon, ghost, spirit, angel, Son of man in glory, Father in heaven, or any other spiritual being whatever, that the will can possibly make itself felt by mortal beings, is a supposition which is repugnant to the philosophy of the day, or rather to the prejudices which were created by science when it was young and insolent, and very ignorant of even its own domain, some seventy or eighty years ago. That the universe, and that even our little surrounding world may have many properties of which there is nothing known, is a speculation with which science easily coincides, notwithstanding what some of its professors may think. The ear, the eye, and the tip of the finger are the chief channels of communication with the universe for men, by their state of nature. But there may be other beings, to whom this earth may be another thing than what mortals see; and to whom it may report itself in ways, of which man may never get a glimpse. And, conceivably, these creatures may be as invisible as electricity is when it is latent; and yet for movement may be as swift as thunderbolts, and, as regards God, be even familiar with what mortals would call "the hiding of his power." Verily, who we are, and what we are, being considered, there is a way of arguing from even our human ignorance, which is truer, more just, and more profitable, than even the logic of science, as it is narrowed by some men.

As to miracles by the will of God, being incredible as acts of divine condescension — that would hardly seem to be a just sentiment, while a sparrow cannot fall to the ground without the knowledge of the Father in heaven; while the lily is arrayed in glory greater than that of Solomon; and while year after year, an inheritance of instinct is perpetuated from worm to worm in the ground. While the glow-worm shines, and while the young ravens are fed for crying, while the turtle, the crane and the swallow are shown the times of their coming, it may well seem credible as to man, that "the inspiration of the Almighty" should be his understanding; and even that, as he draws nigh to God, he should have God draw nearer to him, and lend him perhaps his finger for miracles, and have him pour out of his Spirit for Pentecostal purposes. No doubt, as true philosophy widens, some words also will widen and deepen in meaning. But while "father" means father, and essentially is the same thing in Christian households, and among aboriginal savages, the word "God" will never part with its essential meaning, and will continue to be, for condescension and love and assistance, what Paul felt, when he wrote of what he had been as an apostle "through mighty signs and wonders, by the power of the Spirit of God."

But it is questioned, why one man is not a subject for miracles, or an agent, as well as another. But it might as well be asked why every man is not a poet, and why poets are not all equal. One man is doomed by his constitution to die at his thirtieth year; while another man by birth is heir to threescore years and thirty. But why is that? As to ancient Greece, why were not the periods of history uniform; why did not every age flower with names as great and rich as those of Plato and Æschylus? And after the death of Euripides or the last speech of Demosthenes, why did the inspiration of genius fail; and why was Pausanias a mere antiquarian instead of being inspired like Pindar? Why a thing wonderful is not repeated, — this, instead of being the first objection to be made to a miracle, would seem as though it ought to be even the last, in accordance with human experience generally.

As to the probability of miracles having ever occurred or been vouchsafed, it has been objected that a miracle, with advancing intelligence, cannot continue to be of the same importance, as at the time of its manifestation. But really what inconsideration that is! Shakespeare is a greater man to-day than he was in his own age: and so is Milton. And with the growth of intellect, and the widening of human experience, a miracle instead of meaning less, may actually grow to be more significant with the lapse of time. But as one miracle may gain in expression with the widening of science, so another may lose. For the word "miracle," according to the Scriptures, is a general word, covering wonders of more classes than one. The casting-out of unclean spirits was one of the miraculous works of Jesus Christ, though not one of his "greater works." But to-day, an "unclean spirit," if it could be proved to be existing within human cognizance, would, for the Royal Society of London, be as great "a sign and wonder" as even "though one rose from the dead."

"But," says the modern philosopher, "Oh, but unclean spirits are absolutely incredible, being so utterly foreign to our experience. And if really any ever did exist, why are there none known of now?" But perhaps they are known of, though not very widely reported. Also, if there be any virtue in Christianity, ought it to be expected that unclean spirits should be as common a nuisance to-day as when Jesus Christ and the early disciples first began to cast them out? Also, if our human world changes, may we not also suppose that there may be changes on the spiritual borders of it, and along that line, which "unclean spirits" anciently were supposed to haunt? These questions may appear to be strange; but that they should seem so, is itself, perhaps, a still stranger thing. But indeed as to strangeness, what is there which can be greater than the fact that three, four, and five Christian sects should be in controversy with one another as to what really Christianity itself may be?

For Dr. Büchner and some others, according to their own words, clairvoyance or somnambulism, or a perception of a road or a book, independently of the humors of the eye, would be a miracle. And this would be because of what they think they know by anatomy. For a materialist a clairvoyant is as great a miracle as he can ever be shown. But for a Spiritualist a clairvoyant is no great wonder, even though he manifests the certainty that "there is a spirit in man" by showing that, with bandaged eyes, there may be perfect sight, and what even can see through a wall.

Such cures as were wrought through the Prince Hohenlohe, in Germany, about forty years ago, were believed by Catholics to be miraculous. But at present, cures of the same nature with those of the German Prince are common, at the hands of persons who are not Catholics. Be it allowed that they are done through mesmerism: but that would mean only that they are wrought through a faculty which was particularly strong seventy years since, in a man by the name of Mesmer. But that faculty would better have been named after Greatrex of the seventeenth century, only that even before him the faculty had been manifested by multitudes of persons, not of one country only, nor of one century merely, nor even of simply several regions and ages. At this moment, the writer hereof has on his table an engraving, in which St. Philip Neri, by his handling, cures Pope Clement the Eighth of the gout. According to the Catholic Church, and the text which accompanies the picture, the success of Philip Neri was a miracle: and so it was, in a higher or lower degree. And that miracles are of various grades as to significance, is according to the canons of the Catholic Church, and the estimate of the Middle Ages, and the doctrine of the Scriptures. Miracles of healing are more frequent to-day than they were in the age of St. Philip Neri. But the less wonderful miracles of any kind become by frequency, the more significant also they become in another way. Mesmerism is the recognition of the nervous system of a man, as being through his fingers, more or less, an outlet of power, just as his tongue is. And to-day, mesmerism, with the philosophy thereof, means, that after thousands of years, men have attained to the knowledge of there being one or more psychical laws, through which some persons, under some circumstances can help others medically.

Among the Jews, miracles of healing were accounted as being greater or less in themselves, and also by comparison, as when it was written of Jesus, that "he could there do no mighty work, save that he laid his hands upon a few sick folk, and healed them."

That miracles should ever lose in force by becoming common, is an inconsiderate, unspiritual fear. For that was never the feeling of those who knew best about miracles. At Taberah, the spirit which was in Moses had been imparted by the Lord, to seventy elders of the people, stationed about the tabernacle. But simultaneously also two men in the camp prophesied. "And there ran a young man, and told Moses and said, Eldad and Medad do prophesy in the camp. And Joshua the son of Nun, the servant of Moses, one of his young men, answered and said, My Lord Moses, forbid them. And Moses said unto him, "Enviest thou for my sake? Would God that all the Lord's people were prophets, and that the Lord would put his spirit upon them!" For indeed a miracle in itself is nothing in comparison with the spiritual universe, as to the constitution of which, it is "a sign." As arguing the reality of a spiritual world and of spiritual agencies as affecting men, miracles never possibly can lose their meaning, by becoming common, any more than logarithms by use would dwindle into common arithmetic.

The more common of the phenomena of spiritualism may reasonably be accounted as indisputable facts. But they are not equally impressive for all persons. For by them, one man is converted instantly from materialism to a belief in spiritual power of some kind. While another man can be astounded by them, one day, and then, the next day, forget utterly what an astonished man he had been, and a third person will acknowledge the reality of the marvels, but will hold that they are not so useful or suggestive as the tattooed skull of a Maori, or a potsherd from the mud of the Nile. The four rules of arithmetic have the same meaning for all intelligent beings, but a poetic phrase has not. And in connection with Jesus himself, men were affected by miracles, some in one way and some in another. Nicodemus could say, "Rabbi, we know that thou art a teacher come from God; for no man can do these miracles that thou doest, except God be with him." But the Pharisees could argue and say, "This fellow doth not cast out devils, but by Beelzebub the prince of the devils." This was a strange diversity of opinion as to the same facts; and it was not probably of intellectual origin, but moral; and also perhaps not moral merely. "At that time, Jesus answered and said, I thank thee, O Father, Lord of heaven and earth, because thou hast hid these things from the wise and prudent, and hast revealed them unto babes." And when Simon Peter recognized Jesus as being the Christ, Jesus said, "Blessed art thou, Simon Bar-Jona; for flesh and blood hath not revealed it unto thee, but my Father which is in heaven." Fearfully and wonderfully we are made; and there are conditions in us, both of body and spirit, which may have accrued, since our birth, quite unaccountably; and through which one man is strong in an atmosphere, by which another man is weakened; and through which, also, one person can believe only a very little beyond what he sees; while another, being receptive of "the spirit of wisdom and revelation," sees things, the eyes of his understanding being enlightened.

It illustrates the manner in which the ways of thought have become materialized, that some such a sentiment as this can be published, and can even get the acquiescence of persons, whose business it is to know better. "As to the being of a God and his character, the sons of science must ultimately be the judges. And their verdict will have to depend on controversies and inquiries which are already initiated." What a notion! "Who is this that darkeneth counsel by words without knowledge?" Almost it is the spirit of the age, and what might reply for itself in the words with which Jesus Christ was answered by a demoniac, when "he asked him, What is thy name? And he answered, saying, My name is Legion: for we are many." Wait for geologists to tell whether there is a God or not! Does not the human soul know about that, as well as ever it can be known? It might as well be said, before loving their babies, that women should wait for science to justify them, as to the reasonableness of the maternal instinct. A man who does not feel God can never find him. And it is only as a child of God that ever a man can possibly know of the Father in heaven, however great his science may be. God is not at the end of a telescope, nor to be discovered by search among the primitive rocks. God is an instinct for us, or else he is nowhere. Wait for what science may say, while the human soul itself is higher evidence as to God than all surrounding nature! Words of prophecy, and of the highest, and as true as nature itself, and as simple, are these: "Zion said, The Lord hath forsaken me, and my Lord hath forgotten me. Can a woman forget her sucking child, that she should not have compassion on the son of her womb? Yea, they may forget, yet will I not forget thee."

A scientific examination, completely successful, will report God as he is to the stars, and as he was at the composition of the rocks of the primitive and the last formations, and as he still is for what power he endows the whirlwind with. What God is to the worm may be learned from the worm perhaps; and what also he is to the cricket in the grass may be learned by the study of its habits.

"But ask now the beasts, and they shall teach thee; and the fowls of the air, and they shall tell thee: or speak to the earth, and it shall teach thee; and the fishes of the sea shall declare unto thee." But rocks and barnacles, birds, beasts, and fowls, the sea, and the sands upon the sea-shore, lilies of the field, and cedars like those of Lebanon, — these things all, individually and conjointly, can report no more as to God than what they can, than what they have experienced. And what are they all, altogether, with all their properties and qualities combined, in comparison with a human soul?

What God is to the human soul must be something more than he is to all external nature, and be therefore, probably, something even more hopeful.

That which God is to the human body may be inferred from those laws of nature, by which man is akin to nature. But what God is to the soul there is nothing in nature to suggest, and therefore also nothing to limit.

Of God in the realm of spirit a mere scientist can know nothing from the study of rocks, beetles, and astronomy, though the prophet indeed can speak of him from inspiration, and the true poet, in his highest, happiest mood, from intuition.

God is more to a butterfly than he is to Mount Ararat; and he is more to an eagle than to a butterfly, and he is more to "the natural man" than he is to any eagle. And to man through his spirit God is more than he is through his body. And so there may be methods of God with man, and expectations from him and transcendent hopes, which may be worthy of all trust, notwithstanding that nothing like them has ever been experienced by dogs or oxen, or been even hinted by geology.

But it may be asked, perhaps, whether it is not written that even a sparrow cannot fall to the ground without the knowledge of God. And certainly and happily it is to be read so, and in a connection, also, from which it might be inferred that even its feathers may be all numbered. And, no doubt, the sparrow was one of the fowls of the air which Jesus pointed to, as neither sowing nor reaping, but as being fed by the Heavenly Father. Also in one of the Psalms it is to be read of how the sparrows had built about the temple. "Yea, the sparrow hath found a house, and the swallow a nest for herself, where she may lay her young, even thine altars, O Lord of hosts, my King and my God." But, in the Scriptures, are men and sparrows referred to in the same tone? In the Bible is not man recognized as having faculties, susceptibilities, and for God Almighty an interest, such as the sparrow, the stork in the heaven, the crane, and the swallow have not? "O Lord, thou hast searched me and known me. Thou knowest my down-sitting and mine up-rising: thou understandest my thought afar off. Thou compassest my path and my lying down, and art acquainted with all my ways: for there is not a word in my tongue, but lo, O Lord, thou knowest it altogether. Thou hast beset me behind and before, and laid thy hand upon me.

Such knowledge is too wonderful for me; it is high; I cannot attain unto it. Whither shall I go from thy Spirit? or whither shall I flee from thy presence?"

David was more to God than the sparrow of which he sang in his psalm. And the sparrow, chirping and feeding, and the same from age to age, for what divine care it may exemplify, is surely no argument as to human experience of God, as regards either uniformity or miracles. Nor rightly can it be, by its monotony of life, any presumption against the possibility of there having been "signs and wonders" in connection with "Paul, a servant of Jesus Christ, called to be an apostle, separated unto the gospel of God," or with the early Christians, as they watched the fall of the Roman Empire, or with George Fox, as he waited for the Spirit, or with John Wesley, in his newness of life, after he had been "born, not of blood, nor of the will of the flesh, but of God."

After a sensible, good man has learned everything which is to be learned from ornithology and palæontology, then let him correspond with the mind of Christ, and he will learn that he is of more value than many sparrows, and that he therefore is probably treated in more ways than sparrows are, and for more wants than they have, by the Maker of both men and sparrows, and of all things visible and invisible.

The laws by which the sphere of nature was rounded, and was filled with things animate and inanimate, are no evidence as to the susceptibilities and connections of man as a living soul, within reach of the Spirit, and liable to temptation.

As to the operation of the Spirit on human souls,

there is nothing to be argued from the chemistry of the body, any more than the law of gravitation can hint as to the manner in which the lightning flashes, or the electric current darts and strikes.

As to whether Moses and Elijah could ever have been visited by angels, there can rightly be no hint expected from rocks and fossils, unless it can first be shown that those rocks and fossils, at some time in their history, were what angels could have talked with by the Divine permission.

The providence of God, as sparrows can experience it, through the laws of nature, cannot be the measure of that providence, as it adapts itself to living souls, and wraps man about with a care, which death is not to end, but only to manifest. And whatever the connections of man may be through his body with nature and seed-time and harvest, it is yet not inconsistent with them all, that at one time "man did eat angels' food."

There are Christian divines — blind leaders of the blind, surely — who hope to have the miracles of the Bible made more credible, by the result of a scientific controversy, as to whether creation occurred by development or by stages. But really, whether God made the world with his right hand or with his left, though a very curious inquiry, cannot possibly be any new light as to the way in which he may have treated primeval man when "he led him about, he instructed him, he kept him as the apple of his eye."

By his free will, or what feels like it, a man can turn and twist himself intellectually, to strange effect, and can get himself bewildered by curious fantasies, and can even become like the absurdity of clay upon the wheel criticising the mind of the potter. At this present time there are hundreds of persons who think that, for acuteness, they are intelligences of mysterious growth, because they can ask themselves the question, "Has God self-consciousness; or is the Godhead a blind force?" But actually, ability for asking that question was attained long ago, and twenty-five hundred years since was derided by a prophet in a text, which combines the subtlest philosophy with the rarest wit: "Woe unto him that striveth with his Maker! Let the potsherd strive with the potsherds of the earth. Shall the clay say to him that fashioneth it, What makest thou? or thy work, he hath no hands?" And what is there so like that fancy of ancient prophecy as the modern objection? "A miracle! God allow a miracle! Does not God live and act by laws?" And to this question the answer is, "Yes, by laws, and even also by his Spirit, which is like a combination of all laws in one."

By his senses, which are only four or five, man is limited as to his outlook on the universe scientifically, as though he perceived it, for its grandeur and circumference, merely through a loop-hole. And yet, every now and then, somebody, who has learned all that he knows within seventy years, turns round on the public as an observer, to dogmatize in a manner which an archangel would never attempt, even among mortals. "An angel! This world is everywhere impervious to his entrance, and always must have been. A miracle! It is contrary to experience. A spirit appear! That is impossible, because of the laws of matter, and because of surrounding matter, earthy and atmospheric. Science is the true light; and apostles and prophets were not scientific persons." As to effect, this is a speech which is often made in public, and yet for confidence in self-assertion it is what would not become even a seraph, and "how much less man, that is a worm, and the son of man, which is a worm."

Goethe was a singular combination of worldly shrewdness, scientific perception, and poetic faculty. And, considering the manner of man he was, he was still more remarkable for what spiritual insight he had. Probably there is not a theological speculation of the present day, and of scientific origin, with which his thoughts were not familiar. And he said, once, what may be considered as clenching all the vague, wandering argument of the present time as to the being of a God. And never did he say anything more characteristic of himself. It is a verdict on the evidences of religion, when estimated at their lowest.

Argued out from history, and from the make of the world, and from human nature, there are certain lines of thought which converge at what cannot be anything else than a throne, whether thunderbolts be launched from it or not, and even though at present there be round about it the silence of that state wherein one day is "as a thousand years, and a thousand years as one day."

And very likely it was in rebuke of some scoffers that Goethe said what has been referred to, and which was this, "If there be not a God now, there will be one day."

Is daring speculation, then, at its best, preclusive of the subject of miracles? It is anything but that. And really from the direction and the depth whence we, human beings begin our aspiring path, which is from glory to glory, it cannot be otherwise than that our ascension should be distinguished and solemnized by "signs and wonders."

MIRACLES AND PNEUMATOLOGY.

THERE is, of course, a science of spirit, as certainly as there is of nature. And even if it should be thought to be utterly inscrutable by men, it yet must exist somewhere; and no doubt it is well known to "Michael the archangel," and to Raphael and the rest of "the seven holy angels, which present the prayers of the saints, and which go in and out before the glory of the Holy One."

However men may think or despair about it, pneumatology must exist somewhere, as certainly as geology does, or astronomy. And why should it be inconceivable that men should learn it, to that humble extent, which immediately concerns mortals? Science as to the soul would not seem to be any more improbable of attainment, than formerly science was as to the body, and as to those laws by which the body for its wonderful make is only less wonderful than a spirit itself. It is a subject, however, which has been so confused and embroiled as scarcely even to be mentionable; though it may yet really, perhaps, be very simple. But often simplicity is more bewildering than art. And continually, as to spiritual things, it is as it was at Chorazin and Capernaum, in the time of Christ, when they were revealed unto babes, while kept hid from the wise and prudent.

Pneumatology, as the method by which the universe is informed with spirit and divinely governed, is certainly an impossible attainment for us "living creatures"; nor perhaps will any mere mortal ever fully understand that occurrence in the spiritual world of which Daniel was told in a vision, by a man with a face like lightning, and with a voice like the voice of a multitude. "Then said he unto me, Fear not, Daniel; for from the first day that thou didst set thy heart to understand, and to chasten thyself before thy God, thy words were heard, and I am come for thy words. But the Prince of the kingdom of Persia withstood me one and twenty days: but, lo, Michael, one of the chief princes, came to help me; and I remained there with the kings of Persia. Now I am come to make thee understand what shall befall thy people in the latter days: for yet the vision is for many days."

At the time of this vision, and with a view to it, Daniel had been abstaining from flesh and wine for three weeks. When the vision occurred, the men who were present saw nothing, but they felt what made them quake and run away. Daniel himself lost all his strength, and lay on the ground in what is called a deep sleep. But the sleep was a state in which he could hear and speak and remember. His body was asleep in all its senses, probably; while his spirit was awake, and therefore conscious. For a few minutes, perhaps, and by an experience like the beginning of death, Daniel was in a state in which he could talk with angels, like one of themselves, and see them with the eye of his immortal spirit, and hear them with his inward spiritual ear.

Pneumatology may not be able at present, to explain every word which an angel may have spoken on earth, nor to disclose the higher mysteries of the spiritual world, nor to make us understand what exactly was meant as to angelic superintendence, where it was said to Daniel in the vision, "I will show thee that which is noted in the scripture of truth. And there is none that holdeth with me in these things, but Michael, your prince." But pneumatology can suggest the manner by which Daniel was able to talk with "one like the appearance of a man"; and it can adduce classical narratives and monastic annals, and medical experience, and the facts of animal magnetism, to illustrate from the mortal side what that deep sleep was, by which there were spirits about him, as he "was by the side of the great river, which is Hiddekel."

The New Testament presupposes the pneumatology of the Old Testament; and there can never be a right understanding of the New Testament, until for faculties, susceptibilities, and hopes, the human soul is thought of, agreeably to that opinion of it, which was held in common by Jesus and his first disciples, and along with them, by St. Paul, as he wrote his epistles. There are Christians who philosophically are materialists, and who hold that man is only organized matter, and that indeed the word soul, as it is used in the Scriptures, is a synonyme for a human body. And there are spiritualists who are strongly opposed to these materialistic Christians; yet for whom the soul is in the body, but like a pip in the core of an apple. Joseph Priestley was a materialist; yet his dogma as to the constitution of human nature would include in its sphere all the spiritualism worthy of being mentioned, of more than half of his opponents. It is a common experience, and a common confession, with laymen of clear, discriminating minds, and especially if they have been legally trained, that they can read the Scriptures readily and well, for all the ends of piety and morals ; but that continually at words and points of great interest, perception seems to fail them. And that failure is for want of pneumatology.

There is to be read, " The word of the Lord, that came unto Hosea, the son of Beeri." An intelligent reader, with such earnestness as has availed him in commerce, or with such courage as has sustained him in deep investigations, feels rightly, that it might be a half of the worth of the message to know how it came, and was apprehended as being divine. A rationalist may tell him that the word of the Lord is a figure of speech, and a bishop may advise him to trust the words blindly. But as a sensible layman, even though unable to see any better than his advisers, he will know them both, for blind leaders of the blind, certain of falling into a ditch. Whereas a man, who knows when it is dark about him, and who also believes in light and in its coming, will some time, with patience, find himself in the porch of that temple of truth, where the Lord is the nearer for being called upon ; and wherein are ways which are not as the ways of men ; and from the steps of which once, " holy men of God spake as they were moved by the Holy Ghost " ; and withinside of which, in some coming age, according to the prophets, men even yet " shall be all taught of God.".

There is a pneumatology implied in the Scriptures,

however latent it may be in this materialistic age; and it is of the utmost importance. What would the epistles of Paul be, without the Old Testament being to be known of? And the Old Testament again cannot be fully understood apart from the knowledge which it presupposes as to its earliest readers; and which, indeed, was a pneumatology according to which false gods might be actual beings, and as an effect of which men were predisposed to believe in the supernatural or the spiritually wonderful, rather than to feel, as many men boast of themselves, at present, "I would not believe it, even if I saw it; no, not I!"

Of this science of the soul, the Catholic Church has always had something, while Protestants have never held anything definitely and unanimously. And therefore as fronting the Pope, always Protestants have been a discordant host. And among them all, in these latter days, the most dissonant have been people eminent for science, or divines with a predilection for it, and who have been persons acted upon in a way, which Paul knew of, when "the world by wisdom knew not God."

Science, or information about the ways of God in matter, or with bees and elephants, is at the most but a mere hint as to the power, and intelligence, and will, and intentions of Him who, from outside of nature, and from above it all, proclaims as to souls held in it, at school, "Behold, all souls are mine: as the soul of the father, so also the soul of the son is mine." And unsophisticated souls, as they look upwards, know and feel themselves to be endowed and to be distinguished by faculties, which worms and fishes, and birds and beasts have not. Men live inside of nature, as it is called, as moles and butterflies, and eagles and lions do. But there is not a very fool of civilization, nor an aboriginal savage anywhere, but by the ongoings of his thought is evidence as to a Providence higher in order, and farther reaching as to its purposes, than what even the elephant can be subject to.

And yet as to what God may be meaning with the soul of man, the soul itself is often almost the last witness to be examined. From science, as it anatomizes the human body, theology learns that God is wonderful at the adaptation of means to ends : but theology just at present very seldom asks of pneumatology what the human soul may have been disclosing of its nature, adaptation or correspondences. The theology of the day knows disproportionately much about the Dead Sea, and ancient sites, and as to mint, anise, and cummin, and tithes in the Holy Land ; but it is at fault as to "the first principles of the oracles of God."

A man may be of a name, illustrated in many ways, and through many generations, and at the battles of Bannockburn, and Evesham, and on the field near Hastings. But even though also the man could derive his descent from an age anterior to the Tower of Babel, and even directly from Tubal-cain, what would it all be for glory, in comparison with what probably he would be disabled from feeling by ancestral pride, and that is, the actual height of his descent ! For fleshly parentage is but the channel, through which the universe itself gives birth to human beings endowed with feelings, by which every man is akin to every spirit, in the image of God, everywhere, irrespectively of time and solar systems; and by which also he is blest with faculties, which will manifest themselves afresh to all eternity, as he passes from world to world, or ascends the heavens, one above another.

The preceding sentiment is worth more than a dukedom to the man who can make it his own. But nearly everybody fails of it more or less, and just as the Gospel is failed of, and merely because of "the lust of the eye and the pride of life."

And the theology of the present day is characterized by a similar externality of view. And thus it is that pneumatology or the experience of men, as to the soul, through thousands of years, is what is utterly unknown in many schools of divinity, though actually it may be called the grammar of revelation. Also, commonly persons read the Bible, being ignorant as to the difference between soul and body, and as to what anciently was understood and believed, as to spirit. And even persons of mental training will talk about the spirit as though it were a religious word for the body, and something very simple and familiar. And yet some of these same persons would be very careful as to thinking about an oyster, or how they gave an opinion about the habits and connections of a beetle.

The degradation of sentiment alluded to above is a thing of the last hundred years, and mainly of even the last fifty. For, before that time, the word spirit meant more, religiously, than it now does; and it was more nearly akin to revelation and miracles than it is now thought to be.

It has already been remarked that the best thinkers of the Christian Church have recognized persons of different ages and places as being prophets who were neither of the seed of Abraham nor of the Christian name. Capacity for prophecy is of human nature; while the inspiration itself may be of extra-natural origin.

Christianity and heathenism were in direct, daily controversy, when it was held in the Church, that the philosophy of Plato was the long dawn that preceded the rise of the sun of righteousness. But how different is this opinion from the jealousy of everything spiritual, outside of the Bible, which is so common with Christians to-day!

It has often been a great shock to people, when they have heard, for the first time, that one or two of the moral precepts of Christ had been anticipated by classical writers. As though eighteen hundred years ago it had been possible for Jesus Christ or for an angel from heaven, to have said anything absolutely new as to mere morality. And so there have been persons who have felt as though Christianity were scandalized because Matthew the publican is found not to have written as good Greek as Thucydides, the historian of the Peloponnesian war, and because the style of St. Paul in his epistles is not faultlessly classical. But what says Paul himself as to his language? "Now we have received not the spirit of the world, but the Spirit which is of God; that we might know the things that are freely given to us of God. Which things also we speak, not in the words which man's wisdom teacheth, but which the Holy Ghost teacheth; comparing spiritual things with spiritual." Why did not Paul pick and choose his words for himself? Because he was not always merely himself, when he wrote, and did not wish to be; and because to an argument, of his own apparently, or possibly, he could add, "And I think that I have the Spirit of God."

Some persons suppose that the preceding words are merely Paul's Jewish way of hoping that he was a good man, and therefore entitled to give advice. Than which a more violent misunderstanding of words could not well be, if Paul may be interpreted by himself, and by the tone and purpose of his epistles, or even by his words to Timothy about the world's "sinners, of whom I am chief." For these words of Paul, as to his having the Spirit, are expressive of a pneumatology, presupposed by the Gospel, and in ignorance of which the best lines of Paul's writing fail and fade before the eye of the reader. For it is as being from over and above him that the Spirit is authority for the promises, which are made through him, and as to the communion of saints, to the sense of which Paul would quicken us, and as to the liberty which may be claimed and trusted "where the Spirit of the Lord is."

That the Spirit of God, for inspiration, may operate through human receptiveness, irrespectively of nationality, was an opinion which might well have been held by the readers of Paul's epistles, and even by the ancient Jews generally. In the book of Joshua, Balaam is described as having been a soothsayer. And yet through him was given the grandest prophecy in the Old Testament. And the circumstantial detail connected with that prophecy is what makes it to be its own all-sufficient evidence, for reality, as an historical occurrence, with all such persons as have any right to judge about it. Balaam was famous as a soothsayer, before the Israelites on their journeying came within his sight. Probably he was inspired by the Lord only on that one occasion, when he was confronted with the Lord's people, with a hostile view. Balak, the king of the Moabites, summoned Balaam and said to him, "Behold there is a people come out from Egypt: behold they cover the face of the earth, and they abide over against me. Come now, therefore, I pray thee, curse me this people, for they are too mighty for me." It was Baal against Jehovah. "And it came to pass on the morrow, that Balak took Balaam, and brought him up into the high places of Baal, that thence he might see the utmost part of the people." And probably it was because he was conscious of another kind of inspiration than what had ever come upon him from Baal, that "he went not as at other times to seek for enchantments," or artificial means, by which to fit himself for being spiritually possessed. Balaam was an Ammonite perhaps, or an Edomite, and he was even on one of the high places of Baal, when his spiritual susceptibility was used by the Lord for prophecy.

And if, "when Jesus was born in Bethlehem of Judea, in the days of Herod the king, behold there came wise men from the east to Jerusalem, saying, Where is he that is born King of the Jews? for we have seen his star in the east, and have come to worship him," it could only have been because of their nature as Magi, having been wrought upon spiritually by the God of Abraham, and Isaac, and Jacob, and Moses, David, Isaiah, and Daniel. The star by which they were guided would seem to have been visible only to them, and therefore to them only "in the spirit." On finding "the young child with Mary his mother," at the end of their long journey, "they presented unto him gifts, gold and frankincense and myrrh." And so through that act of theirs was manifested that from the best of the Gentiles, as well as with the Jews, "the testimony of Jesus is the spirit of prophecy."

Plato was for the Greeks what Moses was for the Jews, and was a schoolmaster to prepare men for Christ. This was a Christian opinion in the early days of the Church, and while still Greek meant Gentile. In this sentiment, a belief is implied in spiritual susceptibility, as being an endowment of the soul. And the name of Plato is but the greatest, on a long shining list of natural saints. For, always and everywhere, whether in vile neighborhoods or amidst the splendid temples and monuments of paganism, the simple, longing, unperverted soul does, by its spiritual susceptibility, become of itself a temple of the Holy Ghost, and an oracle for consultation; and has in it an odor of sweet thoughts like grateful frankincense, and strains of sweet music, as though from angelic choirs, high up in heaven.

That the Holy Spirit does not inform men as to natural history, nor correct them as to bad logic, is not inconsistent with the certainty of its effects as to enlightenment and faith. Gregory Thaumaturgus said as to Origen, his master, that he had received from God a large share of the greatest of all gifts, that of interpreting the words of God to men, and of understanding the things of God, as if God himself were speaking. Whatever the special application to Origen may be of these words, they yet illustrate the philosophy of early Christian belief.

Before a man can take, he must have a hand to open and to stretch forth. And for being quickened by the Spirit, a man must be, not a statue in marble, but a living, suffering, craving soul. And it is only as he craves and covets earnestly, that the best gifts can either be attracted to him or be received. The gifts of the Spirit presuppose spiritual receptiveness.

And the variety of the gifts of the Spirit, as they are enumerated by St. Paul, is presupposed the variety of the ways, in which men may be quickened, taught, and endowed from above. It is probable that of all the myriads of millions of human beings, that there are no two souls alike, any more than two faces are. And therefore probably with the Spirit, no two souls quicken in exactly the same manner, or are endowed to precisely the same purpose. The young man through it may see visions, and the old man by it may dream dreams. One man is helped by it, as to infirmities, and another as to prayer. One man abounds in hope through the Holy Ghost; and another man, through the Spirit, is encouraged to wait for the hope of righteousness by faith. By the Spirit of God in his words, one man may cast out devils, without knowing of it, while another man sheds abroad the love of God. "To one is given, by the Spirit, the word of wisdom; to another the word of knowledge, by the same Spirit; to another faith, by the same Spirit; to another the gift of healing, by the same Spirit; to another the working of miracles; to another prophecy; to another discerning of spirits; to another divers kinds of tongues; to another the interpretation of tongues; but all these worketh that one and the selfsame Spirit, dividing to every man severally as he will." And not only as to manifestation may the Spirit differ in different men; but more broadly and more distinctly still, must it differ from one age to another, in the Church. And even it may happen, that a man may have been so instructed about the Spirit, as to think of it mainly for some of its more noticeable manifestations, and as being sharpness in the sword of the Lord, or inspiration in psalms and high thought, or as being a baptism of fire; and so may fear that he may be a stranger to it, while yet himself he is actually walking in it.

And indeed it is as men "walk in the Spirit" that chiefly it is blessedness. For the more marvellous manifestations of the Spirit, which are the exceptional experiences of individuals, are really for the good of all; just as Peter argues that "no prophecy of the Scripture is of any private interpretation."

One man in a generation may be so rapt in spirit, as almost to have his soul thrill to the joy, which there is in heaven, when some fresh word of the Lord is evolved; or he may be so sensitive through the Spirit, as to have some dim sense of angels on the wing, and so appear to have a prophetic instinct as to critical events foreordained of God. Or with being lifted up, in spirit, and breathing, for an instant, what is more than mortal air, a man may have a thought grander than the tone of ordinary thinking, and what may make him famous among his fellow-mortals. But it is scarcely possible for a person to have transcendent experiences, without incurring some earthly disruption.

Just as Paul found, after the visions, in which he was called and qualified to be an apostle, that there was lodged with him a life-long trouble, lest he "should be exalted above measure through the abundance of the revelations." And a man has found himself become like a stranger among his kindred and his acquaintance simply from having been sublimed by a prayer, of agony and faith combined.

The soul of man is susceptible of the Holy Ghost. It is not born with the Spirit, but only with a nature fitted for its coming. The apostle Paul asks, "Know ye not that ye are the temple of God, and that the Spirit of God dwelleth in you?" And it may be, that it is through the same susceptibility of spirit, that one man receives the Holy Ghost, and another man "drinketh iniquity like water." As a young man with his face in the right direction, Saul had the Spirit of God come upon him. Thirty years afterwards, with his face set wilfully wrong, "the Spirit of the Lord departed from Saul, and an evil spirit from the Lord troubled him." And probably the same spiritual susceptibility, by which he had been receptive of the Spirit of the Lord was the channel by which "the evil spirit," sent on its errand, got at him. That spiritual susceptibility, for which perhaps Judas was chosen as one of the twelve, and through which perhaps he received "power and authority over all devils and to cure diseases," was, in all probability, the same susceptivity, through which diabolically it was "put into the heart of Judas Iscariot, Simon's son, to betray him." Demoniacal possession as the Jews knew of it, and as it is known of to-day, in many parts of the world, illustrates human nature, as to its susceptibilities spiritually, and as to its exposure to dangerous, disembodied agencies, and invisible forces. But from the Scriptures, it might seem, as though in the age of Jesus Christ that that spiritual susceptivity, by which the "spirit of an unclean devil" could get entrance into the temple of a human soul, was actually what, with a better man, would have been receptiveness of the Holy Ghost. This spiritual susceptibility is by nature; though one man may perhaps have more of it, than another; just as one man is more tender in heart, or poetic in thought, than another. But perhaps by prayer and other means, it is what a man can get quickened and purified for himself, more surely than he can hope as to the enlargement of any other faculty of his nature.

Let this susceptibility of spiritual influence be called magnetic, if it may thereby seem to be more credible. For man is organized magnetism, as certainly as also organically, he is flesh and blood. A skeleton is human, but senseless. A skeleton properly clothed with flesh and blood is a living creature, with adaptations, by which it is fitted to a world of earth, air, and water, light, heat, and fruits. But as a magnetic man in a magnetic world, I am a creature of affinities and possibilities innumerable. Of many and of most of them, I may have only a faint and scarcely noticeable experience. But whatever anybody has ever felt or seen or known, is testimony as to my nature. Also I am alive with odyle, and by the odic force I am connected with things unknown on the earth and under it.

For indeed man is not born of flesh and blood

merely, nor of two parents simply, but of the universe, both material and immaterial, and with an aptitude, which high angels will respond to hereafter, and with a susceptibility as to spiritual influences of various kinds, which is none the less real because often it is very weak, and because, whether it is seated "in the body or out of the body," not every one can tell.

By means of electricity, it is possible for a person in Boston, simultaneously almost, to be connected, as to intelligence, with persons, in every city in North America, and perhaps in Europe. And that it is possible for one mind to act upon another, without any intervening agency, and from a long distance, is an established fact of pneumatology; and it has been demonstrated artificially, by mesmerism, many hundreds of times. How often and continually mothers are impressed as to critical events concerning their absent children! And how frequently instances occur, in which the dying believe that they see spirits, and hear unearthly music! Also how numerous, even within the last few years, have been the cases, which have been published of strange and irresistible impulses, which proved afterwards to have been prophetic and guardian!

When all the varieties of information which exist as to the human body are collected, science would seem to hint, that possibly in the eyes of an angel, man as a mortal may seem like a spirit aglow with all the colors of the rainbow, though with just enough materiality about him, to keep him at school inside of the walls of nature.

Doubt about miracles as not perhaps being natural

to man! But really even bread is not more so! Miracles — those of the Scriptures, and, as being nearer to our own times, those of the New Testament especially — miracles are true to human nature. But human nature is not like the make of a cast-iron machine working by rule.

And indeed we human beings as children of the universe, and heirs of God, have in us, by birth, a capacity for being born again, and germs also of marvels, which will be opening to all eternity. And thus, too, we find ourselves endowed with some powers and affinities, which appertain especially to a world which is to come; but which yet may manifest themselves faintly and fitfully through individuals, in this present world, and so hint for us all, as by flashes of lightning, that, because of the flesh, life at its brightest, is what "now, we see as through a glass darkly."

Such facts as have been supposed to be supernatural, of the nature of dreams, apparitions, and strange impressions and impulses, and which have happened and been published, within the last twenty years; and such narratives of a mesmeric character as are to be found in the Zoist, — were these things to be gathered, examined, and collated, with as much care as has been given to the lives and classification of butterflies, and with as much acuteness as what caught the lightning in its ways, there would result a pneumatology, by which the Scriptures would be illuminated for darkling readers; and by which men would believe in the immortality of the soul, as they never can, until they have some understanding about the soul itself, and discerningly "have tasted the good word of God, and the powers of the world to come."

But some persons perhaps will exclaim, "Mesmerism! What has that to do with the Scriptures? A thing of the last century!" It is, however, an old thing. And of its connection with the Old Testament, there is this to be read. Naaman from Syria had been directed, for a cure, as to leprosy, by Elisha the prophet, to wash himself in the Jordan, seven times. But he would seem to have felt himself aggrieved by the simplicity of the remedy. "Naaman was wroth, and went away, and said, Behold, I thought he would surely come out to me, and stand and call on the name of the Lord his God, and strike his hand over the place, and recover the leper." That the prophet would move his hand up and down, over the diseased part of his body, was what was expected by Naaman according to a correct translation of his words. And apparently it was a mode of healing, which the Syrian knew of, before his resort to Elisha. And it is certain, that mesmeric practice is to be seen sculptured on ancient monuments in Egypt.

Mesmerism is not the Gospel, and God be thanked that it is not, and that there is come to us "the glorious gospel of the blessed God." But mesmerism is more of a gospel than the doctrine of those who believe in spirits and angels, only as pious words in the Bible, and who know of Christianity, in the letter merely, and as though apart from "the everlasting spirit," and who fancy that there can be faith in Jesus as the Christ, with those who cannot conceive of the possibility of a prophet, in the way in which he was thought of, by the Jews of the Old Testament.

It was one of the parables of Jesus, that "The kingdom of heaven is like unto leaven, which a woman took and hid in three measures of meal, till the whole was leavened." But very unlike the spirit of this parable, is the mental state of some believers to-day, who confess their jealousy of studies, through which any word or incident of the Scriptures, might have its apparent peculiarity diminished. O they of little faith! Would Jesus Christ himself be less important, by having his words fulfilled, "Verily, verily, I say unto you, he that believeth on me, the works that I do, shall he do also; and greater works than these shall he do, because I go unto the Father"? Do the heavens declare the glory of God the less, because now more is known of them, than what David sung of by inspiration? Is man's make any the less fearfully and wonderfully felt, because of the discovery of the circulation of the blood?

That some sentences in the Lord's prayer are older than Jesus himself has been urged as a fact derogatory to Christianity. But it might as well be said in derogation of Jesus, that he made use of common words as well as the common sentiments of his day; and that he was furnished with parables by such common objects as a mustard-plant, a sower going forth to sow, a net that was cast into the sea, and a woman with ten pieces of silver.

There are persons who feel as though ghost-stories infringed on the Scriptures, as to the revelation of another world. And there have been persons who have held that there never was any knowledge of a future life, till the preaching and the resurrection of Jesus Christ. Yet it is plain, from the four Gospels, that Jesus did not address men as apes and gorillas, but as believers in a world to come. Jesus did not invent the words "spirit" and "soul," "heaven" and "hell." And when he first used them, they were very old words, and meant conceptions that were ancient. Actually there are theological writers at this present time who have less knowledge as to the soul than what was taken for granted by Paul with the heathen, and by Jesus with the Jews. In the Middle Ages, and in the sixteenth and seventeenth centuries, theology vindicated for the service of the Church, facts such as are common in the records of animal magnetism. But to-day, animal magnetism is commonly the terror of theologians. Yet men will never be religiously what they ought to be, in the light of these latter days, nor be Christians with Paul's courage, till it shall be understood that pneumatology is a handmaid in the household of faith, and not a suspicious vagabond about the temple, who will not be driven away.

"The word which God sent unto the children of Israel, preaching peace by Jesus Christ," is anything but what ought to be isolated from science, and from the facts of human experience, as they accrue. For, as to the earth, it is as true to-day, for eyes that can see, as it was in the year when King Uzziah died, and when Isaiah saw the seraphims; and when "one cried unto another, and said, Holy, holy, holy is the Lord of hosts; the whole earth is full of his glory!"

Fearfulness for the Gospel, as to geology, or animal magnetism, or the publication of the Talmud, or as to the gates of hell, is utterly uncongenial with "the eternal Spirit," and inconsistent with any experience of it.

Who and what, then, is Jesus Christ? He is "Jesus

Christ our Lord, which was made of the seed of David according to the flesh; and declared to be the Son of God with power, according to the spirit of holiness, by the resurrection from the dead." But for us in this age, individually, what is he? He "is the Lord from heaven"; he is "a quickening spirit." And the Holy Spirit, the Comforter, which comes of him, is what my nature has a sense for; and it is also what my nature has groaned for, and travailed in pain, to have come. And this spiritual susceptibility which I have, by creation, not only argues my want, but as under God, foretells also, as to itself, that it will certainly be met from above. "Blessed are they which do hunger and thirst after righteousness: for they shall be filled." And today, as in the first days of the gospel, by God certainly "the Holy Ghost is given to them that obey" Christ. And therefore through that susceptibility to spiritual influence, which is natural to me, by sympathizing with Christ Jesus as a man, in his heavenward aspirations, I may trustfully expect the Holy Ghost, and be certain of it, even though through me, it may make no "manifestation" of those special "gifts," which though vouchsafed to individuals, yet are for "every man to profit withal."

The Spirit of God may be intimately mine, and so as even possibly to be cunning in the hand for workmanship, as it was with Bezaleel. It may be like a part of myself, and as intimately so, at least, as the strength which results from food. But yet it is what is separate from me; and it is what may be quenched in me. David prays to God, "Cast me not away from thy presence; and take not thy Holy Spirit from me."

And Paul writes to the Ephesians, "Grieve not the Holy Spirit of God, whereby ye are sealed unto the day of redemption." And to the Thessalonians he writes, "Quench not the Spirit." The Holy Spirit is part of me; it is what I can think by: it is what will inform my prayers for me; it is joy in me, and it is as though I myself were it, as long as I myself am right. But with vanity or wrong-doing, it fails me, just as his strength fails a fainting man. The Holy Spirit was in me, like the inspiration of my understanding; it was the life of my higher life; it was the soul of my better soul; and it was the holiness of my spirit. And suddenly with sin, it is gone; and my most familiar connection with heaven is stopped, And though I may not have been certain, as to whether I ever did have the Spirit, yet with the loss of it by sin, I know well what I have been parted from.

A man may never have it but once; and indeed he cannot have it more than once, with the same effect — that strange experience of grieving the Holy Spirit, with a sense of revelation afterwards. For when the Spirit is withdrawn, or fails from a person who has been walking in it, his joy stops, and his prayers grow dry and unbelieving. And it is like a revelation by darkness, what he feels, at finding himself to be left to himself, and cut off from heaven, and from that Holy Spirit, which, among mortals, is like its outer sphere.

In all this experience as to the Holy Spirit there is, what essentially is meant by the word, miracle, for there is the experience of extraordinary, extra-natural, and and therefore occasional forces. "Speak, Lord, for thy servant heareth," said the child Samuel by the advice of Eli, the prophet, in the dark, in the temple, and before he yet knew the word of the Lord. And whatever it may be in high heaven, still among us mortals, every word and influence not from the Lord only, but from withinside of the spiritual world, from any one, is of the nature of a miracle.

Every man is a creature of miraculous possibilities. And by comparison with the uniformity of nature, there are thousands of human beings, at this day, whose lives are of a miraculous character, because of preternatural influences. Miracle! All human intercourse with the world invisible, whether with spirit, or angels, or with God Most High, must necessarily flash with "signs and wonders," as being itself miraculous.

In the Iliad of Homer there is the saying, "The dream is from Jove." And Cicero has the sentiment that "Dreams are the natural oracle." Let these two quotations represent almost two thousand passages, which might easily be cited from ancient authors, as to the philosophy and authority of dreams, and as to the supernatural communications, of which they have been believed to be the channel. But by dreams, of course, are not meant mental movements started by an uneasy stomach or any other accidental cause, nor even such wanderings of the mind in sleep, as idleness can have, when much at its ease, and wide awake. The Greeks and Romans knew very well, that dreams have not all the same origin. And men like Pausanias, and the students of Plato, were little likely to attribute the absurdities of a crude stomach to a heavenly origin.

That "dreams are the natural oracle" is a sentiment which involves the philosophy of revelation. For, it asserts the existence in man, of a susceptibility to the influences of the spiritual world. And that sentiment did not originate in any such nonsense about dreams, as a modern materialist would suppose, but in experiences and traditions, as respectable as the names of Socrates and Plato, as wise as ancient Greece, and broader even than the Roman empire.

But here some one will ask, in the special way of the modern unbeliever, "If it be true that dreams are the natural oracle, why do not I have good dreams? For I am as good as another, certainly." But now it is simply for the same reason, as that for which every man is not a born archangel, nor even a saint of the earth. To justify the sentiment from Cicero, it is enough that one man in a million should have what is called "a remarkable dream." Just as one true poet in an age is enough for enabling men to feel themselves aright, and to know of a glory in the world, surpassing that of Mammon, and an interest, compared with which battles and revolutions are but bubbles.

In the Scriptures, and especially the more ancient, and as though more particularly connected with the primitive, unsophisticated nature of man, dreams or visions in dreams were not uncommon experiences, whence men might infer themselves to be within spiritual reach. The sentiment in Cicero as to oracular dreams, pagan though it be, coincides with what is said in the book of Job by Elihu, "For God speaketh once, yea, twice, yet man perceiveth it not. In a dream, in a vision of the night, when deep sleep falleth upon men, in slumberings upon the bed, then he openeth the ears of men and sealeth their instruction, that he may withdraw man from his purpose and hide pride from man." Spiritual susceptibility during sleep, or capacity for visions like dreams while asleep, would seem to have constituted a prophet. From the pillar of cloud at the door of the tabernacle the Lord said, "Hear now my words: If there be a prophet among you, I the Lord will make myself known unto him in a vision, and will speak unto him in a dream."

But the susceptibility to spiritual influence through which a man in his sleep may have had his soul addressed by angels or spirits, though it may have been a peculiarity with him for its greatness, was yet certainly not so for its nature. It is the action of the Spirit and that susceptibility which all men have, in a greater or less degree, which is referred to in the prophecies of Joel. "And ye shall know that I am in the midst of Israel, and that I am the Lord your God, and none else; and my people shall never be ashamed. And it shall come to pass afterward that I will pour out my Spirit upon all flesh: and your sons and your daughters shall prophesy; your old men shall dream dreams, your young men shall see visions: and also upon the servants and upon the handmaids in those days will I pour out my Spirit." Let there be some change which shall refine the flesh of my body; or let me experience all that is meant by being born again; or let my faculties open heavenwards by the intensity of my faith; or let me be within reach of some Pentecostal outpouring of the Spirit; and I should then know of myself, how it was that "God came to Abimelech in a dream by night"; and how true were the words of Jacob about himself, "The angel of God spake unto me in a dream, saying, Jacob: and I said, Here am I"; and how it was as natural as man talking with man, when Jesus Christ in heaven talked with the spirit of Paul, while his body was asleep in a house hard by the synagogue in Corinth. "Then spake the Lord to Paul in the night by a vision, Be not afraid, but speak, and hold not thy peace; for I am with thee, and no man shall set on thee to hurt thee; for I have much people in this city."

The manner in which Paul was waked up in spirit, while his body was asleep, is a way which is possible with all men, however improbable it may be, that there should ever be common experience of it. And it is of our nature, that in deep sleep possibly our ears might be opened, as Elihu said, and instruction be infused into us. And when Pharaoh and Nebuchadnezzar were inspired with dreams, which were concurrent with Divine Providence, it was through their natural susceptibility to spiritual influence, and not through such an operation of Almightiness, as would be necessary for making a statue of Hercules dream and remember.

The dream was described by Cicero as being a natural oracle, in contradistinction to other oracles, which were got from gods and demons by various artificial means. At Delphi, they were obtained through a woman, who was supposed to be entranced by Apollo; at Lebadea, after certain ceremonies of purification, the oracle was got in the dark cave of Trophonius, sometimes from a voice there, and sometimes by other means. In Greece, there was a cave, which Pausanias saw by the wayside, in which was a statue with a table before it, and at which oracles were to be obtained by the throwing of dice. And there was a temple in Egypt, at which oracles were got by asking questions before a wooden image, which was thought to answer by shaking its arms when possessed by a demon.

To all the preceding ways of obtaining oracles the Jew would have been opposed. He would have acknowledged them as being real, probably; but he would have repeated to himself the commandment, "I am the Lord thy God which have brought thee out of the land of Egypt, out of the house of bondage. Thou shalt have no other gods before me." But the Jew would have joined with Cicero, as to his sentiment about the dream-faculty, and would have acknowledged it, for a part of the primitive religion, which was before Abraham was.

As to dreams, which have been vision-like for veracity, there is an allowance to be made, according to the doctrine of chances, for cases of mere coincidence. But after everything has been said and allowed for, it would seem as though in every country there may always have been occurring dreams of an extraordinary nature, enough, fairly considered, to make everybody feel himself to be a creature of spiritual faculty, and spiritually connected.

But at this point there are persons who would exclaim together, as one man, "Dreams! and meant seriously too! Dreams! as though there ever could be anything in a dream! It is too ridiculous!" But is Plato then ridiculous; or is Socrates? Is Plutarch ridiculous; or are the philosophers and heroes of whom he is the biographer, mostly ridiculous? Ridicule! was Cicero a subject for it; or of the two Plinys, was either the elder or the younger; or was Galen? And can a subject be ridiculous, whereon as to belief, along with the foregoing great names, nearly and probably, all the Fathers of the Church coincide, from Polycarp to St. Augustine? And whether intended or not, it cannot but be a laugh of pitiable inanity, which happens to be turned simultaneously against Cardan and Petrarch; against the Emperor Theodosius and the Emperor Charles the Fifth of Spain; against Francis Bacon and Halley the astronomer; against Sir Christopher Wren and Sir Roger L'Estrange; against Defoe and —

But enough of this! For there is no man but must feel abashed, when actually he finds himself to be lightly laughing in the grand awful face of antiquity, and with the fathers, martyrs, and doctors of the Church against him.

But indeed the man, who is the grandchild of the last century, and the child of this, is almost necessarily a person of contradictory notions. And so it often happens that a person will say philosophically what, if it were true, would be ruinous of the religious belief, which he holds even fervently. And that is, just as there have been many divines, who with pleading for the Church, have made void the Gospel.

Nor, should this argument seem to be novel, is it therefore necessarily the less trustworthy. For, even as to his bodily constitution, man in these latter days is continually discovering something new, and by which he finds his health, or temporal salvation, to be largely dependent on laws, of which Abraham knew nothing, nor Julius Cæsar, nor yet Martin Luther. The primary facts of life, as connected with his skin and lungs, man is but just now learning; and so it may well be supposed, that, as connected with his spiritual nature, there may be common things, of which the full significance has not yet been taken.

A dream of much particularity which comes true,—an oracular dream argues not only that man can have dreams which come true, but that he can dream under influence, and from spiritual connection of some kind. And if one man can dream in that way, so perhaps in that way may another be capable of inspiration, even while wide awake. That kind of dream, which Cicero calls the natural oracle, is presumptive proof as to the actuality of revelation, and as to the reality of those spiritual faculties in man which Christianity presupposes.

There have been some eight or ten dreams, which have been had and published in this neighborhood, during the last twenty years, which, for an earnest thinker, would be more valuable than the whole of some metaphysical libraries. Because one fact accruing from nature is better than all the argument which is inconsistent with it, however ingenious and laborious it may be.

What is properly the dream-faculty may be regarded as the primitive germ of revelation. It is also a simple and good proof that man is spiritually connected; and that therefore also he himself may probably be a spirit.

Actually and with full consciousness to feel himself to be a living soul, by any trial, test, or experience, within the range of his own understanding, is the hunger and thirst of myriads; though also it is a craving, which is as dull as despair itself. And all that merely primitive want might for many a man be satisfied by a dream, which has been had by some poor chastened widow, in his neighborhood, anxious about her absent son; only that theology has got so far away from common life, that it would wish to scout the smallest possible miracle of the present day, for fear of being challenged by science, in the names of uniformity and law. But actually, though those words are good enough for a lecture-room, they are altogether inadequate for what Christians ought to be ready to maintain in the Church.

How many persons there are who sit in church, only to feel as though the darkness about them were growing more visible! How many men of ability there are, who have the gospel sound to them like an unknown tongue! Said the voice which was heard by St. John when he was in the Spirit, "He that hath an ear, let him hear what the Spirit saith unto the churches." But how can he well hear to-day, who cannot well conceive how the Spirit could ever have spoken? Persons whose ways of thinking have been almost altogether materialized, — how should they understand the things of the Spirit? "The God of the spirits of all flesh," — how possibly can they pray to him in the fulness of belief, who think that they themselves, perhaps, are flesh only?

Yet if men were willing to be taught by it, a dream which is a dream in Cicero's sense of the word, or in that of the Bible, would be enough for any ordinary degree of doubt as to the spiritual world. But the dread of acknowledging in any way what science might perhaps challenge for a miracle and a violation of law, is the nightmare of theology at this time. However, it is what is nothing more than a nightmare; and it will probably soon be over.

THE SPIRIT AND THE OLD TESTAMENT.

THE Scriptures are the history of a particular people, or line and succession of persons, as they were acted upon by the Spirit of God.

When everything was nothing, and while as yet darkness was on the face of the deep, it was the beginning when "the Spirit of God moved upon the face of the waters." Also, "by his Spirit he hath garnished the heavens." And said the Psalmist, as he sang in view of both Lebanon and the sea, "Thou sendest forth thy spirit, they are created," — the stork to house herself in the fir-tree, the fowls of heaven to sing in the branches, the young lions to roar after their prey, the wild asses with their instinct for the springs among the hills, grass as it grows for the cattle, and herbs for the service of man. And not these only, even though along with the sea and leviathan! For also "the Spirit of God hath made me, and the breath of the Almighty hath given me life."

But there is another and higher sense of the phrase "Spirit of God" than that use of it. The Spirit of God created man, as it made the elephant, and it might have maintained man as man, at a certain uniformity of intelligence and character, just as, for thousands of years, it has perpetuated nature in elephants. As the Holy Ghost, the Spirit of God finds in man a susceptibility which the elephant has not. And it is this spiritual susceptibility which is the great, grand distinction of man.

Men are the creatures of God, as the elephant and the lion are, and as the dove and the provident, skilful beaver. But the elephant lives from God more largely than the dove; and man, as a biped with his head erect, lives from God more fully than the elephant. But the truth as to man is more than that; for he does not merely live and move like a superior elephant, but also he has and derives his being like a child of God. In the great sphere of life of which God is the fulness, man lives in God, and yet in some way as though detached from him. And it is through that way, and because of it, that man is specially dear to God, and of more value than many sparrows; as being not only a creature of instinct, but also a child capable of instruction, and a soul susceptible of inspiration; and as being possibly a son, for companionship with him, to all eternity, through the Holy Ghost. And the Scriptures illustrate this relation, as it exists and always has existed between God and man.

By the gospel, human beings are invited to become sons and daughters of the Most High. But often persons avert their faces from God, and turn and look along with the people, as to whom, once Jesus said, "Ye are of your father, the devil." And it is only just as we believe in its being possible for us to become the children of God, that the Bible belongs to us, as a thing of any meaning.

In the Scriptures, the special action of the Spirit of God on the soul is called "the word of God." Sometimes it is so called, when it is simply a Divine message to an individual; and sometimes it is so called when it is addressed to a nation; and it is also used for that expressiveness of the Divine will, which was the act of Creation; as when Peter writes "that by the word of God the heavens were of old, and the earth standing out of the water, and in the water."

"The word of the Lord" is a special completed act of "the Spirit of the Lord"; and always it is inspiration, as unto the formless, void world for creation; or into the consciousness of a prophet, for a communication; or into the mind of a man, like David, for the beauty of a psalm. And in the personality of Jesus, the word was so completely incarnated, as that himself Jesus became "the word" itself. "And the Word was made flesh and dwelt among us (and we beheld his glory, the glory as of the only-begotten of the Father), full of grace and truth."

Sometimes the word of the Lord was a voice in the ear of a prophet; and sometimes it was a picture before the eye of his mind; and sometimes it was the appearance of an angel. And there are two or three other ways, by which the word of the Lord was given, which are mentioned in the Old Testament, though obscurely, and which perhaps were never commonly used.

What books have been written and what nonsense has been talked about the Jewish theocracy! It has been supposed to have been the government of a priesthood, which is exactly what it was not. And it has been supposed to have been mainly and characteristically the sacerdotal ministration of a written law, which also it was not. Prophets were the theocracy, — men who could even denounce the priesthood, and who were not necessarily even Levites. They were men of God, and not merely men of the temple of God.

As was said to the Jews in the wilderness of Sinai, "Hear now my words: If there be a prophet among you, I the Lord will make myself known unto him in a vision, and will speak unto him in a dream." But then it is added as to Moses, "with him will I speak mouth to mouth, even apparently and not in dark speeches." And of how that was, this is an instance. In the wilderness, two men appealed to Moses about a ceremonial difficulty. "And Moses said unto them, Stand still, and I will hear what the Lord will command concerning you." And standing still with the people about him, under the eastern sky, Moses listened for a voice, which nobody else could hear. And that voice he heard spiritually. "And the Lord spake unto Moses, saying, Speak unto the children of Israel, saying, If any man of you or of your posterity shall be unclean by reason of a dead body, or be in a journey afar off, yet he shall keep the passover unto the Lord." Also that precept, as being got and given in that manner, is an instance of theocracy.

And now, how were prophets commissioned, or how did a man know himself to be a prophet? David became a prophet, with being anointed for king; though perhaps his spiritual susceptibility may have been a reason for his being chosen as king. He was fetched into the house from keeping the sheep. "Now he was ruddy, and withal of a beautiful countenance, and goodly to look to. And the Lord said, Arise, anoint him: for this is he. Then Samuel took the horn of oil, and anointed him in the midst of his brethren. And the Spirit of the Lord came upon David from that day forward." Very different from that is the account Jeremiah gives of himself. "The word of the Lord came unto me, saying, Before I formed thee in the belly I knew thee; and before thou camest forth out of the womb I sanctified thee: and I ordained thee a prophet unto the nations. Then said I, Ah, Lord God! behold, I cannot speak; for I am a child. But the Lord said unto me, Say not, I am a child: for thou shalt go to all that I shall send thee, and whatsoever I command thee thou shalt speak. Be not afraid of their faces: for I am with thee to deliver thee, saith the Lord." And very different again from the call of young Jeremiah, the son of Hilkiah, was the experience of the prophet Amos. "Then answered Amos, and said to Amaziah, I was no prophet, neither was I a prophet's son: but I was a herdman, and a gatherer of sycamore fruit: and the Lord took me as I followed the flock, and the Lord said unto me, Go, prophesy unto my people Israel." And when Barak received the commandment of the Lord, in connection with a striking episode in Jewish history, it was through Deborah. And what is to be read about her is like a wonderful little picture. "And Deborah a prophetess, the wife of Lapidoth, she judged Israel at that time. And she dwelt under the palm-tree of Deborah, between Ramah and Beth-el in Mount Ephraim; and the children of Israel came up to her for judgment."

And it would seem also that "the word of the Lord" found its recipients or prophets, quite irrespectively of worldly circumstances. Kings and peasants were alike to it. Solomon was a youthful king when "in Gibeon, the Lord appeared to Solomon in a dream by night: and God said, Ask what I shall give thee." And it was while he was "in all his glory" that "God gave Solomon wisdom and understanding exceeding much, and largeness of heart, even as the sand that is on the sea-shore." And when the Queen of Sheba, having heard of what Solomon had become through "the name of the Lord," journeyed to Jerusalem to try his wisdom, she found him surrounded by pomp and grandeur. But his magnificence was no bar to the attendant power which fed his intellect with wisdom. And as he heard questions she asked, answers like miracles rose in his mind. "And Solomon told her all her questions: there was not anything hid from the king which he told her not." At one time Elijah lived by a brook and was fed by ravens; and at another time he was lodged by a widow whose mind had been miraculously prepared for receiving him. "And when he came to the gate of the city, behold, the widow woman was there gathering of sticks." A priest was always probably far above want, because he was always well provided for, by his birthright. But for the prophet, there was no provision in life, which might be called special; unless indeed that quality might be so called by which nature answers to nature, and persons who are spiritually-minded are drawn towards those who are in any way like themselves, such as prophets, men of genius, and sufferers living by faith. Owing to the kind impulse of a Jewish lady, there is to be read, what is like a sudden distinct glimpse of a prophet moving about. "And it fell on a day that Elisha passed to Shunem, where was a great woman; and she constrained him to eat bread. And so it was, that, as oft as he passed by, he turned in thither to eat bread. And she said unto her husband, Behold, now, I perceive that this is a holy man of God, which passeth by us continually. Let us make a little chamber, I pray thee, on the wall; and let us set for him there a bed, and a table, and a stool, and a candlestick: and it shall be when he cometh to us, that he shall turn in thither. And it fell on a day that he came thither, and he turned into the chamber, and lay there." The prophet was very unlike a priest in his mind, and so he was in his experience, usually, in one way or another. Says St. James, "Take, my brethren, the prophets, who have spoken in the name of the Lord, for an example of suffering affliction, and of patience."

And now what was the position of the prophet socially? He had a right to utter himself, but on certain conditions, which might involve even his life. Ahab the king wanted the word of the Lord from the prophet Micaiah; and was enraged by what he got; notwithstanding that the prophet had said, "As the Lord liveth, what the Lord saith unto me that will I speak." Whereupon a false prophet, a prophet of Baal, probably, who had been flattering the king along with four hundred others, Zedekiah, "went near and smote Micaiah on the cheek, and said, Which way went the Spirit of the Lord from me to speak unto thee? And Micaiah said, Behold, thou shalt see in that day, when thou shalt go into an inner chamber to hide thyself. And the king of Israel said, Take Micaiah, and carry him back unto Amon the governor of the city, and to Joash the king's son, and say, Thus saith the king, Put this fellow in the prison, and feed him with bread of affliction, and with water of affliction, until I come in peace. And Micaiah said, If thou return at all in peace, the Lord hath not spoken by me. And he said, Hearken, O people, every one of you." Then the king went up to Ramoth-Gilead to battle, and never came back; and the prophet with having his prophecy fulfilled, saved his life, according to the law.

And of what the prophet was among the people, for his work, as compared with the priest, there is an illustration in one of the prophecies of Hosea. The priest was the man of ritual, and the prophet was the man of the Spirit. "O Ephraim, what shall I do unto thee? O Judah, what shall I do unto thee? for your goodness is as a morning cloud, and as the early dew it goeth away. Therefore have I hewed them by the prophet; I have slain them by the words of my mouth: and thy judgments were as the light that goeth forth. For I desired mercy, and not sacrifice; and the knowledge of God more than burnt-offerings." And as Christianity becomes, as certainly more and more it will become, a ministration of the Spirit, it will be well to remember and know thoroughly, that the Holy Ghost may probably get itself uttered, not so much through functionaries of the Church, as through those whom the Spirit, for any reason, may find to be approachable; and who perhaps may often seem to be but mere earthen vessels, when compared with honored and honorable personages, arrayed, it may be, in official robes, and invested with the privileges of high places.

But now how was the prophet received? Exactly

as conscience is received to-day; and those who did not want to know of him could ignore him. And those persons, who were actually reached by his words, could do with God in his words, just as they were in the habit of doing with God in the suggestions of their own consciences; they could exclude him, in some way, or else elude him. There had been the grossest wickedness; and with an impulse from the Lord, "Nathan said to David, Thou art the man." And being charged thus and threatened, "David said unto Nathan, I have sinned against the Lord. And Nathan said unto David, The Lord also hath put away thy sin; thou shalt not die."

But David was a man of conscience, as well as passion. Two or three hundred years after him there was a prophet, who did not get even from a priest that acknowledgment of his character which David would have left his throne to yield. Amos, the prophet, had terrible truths to utter. But it was not precisely so; for Amos himself actually had nothing whatever to say, as being simply a man of the country, and specially of sheepfolds and sycamore-trees. But it happened to him that he became at a particular time the mouth-piece of the Lord, because, as he said, the Spirit of the Lord took him. And, at Bethel, he had visions, which he told of, as of the Lord, in awful action among men. But Amaziah, the priest of Bethel, was thereby greatly scandalized, as indeed well he might have been, as a chaplain to royalty. "Also Amaziah said unto Amos, O thou seer, go, flee thee away into the land of Judah, and there eat bread, and prophesy there: but prophesy not at Beth-el, for it is the king's chapel, and it is the king's court." The way of this priest of the court held good for eight hundred years, so as that when there was a great excitement about John the Baptist, in speaking to the people, Jesus said, "Behold, they which are gorgeously apparelled, and live delicately, are in king's courts. But what went ye out for to see? A prophet? Yea, I say unto you, and much more than a prophet." But even though the Baptist was worthy of this testimonial, and was "more than a prophet," yet not only was his life apart from the court, but even it was passed outside of the region of respectability. And also said Stephen to the bigots about him, just before he was stoned to death, "Ye do always resist the Holy Ghost: as your fathers did, so do ye. Which of the prophets have not your fathers persecuted?" But about the prophets, complaint was not always of persecution, but sometimes of something else, as bad or worse perhaps than that. Ezekiel, man of wonder and fire and vision, — prophet and man of God! How was Ezekiel treated? He was treated in his own land, just probably as he would be to-day in Boston or Washington. For proportionately there are no more people with a true ear for prophecy, to-day, than there were anciently in the worst of times. And in what follows, let it be noticed that the audience were people of what may be called literary taste. "Also, thou son of man, the children of thy people still are talking against thee by the walls, and in the doors of the houses, and speak one to another, every one to his brother, saying, Come, I pray you, and hear what is the word that cometh from the Lord. And they come unto thee as the people cometh, and they sit before thee as my people, and they hear thy words, but they will not do them: for with their mouth they show much love, but their heart goeth after their covetousness. And, lo, thou art unto them as a very lovely song of one that hath a pleasant voice, and can play well on an instrument." The Spirit of the Lord might speak, and actually the style only of the words be noticed!

And furthermore the prophet was the prophet of the Lord, and not of Baal or any other heathen god. The prophetic was a natural susceptibility, through which a man might be a channel either for the word of the Lord or for the influence of Baal. And indeed Balaam was up at the high place of Baal with his mind and will against the Israelites, when words not of his own thinking passed from his mouth: and it was because "the Lord met Balaam and put a word in his mouth." On finding himself overmastered, Balaam yielded, and "the Spirit of God came upon him": and the grandeur of his prophecy was because of his being a man "which heard the words of God, which saw the vision of the Almighty, falling into a trance, but having his eyes open." It was through the prophet that the Spirit had its utterance against those who succumbed to the vile seductions of heathenism.

The Lord said to Moses that sacrifices should be offered only at the door of the tabernacle of the congregation: "and they shall no more offer their sacrifices unto devils." For indeed it had been only a little while before that "they sacrificed unto devils, not to God: to gods whom they knew not, to new gods that came newly up, whom your fathers feared not." And the Scriptures of the Old Testament are largely the history of the Spirit of God, as to its conflict with the devils, and altars, and prophets, and villanies of heathenism.

As soon almost as the Israelites of the desert had all of them been buried in the land of promise, "the children of Israel did evil in the sight of the Lord, and served Baalim. And they forsook the Lord God of their fathers, which brought them out of the land of Egypt, and followed other gods, of the gods of the people that were round about them, and bowed themselves unto them, and provoked the Lord to anger. And they forsook the Lord, and served Baal and Ashtaroth." It was eight hundred years later than that, that through the prophet Jeremiah the Spirit complained of the persistent rebelliousness of the Jews. And in this passage, let it be noticed, that a prophet was a man of prophetic susceptibility, who could let himself even prophesy from Baal. "The priests said not, Where is the Lord? and they that handle the law knew me not: the pastors also transgressed against me, and the prophets also prophesied by Baal, and walked after things that do not profit." And it was not till after the Babylonish captivity that the Jews became safe from idolatry, and able to believe and glory in the proclamation, "Hear, O Israel: the Lord our God is one Lord."

Five hundred years had the Jews been in Palestine, and the adventures of Samson had become an ancient history, and Eli and Samuel, Saul, David, and Solomon had been successively gathered to their fathers, when Jeroboam "ordained him priests for the high places, and for the devils." And what follows was still eighty years later than the age of Jeroboam. "And Ahaziah fell down through a lattice in his upper chamber, that was in Samaria, and was sick: and he sent messengers and said unto them, Go, inquire of Baal-zebub, the god of Ekron, whether I shall recover of this disease. But the angel of the Lord said to Elisha, the Tishbite, Arise, go up to meet the messengers of the king of Samaria, and say unto them, Is it not because there is not a God in Israel that ye go to inquire of Baal-zebub, the god of Ekron? Now, therefore, thus saith the Lord, Thou shalt not come down from that bed on which thou art gone up, but shalt surely die. And Elijah departed." The messengers thereupon returned to the king. "And he said unto them, What manner of man was he which came up to meet you, and told you these words? And they answered him, He was a hairy man, and girt with a girdle of leather about his loins. And he said, It is Elijah the Tishbite."

It was just about the time of the preceding incident that there happened what marks the heathen notion of the Jewish theocracy. "And the prophet came to the King of Israel, and said unto him, Go, strengthen thyself, and mark and see what thou doest: for at the return of the year the King of Syria will come up against thee. And the servants of the King of Syria said unto him, Their gods are gods of the hills, therefore they were stronger than we: but let us fight against them in the plain, and surely we shall be stronger than they." Three hundred years later even than the period just mentioned, and just before the captivity, the Spirit spoke through Jeremiah and said, "Seest thou not what they do in the cities of Judah and in the streets of Jerusalem? The children gather wood, and the fathers kindle the fire, and the women knead their dough, to make cakes to the queen of heaven, and to pour out drink-offerings unto other gods, that they may provoke me to anger." But what was threatened through Moses was close upon them, and though it was predicted as being imminent, it was not believed. "I spake not unto your fathers, nor commanded them in the day that I brought them out of the land of Egypt, concerning burnt-offerings or sacrifices: but this thing commanded I them, saying, Obey my voice, and I will be your God and ye shall be my people: and walk ye in all the ways that I have commanded you, that it may be well unto you." Also says the voice, which they had not obeyed, "Since the day that your fathers came forth out of the land of Egypt unto this day, I have even sent unto you all my servants the prophets, daily rising up early and sending them: yet they hearkened not unto me, nor inclined their ear, but hardened their neck: they did worse than their fathers."

During the eight or nine centuries, of which the last lines were a retrospect, there were many more prophets than are known of now. And of some prophets, the experiences were once extant as books, of which now only the titles survive. In connection with Solomon alone there were three books of prophets, which are lost; as is evident from a passage in the Second Book of the Chronicles. "Now the rest of the acts of Solomon, first and last, are they not written in the book of Nathan the prophet, and in the prophecy of Abijah the Shilonite, and in the visions of Iddo the seer against Jeroboam the son of Nebat?"

Prophets may have been numerous or few in different ages. At one time there may have been "no open vision," and at another time, for some cause, the prophets may have "become wind." And it might also often have been perhaps that individuals may have failed of getting their inquiries of the Lord answered; as Saul failed, just before he applied to the woman at Endor. "When Saul inquired of the Lord, the Lord answered him not, neither by dreams, nor by vision nor by prophets." But it would seem as though always "the Spirit of God — the word of the Lord" — the voice had been more or less near and ready for communication, through angel or prophet, vision or dream, or some other authorized oracle, from Abraham to the captivity.

According to the Book of Judges, during a space of a hundred years, apparently there was no experience of a vision, by any one; but there was a wonderful experience as to angels at two or three critical seasons. Gideon saw an angel of the Lord, face to face, and talked with him, and had from him one sign and another. And his experience illustrates the Divine action, and the manner in which one man can be reached in one way, and another man in another way, and even the same man by means, both direct and circuitous. Gideon had been addressed and commissioned by an angel, and had had the Spirit of the Lord come upon him: and yet it was by a dream, which one man had in the camp, and another man interpreted, that he learned that the hour had come for him and the Spirit, and for "the sword of the Lord and of Gideon." There may be various ways, through which the souls of men may be affected, as to their spiritual susceptibility. An age of fierce excitement from battle, and an age of long-continued, contented quiet must necessarily differ as to what manifestations they may be ready for, from the Spirit. The age of Samson or that of Jephthah was not likely to have had the visions of Ezekiel disclosed to it. And whenever people were secretly longing for the licentiousness of Baal, they could hardly have been approachable by the Spirit of the Lord, in any other way than through an indignant prophet.

It was a belief with the Jews that fasting or a simple diet might end in fitting a man for spiritual experiences. And even a prophet would sometimes try to prepare himself for the Spirit by the soothing effect of music. And so experiences from the Spirit of God may well be supposed to have been affected by the varying spirit of the centuries. Also, prophets open to the Spirit of the Lord, evidently had that Spirit affect them, according even to their state by education. The prophecies of Amos have an odor of the country, which is sensible to everybody: and the prophecies of Jeremiah are uttered in imagery, with which he was furnished by his personal experience. And similarly, the epistles of Paul are the penmanship of a man whose learning had been gained at the feet of Gamaliel, but whose enlightenment had been on a journey to Damascus, from a vision of Christ in glory. And thus it may have been, as between mortals and the world immortal, that at one time, influence from above may chiefly have been by dreams and visions, and at another time, through angels, and at still another time, through prophets, more or less entranced.

But besides the preceding, there were ways of obtaining oracles from the Lord, of which but little is known, and which may have answered, only perhaps at intervals, such as Teraphim, and Urim, and Thummim, and casting of lots.

And now through these various agencies, with what results were men affected by the Spirit of God? There would seem then to have been scarcely anything human, on which "the word of the Lord" might not have been had. And it would seem to have been obtained much more commonly than might, at first, be thought. Rebekah, the wife of Isaac, when she was about to become a mother, "went to inquire of the Lord" as to her condition, and was answered by a strange and wonderful prophecy. It is the only occasion recorded, but it cannot probably have been the only time in her life of her inquiring of the Lord. It is only incidentally that it appears what a place of resort the house of a prophet may have been sometimes, and on what merely personal matters he may have been approached. "And when they were come to the land of Zuph, Saul said to his servant that was with him, Come and let us return, lest my father leave caring for the asses, and take thought for us. And he said unto him, Behold now, there is in this city a man of God, and he is an honorable man; all that he saith cometh surely to pass; now, let us go thither; peradventure he can show us our way that we should go." And it was only by an accident, that the fame of Elisha as a healer is known to-day. The Syrians had gone out by companies, and had brought away captive out of the land of Israel a little maid; and she waited on Naaman's wife. "And she said unto her mistress, Would God my Lord were with the prophet that is in Samaria! for he would recover him of his leprosy." And only in the same incidental manner is the wide reach of his spiritual hearing or information told of. During a war with the Israelites, the King of Syria was troubled at the discovery of his plans and secrets, and thought that among his servants there must certainly be some traitor. "And one of his servants said, None, my Lord, O King; but Elisha the prophet that is in Israel, telleth the King of Israel the words that thou speakest in thy chamber."

In art, in architecture, and in poetry also, the Spirit was inspiration. For work in the tabernacle "the Lord spake unto Moses, saying, See I have called by name Bezaleel, the son of Uri, the son of Hur, of the tribe of Judah; and I have filled him with the Spirit of God, in wisdom, and in understanding and in knowledge, and in all manner of workmanship, to devise cunning works, to work in gold, and in silver, and in brass." David wished to build a house for the Lord; but he was forbidden by the Lord, because of his having been a man of bloodshed and war. But he was allowed to make preparations for it, for his son Solomon to make use of. Gold and silver, and iron and timber, David made ready. And along with all this material, he delivered to Solomon building-plans, of which the account is very noticeable. "Then David gave to Solomon his son the pattern of the porch, and of the houses thereof, and of the treasuries thereof, and of the upper chambers thereof, and of the inner parlors thereof, and of the place of the mercy-seat, and the pattern of all that he had by the spirit, of the courts of the house of the Lord, and of all the chambers round about, of the treasuries of the house of God, and of the treasuries of the dedicated things." And still more explicitly as to the plans and patterns, and the way in which he had obtained them, "All this, said David, the Lord made me understand in writing by his hand upon me, even all the works of this pattern." And as to that poetry, in which men have gloried and worshipped so long, "Now these be the last words of David. David the son of Jesse said, and the man who was raised up on high, the anointed of the God of Jacob, and the sweet psalmist of Israel said, The Spirit of the Lord spake by me, and his word was in my tongue."

For war also, the aid of the Spirit was promised to the peculiar people. And on going to battle, the priest was to exhort the people and to tell them "The Lord your God is he that goeth with you, to fight for you against your enemies, to save you." On one occasion, we read that the Lord said to Moses, "Say unto them, Go not up, neither fight, for I am not among you: lest ye be smitten before your enemies." And on another occasion it is to be read, "And, behold, there came a prophet unto Ahab, King of Israel, saying, Thus saith the Lord, Hast thou seen all this great multitude? behold I will deliver it into thy hand, this day: and thou shalt know that I am the Lord." And then the prophet directed him as to his battle array. Samaria was besieged and at the worst extremity from famine. Elisha sat in the house and the elders with him. The king had just lost his faith, and was abjuring the Lord: and a messenger was on his way for the head of the prophet. "Then Elisha said, Hear ye the word of the Lord: Thus saith the Lord, to-morrow, about this time, shall a measure of fine flour be sold for a shekel, and two measures of barley for a shekel, in the gate of Samaria." And so it happened, because the Syrians deserted their camp. "For the Lord had made the host of the Syrians to hear a noise of chariots, and a noise of horses, even the noise of a great host: and they said to one another, Lo, the King of Israel hath hired against us the kings of the Hittites, and the kings of the Egyptians to come upon us. Wherefore they arose and fled in the twilight, and left their tents, and their horses, and their asses, even the camp as it was, and fled for their life."

In a psalm, which is like his autobiography set to music, David says of the Lord, "He teacheth my hands to war, so that a bow of steel is broken by mine arms." And by these words, doubtless, he meant something of what Jephthah felt, when "the Spirit of the Lord came upon him," and like what Samson experienced, when "the Spirit of the Lord began to move him at times in the camp of Dan."

Also, the Spirit, for the Jews, was as a judge. One day, Moses sat in judgment among the people, from the morning to the evening. "And Moses said unto his father-in-law, Because the people come unto me to inquire of God: when they have a matter, they come unto me; and I judge between one and another: and I do make them know the statutes of God, and his laws." Moses needed as a judge to have a successor. Joshua was appointed as being a man in whom was the Spirit. And now how was he to judge, how was he to be guided and directed as to his judgments? "He shall stand before Eleazar the priest, who shall ask counsel for him, after the judgment of Urim before the Lord." And indeed this judgment from God became an institution, to which appeal was made in difficult cases of the highest importance. "Then shalt thou arise and get thee up into the place which the Lord thy God shall choose; and thou shalt come unto the priests, the Levites, and unto the judge that shall be in those days, and inquire; and they shall shew thee the sentence of judgment." And refusal to submit to the sentence thus rendered was a capital offence; on which judgment was to be executed. "And all the people shall hear and fear, and do no more presumptuously."

Also over the Israelites, the Spirit of the Lord was king; though commonly the subjects were in rebellion against it, in much the same way, and with much the same results, as at the present time, when men rebel against God, and equivocate with him, and hide themselves from him, as he looks in upon them, and talks with them through their consciences. The Spirit was King of kings, after the Israelites, by asking for a king to be set over them, had Saul and his successors; and after it had been said at the inauguration of Saul, "Ye have this day rejected your God, who himself saved you out of all your adversities and your tribulations, and ye have said unto him, Nay, but set a king over us." Saul was chosen by the Spirit of the Lord, and so was David. And even than in those instances, a still more striking intervention of the Spirit was in connection with Jehu. It began with Elijah at the end of his wonderful experience at the cave of Horeb. "And the Lord said unto him, Go, return on thy way to the wilderness of Damascus; and when thou comest, anoint Hazael to be king over Syria: and Jehu the son of Nimshi shalt thou anoint to be king over Israel: and Elisha the son of Shaphat of Abel-meholah, shalt thou anoint to be prophet in thy room." Years passed on. "And Elisha the prophet called one of the children of the prophets, and said unto him, Gird up thy loins, and take this box of oil in thy hand, and go to Ramoth-gilead: and when thou comest thither, look out Jehu the son of Jehoshaphat, the son of Nimshi, and go in, and make him arise up from among his brethren, and carry him to an inner chamber: then take the box of oil, and pour it on his head, and say, Thus saith the Lord, I have anointed thee king over Israel. Then open the door, and flee, and tarry not." After this was done, the first thing said to Jehu was, "Is all well; wherefore came this mad fellow to thee?" But the end of it was that Jehu became king, and the instrument and object of the fulfilment of other prophecies.

The Spirit of the Lord intervened as to the election and dethronement of kings, and with advice and commands, as to foreign powers; and also, apparently it was accessible to the petitions of the humblest inquirer. Sometimes "the word of the Lord came" to a prophet, wherever he might happen to be, and started him off, with a sudden message, beginning, "Thus saith the Lord," to be delivered in a market-place perhaps, or at a palace. And sometimes it would be as thus: King

Jehoshaphat and Jehoram, the idolatrous King of Israel, were in trouble together. "But Jehoshaphat said, Is there not here a prophet of the Lord, that we may inquire of the Lord by him? And one of the King of Israel's servants answered and said, There is Elisha the son of Shaphat, which poured water on the hands of Elijah. And Jehoshaphat said, The word of the Lord is with him. So the King of Israel, and Jehoshaphat, and the King of Edom went down to him. And Elisha said unto the King of Israel, What have I to do with thee? Get thee to the prophets of thy father, and to the prophets of thy mother."

And now, how was it with Elisha at that moment? He was very likely affected in some such manner as Stephen was. He certainly had not needed to take thought beforehand what he should say. Nor could there have been any resisting of the wisdom and spirit which he spoke with. And not improbably because of the Spirit, his face may have shone like the face of an angel.

Sometimes the Spirit of the Lord expressed itself through a visible angel; as Zechariah writes was his experience. "And the angel that talked with me came again and waked me, as a man that is wakened out of his sleep, and said unto me, What seest thou?" And sometimes the Spirit was "the word of the Lord" in human words, which could, at first for the sound of them, even be taken for the voice of a man. Of this the experience of Samuel was an instance, before he yet knew the word of the Lord. In the night, hearing himself called by name, once and again, he answered Eli, and went to him. And at the third time of his answering so, "Eli perceived that the Lord had called the child." The Spirit of the Lord spoke through Jeremiah, when he was but a child; and through Elijah, a hairy man girt with a girdle, it confronted Amaziah the king; of whom it is written, "So he died, according to the word of the Lord, which Elijah had spoken."

Not only was Jehovah the Lord God of their worship, for the Jews, anciently, but also he was their king, the commander-in-chief of their armies, their supreme Judge, and was also amongst them inspiration from the highest, as to art and poetry. But indeed against him as king, and perhaps against his influence in all other ways, they were almost continually in rebellion. At the first thought of it, it seems incredible that a nation, or even an individual, could possibly rebel against Jehovah as a king. And for this seeming improbability men have doubted the Old Testament, as a history; while actually they themselves, more or less, every day, were rebelling against God, and prevaricating with him, in the chamber of conscience, just as the Jews did with God as connected with their temple.

The Old Testament is the history of the Spirit of the Lord, as a fountain-head of influence for men, and supremacy over human rebellion and helplessness. That Spirit, Saul might have, and might have it withdrawn, and Solomon might have and lose it with his becoming foolish. The Israelites, as its subjects, might be faithful, or be apostates to Baal; or in their fear of Syria, they might look to Egypt for help. But whether they were dutiful or rebellious; whether they were judged by Deborah the prophetess, or lived prosperously under

King Solomon, or were captives by the river of Babylon, there was over them always the supremacy of the Spirit, as it vindicated itself by judgments, and fulfilled upon them the prophecies of its own inspiring, and got itself as to its ends, praised by even the wrath of man.

Jehoram might reign in Samaria, and Jehoshaphat be King of Judah, and Mesha might be King of Moab and be also a great sheep-master; and the King of Syria might war against Israel, and compass Dothan with his army; but it was the Spirit, as it spoke from Elisha, which was the ruler of events. From the prophecies of Balaam to those of Malachi are a thousand years, but all through, it was from the selfsame Spirit, that the judges judged divinely, and the seers had visions, and the prophets prophesied, and the psalmist sang sweetly. "But the word of the Lord was unto them, precept upon precept, precept upon precept; line upon line, line upon line; here a little and there a little." And by inheritance in Christ, that word in its development is ours.

And here there are persons, who will be ready to exclaim with one voice, "The Old Testament! The miracles of the Old Testament! Does the man know what he is writing about? Does not he know even about the Book of Genesis? Does he not know of what Ezra the scribe has been suspected of having done? Does he not know what is as good as certain about the Book of Daniel? Baur and De Wette, — has he never even heard of their names; Does he not know about the earlier Isaiah and the later? Does he not know what has been done with the Old Testament so admirably and so thoroughly, by criticism, that is to say, by theology?

Truly, the writer is humbly aware of all that. But he thinks also that as to the study of the Scriptures, an instinct for the Spirit is quite as important as mere lexicology. "Oh, oh!" they exclaim again, "but do you believe in the tower of Babel, and in the whale that swallowed Jonah? Do you believe that ever the sun stood still upon Gibeon? And if you do not believe in those things, what right have you to believe in other things of the same kind?" Perhaps my believing faculty may not be very large; but would that be a good reason for my wishing to have none at all. Because my eyes will not reach the Pyramids, ought I therefore to shut them, as I walk about the streets of Boston? A real believer is a man who believes intelligently and not indiscriminately. And now as to the sun standing still, — have my opponents never heard of figures of speech: and though they often say that it does, yet is there even one of them, who believes that ever the sun does actually rise? And as to Jonah, — is there one of all my opponents who can inform a good Hebraist as to the origin and undoubted meaning of the word which is translated whale? And as to the tower of Babel, has it never occurred to them, as it does occur to me, that perhaps some time that tower will be regarded as having been singularly monumental in human history; and that the confusion of tongues may perhaps come, on good reasons, to be accounted as evidence of some great psychical change in human nature, analogous perhaps, in the infancy of the race, to the change which takes place with a child, when instinct begins to yield to the growth of reason.

As derived by creation from the Godhead in its

unity, it might be expected that religiously and spiritually there would be analogies which might correspond with the world geologically. And in the early part of the Book of Genesis there are what seem like hints of such things. Whether regarded as literal or as symbolical, the narrative as to Adam and Eve and Paradise means something. There is a curious mention of the time concurrently with the birth of Enos, when "men began to call upon the name of the Lord," which would seem to mark some change with man, rather than simply his having begun to ejaculate devotional words. "And the Lord said, My Spirit shall not always strive with man, for that he also is flesh; yet his days shall be a hundred and twenty years. There were giants in the earth in those days; and also after that, when the sons of God came in unto the daughters of men, and they bare children to them; the same became mighty men, which were of old, men of renown." What this may mean there is no knowing, at present. But it will probably some time dawn on some mind, and become apparent, and be like the deciphering of some primeval inscription.

Is it not in analogy; is it not in recognition of that great law of progress, attendant on the earth's creation, to suppose that its human inhabitants have been under a similar dispensation of advancement by convulsion, and thereby also under a corresponding law as to spiritual assistance? Jesus was a communication of God, after another manner than Moses was: and so was Moses after another manner than what Abraham knew of. And the terrible miracles from which the Egyptians suffered, and of the like of which there was some manifestation in the time of Elijah, when the Israelites were succumbing to the devil-worship of their neighbors, — these would seem to have been in some kind of keeping with the convulsive forces by which the earth was rounded and enriched, and made ready for men.

The philosophy of the phrase, "the word of the Lord," is spiritually as much in advance of mere rationalism as a rationalist himself is in advance of an elephant. What calls itself rationalism, walks and talks by a lamp, which it does not know, has a hundred slides, of two or three of which there is some experience with a few persons, even in this life. One man discerns acutely as to things within his vision, while yet he is blind to things which to another man of inferior acuteness are very plain, because of his seeing by a lamp with another slide. What! shall we go on to all eternity, seeing just as we now see? But truly we are already in germ what we shall be to all eternity. And the germinating principle is already active in us; and in some persons it is more developed than it is in others, as may very credibly be supposed for many reasons.

Most men have eyes only for material objects, but some men have had eyes for angels, and for seeing in vision. And at this present time there are persons who see spirits occasionally, as always there have been such. Spiritual sight is an attribute of all persons, though commonly it exists only as against the world to come. There is the understanding of the natural man; and there is also a spiritual understanding: and a man may have the one actively, while of the other he may never have had the least opening. To the merely natural man, miracles, and angels, and spirits are necessarily incredible.

The different look, which the Scriptures may have to two persons of the same intelligence is to be accounted for, very often, by a difference between them as to spiritual condition, not moral nor religious, but simply psychical. There are persons who cannot possibly believe the Scriptures, nor love them, and who never will, until they shall have been baptized in the sea of affliction, and so have had their souls waked up.

"Oh, oh! but what would that have to do with criticism?" Much and justly. Because, for lexicology the Spirit has no meaning but only words: and science is no more a judge as to miracles than it is as to the chronology of the Amorites. The appeal of the Scriptures as to credibility, is not to the science of either words or matter, but to the soul of man, learned with all possible learning, and alive through all its faculties.

The Old Testament is its own evidence as to authority, to all persons competent to judge about it, and who also believe in the unity of God, and are well informed as to ancient nations, and as to the religions of primitive tribes and peoples, outside of Christian civilization. For the Old Testament is the history of the manner in which that happened which is the greatest miracle, of which it has to tell, and by which a whole nation, man, woman, and child, priest, rabbi, and fisherman, became intelligent, persistent, enthusiastic, devoted believers in that doctrine as to the unity of God, of which it has been the distinction of Plato, that he caught a glimpse of it, as of some distant starry truth.

It has been a common confident objection to the credibility of the Old Testament, that it recognizes necromancy as a real thing. And the account of the woman of Endor has been reckoned sufficient to vitiate the whole history of the Old Testament. But that strange narrative, by every word with which it is worded, authenticates itself to-day, for those who are willing to learn. From Spiritualistic experiences, at the present time, any one can learn, that the Scriptures were written about realities, when they mention Baal and Baalim, and the God of Ekron, and divination by unclean spirits. Nor am I to be deterred from this position, by being asked whether I will support the Bible by reasons drawn from hell. For do not most men believe that even their respective churches are so supported? Baal and his crew, however, are not the only spiritual agencies in the Old Testament, which are made certain by Spiritualism; but even if they were, they would be enough for our present purpose, with a little thinking. Hell and its ways are exactly the opposite of heaven and those ways which lead up to it. Always there is good reasoning from the obverse. And if I am made certain as to the devils, who got themselves worshipped anciently, then also as a thinking creature, I am assisted as to my belief about the prophets of the Lord, and about ministering angels, and the angels that encamp about the righteous. And so it is, to-day, that a man can affirm of his own knowledge, that the scriptures of the Old Testament are true to the facts and powers of the spiritual universe.

There are persons, who profess to be theologians,

who are light and derisive as to the Old Testament, and who obstinately and contemptuously harden themselves in their blind leadership of people, by ignoring what might be learned from Eastern travellers, and from the long-continued experiences of the Catholic Church. But the theology which cannot eagerly appropriate facts, instead of eschewing them, is no theology at all.

The Old Testament authenticates itself for all those persons, who have a sense for the perspective of history, good for the length of fourteen hundred years, and who have also along with that sense, some instinct as to spirit, and its laws and ways.

On the subject of anthropomorphism, both among those who have assailed and those who have defended the phraseology of the Old Testament, the ignorance often has been indescribably great. And on neither side do the partisans ever seem to have suspected that perhaps the writers of the Scriptures may have written from an understanding into which they themselves may not have entered. That the law "was ordained by angels in the hand of a mediator" is a controlling fact, which it is always necessary to remember as to the Old Testament, and which yet has never been thought of by some of its censors. And so they have been like persons, undertaking with a foot-rule and compass to measure and criticise the perspective of Raphael's great picture of the Transfiguration. The writers of the Books of Samuel and of the Kings were certainly readers of the Book of Genesis; and therefore whatever words or figures of speech they may have employed as to what God may have done or said or felt, are manifestly to be understood in some manner which may be consistent with the sublimity and spirituality of the account, in which creation is said to have begun, when "the Spirit of God moved upon the face of the waters."

But it will be objected perhaps, "Do you then really believe that the Canaanites were slaughtered at the instance of the Lord? And you do believe that the disobedient prophet was killed by a lion in fulfilment of a Divine prediction! And you believe that the Lord sent a pestilence among the people when he was displeased with them!" Well, yes; I do believe all those things. But then I think about them with a better belief than some persons can conceive of. It is certain that the earth is the Lord's, and yet somehow the Canaanites were slaughtered in it. And it would seem probable, that, like many another man, a disobedient prophet was killed by a lion. And that a plague wasted the people of Israel two or three times is certain, just as hundreds of pestilences have wasted other nations, whether they were sent or incurred or encountered. And how can a pestilence possibly ever waste men, without the Divine concurrence being in some way implicated? "Shall there be evil in a city, and the Lord hath not done it?"

Was there necessarily a greater amount of suffering in the world than usual, in those years when a part of it was specially directed? And if a man died a death, which was foretold as well as foreknown by the Lord, should it be hard to be credited as a fact, or be counted for an incredible thing as to the Lord, by us human beings, who, at this moment, have, every one of us, "the sentence of death in ourselves," either by a lion, or a railway car, or through violence in some other form, or else by disease? We shrink from thinking as to a few individuals, that certain things were divinely done, which yet, a million times over, we say, are the divine will as to the human race. It is the old reluctance, which can believe in God easily and grandly as the Lord of hosts, but not so readily as being "him with whom we have to do."

It was asked of the Jews, through Moses, "For what nation is there so great, who hath God so nigh unto them, as the Lord our God is in all things that we call upon him for?" And really it is simply for nighness, and not for quality of action, that exactly objection is made to the credibility of Jewish history, as to the Lord. And on the foregoing understanding, nighness is simply and fairly a matter of historical inquiry; and it is not of that utter improbability, which is sometimes lightly supposed.

As to some actions, which purport to have been directed by the Spirit of the Lord, objection has been made, as not having been as merciful as Christianity, or as vigorous as Almightiness might have made them, or as being even of the nature of repentance. But the action of the Spirit among men is not to be judged of as human actions are: because the everlasting Spirit is not as the spirits of men are. The spirit of a man, to be its best, must strive to the uttermost: but the Spirit of the Lord, to be at its best with men, must temper itself for them as being weak and ignorant, and must adjust itself to those human circumstances which cannot be changed, without changing man himself, to an extent which would be almost like annihilation. Nor is the Spirit to be judged of as to its manifestation in time and space, by what men may think it ought to show itself: since the Spirit is unchangeable, because of its being actually of the essence of all possible changes, and of all creations which ever have been, or can be.

The Spirit of the Universe in action, is necessarily manifested for men withinside of their human conditions: and for the Jews, that it might be the better humanized for human apprehension, it even gave "the law by the disposition of angels."

In the Old Testament, instead of the Lord, or the Lord God, or the angel of the Lord doing things, let it be supposed that it was written that the Spirit of Nature favored one race and extirpated another, and that for violation of her laws she suddenly visited men, with what truly were simple effects, but which apparently were like magical punishments. And let it be supposed, besides, that it were found to have been written, that the Spirit of Nature was recognized by the Jews as blasting the fields at one time and blessing them at another, at her will. Would that sound incredibly to-day; and is it not indeed what is actually going on about us, always?

Now the Lord God is the soul of nature. He may be more than that and infinitely more. And he may be the soul of various other natures, than this one, inside the circumference of which we live. But nevertheless, in a sense, God is nature. And now plainly does not nature favor individuals, one above another; and one family more than another; and one nation above other nations, as to strength, or beauty, or intellect, or wealth, or even sometimes as to all of them combined? The word "luck" is derived from the name of a heathen deity; and is it not still felt, as though by nature some persons were more lucky than others?

For a special purpose, the Lord, as regards a particular people, acted avowedly through the forces of nature, but yet not more certainly than he is always acting. Spirit is the God of nature; and also it is animal life with man. Also the Spirit is God Most High, and in the souls of good believing men it is the Holy Ghost. And as to whatever spiritual plane men may choose to live upon, or may be raised to, the words of Christ are true, "With the same measure that ye mete withal, it shall be measured to you again." It was from the Spirit, with which his soul was quick, and from his being like the mouthpiece of Divine Necessity, that Hosea at one time said of the Jews, "For they have sown the wind, and they shall reap the whirlwind."

God as he is known to the seraphs, and is experienced on the seraphic plane, is not God as possibly he could be felt on the human plane, intelligibly and according to human wants, any more than a pious book by William Law could answer religiously such wants as a Kaffir may have. And God, as he is thought of, on steps far lower down, before his throne, than where seraphs and cherubs have their regions, is not God as he would be intelligible to persons living on this earth, and limited as to their capacities of thought, by the narrowness of their experiences, and by prejudices and feelings connected with their cradles, and which they can never get clear of, but along with their bodies. God can possibly have to do with us, only as being ignorant. For if he should approach us, as seraphs, we should never know of him, because of our senses and susceptibility being inferior to the seraphic. "Every good gift and every perfect gift is from above, and cometh down from the Father of lights." Yet it reaches this earth through agencies, and perhaps even through angelic intermediations. And certainly as it enters into this world, it is through some particular channel; it is through the mind of a poet, or the apprehension of a philosopher, or during the meditative mood of some religious genius; and it is, therefore, through a certain few persons, who, whether they know it or not, are in their time and place, more or less successfully, and more or less faithfully, like ministering Levites, standing before the Lord. And it was through a similar ministration of the Spirit, that the Old Testament was made the long preparatory introduction to the New. Also, of the Gospel, the first believers and preachers as being Hebrews, were men of hereditary fitness, as being members of a family, whose minds had been shaped as to apprehension, expectation, and belief, by the manner in which their forefathers had been divinely dealt with, during more than a thousand years. And it was from this point of view, that St. Paul wrote to the Galatians, "Wherefore the law was our schoolmaster to bring us unto Christ."

And now let another point be considered, connected with the miraculous. The natural eye, it may be, with infinitely various splendors before it, can see only what, by its nature, it is ready to perceive : and so it is with the spiritual eye. The natural eye is fixed as to its constituents, and therefore as to its capability of being strengthened, and its ability of perceiving. But the spiritual eye is not so fixed, because of its being an organ not only for ever-widening fields, but also for states, which may become more and more interior, to all eternity. The eye of the spirit, therefore, when it is open, is probably the eye of that state, in which the spirit is, for a time, by information and faith.

It is one of the primary and deepest truths, as to human nature, "Draw nigh to God, and he will draw nigh to you." But a man can see only what he is ready to see. And a Divine communication pressing into the mind of a prophet, has shape and coloring, from the imagery and religious expectations, with which the receiving mind may be furnished. And so it was, that the Father Everlasting, without beginning or end of days, seemed to Daniel, in his vision, as though "the Ancient of days did sit, whose garment was white as snow, and the hair of his head like the pure wool." Also, in the first vision of the prophet Ezekiel, there was a manifestation of the Spirit, through which "when the living creatures went, the wheels went with them : and when the living creatures were lifted up from the earth, the wheels were lifted up. Whithersoever the spirit was to go, they went." And of this imagery, it may be, that the original, as Ezekiel saw it, or what is some copy of it, is to be seen to-day, among the sculptures, Assyrian perhaps, which are preserved in the British Museum.

World beyond world, and state within state, — this is the condition by which we live. Are there varieties of report amongst us resulting thence spiritually? Certainly there are, and there must be; just as in England, a coal-heaver, a mason, a brass-founder, a glass-polisher and an astronomer-royal, would vary infinitely about what the heavens may be, or may have to show, though even they may all of them actually have worked together, for the construction of the same observatory.

And if a star can shine differently into different minds, because of their being informed, some more than others and some less; so may some primal truth of the spiritual world, shining on the minds of men, be apprehended by one person in one way, and by another person in another way. And thus it is that for saints in the same spiritual sphere with St. John, "God is love"; while yet for men, in a lower sphere, wanton against grace, brutish, and rebellious, "Our God is a consuming fire." And that indeed he must be, or else be nothing. And perhaps revelation and the probabilities of human expectation as to the next world, will all be fulfilled in spirits having the scene about them change with their love of God.

Much difficulty has been felt about the Old Testament, as though it were inconsistent with the impartiality of God; and as though it were a thing incredible, that God should have had "a chosen people." But now in what manner, and for what end were they chosen? Was it favoritism? But really that could not be argued from their history, from the pestilences and the famine which they endured, and from the manner in which their sins were visited upon them, and from their captivity in Babylon, and their dispersion by the Romans. And certainly with the prophets, age after age, "the word of the Lord," as it came, was commonly reproach, indignation, and warning. A chosen people they were; but they were chosen for the good of others, just as much as for their own. The promise, as it was made to Abraham, at his call, was "And in thee shall all families of the earth be blessed." But why through the Jews was this blessing to accrue, rather than through any other people? Simply perhaps because, as it had got to be given through some nation, they were as good for the purpose as any other. Or, it may be, that without being morally either better or worse than other nations, there was in them some constitutional peculiarity, through which they were eligible for a particular purpose. But the use to which God puts a man is no pleasure for him, unless first his heart be right with God. And if a man be a born poet, it is only with his singing aloud and well and rejoicing others, that he can truly know and feel himself. In what way, then, have all the families of the earth been blessed through Abraham? They have not all yet been blessed, but are many of them only about to be. But Christ was the blessing predestined. And the Jewish mind, as it was schooled by experience, and solemnized by the Lord, and taught of God, was in the fulness of time, like flesh for "the Word," when it was to dwell among us.

The experiences of the Jewish people, as they are written in the Old Testament, regarded as mental, domestic, political, and spiritual preparation, are what is meant in the epistle to the Hebrews, where Jesus is described as contemplating an entrance into this world, in concurrence with prophecy, to do the will of heaven; and when he says, as before God, and looking down upon the earth, "A body hast thou prepared for me." And thus it was actually towards us Christians of to-day that God condescended, when he called Abraham. And it was for us that the prophets prophesied. And when the psalmists sang, they really sang for us of this age, and more effectively perhaps than even for their own immediate friends. In the Babylonish captivity, it was what might have been our faithlessness, individually, which was chastened; and it may be, that through the punishment of the Jews, and their "stripes we are healed."

The marvellousness of Jewish history is the glorification of my nature. And whatever the graciousness of God may have been towards Saul, it may yet avail me to-day in the flesh, as a mere history, more than it ever did him. And that wisdom, of which Solomon was the channel, but which he failed to appropriate for his own good, has been of some profit for me, through perhaps ten thousand unknown channels.

As to every true poet that ever sung, as to every person of spiritual insight that ever spoke, as to every man that ever God raised up, for an emergency in human affairs, and also as to those nations, who may have been receptive of it in any way, whether in Greece, Italy, or Palestine, the Spirit has been manifested "for every man to profit withal." And it is the explanation and the justification of Jewish history, as to the peculiar people, and the covenants and the fathers and the promises, and the glory, that out of it all "as concerning the flesh, Christ came, who is over all."

It would seem as though there were descent by spirit as well as by blood; and it would appear also as though there were a descent by spirit, in connection with blood. And it would seem too, with living together earnestly, that people strengthen and perpetuate ways of thinking, and even generate a spirit which, for intensity and thoroughness, is like infection for those who come within its reach. And by the manner in which the Jews were secluded from other nations, and through their sympathy with one another as fellow-worshippers, manifestly there was induced an intensity of belief as to the unity of God, which has been like leaven for leavening the whole world. And, but for the Old Testament, there never could have been the New, nor ever could the Son of God have been manifested, nor possibly could the Holy Spirit have had its right action on believers.

And now, not unreasonably, it may seem, as though a man of the highest science, and of the truest intuitions, and of the widest information as to history, might say, "When I pray, I pray out of my heart, trusting that the Spirit of God's sending will inform my prayer and quicken me. And at times, also, I am glad to think, as I kneel before my Father in heaven, that I am looking in the direction of the God of Abraham, the God of Isaac, and the God of Jacob."

Glory to the Lord my God, who knows me better than I know myself, and who, whatever else he may be, is surely better than my goodness!

Glory to God, who "created the heavens and the earth," and because of whose outflowing Spirit things seen and temporal are but like the dark shadows of things unseen and eternal!

Glory to God, whose word as it goes forth lights high heaven with splendor, and kindles every seraph, and enlightens every angel, and is an impulse among men, which utters itself more or less effectively in the languages of many lands!

Glory to God in the highest, as that archetypal mind, whence the elements derive their properties, and whence also are evolved the ages as they come and pass; wherein, too, the first man existed as a thought, before he walked this earth in form; and without which, no kingdom can rise to its destiny, nor even a sparrow fall to the ground!

Glory be to God, for he makes spirits be his angels, and flaming fire do him service!

Glory to God! "who at sundry times and in divers manners spake in times past unto the fathers by the prophets."

THE OLD TESTAMENT AND THE NEW.

THE New Testament is no detached piece of history; and the documents of which it is composed have other connections than simply with one another. Its title as the New presupposes the Old Testament: and throughout, it is alive with the spirit and phraseology of Isaiah and Jeremiah and David and Elijah and Moses. And just as a government may for continuity and spirit be the same government, throughout many generations of ministers and subjects connected with it, so was the era of the New Testament a continuation of the line of ages, which dates from Abraham.

At the birth of Jesus there was present a continuity of custom, thought, and hope, which began, as all the Jews of the age gloried in believing, "with the faith of Abraham, who is the father of us all." At that time, for everybody, everywhere, with the exception of a Roman garrison, for everything it was the law of Moses. The smoke of the morning and of the evening sacrifice went up from Mount Moriah, over Jerusalem, just as it had been commanded in the desert. The foundations of the temple were what Solomon had laid. And as the priests chanted their psalms, often it was in the words of David and of a thousand years before. The prophets indeed were dead, but in every synagogue, on every Sabbath, still they were to be heard, speaking from their books. And outside of Judea, in Rome probably, and in Corinth, and in many other places, there was a state of things, like what was pleaded as a fact, in a conference of the earliest Christians about the Gentiles, and which is thus written of in the Book of Acts: "Moses of old time hath in every city them that preach him, being read in the synagogues every Sabbath day." And throughout Palestine, all the localities, loudly as they speak to-day, yet spoke still more impressively, eighteen hundred years ago, of Samson, Samuel, Saul, David, Solomon, Elijah, and Elisha. And at that time, no doubt, there were places, which seemed, as though still glowing with the presence of Isaiah, or mourning along with the spirit of Jeremiah, and as though still fresh from the footsteps of Hosea and Amos, or as though made holy by the life of Malachi, the last of the prophets. Nor, as it would seem, had the voice of prophecy then been quite suspended, because with his annual entry into the holy of holies, in the temple, it was believed that the high priest for the year became prophetic for some particular purpose. And indeed, at that period, all the land of Judea was alive with traditions of what the angel of the Lord had been; and of what judgments had been incurred, and what hopes had been imparted from the Lord; and of what miracles had been wrought, at one place and another, and what visions, also, and dreams had been vouchsafed to one man and another. By its nature, time past in Judea, for effect had become prophetic of a future wonderful and miraculous.

The Old Testament was like the soul of the Jewish people. It was what they thought from, what they prayed by, and what they trusted to. The God of Abraham and of Isaac and of Jacob was the God they looked to, and towards whom their souls were open. Historically, they were the Lord's people, but not therefore spiritually, all of them, and altogether; for it was then, as it is to-day, when Christians pray for that coming, which would destroy many of them with its brightness. And so it was that, at the commencement of our era, every mountain and valley and city from Beersheba to Lebanon, every fisherman on the lake of Gàlilee, and at Jerusalem every member of the Sanhedrim, and every man in the market-place, Scribes and Pharisees all, and every worshipper also, that went up into the temple to pray, was alive with the spirit of the past, and with hopes accruing from it.

From the termination of the Old Testament to the commencement of the New, there was a space of four hundred years, which, however, was not without its documents, which are to be found in the Apocrypha. During this interval, the Jews had become more and more a peculiar people, so as indeed to have hold of a right belief, many of them, in a most unrighteous spirit. And indeed they had become, and they were what they were, a mere earthen vessel, wherein was held aloft and before the whole world, the golden, heavenly, eternal truth of the unity of God.

The day, which Jesus Christ said that Abraham had rejoiced at foreseeing, was coming. And for many and perhaps a thousand converging reasons before the throne of God, "now the fulness of the time was come." These are the first verses of the Gospel according to St. Mark. "The beginning of the Gospel of Jesus Christ, the Son of God: as it is written in the prophets, Behold, I send my messenger before thy face, which shall prepare my way before thee. The voice of one crying in the wilderness, Prepare ye the way of the Lord, make his paths straight. John did baptize in the wilderness and preach the baptism of repentance for the remission of sins. And there went out unto him all the land of Judea, and they of Jerusalem, and were all baptized of him in the river of Jordan, confessing their sins. And John was clothed with camel's hair, and with a girdle of skin about his loins; and he did eat locusts and wild honey; and preached, saying — "

And here now on the instant starts up our modern scepticism and exclaims, "Written in the prophets, the old prophets! That is a very good beginning certainly! But preaching in the wilderness! A popular preacher keeping to the wilderness, — that is too ridiculous. And who was John? who was his father? O, Zacharias, indeed! But who then was the Scribe that registered his birth? For, it is pretended, that the Jews had registers of births among them. Preaching the baptism of repentance! What an audacious undertaking! Why was he to preach in that way, rather than anybody else? And then for his food, locusts and wild honey! Did anybody ever hear of such a diet? But, no doubt, he was secretly supplied from the city with something better than that; was not he?" And to this, answer is proper thus: "No, he was not, probably. Go away, poor child of self-conceit and misfortune, go away. What have you to do with the time and scene and spirit, which we are trying to realize? Get away into the fields, and find, if you can, the prodigal son; and, far away from the flippancies and fashions of the day, think with yourself till you come to yourself, and feel yourself to be a living soul with the feelings, responsibilities, and connections of a soul immortal." Reason in its majesty ought to be welcome everywhere; and it has a place, indeed, immediately under the throne of the Most High. But what has mere pertness to do at the gate of the holy of holies? It can really do nothing there, except incur penal blindness; as the Syrians did at Dothan, when they reached out their hands for the life of the prophet Elisha.

At the birth of Jesus Christ, it was, as St. Paul wrote to the Galatians, because "the fulness of the time was come." And not improbably, it was, for the whole world, a more complete fulness of time than what Paul of himself could ever have thought. Because, as to the providential agencies concerned with a great crisis in human affairs, the chief actors in it may personally know no more than many other people of the time. For, persons may meet together for a settlement of their differences, by argument, fight, or otherwise, and yet be merely the representatives of forces, external to themselves, and of the potency of which they may be quite unaware. A great crisis like "the fulness of the time" is to be known of by men thoroughly, only from some watch-tower commanding the stream of time. And so it is possible, that Paul as to the fulness of time, wrote by the Spirit, more truly than he himself knew of.

Four hundred years previously, Plato had written, that in his view, there was no hope of deliverance for man, from the vile slough into which they had fallen, but through the intervention of that Power, by which they had been created. And as appears also, from classical authors, there was, about the commencement of our era, in the Roman Empire, a strange, wandering, prophetic sense abroad, that there was a crisis rising as to human affairs. In describing the capture of Jerusalem by Titus, it is said by Tacitus in his heathen way, "Omens had happened, for averting which, there is no rite practised by a people, who are opposed to all religion, though actually very superstitious. Troops were seen to meet in the sky, and arms to glisten, and the temple was suddenly illuminated by light from the clouds. The doors of the inner temple were suddenly thrown open, and a voice more than human was heard saying that the gods were going. These things frightened some people. But most persons were thereby more fully persuaded, that what was contained in the ancient writings of the priests was coming true, that the East was about to be magnified, and people from Judea about to rise to power." And Suetonius writes to the same effect and says, "A certain ancient and persistent notion had overspread the East, that by Fate, people from Judea would become supreme." And in the same way, Josephus wrote, after the fall of Jerusalem, that what had emboldened the Jews, to resist the Romans, was an uncertain oracle contained in their sacred books, that some of them, about that time, would rule the world. Very singular indeed was that expectant state of the public mind, which there was, among both the Jews and the heathen, during that century, in which Jesus Christ was born. No doubt, the world had grown ripe for a great change, and was also conscious of that ripeness, through the best intellects of the age.

Greece had yielded its best as to intellectual preparation, for the world. And Rome had subordinated all nations to itself, from Britain to the borders of Persia, and by permeation, had made them like one people, and had tied them together with roads, opening in every direction, from the Forum. The Gentiles had been working for an end beyond their thought, and had unconsciously been fulfilling ancient prophecy, and preparing the world for the new doctrine that should proclaim the brotherhood of man. Rome had unconsciously been making ready with its work, and Judea, without knowing it, had been producing the man, against "the fulness of the time," and the fulfilment of the prophecy of Isaiah: "The voice of him that crieth in the wilderness, Prepare ye the way of the Lord, make straight in the desert a highway for our God. Every valley shall be exalted, and every mountain and hill shall be made low: and the crooked shall be made straight, and the rough places plain; and the glory of the Lord shall be revealed, and all flesh shall see it together: for the mouth of the Lord hath spoken it."

Probably it was as the earth answers to heaven, electrically; but any way, so it was, that the world, at its best, was as though expectant, about the time when Christ was manifested. This state of expectation may perhaps have been from what Plato had said, or it may have merely been occasioned by some Sibylline prophecy, such as every now and then got wandering about the world and exciting men's minds; or it may have been caused simply by the shadow of a great event, forthcoming from the gates of destiny. There is an eclogue of Virgil, which has always had a fascination for some minds, as seeming like what might have been written from inspiration at Jerusalem. And certainly it is a strange, singular poem; for it is in the spirit of Isaiah, rather than like the Muse of Theocritus. And it is as though in some high mood, while Virgil was thinking to express his best wishes for the newly born child of a friend, he had actually been caught by the spirit of prophecy, and been lifted up like Ezekiel, and been made to shape his words, as though for a Messiah just born. And if any one should think that so this may have been, he might maintain his belief by many analogies and instances. For, through being possessed and overmastered by a mighty spirit, often a man has said grandly what he never thought, and been even like Balaam, who blessed sublimely, while wishing only to curse. But, however that may have been, there was, at the time of the birth of Jesus Christ, a prophetic sense abroad of something great about to happen, and not in Judea only. And so it was, "now when Jesus was born in Bethlehem of Judea in the days of Herod the king" that the words of Haggai came true, which had been uttered five hundred years before, not out of his own mind, but by the spirit of prophecy, "And I will shake all nations, and the desire of all nations shall come: and I will fill this house with glory, saith the Lord of hosts."

And here abruptly our modern captiousness calls out, "Somewhat indefinite that, is it not? If there was to be a prophecy, why was it not accompanied by the names of persons and places, and by exact dates, and by the names of the kings, or emperors, that were to be?" To which the answer is, But now the end of that course of thought is, that you can have nothing to do with God Almighty, unless he will show himself in a court constituted after human methods, and be examined and cross-examined as to his right to own human creatures and to deal with them. Woe unto him that striveth with his Maker! Potsherd of earth, is that the temper, in which you can even treat with your fellow-potsherds? Or is that the spirit, in which men of the least success have ever contemplated the earth, geologically? Also, what, necessarily has Spirit, foretelling its course, to do with names; for, what has the mere name of a man to do with the spirit of an age?

This matter of prophecy is not for a man, whose mind has been narrowed to the mere methods of science, nor yet for a bigot of the Talmud, nor yet for a bigot of any Christian kind, because really it is the affair of human nature at its highest and truest. And indeed it is a subject for men, not of mathematics merely, but of poetry and intuition, and of wide learning as well as modern sharpness; and who also have had personal experience of the Spirit, as dealing with them, for sin, and redemption and hope. And for such men, the Old Testament is one long grand prophecy as to the "desire of all nations," and the manner of his coming.

The people of Israel were a chosen people; were

they? They were; but yet not to the exclusion or detriment of other nations; because, through the choice of them, divinely, all other nations were to be blessed, and to know the Lord, and have a Messiah, and receive the Spirit.

The beginning of Christianity was not at Bethlehem, nor yet at Nazareth; and it was indeed, very long before Cæsar Augustus became emperor: for it was when there was "preached before the gospel unto Abraham, saying, In thee shall all nations be blessed." And if it were as Paul writes, that it pleased God "to reveal his Son in me, that I might preach him among the heathen," it was because, first, as he says, God "separated me from my mother's womb, and called me by his grace." And before the words, God, Father, faith, and Spirit could have their right meanings, as spoken by the apostles, it was necessary that they should have been used in joy and sorrow, and hope and fear, by one generation after another, and by Moses as a lawgiver, and by David as a Psalmist, and by the prophets, one after another, in their various messages of love, or anger, or direction, or encouragement.

There is not an age of the ancient Church, but lives to-day, by its influence, in every member of the Church of God. If faith avails me to-day, for righteousness or a hereafter, it is because I am "blessed with faithful Abraham." The heathen are the majority in the world, as yet, and according to them, "there be gods many, and lords many." And "the fool hath said in his heart, There is no God." And that everything is God, is what a student is liable to think, if he forgets himself, as a finite limited creature, with whom sometimes inquiry must grow microscopic as it grows intense, and therefore must report less and less of the infinite and eternal. And if my soul has in it provision against its times of trial and agony, it is because of something in me, which is like an instinct; it is because of spirit by descent; it is because of an inherited feeling, from ages long before the commencement of our era, as to the God of heaven and earth being the God of persons, the God of Abraham, and of Isaac, and of Jacob; and it is because of great souls, that were before Christ; because of the manner in which David agonized, and had his spirit drawn, that myself I can exclaim and plead, "O God, thou art my God."

Jesus said to the Jews, in the temple, on an occasion when he was charged, somewhat indiscriminately, with being a Samaritan, and also with having a devil, "Your father Abraham rejoiced to see my day: and he saw it, and was glad." This prophetic view of the future had been a grace vouchsafed to Abraham by the Spirit; and apparently also it was through the Spirit, that Jesus was enabled to speak of it.

The Spirit of the Lord, as it legislated for the Jews, anciently, was making ready for that wonderful liberty, wherewith Christ was to make the whole world free. The Spirit, through the prophets and through the agency of nature, taught and guided the people of Israel, and warned and punished them, and cheered and blessed them, not for the sake of them, as individuals, merely or mainly, but because they were to be a people, "of whom as concerning the flesh, Christ" was to come. The Spirit, as it ruled the Jews, foretold in its action, the future of the Gentiles. These words were from the Spirit, through Isaiah, nearly eight hundred years before the birth of Jesus Christ. "And it shall come to pass in the last day, that the mountain of the Lord's house shall be established in the top of the mountains, and shall be exalted above the hills; and all nations shall flow unto it. And many people shall go and say, Come ye, and let us go up to the mountain of the Lord, to the house of the God of Jacob; and he will teach us of his ways, and we will walk in his paths: for out of Zion shall go forth the law, and the word of the Lord from Jerusalem. And he shall judge among the nations, and shall rebuke many people; and they shall beat their swords into ploughshares, and their spears into pruning-hooks: nation shall not lift up sword against nation, neither shall they learn war any more." The vision is not yet as to accomplishment, on the subject of war: but it is not therefore the less wonderful for any man, who has an eye for history, and the workings of the human spirit, and for those many other signs of the times, which are to be discerned to-day, besides what glitter from the points of bayonets. Ten or twelve generations had lived and died in the knowledge of the preceding prophecy, when, through Malachi, the Spirit predicted as to its own course, "Behold, I will send my messenger, and he shall prepare the way before me; and the Lord, whom ye seek, shall suddenly come to his temple, even the messenger of the covenant, whom ye delight in; behold, he shall come, saith the Lord of hosts. But who may abide the day of his coming? and who shall stand when he appeareth?" This anticipation of the Spirit was what, four hundred years later, was to be continued as a lamentation of the Spirit, by the utterance of Jesus Christ, " O Jerusalem, Jerusalem, thou that killest the prophets, and stonest them which are sent unto thee, how often would I have gathered thy children together, even as a hen gathereth her chickens under her wings, and ye would not! Behold your house is left unto you desolate." As to the preceding prophecies, the Spirit justified itself. For, to Jerusalem, it happened, just as was said by Jesus Christ, as he looked at it, from the Mount of Olives. And we Christians all, do we not worship in a temple, which though not made with hands, has yet for its porch and entrance, that house of God upon the mountain, which Isaiah knew of? And are we not Christians, because of what the Jews were anciently?

They were almost the last words of the last of the prophets, " Behold I will send you Elijah the prophet, before the coming of the great and dreadful day of the Lord." They had been pondered by the Jews for four hundred years. And so, on his appearance, John was asked if he were the Christ, and if not the Christ, then if he were Elias. Both which things he denied. That the Christ was near him, he felt, but apparently without being certain as to who it was. "And John bare record, saying, I saw the Spirit descending from heaven like a dove, and it abode upon him. And I knew him not; but he that sent me to baptize with water, the same said unto me, Upon whom thou shalt see the Spirit descending and remaining on him, the same is he which baptizeth with the Holy Ghost. And I saw and bare record that this is the Son of God."

But it is asked, "Why was that particular person

chosen rather than anybody else; and why was Christ manifested at that particular time, rather than a hundred years earlier or later? But it might as well be questioned, as to why Milton should have been more of a poet than all other men of his generation; and as to why some plant should flower certainly, and yet only once in a hundred years.

"When the fulness of the time was come, God sent forth his Son, made of a woman, made under the law, that we might receive the adoption of sons." The Jewish people were ripe for his production; and all nations were awaiting him, as their desire. And for the fulness of the time, it was as though the whole world were folded about by eternity, with forces and tendencies converging for a crisis. The air felt as though it had grown prophetic; and men were "waiting for the consolation of Israel," as Simeon was, before it was revealed to him about the Lord's Christ. And indeed nature now was about to let in "a multitude of the heavenly host," for praising God, within the hearing of mortals: and about to be ready also for admitting inside of its walls more than twelve legions of angels, should Jesus pray for them to the Father.

For "the fulness of the time," other conditions may have contributed, besides those which are deducible from prophecy and history. The philosophy of what is called a Revival of Religion might perhaps be made to yield some information on this subject. Indeed, historically, it is evident that there are times of what the Scriptures call refreshing from the Lord. And to philosophers, who even have been irreligious, it has seemed as though at certain emergencies, there certainly must have been a force, extraneous to men, individually, which quickened and whirled them, and disposed of them by a will of its own, independent and irresistible.

And perhaps, also, we mortals may be spiritually affected, for numbness or quickness, by conditions dependent on even the particular quarter of the universe, wherein our earth may happen to be carrying us. It is common experience that we are dull or lively, with the state of the atmosphere, and especially as to electricity. Also, at present, we are borne, annually, through showers of what are called falling stars, but of which, anciently, there would seem to have been no knowledge. Men "are fearfully and wonderfully made"; and as being possibly children of God, they are the creatures not of a Commonwealth simply, nor a continent, nor even of a planet, but are natives of the universe. And a grand and worthy saying was that of Paul, as to the coming of Christ, and sounding like what he might have been taught of God, — "The fulness of the time was come."

But why did not everybody know it, when the time was come? But further yet than that, why has not everybody since Adam known all that the heavens have been proclaiming: and why do so few people know even to-day what the best astronomers have caught? John the Baptist could scarcely believe in himself. He knew that he was the "voice of one crying in the wilderness"; but he did not know that he was Elias. As indeed how could he know that at a time, when all that he knew of the one behind him was, that himself he was not worthy to take off his shoes. By the Spirit, afterwards, he was shown that the Christ was Jesus. And Jesus subsequently was enabled to say of him, "This is Elias which was for to come." Truths from the highest are not readily subordinated by the earthly understanding: and the monitions of the Spirit are but slowly translated into the dialect of common life.

Of the preceding remark, there is some illustration even in the life of Jesus. When the Spirit came upon him, in John's sight, there had to be a reception of it and appropriation. And Jesus did not on the instant, begin to teach on the river-side, nor look round for the nearest sick person to heal. "And immediately the spirit driveth him into the wilderness. And he was there in the wilderness forty days, tempted of Satan; and was with the wild beasts; and the angels ministered unto him." This was not unlike what happened to Ezekiel, when the word of the Lord first came to him. "So the spirit lifted me up and took me away, and I went in bitterness, in the heat of my spirit; but the hand of the Lord was strong upon me." For solitude and fasting, Jesus was, for the time, like some prophet of the Old Testament. But not even once would he seem to have been a subject of that ecstasy, which was characteristic of the prophets. Nor even would he seem to have had what was a common experience with Daniel. "And I Daniel fainted, and was sick certain days; afterward I rose up, and did the king's business; and I was astonished at the vision, but none understood it." But still apparently, Jesus was not on the instant, both as to body and mind, absolutely congruent with the Spirit, which had come upon him. And indeed long afterwards, the Son of man prayed in regard to his suffering greatness as the Son of God, " Saying, Father, if thou be willing, remove this cup from me: nevertheless, not my will, but thine, be done. And there appeared an angel unto him from heaven, strengthening him."

And so when Jesus was "led up of the Spirit, into the wilderness," it was that he might be tempted, as indeed he could not but be; it was that he might manifest his temper, while growing suddenly out of the condition of a humble Nazarene, into something even greater perhaps than "the nature of angels"; it was that he might commence his Messiahship with overcoming Satan, at his greatest advantage; and it was, that in quiet and apart from the world, he might have his soul quicken, and fill, and strengthen with that Spirit, which was to become his without measure.

THE SPIRIT.

THE Spirit, the Spirit of the Lord, the Spirit of God, the Holy Ghost! There is nothing which more intimately concerns us than that, and nothing, also, which is more difficult to know about, theologically. And yet perhaps it is simple enough, for willing and simple people. However, of all the various kinds of knowledge, proverbially self-knowledge is the most difficult. And perhaps it is because the Spirit is so near to us, and is indeed part of us, at times, and like the breath we draw, and the strength we have, and the light we see by, that it has been so hard to think about.

Says Baumgarten: "The doctrine of the Holy Spirit remained a long time undecided. It lay near to the first church in a practical respect only." And says Neander: "Some believed him to be a mere power; some confounded the idea of person with the charism; others supposed him to be a creature; others believed him to be God; and others still were undecided. The practical recognition of him, however, as the principle of the divine life in man, was almost universal in the early church." It would seem, however, as though perhaps the uncertainty of the primitive Christians may have been a better thing than the certainty of their successors could possibly have been, two or three hundred years later. For, in the fourth century of our era, the Christian Church was permeated through door and window, by influences from the surrounding world of heathenism and "philosophy falsely so called." The Apostles' Creed, as it is called, would seem to have been the earliest creed of the Church. And as to the Spirit, this creed says simply, "I believe in the Holy Ghost." And for a more particular belief than that, the Creed would certainly commend us to the Scriptures, and not to the controversialists of the third and fourth centuries.

What, then, is to be understood by the Spirit of God, the Holy Spirit; that Spirit which was promised and poured out; which rested on a person, and with which people were baptized? Like "the Word," it is a phrase both generic and special, and of various meanings. The primary meaning of the Scriptural word for Spirit is breath or wind; just as the primitive meaning of "Logos" is that by which men word their thoughts. Other meanings of the word "spirit" are the spirit of a living man, and the spirit of a man which has departed the body. Angels are called spirits. God is described as being spirit; and his action in nature and on man is said to be through the Spirit.

Jesus Christ said that God is spirit. At the beginning of creation, "The Spirit of God moved upon the face of the waters." And said Job, "By his spirit he hath garnished the heavens." And said Elihu to Job, "If he gather unto himself his spirit and his breath, all flesh shall perish together, and man shall turn again unto the dust." It is true that "there is a spirit in man";

but it is from another spirit than itself, that it lives to any good purpose; for it understands aright only by "the inspiration of the Almighty." Spirit is the life of everything. And it is the life of my life; and it is also what must be with me, as a foreign presence, or else I could not be myself, nor think, nor have a word on my tongue. "Such knowledge is too wonderful for me; it is high, I cannot attain unto it. Whither shall I go from thy spirit?" But besides this pervading, life-supporting presence of the Spirit, there is an action of it which is intermittent, conditional, and occasional.

When "all the sons of God shouted for joy" at the beginning of our earth, no doubt, it was mainly, because for them, the new house prophesied of its inhabitants, that were to be, age after age.

And as to the human body merely, it is plain now, that type after type in creation, it is what nature had been forecasting, from the first saurian that ever crept, and from the time when the elephant was endowed with a trunk, so wonderfully like the arm and hand of a man, for pliability, adaptability, and delicacy of touch. Yes, and from a period long before Adam, by a hundred symptomatic creations, nature prophesied of man, as he was to be, not merely as to the shape of his body, but even also as to those instincts which largely determine his manner of life.

Out of the same dust of the ground as an elephant was the body of Adam formed, by the Lord God; but into that human body, as being a temple, wherein there was to be worship afterwards, there was breathed "the breath of life; and man became a living soul." That breath! to all eternity, it is the difference of a step between the highest bestial and the lowest spiritual; it is the width of a proper miracle, on the scale of creation.

He is liable to be confused by light, for which incidentally he may not be ready; but otherwise by nature, man is all that the best beast is, and additionally, he is created with a susceptibility as to influences, from what is super-bestial, and even supernatural. What was written as to a higher plane spiritually than what Adam started on, is yet applicable as to the coming of the first man into the world, — "A body hast thou prepared for me." And because of its adaptation as to the world which now is, and because also of its porch-like nature as to the world which is to come, the frame of man, as connected with the book of nature, is what might well prompt the soul to say, "Lo, I come (in the volume of the book it is written of me) to do thy will, O God."

A living soul, that could be spoken to, spiritually, and that could hear, and that was even also free to hear or not to hear, to obey or not to obey! A new creation this! And also this was the commencement of a new era under the skies. For "the Spirit of God" which had been moving "upon the face of the waters" had become now a voice in the garden of Eden, — the Lord God speaking.

"The Lord God speaking!" exclaims our modern scepticism. "That could not have been, for he was not obeyed; and so on any understanding of it, symbolic or otherwise, there can be no meaning in that narrative." And who are we that think so? We are persons certainly that own to conscience, and who have therefore been like Adam and Eve, over and over again, for that disobedience, which seems so incredible in them. For, certainly, we cannot say that the voice of conscience would be more authoritative than it now is with us, merely for quivering on the air before reaching us spiritually.

When man was created, it was by the same Spirit as that which garnished the heavens, though by a diversity of operation. And when that Spirit which had coerced and informed the elements began the training of creatures in the image of God, it was necessarily through adaptation, and by being fatherly as well as almighty, and by being perhaps a voice, while as yet conscience had not begun to speak, and by being companionship for the first human beings in the solitude of an unpeopled world.

In the Scriptures, when it is said that God spoke, the right understanding would seem to be, that it was through an angel. Jacob had a dream, or more precisely perhaps, a vision in a dream, as to which he says what follows. "The angel of God spake unto me in a dream, saying Jacob: and I said, Here am I." But then that same personage, which had commenced speaking as an angel, as he continues his speech, says, "I am the God of Bethel, where thou anointedst the pillar, and where thou vowedst a vow unto me." When Moses was keeping his flock of sheep near Mount Horeb, "the angel of the Lord appeared unto him in a flame of fire out of the midst of a bush." And when Moses went near to see how there could be such a fire, and the bush not be burning with it, the voice which called to him out of the bush was from God, and it said, "I am the God of thy father, the God of Abraham, the God of Isaac, and the God of Jacob." And similarly, it is to be read, "The Lord went before them by day in a pillar of a cloud, to lead them the way." And almost immediately afterwards it is written, "And the angel of God, which went before the camp of Israel, removed and went behind them: and the pillar of the cloud went from before their face, and stood behind them."

In the Book of Numbers, it is to be read that Moses talked with the Lord, and said as to the Egyptians, "They have heard that thou Lord art among this people, that thou Lord art seen face to face, and that thy cloud standeth over them, and that thou goest before them, by daytime in a pillar of a cloud, and in a pillar of fire by night." And yet at the commencement of the Gospel of John it is written, "No man hath seen God at any time." Now, how are these two very distinct statements to be reconciled? It is to be done through a third, very simply; and it is to be read in the Book of Exodus, along with many laws, which were given at Sinai. "Behold, I send an angel before thee, to keep thee in the way, and to bring thee into the place which I have prepared. Beware of him, and obey his voice, provoke him not; for he will not pardon your transgressions: for my name is in him. But if thou shalt indeed obey his voice, and do all that I speak; then I will be an enemy unto thine enemies, and an adversary unto thine adversaries. For mine angel shall go before thee, and bring thee in unto the Amorites and the Hittites."

When then by the letter of the Scripture it would

seem as though God had been seen or heard, it is to be understood that it was through his angel that God was manifested. No doubt, in the preceding text, there is implied a philosophy of revelation which has not been common, for many ages; but it is not therefore the less certainly Scriptural: and it is indeed the philosophy of the Spirit.

Seven hundred years later than the giving of the Decalogue at Sinai, was this utterance through Isaiah the prophet, as to the Lord, and the angel of God. "For he said, Surely they are my people, children that will not lie: so he was their Saviour. In all their affliction he was afflicted, and the angel of his presence saved them: in his love and in his pity he redeemed them; and he bare them, and carried them all the days of old. But they rebelled, and vexed his holy Spirit." Later still than these words by three hundred years, were the prophecies of Malachi. The last of the prophets he was. And the Spirit as it spake through him anticipated the Gospel. And the following words would seem to foretell that the inauguration of Christianity would, in some way, be attended by that angel of God who had been "the angel of his presence" for the Israelites. "Behold, I will send my messenger, and he shall prepare the way before me: and the Lord, whom you seek, shall suddenly come to his temple, even the messenger of the covenant, whom ye delight in: behold, he shall come, saith the Lord of hosts." What a strange and wonderful utterance this is to think upon! It is the Spirit speaking from afar off, but for effect at the present day, almost as though in an unknown tongue. For it implies probably knowledge which is lost, though not perhaps irrecoverably. The words of that prophecy are to be read to-day by the natural eye. But some time they will be spiritually discerned; and then they will be like an angel testifying as to the Gospel, from his own connection with it.

In the Scriptures, then, an angel of God is God himself, as it were. And it would seem also as though a spirit in the service of God might some time have been accounted as the Spirit of God. And this perhaps is an import of the phrase which is illustrated by the saying of a Jewish Rabbi, as quoted by Lightfoot, in his *Horæ Hebraicæ et Talmudicæ*. The Jews believed anciently that a man who wished to become a diviner might get a demon or unclean spirit to enter him, by a preparation of the nervous system through fasting, and by waiting in a graveyard. Said the Rabbi Akibah, "Does the unclean spirit come upon him that fasts for that very end, that the unclean spirit may come upon him? Much more would the Holy Spirit come upon him that fasts for that very end that the Holy Spirit might come upon him." But more precisely still to the point is the statement of Lightfoot that "the seven spirits" was an ancient phrase with the Jews for the Holy Ghost; and that that is the meaning of the words in the Book of Revelation. "Grace be unto you, and peace, from him which is, and which was, and which is to come; and from the seven Spirits which are before the throne; and from Jesus Christ, who is the faithful witness, and the first begotten of the dead, and the prince of the kings of the earth." Of the manifestation of the

Spirit, prophecy was one form. But by St. John it is distinctly implied that spirits from the spiritual world might be the manifestation of the Spirit of God. "Beloved, believe not every spirit, but try the spirits whether they are of God: because many false prophets are gone out into the world. Hereby know ye the Spirit of God: every spirit that confesseth that Jesus Christ is come in the flesh is of God; and every spirit that confesseth not that Jesus Christ is come in the flesh is not of God." Also, that the Spirit may manifest itself through individual spirits, and through the manner in which those disembodied, invisible spirits may actuate human beings, appears by the words of St. Paul, addressed to the church at Corinth, as to how people were to behave during an actual manifestation of the Spirit. "Let the prophets speak two or three, and let the other judge. If anything be revealed to another that sitteth by, let the first hold his peace. For ye may all prophesy one by one, that all may learn, and all may be comforted. And the spirits of the prophets are subject to the prophets." Hence, it would seem as though sometimes and for some purposes spirits might be the channels between men and God for the Holy Ghost, and be indeed themselves as spirits, the manifestation of the Spirit. Among the gifts of the Spirit to the early Church, one was "discerning of spirits," or an instinct as to inspiration, — ability for knowing the quality of the influence from which a prophet might speak.

The spirits by whom the prophets were made to prophesy in the early days of the church at Corinth, may perhaps have been some of them of another nationality than the Jewish, or of some age earlier than that of the captivity. And thence perhaps may have resulted the phenomenon of persons speaking in unknown tongues. It does not seem necessary to suppose that always these tongues were absolutely new, or even certainly foreign to this earth. Commonly they may simply have been unknown languages to such persons as were present to hear them. And indeed just as the spirits who were attendant on the prophets were to be restrained as to utterance at times, so also were these unknown tongues to "keep silence in the church," unless there were interpreters present. This speaking in unknown tongues would seem to have been somewhat of an incidental manifestation of the Spirit. Says St. Paul to the Corinthians, "I thank my God, I speak with tongues more than ye all; yet in the church, I had rather speak five words with my understanding" — what a positive saying! — "than ten thousand words in an unknown tongue." And as to the nature or manner of these tongues, as they were spoken with, perhaps there may be some suggestion latent in those words, which Paul could imagine might be true as to himself, when he said, "Though I speak with the tongues of men and of angels."

And analogous with what precedes is the remark by Maimonides, on the subject of prophecy, that "on a man intelligent, wise, holy, removed from all worldly associations, and absorbed by heavenly contemplations, the Holy Spirit will rest: that he intermingles with that grade of angels called 'ishim,' and becomes quite a different being from what he was before." That the Holy Spirit might come on a holy man, from his being in affinity with holy angels, was the doctrine of a Jewish Rabbi of the twelfth century. He is still accounted the greatest Rabbi that has ever been: and he probably read *his Bible* by light as purely Jewish almost, as though it had been from the seven-branched candlestick.

Said John the Baptist as to Jesus, "God giveth not the Spirit by measure unto him." And Jesus said of himself what apparently was the same thing in other words, "Hereafter ye shall see heaven open, and the angels of God ascending and descending upon the Son of man." It is noticeable that the words of Jesus, as to the angels, are the same words which are used in Genesis, in the history of that vision which Jacob had, as to the nearness of God. "Behold a ladder set up on the earth, and the top of it reached to heaven: and behold the angels of God ascending and descending on it." Carrying prayers heavenwards, and bringing back answers and help, "the angels of God ascending and descending" would seem to be at times the same as the Holy Spirit. And indeed are not angels under God, like "the seven spirits which are before his throne"; and "are they not all ministering spirits, sent forth to minister for them who shall be heirs of salvation?"

The Spirit must have laws and ways of which mere mortals can never possibly know. Results from it they may experience personally, while yet the manner thereof may transcend all conjecture. Till within the last two or three hundred years, universally men had lived and died in ignorance that blood is reddened and vitalized by the process of breathing. And so it may well be supposed that the philosophy of human nature, spiritually, will never be known perfectly by anybody in the flesh. With an unperverted man, prayer is as truly an instinct as breathing is. But as to how prayer is power, and as to how God feels it, as man breathes it, mortal man may never know; nor is it necessary that he should. Indeed, it cannot be otherwise, religiously, than that we ought to be confident as to some things which we cannot see. We may be ever so prosperous in this world, and great, but yet as human beings, we are at our best and truest only when "we walk by faith, not by sight." And to persons who live more sublimely than they can possibly know, and as "kings and priests unto God and the Father," there must occur things higher as to origin than what they can possibly trace; because spirits living by the Spirit have infinite, and infinitely various connections.

It has already been quoted, in another connection, what was the last prophecy of the last of the prophets. "Behold, I will send you Elijah the prophet, before the coming of the great and dreadful day of the Lord." Four hundred years after this prophecy was on parchment, Jesus said as to John the Baptist, "What went ye out for to see? A prophet? Yea, I say unto you, and more than a prophet. For this is he, of whom it is written, Behold, I send my messenger before thy face, which shall prepare thy way before thee." And then Jesus added, "If ye will receive it, this is Elias, which was for to come."

Elijah back again on the earth, after more than eight hundred years! So indeed it would seem that men might have thought. And if there be any connection between this world below and the world above, as to intercommunicating agencies, it may well have been, that Elijah of the age of Ahab and Jezebel, who had vanished from earth, on a highway of the Spirit, and in a chariot like fire, might have been expected to "first come and restore all things" against the coming of the Messiah and the kingdom of heaven. And of his nearness to the earth and his connection certainly with Jesus, the narrative of the Transfiguration is evidence, wherein it is written, "Behold there talked with him two men, which were Moses and Elias: who appeared in glory, and spake of his decease which he should accomplish at Jerusalem."

Moses and Elias then had known of Jesus in their world, and had conversed together about him, many a time probably, before they were seen talking with him on the Mount. And, no doubt, their discourse as to his decease was from their angelic foreknowledge, and from their sensitiveness as to that Spirit, through which an acorn is an oak-tree in a shell, and Christianity is the development of Judaism, and the world of to-day is the germ of some distant millennium.

But Moses and Elias knowing of Jesus, so as to meet him on the Mount! Certainly, there are persons to be startled by that wording of the fact, who, all their lives, have been reading of it in the Bible, very devoutly indeed, but yet very thoughtlessly. Moses and Elias in glory not know of Jesus of Nazareth! They must have known of him, and of the purpose as to which one day he would say, "For this cause came I unto this hour. Father, glorify thy name." And Moses and Elias may well have been not only knowing of Jesus, but concerned also with his way and work in the world. For, indeed, — another thing so often read and so seldom believed, — actually "there is joy in the presence of the angels of God over one sinner that repenteth." That grace which had reached the earth in the person of Jesus Christ, — it may well be that Moses and Elias had been accessory to it, and that they had even, during the captivity in Babylon, been inquiring among the spirits of the prophets Ezekiel, Malachi, and Isaiah, "searching what or what manner of time the spirit of Christ which was in them did signify, when it testified beforehand the sufferings of Christ, and the glory that should follow."

It should be observed, what is rarely and almost never noticed, that on the Mount at the time of the Transfiguration, what happened was seen by Peter, James, and John in a vision, and while they were in a trance-like state. "And as they came down from the mountain, Jesus charged them saying, Tell the vision to no man, until the Son of man be risen again from the dead." They had seen in a vision, and after an unearthly manner, just as afterwards "Cornelius saw in a vision evidently about the ninth hour of the day an angel of God coming in to him"; and just also as, by a corresponding vision, Peter was prepared for hearing of what had happened to Cornelius the devout centurion; because having gone up upon the housetop to pray, "he fell into a trance, and saw heaven opened." And similarly, Daniel says as to the commencement of a revelation which was made to him from an angel, that his strength failed him, "And when I heard the voice of his words, then was I in a deep sleep on my face." That sleep was of the body, merely, and not of the soul. It was the same state as that in which Abraham was, when a covenant was made with him by the Lord; and when "as the sun was going down a deep sleep fell upon Abram."

That sleep or fitness for visions is something like the same thing, apparently, as being "in the Spirit." It is a condition in which the ear is closed against thunder, and in which the eye is as though it were dead, and in which the skin is insensible even to fire. It is a state in which the soul is purely itself, and hears through its spiritual ears, and sees through its spiritual eyes, and is conscious of another atmosphere than this of earth.

Also then being "in the Spirit" means often, being in a state in which the body is nothing, and through which, also, the soul is among spirits and may see angels. At the time of the conversion of St. Paul, Ananias told him, "The God of our fathers hath chosen thee, that thou shouldest know his will, and see that Just One, and shouldest hear the voice of his mouth." And now how were these words made good; and how was Jesus Christ seen by Paul? This is what Paul himself says: "And it came to pass, that, when I was come again to Jerusalem, even while I prayed in the temple, I was in a trance; and I saw him saying unto me, Make haste, and get thee quickly out of Jerusalem; for they will not receive thy testimony concerning me." And that the trance which he wrote of is as though his body had been abolished for a time, or as though the soul's connection had been suspended with it, is plain by what St. Paul says as to his having been in Paradise, when he heard things, which, though he might have felt, he was unable to utter for want of words. The Principia of Newton never have been and never can be translated into Erse. Nor possibly, therefore, could the sublimities which Paul heard in Paradise have been reducible into Greek, by any human skill. And as to that abnormal state which he experienced, his words about it are for simplicity almost as wonderful as what he narrates. And indeed they are the words of a man familiar with miracles. These are the words: "I knew a man in Christ above fourteen years ago (whether in the body, I cannot tell; or whether out of the body, I cannot tell: God knoweth), such an one caught up to the third heaven."

During the trance which Paul had in the temple, at Jerusalem, it is possible that his spirit may have parted from his body, and by some spiritual law may have reached either Paradise or the third heaven, like a ray of light. But also it is conceivable that while Paul was entranced in the temple, his soul may simply have been wearing the body like insensate clothes, and been receiving some influence from above, by which it became more and more intensely spiritual, and by which also it found itself successively in affinity with one heaven, and another, and even a third. And of that preternatural experience, as to the manner, either understanding well corresponds with such texts as these, in the Book of Revelation, "Immediately I was in the spirit," and "He carried me away in the spirit."

This being "in the Spirit" would seem to be concurrently with nature. Man by his nature is capable of intromission as to spirit, and of being caught up into Paradise, and of hearing what the Spirit says, and what also angels may have to say or show. And in regard to revelation, the deep sleep of the body which was experienced by prophets and apostles may have been but a consequence of their souls having been intensely quickened in some way, at some point. For often persons, with great excitement, mentally, have found that there had been thunder without their notice, and that even they had been severely wounded, without knowing that they had been struck. And indeed many times, martyrs and confessors have testified, as to their having had no sense of pain, while the torturers were at work upon them.

But how are men approached or reached or affected by the Spirit? In many ways perhaps, and contingently on many conditions, as to person, time and place; as indeed may well be supposed, when it is remembered how persons differ from one another, mentally, and by education and by nationality, — and also how men of the same descent must necessarily be differenced by the varying tone of the successive centuries into which they are born.

In one age, a man may live by the Holy Ghost, and be strong and joyful in it, without a wish for a miracle or a thought of one. While in another age, a man cannot think but that he grows from birth to death simply from out of his earthly self, like a plant rooted in the earth; and for him, therefore, some gift of the spirit, or some miracle or sign, might be of infinite importance, as a thing for thought; because of its manifesting a connection for him with a world invisible of spirit.

A royal miscreant like Ahab was not approachable by the Spirit, as though he had been some "bruised reed." Isaac, the patriarch and shepherd, may have been capable of having the Lord appear to him in a vision, in the night, while yet he may have been utterly incapable of having the Spirit of the Lord breathe through him, for the wording and soul of a psalm. Just before his death, Jacob was more fully prophetic than in all his life before. "And Jacob called unto his sons, and said, Gather yourselves together, that I may tell you that which shall befall you in the last day." And why, and how was this? It was because almost his spirit was inside of the spiritual world, and was within hearing perhaps of the angel of the covenant; and it was because he would within a few minutes have "gathered up his feet into the bed, and yielded up the ghost."

Before the prophet Samuel was called, there had been a time, for the Jews, when "there was no open vision." And that time would seem to have been so long as that even there had occurred with it a change in the use of words. For, in connection with Samuel, it is to be read, that in Israel "he that is now called a prophet was beforetime called a seer." And indeed it was not because of a long time having elapsed, or because of mere worldly craving, that ever the word of the Lord was vouchsafed. Nor ever was the Spirit receivable by everybody alike. While the Jews were yet on their journey from Egypt to the promised land, the Lord had said, by way of magnifying Moses, over his successors, "If there be a prophet among you, I the Lord will make myself known unto him in a vision, and will speak unto him in a dream." Before there can be a revelation from the highest, there must be a receptive state in some person on the earth. And it is but a development of this truth, according to the philosophy of revelation, to say that certain persons of a prophetic temperament, must have been faithful to their nature and have been welcomed among their fellow-creatures, before God can draw nigh to men through the Spirit, rather than by convulsion, pestilence, and the terrors of the Lord, or by that penal blindness, which is none the less fearful because it does not know of itself.

As to the preceding statement, worldly objection of any kind is nothing. What is all the state of Bœotia to-day, in comparison with Homer? Poetry is a mighty influence; for it glorifies the earth and man's life in it; and it can prepare in the mind the way of the Lord. And yet not every man, but only one man in the seventeenth century, was born with a soul which could so live on earth as to leave behind, on its departure, the works and the glory of John Milton.

Thoughts from on high as to God, or high thoughts concerning God, can reach mankind only through such minds as may, at any time, be open and willing to receive them. This gentle manner of approach is not however of necessity. Though certainly the way of the Spirit, in this world, at present, would be confusion worse than what happened at the tower of Babel, and would even be suffering worse than what the Israelites were punished with, in the desert, but that it is tempered for us and administered, by what in a Christian way, may be called the fatherhood of God. And indeed the condescension of God, toward this world, as he wraps it about and fills it with his Spirit, is not by acts dating from eras, but it is continuous, and like a stream, for "ho, every one that thirsteth."

Man must think of God, before he can feel that God remembers him. "Draw nigh to God, and he will draw nigh to you." A lonely disciple is not without Christ, and yet also these words are not a mere truism, however they may be interpreted, "where two or three are gathered together in my name, there am I in the midst of them." And in these words, there is something spiritual meant, and beyond what Novalis may have intended intellectually when he said, "Certainly my belief gains infinitely as to strength, as soon as it is shared by another person."

"The assembling of yourselves together" is a form of waiting for the Spirit, whether or not it be so understood by mere church-goers. Men are approachable by the Spirit, not only as individuals, but as societies. Any day, by the mysterious alchemy of the universe, seekers after God may suddenly have their earnestness open out into the Spirit, and have the Spirit come in upon them. And with taking "sweet counsel together," and walking "unto the house of God in company," and with looking steadfastly towards heaven, Christians are in a way to see it open, and to have their hearts fill with a strange, unearthly joy in the Holy Ghost. "He that cometh to God must believe that he is, and that he is a rewarder of them that diligently seek him." And so also is it as to the Spirit. It was on believers in an expectant attitude, and on those who did "wait for the promise of the Father," that the Spirit was poured forth, after the ascension of Jesus Christ. They were drawn together by their faith; and the thoughts of all of them were conjointly a longing expectation. "And when the day of Pentecost was come, they were all with one accord in one place."

According to the Scriptures then the Spirit was that of which there can be an outpouring in one age and a dearth in another. It is what can be imparted to a man, and what can be withdrawn from him, and it is what also he can quench as to himself. Occasionally, also, it is what can be imparted by one man to another, not however as arbitrary grace, but only like some angelic whisper, for the inmost being of the recipient. In the evening after his resurrection, the disciples being assembled together in a room, of which the doors were closed for fear of the Jews, Jesus became present among them and breathed on them, and said, "Receive ye the Holy Ghost." The Holy Spirit was also communicable, occasionally, by the apostles, through their hands, while placed on right-minded persons. Arguing with the high priest and the council, at a very early day in the Church, Peter said of the Holy Ghost that it was what "God hath given to them that obey him." And at a later period than this, when Peter was preaching to hearers who were not all of them Jews by blood, to the astonishment of them of the circumcision, "the Holy Ghost fell on all them which heard the word." Spiritual affinity had met the Spirit, through the agency of Peter, at Cæsarea, and then and there and thereby began to be fulfilled that promise which was made to

Abraham by the Lord, almost twenty centuries before, "I will make of thee a great nation, and I will bless thee, and make thy name great; and thou shalt be a blessing; and I will bless them that bless thee, and curse him that curseth thee; and in thee shall all families of the earth be blessed." Also apart from all human agency, and at all times and everywhere, on the assurance of Jesus Christ, the Holy Spirit is what can certainly and even perhaps suddenly be obtained by everybody, by prayer. "If ye then, being evil, know how to give good gifts unto your children, how much more shall your heavenly Father give the Holy Spirit to them that ask him?"

The Spirit of God may be poured out on men, in multitudes; or it may spread from heart to heart like a flame; or by possessing itself of the body of some man, it may even speak expressly. It may reach one man, like some "word of the Lord" suddenly revealed in the mind; and to another man it may be imparted by angelic agency. It may strike a man with conviction, while he is in a crowd: and conceivably it may get lodged with him, during deep sleep, when sometimes God "openeth the ears of men and sealeth their instruction, that he may withdraw man from his purpose, and hide pride from man."

The Spirit is always the selfsame, but in operation it may be of infinite diversity. And for this reason, it is variously described. The Spirit is the Holy Ghost; but the Holy Ghost is a phrase, which cannot always be used for the Spirit of God. Chaos became order and was made to blossom with beauty, and the heavens around were garnished by the Spirit of God, but not by the Holy Spirit; because fire and water, trees and animals, are all alike incapable of holiness; and so too are all the stars, however they may differ from one another in glory. Prophetically what came upon Balaam was the Spirit of God; and it was by the same Spirit that prophets and apostles were inspired: but if in them it was the Holy Spirit and differed from what Balaam felt, it was because of their having been better men than he, and sensitive to holiness; and because it was, as it is written, "holy men of God spake as they were moved by the Holy Ghost."

In the Gospel of John, the following words were spoken, with a view to the distress which the disciples were soon to feel, and what also would be their need of instruction. And in these passages the Spirit is the Holy Ghost, and it is the Comforter, and also it is the Spirit of truth. "I will pray the Father, and he shall give you another Comforter, that he may abide with you forever; even the Spirit of truth." And then soon afterwards Jesus says, "The Comforter, which is the Holy Ghost, whom the Father will send in my name, he shall teach you all things, and shall bring all things to your remembrance, whatsoever I have said unto you."

In the New Testament, what is "the Spirit of your Father," as mentioned by Matthew, is "the Holy Ghost" as recorded by Luke.

Men are reached by the Spirit, on one plane and another. As walking, thinking, working creatures on the earth, "the inspiration of the Almighty giveth them understanding." But for men "in the image of God created," the Spirit can be the Holy Spirit. And by still other persons, the Spirit of God can be felt like the spirit of the Son of God, for tenderness and encouragement, and sweet loving assurance. And to men who feel as Jesus felt, and who feel also that certainly it cannot be otherwise than that "the Father loveth the Son," Paul would say, as though it were the way of the universe, "and because ye are sons, God hath sent forth the Spirit of his Son into your hearts, crying, Abba, Father."

God, that made all things, is "all things to all men" to a greater extent than ever Paul was made. From north to south, from the earth to the sun, and from one sun to another, it is by the Spirit of God, that the universe is coherent. And it is by the same Spirit, that men are made to differ, and the stars also from one another in glory, and one era on this earth from another, as time wears on. When the beasts of the field were made, it was by the Spirit, but not by as much of the Spirit of God as what created man in his own image. And man, as he lives, is more and more receptive of that Spirit.

There are persons who believe in the Spirit as a pious word, but cannot conceive of it as an actuality which concerns them. And there are some who say scornfully, "What sign is there of the Spirit, any more than there is of spirit, at all? A mere Hebraism! Who but the Jews ever thought of it? And what way is there by which it could ever get at us? There is no possibility of it between us and the sun; and under the earth, there is certainly nothing of the kind." But now the argument from ignorance is good only as it is used by persons who know a great deal, which those scornful ones never do.

The susceptibilities of human nature as to spiritual action, are many, as may perhaps have already appeared. And additionally this is conceivable. As the body is the case of the soul, so may animal magnetism serve for the corporeity of the Spirit, sometimes, and for one or two purposes. Just as it is written as to Peter and John among the Samaritans, "Then laid they their hands on them, and they received the Holy Ghost."

But indeed myself already I am spiritually insphered, and so I have been ever since I was born as a living soul. It is true, as I look up, that there is nothing between me and the sun, for such eyes as I can open as yet. Nor is it likely that ever my spiritual sight will be opened, till I shall have got through the valley of the shadow of death. But still if I could look to-day, with those eyes, through which it is possible that hereafter I may even see Uriel in the sun, I should discern between this earth and the altered look of that luminary, at various distances, signs probably of principalities and powers, and ways of communication with the New Jerusalem; and I should be sensible of the magic properties of another atmosphere than this of earth; and I might thereby also perhaps become conscious of strange affinities drawing me like old friendships, towards Paul or Dante; and toward some angel, who may at some time have encamped about me in a time of trouble, without my knowledge; or toward some remote ancestor, whose name I may never have heard of; or toward some spirit, whose course in his earthly life was marked by like lines with my own; or toward some fellow-Christian, who may have thrilled, in church, without my knowledge, to the same movement of the Spirit as what quickened me.

Is it said that there is no avenue for the Spirit, as to human nature? It might as well be said that there is no channel in the air, whereby words can pass from man to man!

The universe is alive with the Spirit and with spiritual occupants, and has always been thought to be so, except by a few people now and then, and here and there, — persons of a nature somewhat elephantine as to outlook, and unfortunate as to education. According to an old word for a prejudice on the subject, there are those who cannot believe in the existence of spirit. There have been persons, especially in France, who have been even bigoted against a belief in human immortality or in spirit. During the first half of this century, magnetism was ardently studied in France, but when it began to give signs of being spiritually connected, some of its greatest adepts were shocked and scandalized as being men of "the world that now is." The Baron Dupotet was so affected; but yet he could not but say, "There is an agent in space, whence we ourselves, our inspiration and our intelligence proceed; and that agent is the spiritual world which surrounds us." Those are the words of a French adept and scholar as to magnetism, and which were true to his own knowledge, as he thought. And these words following are by Confucius, the contemporary, indeed, of the prophets Zechariah and Haggai, but yet who was also a Chinese, "An ocean of invisible intelligences surrounds us." Plotinus has been quoted in opposition to Christ and the apostles by anti-supernaturalists, who apparently were quite unaware of his claims to be an ecstatic. But Plotinus said, what, no doubt, was of his own experience, as he believed, "All things are full of demons," or in plain English, "Everywhere there are spirits."

This spirituality of the universe is the testimony of almost all tribes and nations, in every age. It was the persuasion of Greece, and Egypt, and Chaldea. Under the light, conjointly of history and criticism, what the Scriptures were especially given to teach is not the reality of the spiritual world, as many people think, but rather the certainty and nature and operation of the Spirit of God; or the Holy Ghost.

It is of the nature of the godhead, that it should be always revealing itself, in one way and another; in the make of a diamond, in the beauty of a fern; in the cry of a young raven and the manner in which it gets answered; in the appearance of the first man on earth; and in that glimmer of Providence, which is perceptible on the stream of time historically, and which to some eyes is as dubious as phosphorescence, and yet still as certain.

Geology is science as to the Spirit of God, while it was shaping the earth. And the Bible is the history of the Spirit, in its relations with man. The tent of Abraham, the sojourn in Egypt, the captivity in Babylon, Moriah, and the lake of Galilee are but accessories to the history. The Old Testament and the New are a revelation of every man to himself, through the Spirit, and a revelation also of the eternal Spirit as it acts in time.

And now perhaps we are in a way, wherein can be resumed more intelligently what was being discussed about Elijah as the forerunner of Jesus Christ. And it should be remembered, that what is now being considered is in connection with the reign of the Spirit, made visible. During the transfiguration, the disciples saw Elias in the spiritual world, and so when Jesus referred to his death, as being perhaps not far off, "his disciples asked him, saying, Why then say the Scribes that Elias must first come? And Jesus answered and said unto them, Elias truly shall first come, and restore all things. But I say unto you, that Elias is come already, and they knew him not, and have done unto him whatsoever they listed. Likewise shall also the Son of man suffer of them. Then the disciples understood that he spake unto them of John the Baptist." John the Baptist was a man like any other Jew, and yet also he was Elias. The philosophy of this matter is the same as that which was entertained by the sons of the prophets, after Elijah had vanished in heaven, when they said, "The spirit of Elijah doth rest on Elisha. And they came to meet him, and bowed themselves to the ground before him." And so according to this account, John the Baptist, in the flesh, may in some way possibly have been influenced by Elijah, while dwelling in a state altogether foreign to flesh and blood, and sun, moon and stars. For the spirit indeed, time and space are nothing, or nearly so; while sameness of mind or spiritual affinity may, under God, be almost everything.

But why should John the Baptist have been inspired by Elias, or in any way have been Elias? It was, no doubt, because of the spiritual constitution of the universe. And thereby it was not an exceptional event, but was in conformity with other things, which concern us, and of which some perhaps affect us frequently. In Patmos, John received a revelation from an angel, which revelation the angel had received from Jesus Christ. And it was in a similar manner, probably, that Elijah was concerned with Christ, as making the Baptist "go before him in the spirit and power of Elias." And indeed the whole ministration of the world, intellectually, morally, and spiritually, is largely by mediation. For when influences from above reach men, commonly it is through a certain few, who are like mediators for the rest. And according to St. Paul, not only was the law "ordained by angels," but also it was "in the hand of a mediator."

It was by the foreknowledge of God, and through the operation of spiritual laws no doubt, and of his own free-will also, that Elijah was the spirit and power of John the son of Zacharias the priest. But now Elias had left the earth nine hundred years, when he intervened through the Baptist. And yet also, nineteen hundred years before Jesus was born, there had been "preached before the gospel unto Abraham."

Often on earth, that which is a mystery of the kingdom of heaven had its beginning with the Spirit, and is outside of the reach of mere reason, and is what only the Spirit can ever show, or even hint about.

According to the Book of Revelation, "Behold the tabernacle of God is with men, and he will dwell with them, and they shall be his people." In a state of more or less intelligence Archbishop Fenelon, Jacob

Böhme, George Fox, and William Law, and Swedenborg, and Charles Wesley and his brother John, and multitudes, more or less like them, have entered into the court itself of that temple, during the last two or three hundred years. But nevertheless, one generation after another, for, now, a long time, while Christians have been going up to the temple for worship, commonly they have had but a poor belief, and often none whatever, as to the holy of holies, and the positive, kind, familiar, human nearness of the Spirit.

The holy of holies! Now under Christ Jesus, the actual place of it is in the soul itself, if only men had faith in it, and could believe in the Spirit.

And indeed it is in the Spirit, and from the Spirit, that man is to live to all eternity, and even just as he does already. For, truly the human body is the highest formation of the Spirit which there is in connection with this earth. And indeed, optically, diamonds of the purest water are but ancient experiments in the workshop of nature, with a view to the human eye.

The recent discoveries, through which the powers of nature lend themselves to human use, and under the application of which the fields grow more fertile, and the depths of the earth yield up their treasures, are often spoken of, as nature unveiling herself. Nature unveiling herself, — what is that? O thou poor idolater of second causes, what is nature? Nature is but one of the lower titles of God. And "nature unveiling herself," if it means anything, means the Spirit of God, revealing itself of its own good-will on a plane which is level with human intellect.

But, at its best, what is all that eases our bodily

life, or even that glorifies existence for us, as mere denizens of this earth, in comparison with that revelation of the Spirit, of which man spiritually is susceptible? Fearfully and wonderfully made as man is as to his body, he is yet more wonderful still as to his soul. And of all the creatures that have ever been on this earth, man only is what can answer, in any way, to the fatherhood of God. And we human creatures, at this late time, ought to be able to understand readily the meaning of St. Paul, when he asks, "Know ye not that ye are the temple of God, and that the Spirit of God dwelleth in you?"

JESUS AND THE SPIRIT.

THIS essay is simply what it purports to be, and is not a treatise on Christology.

During his stay in the wilderness, Jesus was qualified for his work, by having his spirit tried to the uttermost by what he was to preach against. His trial was probably like the trial of Abraham as to his faith, and was while his soul was in a state wherein it was exercised independently of his bodily senses, and irrespectively of geographical limitations. And if that condition should be called a state of vision, it should be remembered that a vision differs from a dream much more widely and profoundly than even waking does. From out of his inmost being Jesus withstood that concentration of all temptation, for which as to subtlety the word is Satan. " And he was there in the wilderness forty days, tempted of Satan; and with the wild beasts: and the angels ministered unto him."

On his reappearance, after his seclusion in the desert, he received a message from John the Baptist. The day of the Lord is light only for the children of light. And by some persons it is never known of while it is passing. John the Baptist was to be famous forever, in connection with the gospel, and yet for discernment, spiritually, of the time in which he was living, "he that is least in the kingdom of heaven is greater than he." John was the forerunner of Jesus, and also he had borne " record, saying, I saw the Spirit descending from heaven like a dove, and it abode upon him" ; and yet " when John had heard in the prison the works of Christ, he sent two of his disciples, and said unto him, Art thou he that should come, or do we look for another ?" It was a " day of visitation." It was the time of the Spirit, and by the Spirit, judgment was to be formed. John, as well as Jesus, was withinside of its sphere. John was in mortal danger of his life; and Jesus probably felt that he was himself on the way to Calvary; and so, as though death were nothing, because of the surrounding light from heaven, " Jesus answered and said unto them, Go and show John again those things which ye do hear and see; the blind receive their sight, and the lame walk, the lepers are cleansed, and the deaf hear, the dead are raised up, and the poor have the gospel preached to them. And blessed is he, whosoever shall not be offended in me."

This answer to John was exactly like the claim which he had made on his return from the wilderness. He had taught in various synagogues acceptably. " And he came to Nazareth, where he had been brought up: and as his custom was, he went into the synagogue on the Sabbath day, and stood up for to read. And there was delivered unto him the book of the prophet Esaias. And when he had opened the book, he found the place where it was written, The Spirit of the Lord is upon me, because he hath anointed me to preach the gospel to the poor; he hath sent me to heal the broken-hearted, to preach deliverance to the captives, and recovering of sight to the blind, to set at liberty them that are bruised, to preach the acceptable year of the Lord. And he closed the book, and he gave it again to the minister, and sat down. And the eyes of all them that were in the synagogue were fastened on him. And he began to say unto them, This day is this scripture fulfilled in your ears. And all bare him witness and wondered at the gracious words which proceeded out of his mouth. And they said, Is not this Joseph's son?" Those gracious words are not to be known of now; but it would seem, that in some way, they were provocative, as they were thought about. And then miracles, like what had been heard of, from Capernaum, would seem to have been expected. And thereupon by Jesus, it was stated that a miracle was not a thing for everybody, nor forthcoming always at demand. Very instructive is the narrative of this matter by Luke. More and more devilish always does the spirit of the world become with arguing against the Spirit of God. And so it was, that in his own city, on a Sabbath day, and after having been admired for his gracious utterance, that Jesus was in danger from all who heard him, for "they led him unto the brow of the hill whereon their city was built, that they might cast him down headlong."

In the synagogue on that Sabbath day, as Jesus read and spoke, it was because of his having "returned in the power of the Spirit into Galilee." The power of the Spirit! what was that? It was the same thing as what is implied in this text, "And Jesus being full of the Holy Ghost returned from Jordan, and was led by the Spirit into the wilderness, being forty days tempted of the devil." It was that controlling, inspiring power, by which, on account of his nature, it is conceivable that practically he may have been like almightiness in a robe of clay, and like omniscience, as far as the scanty words of a poor dialect could afford it utterance. Said Jesus of himself, "He whom God hath sent speaketh the words of God: for God giveth not the Spirit by measure unto him. The Father loveth the Son, and hath given all things into his hand." And as further illustrating this union of Jesus with the Father, by the Spirit, for the manifestation of the Father on earth, Jesus said, "The Father loveth the Son, and showeth him all things that himself doeth: and he will show him greater works than these, that ye may marvel."

As used by Jesus, the phrase, "the Father that dwelleth in me," would seem to be of the same import as "the Spirit of the Lord is upon me." And like this variety of phrase is what follows. In the Gospel of Mark, Jesus tells his disciples, "Whatsoever shall be given you in that hour, that speak ye: for it is not ye that speak, but the Holy Ghost." But according to Matthew it was worded thus, "For it is not ye that speak, but the Spirit of your Father which speaketh in you."

After his temptation, Jesus "returned in the power of the Spirit into Galilee." It may help to elucidate the phrase, to remember that Simeon was a just man and devout, and one of whom it is written that "the Holy Ghost was upon him;" and that at the presentation of Jesus, "he came by the Spirit into the temple."

To the modern mind it is something strange, and a thing to be challenged, that Jesus should have arrived in Galilee "in the power of the Spirit." Whereas the phrase was easily and naturally intelligible till within less than the last two hundred years; and indeed had been so in every age of that spiritual descent, by which we Christians derive from Abraham.

As to familiarity of belief, connecting heaven with earth, first an angel disappeared, and then a spirit became improbable, and then by degrees the Holy Ghost became less and less intelligible, and more and more limited as to what it might seem to mean. And this has been as a murky effect of those various philosophies of a materialistic origin, which have obtained during the last two hundred years. It is at this point that the records of revelation are liable to be obscured to minds thus accidentally darkened. But the reliability of the Scriptures, as to meaning, is not therefore invalidated. For a dictionary may be lost; but if it should be found again, and answer its purpose as an interpreter, it is not therefore the less trustworthy. And indeed the mere records of Christianity, with their multitudinous corroborations, historical and psychological, are in the high court of reason, and by comparison, far superior, as to credibility, to all the evidences, on the strength of which geology prides itself. But apart from this all and above it, is what is the main evidence as to Christianity, as soon as ever a man begins really to hear the gospel; because "the Spirit itself beareth witness with our spirit, that we are the children of God," and because further "it is the Spirit that beareth witness, because the Spirit is truth."

For a moment, on that Sabbath day in Nazareth, while prejudice was asleep, and while he was being listened to in the synagogue, with all eyes fastened upon him, Jesus was probably for everybody a man of prophecy, and for some, perhaps, even the Messiah. But with being offended in him, his hearers had him change in their sight, to what apparently was worthy not only of excommunication, but even of death, according to the law of the synagogue.

Said Nicodemus to Jesus, "Rabbi, we know that thou art a teacher come from God: for no man can do these miracles that thou doest, except God be with him." But notwithstanding these miracles, soon afterwards this happened. Said Jesus, "He that is of God heareth God's words: ye therefore hear them not, because ye are not of God. Then answered the Jews, and said unto him, Say we not well that thou art a Samaritan, and hast a devil?" On the same facts such different judgments, because of such different judges!

And in a similar manner, and to a great extent, Christ Jesus was even to his believers, what they were ready or qualified for calling him. And thence perhaps he may have been apprehended variously by persons of different schools, rabbinically, and otherwise, and according also as they may have had right of entrance into the temple, as converts, or as Hebrews of the Hebrews, or as priests. And indeed before the birth of Jesus, some of the various descriptions as to his office, were certainly phrases which were in use among the Jews, and were not improbably employed as synonymes, though of diverse origins scholastically.

And so in the first age of the Church, Jesus "was a prophet mighty in deed and word before all the people"; and also he was the angel of the covenant: he was the Son of man and the Son of God: he was the light of the world, and he was the Word made flesh: and he was the Saviour of the world, and also its Judge. He was "the Lamb slain from the foundation of the world," and he was the "great high priest that is passed into the heavens," and also as Christ, he "through the eternal Spirit offered himself without spot to God." And further it is as to Christ Jesus, that it is written in the epistle to the Hebrews, "After the similitude of Melchisedec there ariseth another priest, who is made, not after the law of a carnal commandment, but after the power of an endless life." A grand statement this! But yet at the time when it was made it must certainly have been much more readily intelligible by "a Hebrew of the Hebrews," or by one brought up at the feet of Gamaliel, than by "devout Greeks."

The sun is a thousand things for operation, as it rises, and so also was the sun of righteousness. Said Jesus as to John, "A prophet! yea, I say unto you, and much more than a prophet. This is he of whom it is written, Behold I send my messenger before thy face, which shall prepare thy way before thee." And that, by which Jesus Christ was the fulfilment of the various conceptions, which his contemporaries had of him, was that by which he could say of himself, "God giveth not the Spirit by measure unto him."

The Spirit of God is equivalent to all miracles in one, just as it is the essential spirit of all the developments or creations which have been since the time, when what was "without form and void" began to grow into the forms and powers of that nature, which surrounds and supports us. It is "the spirit of life," from insect to man, and more divinely still it is "the spirit of life in Christ Jesus," through a sense of which any man may become "a new creature." It is the spirit of the universe waiting on man, as far as what is universal and eternal can possibly express itself through what is merely temporary and local, or as far as human nature is possibly susceptible of it.

But here it may be said, "What then? and how is it? Human nature, at its best — dust of the earth, however divine the soul may be that wears it — human nature, how is it approachable by that Spirit? For indeed credibility is something and indeed it is a great matter." And so it is: and every seed is a presumption of there being somewhere a soil fitted for it; and "every word of God" implies that properly somewhere there are "ears to hear." And whatever gift in any age has come "down from above," must certainly have reached man, through some channel of which his own nature was the receptiveness. A kind word can soothe a man mentally: and why then should not a man full of "the spirit of life," be able to attune fellow-creatures, bodily, and heal them with a touch? Some people have a wonderful sense as to character, and a singular instinct as to the spirit of their times, and the significance and connections of events: and is it not conceivable that such persons, if quickened from above, would readily grow prophetic? Certain people have remarkable experiences as to dreaming; and it would seem that by nature they may be like those persons who were susceptible of visions in Pentecostal times. This is certain and very striking, psychologically. At a time of great excitement, as to some high matter, social or religious, a thousand persons will suddenly feel themselves affected towards one another like brethren, and as though pervaded and possessed by a common spirit. And by the transforming and elevating effects of this spirit, every man in the crowd will feel as though he had become a new man. And so indeed he may be, for the moment, because of the affinity which he experiences as to all the souls about him; and through which he thrills to whatever is strongest spiritually, in the living crowd of which he is a member. And what is this, but a manifestation of some of those susceptibilities, on which as a preparation, when the heavens are willing, the Spirit is poured out? The body of man may be clay, but it is alive with spiritual possibilities, because of the indwelling soul.

But Jesus was not accessible to the Spirit, simply as the prophets were. He was never convulsed, nor after his return from the desert, with his nature explored by his resistance of Satan, was he ever entranced. Nor for mood was he dependent on external assistance of any kind, as sometimes the prophets were. But through him, as a serene atmosphere, the Father that dwelt within him, did the works which were wondered at, and spoke the words.

Jesus Christ was, on this earth, the Spirit of the Highest, in action among men, as condescendingly as when with that Spirit chaos was first agitated, and those ways were started through which by development and concurrence, and by "word upon word" injected into nature, and with, at last, the breath of God for inspiration, there was produced a living soul in the image itself of God.

And the Father, who was in Jesus, was the Spirit. But also that presence was the Spirit, as it never was or could have been in any other person on this earth, because there never was another, who could have been called Son of God, as he was. And under the high heavens, it was because of the sonship of Jesus, that the Spirit in him was the Divine fatherhood.

When Jesus visited his own country, it is written because of unbelief about him, though he healed "a few sick folk," yet that "he could there do no mighty work." And therefore the Father in him, was not the almightiness of the universe bearing down upon men for its own way as mere power, but was a spirit more tender than that even of the prophecy by Isaiah, wherein it is written, "Come now, and let us reason together, saith the Lord."

Jesus slept, and no doubt it was that he might wake the better. And sometimes his soul was joyous, and sometimes sorrowful. And therefore the eternal Spirit was expressive through him humanly. And it is not therefore necessary to suppose that every word of his in the cottages of Nazareth, or in Decapolis, or on the Lake of Galilee, or in Jerusalem, were his words as the Messiah; for, between his baptism by the Spirit and his crucifixion, he must necessarily have uttered a thousand times more words than what his Messiahship could have been concerned with, and especially as the

Son of man "came eating and drinking," and as though in the fair fulness of human nature.

The cry from the cross, "My God, my God, why hast thou forsaken me?" argued probably in Jewish ears, not despair, but simply wonder, humanly, that he was not more distinctly conscious of the Spirit. And not improbably, by the state in which he was upon the cross, that cry was uttered from something like that same level in his nature, as that from which at the river Jordan, he said to John, as to his being baptized, "Suffer it to be so now: for thus it becometh us to fulfil all righteousness."

Such a consideration as the foregoing is to be entertained by us human beings reverently and humbly, separated as we are from the first century of our era by so many days and nights, and so many varieties of thought and speculation.

According to John Smith, an eminent theologian of the seventeenth century, it was in conformity with what had been the practice of the old prophets, when Jesus associated with him the apostles as eyewitnesses and hearers. And, no doubt, the gospels are records, like what were kept among the Jews, in all ages, of the utterances of persons, who were believed to have the Spirit. Of the ancient prophets, according to Jewish history, the utterances of some which were once in books are now lost. And of the life of Jesus, of course, there was much of what was wonderful, which was never recorded,—"many other things which Jesus did." But as to the Spirit, for those who read by the Spirit, ten pages are almost as good as a thousand. And if not "spiritually discerned," the world itself full of books as to Christ, would not mean more than what the pages of the Four Gospels do.

Said Jesus to the apostles, "Ye also shall bear witness, because ye have been with me from the beginning." And as what they might rely upon for assistance, after his death, Jesus told them of "the Comforter, which is the Holy Ghost, whom the Father will send in my name, He shall teach you all things, and bring all things to your remembrance, whatsoever I have said unto you." The prophets spoke from the Spirit, in the respective dialects of their various times and circumstances. And it was in some similar way that Matthew and John are such different biographers. In writing the life of Jesus, Matthew evinces the faculty of the publican, and the man of business and facts. And perhaps by no inspiration that was possible could some of the discourses of Jesus have ever been brought to his remembrance, as they were to the mind of John: because he could never, in hearing, have apprehended them, even momentarily, as John did. And of all the apostles, the "disciple whom Jesus loved" was evidently the one in whose mind, with the quickening of the Holy Ghost, the words and image of Jesus would most readily revive.

The Gospel of John has latterly been regarded by some critics as less certainly authentic than its three companions. It is manifestly more spiritual than they are; and it was therefore, no doubt, less popular than they were in the earlier ages of the Church; and therefore, also, it was not quoted by writers, as the other Gospels were. That the Gospel of John differs in tone from the Gospels of Matthew, Mark, and Luke, and also in amplitude of remembrance is actually evidence as to its authenticity, when it is remembered who John the evangelist was; for because of what he had been to Christ he was probably beyond all the other apostles, receptive of the Spirit, which, as Jesus said to them, was to "bring all things to your remembrance, whatsoever I have said unto you."

But there are persons who demur to this, and who say, "The Spirit! That is a possibility. But how possibly could any man ever have been affected by it, and how did it operate upon him?" But now how is the spirit immortal of a man connected with his mortal body: or how even does the will of a lion strike with his paw? Indeed, the universe may resound ever so loudly with that stream, which is the spirit of life, and there will be some, at times, who will say, "I do not hear, because I do not know how I ought to." And there is many a philosopher, at the present day, who does not consider that perhaps he may be partially insensate as to spirit, by wrong education; and who is like some blind man under the Falls of Niagara, who should say, "It might be by the sound. And intelligent men, for a long while, have fancied it so. But as I do not myself see that it is so, I will not believe in the roar, as being an effect of these incredible Falls. And what for the multitude is the apparent sense, must be explicable, philosophically, in some other way." But there are people who are in a still worse condition, mentally, than that blind man under the Falls. For they hold seriously that they ought not really to believe in anything at all, because they have never been admitted behind their own eyes, where they could watch that mechanism of nature with its spiritual connections, through which external objects become thoughts in the mind. A man who is not to be contented in any other way, than by being not only himself, but also a witness with his own eyes, apart from himself, is necessarily in some way beside himself. But enough as to this scepticism of the day! For it is twenty-five hundred years out of date as a novelty; as is evident by these words in the prophecies of Isaiah, "Woe unto him that saith unto his father, What begettest thou? or to the woman, What hast thou brought forth?"

And like the absurdity denounced through the prophet Isaiah, is the folly which demurs to the Spirit of God, simply as not being concurrent with such laws of nature, as have been ascertained at the present day, and as not apparently being willing to be classed and manipulated, like the laws of chemistry.

The Old Testament and the New, and the Apocrypha also, in its degree, together with ecclesiastical memoirs of all ages, and along with them many a passage also in pagan literature, — these are the history of man, as the subject of the Spirit of God, the Holy Ghost. And Christians differ from one another doctrinally, not altogether because of more or less learning, or because of more or less intellect, but because also as to the Spirit, some persons are more susceptible than others are, and some less. And this may be just simply as one man differs from another man, as to poetic sensitiveness. Nor in this statement is there anything of presumptuousness implied. For the action of the Spirit is but one among many influences, by which character is formed, as is evident from the fact that Judas was one of the twelve. The Scriptures are like a labyrinth, which may be forced and broken through by self-will; but the clew to them, and that by which alone there is any intelligence as to the ways involved, is the Spirit, as a subject of belief. And indeed the Spirit of God may well be credited as what made the rod of Aaron to bud and blossom, and as being also what, at its will, might make a child of God display himself like an archangel, and hold all surrounding nature like a servant.

The Spirit is everything as to power and adaptation and knowledge. By it coral insects build their cells, and through it new worlds are being evolved. And the "Spirit of life in Christ Jesus" is that same Spirit which seraphs glory in, and which also so clothes "the grass of the field." And so now what is there in the Gospels, for which the Spirit cannot be credited, as it was embodied in the person of Jesus of Nazareth, and spake in his words, and acted in his deeds? "O, but," it is said, "no evidence as to the Spirit can be strong enough to upset belief as to the invariableness of nature." And this is said in easy forgetfulness of the fact, that there must have been ten or twenty different systems of nature known to men, as they have fancied. But such indeed is the unspiritual state of the Christian Church in some places, that Doctors of Divinity might be taught things of primary importance by the paganism of Greece and even of Madagascar.

As to the miracles of Jesus, the age in which they occurred is an important witness for their credibility, though it is seldom remembered. Jesus appeared in the world, announced and also welcomed by prophetic voices; and his appearance was "when the fulness of the time was come." His era was "the day of the Lord." And while it was passing, spiritual agencies were unusually active in Palestine, at least; and even the common air seemed to be a vague inspiration, as it was breathed.

The age of Jesus Christ was what Micah had prophesied for his people, and those in authority over them; "The day of thy watchmen and thy visitation cometh; now shall be their perplexity." It was the time which had been foretold by Malachi, four hundred years before, and which the people of Israel thought they would know by the token, which he gave. "Behold, I will send you Elijah the prophet before the coming of the great and dreadful day of the Lord." How that token as to Elijah was given has already been stated. But of the manner in which it was regarded by the Jewish mind, this is evidence that the disciples said to Jesus, "Some say that thou art John the Baptist; some, Elias; and others Jeremiah, or one of the prophets." And this incident is also of the same nature, that during the crucifixion, when Jesus uttered a cry which was not properly heard by some persons, they said, "This man calleth for Elias." And all the while it had been as Jesus had said himself, as to John the Baptist, and after his execution, "Elias is come already, and they knew him not, but have done unto him whatsoever they listed. Likewise shall also the Son of man suffer of them." O, words so simple and so wonderful, and out through which spoke the Spirit of the Most High, and as to which, by comparison, the prophecies of Isaiah and Ezekiel themselves are but those of minor prophets!

Elias not recognized at his spiritual coming, — Jesus on his way to be crucified, — and Jerusalem with that fate becoming certain for it which Jesus Christ had predicted, — and all the while the Scribes and Pharisees triumphant, — this all was because of the Spirit of God; which, when it is active, attracts some and repudiates others, inspires a Messiah and his witnesses, and also makes still more distinct the temper and ways of them that would kill the prophets, and stone them that are divinely sent.

That special spirit-power, under which the Jews had been living ever since the call of Abraham, was drawing in the first century of our era all the tendencies among them, open and latent, towards one point. And that point was Jesus of Nazareth, as connected with the Spirit. The question was asked, in one way and another, of Jesus, "Art thou he that should come?" And answer was made not only by Jesus personally, but also by the Spirit to which he appealed, and even also by "the signs of the times." Said Simeon, prophetically, at the presentation of Jesus in the temple, "Behold, this child is set for the fall and rising again of many in Israel; and for a sign, which shall be spoken against." And Jesus as the Christ, was the trial of his people; and his day was that of their visitation. Faithfulness to the Spirit, in the past, would have recognized him at once as the Christ. But the penal blindness of the people was such, that at the sight of Jerusalem, Jesus could but weep and say, "If thou hadst known, even thou, at least in this thy day, the things which belong unto thy peace! but now they are hid from thine eyes. For the days shall come upon thee that thine enemies shall cast a trench about thee, and compass thee round, and keep thee in on every side, and shall lay thee even with the ground, and thy children within thee, and they shall not leave in thee one stone upon another; because thou knewest not the time of thy visitation."

It was a "day of the Lord," and an age of prophecy. During the ministry of Christ, Vespasian was but an obscure youth in Italy; but also he was fitting himself unconsciously, as an instrument for the hand of the Lord,—he under whom, as the emperor of Rome, Jerusalem was to be captured, and the temple destroyed. The eagles of the legions were scattered over the vast empire, but in Jerusalem, there was a spirit working like destiny, which inevitably would draw the armies of Rome round the city, like eagles about a carcass.

Peter, James, and John in vision saw Moses and Elias talking with Jesus, as they believed. And as a simple matter of history, it is certain that at that time all the ancient warnings in the law, as to disobedience in regard to the Spirit, were immediately about to be made good, by the dispersion of the Israelites among all nations; and in a manner, as to the thoroughness of which, the last eighteen hundred years are solemn witnesses. O Jerusalem, Jerusalem! there was coming on thee, as Christ said to thee at the time, and as to thy people, "all the righteous blood shed upon the earth, from the blood of righteous Abel, unto the blood of Zacharias son of Barachias, whom ye slew between the temple and the altar." And the next words after these are of prophecy, and are very wonderful. They are the Spirit in judgment on its subjects. "Verily I say unto you, all these things shall come upon this generation." And those things, as prophecies of trouble, are to be found recorded in the Gospel of Matthew; and as the actualities of history, they are to be read of in the Wars of the Jews, by Josephus.

In a full view of history, it is hardly possible to think otherwise, than that nations are subject to waves of rise and fall spiritually. But the age of Jesus was the outcome of nearly two thousand years of administration by the Spirit among the Jews, and in a way more special than any other people ever experienced.

Those years, which were the last of the Jewish people in Palestine, and which also were the first of our Christian era, — they were truly, as Malachi had foretold, "the great and dreadful day of the Lord"; and yet also, at the very beginning, they were what Zacharias could sing of, on the prompting of the Holy Ghost, saying, "Blessed be the Lord God of Israel; for he hath visited and redeemed his people, and hath raised up a horn of salvation for us, in the house of his servant David; as he spake by the mouth of his holy prophets, which have been since the world began." That wonderful season! As the like of it, there is nothing else to be conceived of, than the movement of the Spirit of God, for a new world, and the quickening of the elements, once, out of what was without form and void.

It was a period in which "unclean spirits" were unusually numerous; and during which it felt almost as though "the rulers of the darkness of this world" might even loom upon the sight. It was an era in which often "the word of God" gleamed like "the sword of the Spirit." It was a time singularly charged with spirit. And when the marvellousness itself of that age is considered, miracles, as "signs of the times," would seem to have been almost as natural as fireflies are to the umbrageousness of a tropical climate.

It is not in the scope of this essay, to argue the credibility of the miracles recorded in the Gospels, one by one, nor yet to join in the controversy as to the reasonableness of the miracle concerned with the withering of the fig-tree. Everything, which is to be learned about these miracles, circumstantially and historically, is easily accessible. The miracles of Christ, however, were not universally believed, in his own day; nor were his miraculous words always understood. Said Jesus even as to great multitudes, "In them is fulfilled the prophecy of Esaias, which saith, By hearing ye shall hear, and shall not understand; and seeing ye shall see, and shall not perceive." The miracles of Jesus, not believed in his own time, as certainly they were not by the Sanhedrim! How, then, can it be expected that they should be credible to-day? Simply, because it is possible, that even to-day, there may be a better judgment as to those miracles, than even what the members of the Great Council could have formed. For, at this day, we are living long after the events, and can see and estimate, and allow for the prejudices, by which the Pharisees and Sadducees were blinded. It may be said, that to-day, men may be prejudiced as to retrospect. And of course, that is true. But yet candor, at this present time is not liable to a tenth part of the offuscation, to which a member of the Sanhedrim was subject by the mere act of entering the chamber of the Council.

In favor of the Messiahship of Jesus, that Council itself is evidence now, by the manner in which it came to an end. And at the siege of Jerusalem by Titus, every soldier round the city, in his place, was an unconscious witness for Jesus as a prophet. And at the destruction of the temple, because of what Christ had said, every stone, as it was thrown down, cried out as to "the name of the Lord."

The miracles of Jesus were "signs of the times." And the times, as they seemed to be signified, were abundantly fulfilled.

That "day of the Lord," that great era of the Spirit, how can it possibly be understood, without even a belief in the Spirit? And it cannot be but that the commentary of many a famous divine, upon its occurrences, trying to reconcile them to one another and to reason as he thinks, must be what the angels concerned therewith would utterly disown.

And especially, it is only as a man stands within the light of the Spirit, or as he apprehends what may be called the science of the Spirit, that the evidence as to the resurrection of Jesus becomes fairly intelligible. Why did one man see, and another man not; and why on one or two occasions, with seeing, was there not instant recognition? Simply because it was seeing by the Spirit, and with eyes which were opened by it, in some persons more than in others. It was seeing Jesus by eyes adapted to a body which had become of that nature, that it could appear in a room, "when the doors were shut, where the disciples were assembled for fear of the Jews."

The Scriptures are not fully and fairly intelligible, when read according to the Analysis of the Human Mind by James Mill, or any other such philosophy. For they presuppose a pneumatology, by which man is soul as well as body; and by which while he is chained to the earth, he is yet also a nursling of the skies.

JESUS AND THE RESURRECTION.

AS the Mosaic dispensation was drawing towards its close, more and more express became the ministration of the Spirit through it. Moses had been a lawgiver, and David and Isaiah had been prophets; and Gideon had been like the sword of the Lord, and Solomon like a miracle of wisdom. But patriarchs and prophets, and all the angels who had ever been concerned with them, religiously, were but like servants, when compared with him to whom "God giveth not the Spirit by measure." For "when he bringeth in the first-begotten into the world, he saith, And let all the angels of God worship him."

To the foregoing does any one say, "Ancient Hebrew idiom!" disdainfully? And so perhaps it is. But what then? Was there ever a philosophy which did not have its peculiar terms and phraseology? Or is science, in the least degree discredited, because its nomenclature is foreign to the mind of a Kaffir? And is craniology, or is the science of even dead bones, so simple, as that a person can read a treatise on osteology with the same intelligence and words which suffice him perfectly as a merchant? And history and science, in combination, as to the connection of man with God by the Spirit, ever since there was first a manifestation of the divine image on the earth, — is it anything strange as to this, that it may perhaps need interpretation, in some degree, even as geology does, or astronomy? How many men there are who grow spiritually blind through self-sufficiency! and with their flippant speeches, how many more persons there are who are perverted from the simplicity of truth!

No past age can ever be known as it was, except by a lamp like what the light of that time was. And mere self-assertion on a subject like that of "the fulness of the time" would be of the nature of blasphemy, except as desecration about a temple was never possible from mere chirping sparrows, because of their being ignorant.

Does a man deny the resurrection of Jesus, as having any pertinency for him, because of its involving considerations for which he has not the requisite learning, or for which he thinks that he has not time? or because it claims to be something so very unlike to the tenor of his daily newspaper. Or does he demur to the New Testament as being of any special concern for him, because of its antiquity? Then let him remember, that from this present hour to the first day of the first year of our Lord is a shorter space of time, than it was from the birth of Jesus Christ to the promise which was made to Abraham at his call, "In thee shall all families of the earth be blessed."

By every drop of blood in his veins; by every modification of every thought which he has; and by every stripe of suffering, ever endured in the world, and through which, in any manner, bodily or spiritually, he is healed, man is a child of the past, throughout all its generations. Men are historically born, and are bound historically. And the more of a man that any individual may be, so much the more solemnly is he responsible as to the ages behind him, for what they may have to testify. Disown the past simply as being ancient! a man might as well disown God as not being his own little self!

Length of time, merely, does not separate human beings. After three thousand years, the Book of Ruth is like a tale of yesterday. And yet at this very hour hate cannot possibly understand love, and is separated from it by what, as to space, may be called infinity. As to historical events, time is almost nothing in comparison with distance by philosophy, or spiritual state.

The state of mind being changed in which documents are read, it is as though the documents themselves had been written afresh; and then what had seemed to be discrepancies according to a materialistic understanding, when read according to a spiritual philosophy may become parts which even corroborate one another.

How strangely and often figures of speech have become disfigurements of facts! And how often, also, an earnest man has been reduced to mere rationalism in theology, because of the manner in which "the things of the Spirit" have been argued, as though they were material monuments, and properly the subjects of arithmetic, geometry, and mere logic!

The age of Jesus Christ,— that day of the Lord was not exactly like yesterday, though yet to-day there are means by which, critically and historically, it is to be known of as it was. The resurrection of Jesus is not a mere incident in history, because it is infinitely connected. "For as in Adam all die, even so in Christ shall all be made alive." That "new sepulchre wherein was never man yet laid" was about to be the birthplace, as to manifestation, of "the Lord from heaven." And that same place, when left vacant by the resurrection of Jesus, was about to become the cenotaph of mere Judaism.

When Jesus was transfigured on the mount, it was because of the Spirit; and through the Spirit it was that the apostles saw him, and Moses and Elias with him. And it was because of the Spirit, that there was "heaven open and the angels of God ascending and descending upon the Son of man."

A voice from heaven had just borne him witness; when Jesus said to his hearers, "And I, if I be lifted up from the earth, will draw all men unto me. This he said, signifying what death he should die." O wonderful age and day of the Lord! A day which in vision Abraham had desired to see, and also had seen! And yet, too, it was a day as to which, fourteen hundred years later than Abraham, it was doubtful, prophetically, how people would be able to endure it on its coming! And what a time, indeed, that time was! And indeed otherwise than wonderful how could that age have been, wherein he was living through whose death the human race was to be born again!

"Now Herod the tetrarch heard of all that was done by him: and he was perplexed, because that it was said of some, that John was risen from the dead; and of some, that Elias had appeared; and of others, that one of the old prophets was risen again. And Herod said, John have I beheaded; but who is this, of whom I hear such things?" Herod was a Sadducee, probably, and yet with his ears a little open for hearing.

Astonishing times they were! as, indeed, well they might have been, while destiny as to Jerusalem was making itself sure; and while the prophets seemed to be calling out aloud and afresh their old predictions, and while those events were occurring, of which the four gospels were to be the long-enduring records. The promise to Abraham was about being fulfilled; and what anciently was but a germ of destiny, was about to become full-orbed, and to rise upon the nations, spiritually, as the sun of righteousness with healing in its wings. A wonderful age it was; for it was the greatest age, as to crisis in history, which has ever been. It was an age as to the full manifestation of which imperial Rome was but a servant for making ready highways for its great news; or, at best, but an unquestionable, though unconscious, witness as to the keeping of the sepulchre, in and from out of which Jesus rose again. Plato and Æschylus, and also Aristotle, — what has their worth been, in comparison with the language which they used, and through which Greece was but like an intelligent secretary, for helping apostles and others to publish their histories, epistles, and visions, in the best manner possible, for the best intellects of the age!

It was under heaven, and on the earth, "the fulness of the time," more completely than Paul himself, perhaps, ever thought, and in ways of which it is conceivable, that hereafter science will have much to say as to the conditions which concurred, telluric, magnetic, and celestial, and also as to something psychologically, by which human nature may itself have been ripened for fresh conditions of growth. Let the wisdom of Egypt have been all which can possibly be claimed for it; and let the wise men of the East have been informed ever so mysteriously; yet, as a fact, historically, was not there once familiarly named in the cottages of Galilee, and current in the streets of Jerusalem, a name which has proved itself, up to this time, to have been above every other name? And therefore that age may well be credited for having been what Paul claimed for it as "the dispensation of the fulness of time," and thereby also, under Heaven, as the concentration of all those forces, by which human beings live and move and are lifted up.

When Jesus cried out, "O Jerusalem, Jerusalem! thou that killest the prophets!" he was at a point, both as to time and place, where the general effect of Jewish history was becoming manifest, as to the law which was given by Moses; and as to the long rebelliousness, which was punished by the captivity in Babylon; as to what Samuel and Saul had been in regard to one another; and as to what David had sung, and what so very differently he had sometimes done; also as to Solomon so wise and so foolish; and as to the time in which Ahab and Elijah knew of one another; and as to the ages respectively of the prophets from Isaiah to Malachi.

The world was at the beginning of a new era, which was to date from Jesus of Nazareth, as he was popularly called, but yet "the world knew him not." For indeed, at that time, it was a crisis of that nature, and so great, as that what is light to one is darkness to a thousand. And, indeed, otherwise than from that reason how could there have been "killed the Prince of life"? And, indeed, that Prince himself said as to the people of his time, "If therefore the light that is in thee be darkness, how great is that darkness!"

When heaven draws nigh to earth, it is with a light, which is blinding darkness for some persons, while yet for others it is like what angels might emerge from. Heaven draws nigh to earth for quickening. And with quickening they are the latent faculties of men which specially are made remarkable. And it is with remembering that the spiritual atmosphere at the beginning of our era would seem to have been intensified, that many of its incidents become intelligible, such as the revival of prophecy, and the incursion of unclean spirits. A day of the Lord is a time in which men spiritually are under pressure, for the better if they are good, and for the worse if they are bad. And such a time was that wherein were included the life, crucifixion, death, resurrection, and ascension of our Lord and Saviour, Jesus Christ.

And even as it was as to Jesus Christ, that on being "put to death in the flesh" he was "quickened by the Spirit," so also there were those as witnesses who were raised as to their latent spiritual faculties, and which were those by which they saw and heard him; and so, also, there were others more numerous still than they, who felt, spiritually, as to Jesus and death that "it was not possible that he should be holden of it."

The resurrection of Jesus was the manifestation of a

crisis as to mankind, under heaven; and it is not to be understood, at all, apart from time and place and a belief in the Spirit.

In regard to the resurrection of Jesus, many of the objections as to belief in it originate in such a state of mind as what would say this, "Anatomists and chemists standing round, let a dead body, on a table, get up and talk, and then perhaps men will believe." And the brothers of the people who talk thus would say, "Seeing is believing; and as we did not see, we do not believe." But what is Supreme in the Universe would seem to be careless of human pettiness, even at its grandest; and sometimes even it would seem to have "chosen the foolish things of the world to confound the wise."

The resurrection of Jesus was the greatest fact of a great age, and it was the culmination of the greatest earthly crisis under heaven, and as to the significance of which, not Jerusalem only, but Egypt and Assyria, and Greece and Rome, and all time, also, by the way of prophecy, were concurrent.

In the Gospel of Matthew, it is written, as to Pilate, while Jesus was on his trial before him, that "when he was set down on the judgment-seat, his wife sent unto him, saying, Have thou nothing to do with that just man: for I have suffered many things this day in a dream because of him." A sign of the times this was, and as to what the atmosphere was, spiritually. Pilate's wife had this experience. And so strange it is, that it has been so little noticed. The prediction of his Lord as to Peter, that he would deny him thrice in one short night, is accounted as having been wonderful because of the manner of its fulfilment; and surely so it was. But this dream of Pilate's wife is evidence as to what the state was of what may be called the atmosphere, spiritually, in Jerusalem, at that time. And of like proof is the opinion of Caiaphas as to the expediency of killing Jesus, which "spake he not of himself; but, being high priest that year, he prophesied that Jesus should die for that nation."

As to the picture of the crucifixion which the gospels give, how many wonderful lines there are, which could never have been drawn except from life! And also they are lines which are self-sufficient, as to evidence, for a critical understanding! For a man with "ears to hear" that incident is as true as truth itself, as to what the thieves said to one another as they hung on their separate crosses, and as to what Jesus replied to one of them. Such words, at such a time, and from such lips! "And Jesus said unto him, Verily, I say unto thee, To-day shalt thou be with me in paradise." This paradise was certainly not heaven, because even after his resurrection Jesus said to Mary, "Touch me not; for I am not yet ascended to my Father." The state into which Jesus passed after his death as a mortal was that apparently wherein, on his entrance, he "preached unto the spirits in prison." That place or state, therefore, of paradise was probably one of hopefulness. And on this understanding, these words of Jesus to the penitent thief are intelligible and also infinitely tender.

As to the time during which Jesus was dying on the cross, it is written, "Now from the sixth hour there was darkness over all the land unto the ninth hour."

And by another evangelist, it is said that "the sun was darkened." According to the use of language, it is not necessary to suppose that there was an eclipse of the sun, either natural or supernatural. Nor yet fairly ought the historian to be considered as being held by his words to mean anything more than a preternatural darkness in perhaps the region round Jerusalem. As to whether that darkness was noticed in Rome, or experienced by Caractacus in Britain, is simply a superfluous question.

It has been sometimes supposed that this darkness was an effect in nature occasioned by her conscious sympathy with the sight of the crucifixion. But that, of course, is mere sentimentalism. There are some illustrations which might be adduced on this subject, which would be abundantly credible to some persons, but which yet cannot be pleaded here without an argument, which would be a book in itself.

That darkness was probably not a special but an accompanying miracle. It was simply an incident in connection with the death of Jesus; and what was miraculous in it was because of that miracle of organization which Jesus Christ himself was. And probably that strange darkness round Golgotha was because of the greatness of that soul, which mortally was connected with nature, and which by that connection was in agony. With every breath which any man draws, the air about him is changed and impoverished. Nor is man connected with the air, merely as concerns oxygen and nitrogen, but by electricity and magnetism, and also, probably, by other ways which are unknown. And so it is readily conceivable, that in some manner the forces of nature may have been unbalanced and darkened, whilst the soul of Jesus Christ was being loosened from connection with them. And as to this supposition, there are some things analogous, historically and psychologically, of which some great minds have been well persuaded.

The thought of there being any possible connection between a tempest and an earthquake was once accounted superstitious, but at present it is scientific. That by pestilence, there could be an obscuration of the atmosphere, was once supposed to be merely a fancy, but now it is an ascertained fact. And like what immediately precedes, let also what follows be mentioned for what it may be worth. Several times in history, as to men who had been like the right arm of direction for their times, it is recorded that on dying, the atmosphere about them seemed to signify itself by darkness or by tempest. And now let it be remembered that by a spiritual philosophy, which is not likely to become extinct, Christ Jesus was the "one mediator between God and men." And then the darkening, which there was round about, at the time of his crucifixion, will not seem so strange as necessarily to be incredible; nor yet so anomalous but that even science may be expected some time to demonstrate the manner of it.

"Jesus, when he had cried again with a loud voice, yielded up the ghost. And behold the veil of the temple was rent in twain from the top to the bottom." In the temple there were two veils; but the one which was specially "the veil" must have been the second veil, behind which was "the tabernacle which is called the Holiest of all; which had the golden censer, and the ark of the covenant overlaid round about with gold, wherein was the golden pot that had manna, and Aaron's rod that budded, and the tables of the covenant; and over it the cherubims of glory shadowing the mercy-seat." These things were memorials of the past, as to the Spirit. And they were also signs of what the Jewish people had been to God, as "a peculiar people." And the tearing of the veil before them was emblematic that thenceforth "the things of the Spirit" were open to all persons, who should anywhere ever be quickened by the Spirit. And it was the work, perhaps, of "the angel of the covenant." And it was done, probably, as a preparation of the minds of men against the day of Pentecost, and what ensued upon it.

By the same evangelist who has just been quoted, it is said, in continuation, that "the earth did quake and the rocks rent." This probably happened in the same way as at the resurrection. "And the graves were opened; and many bodies of the saints which slept arose, and came out of the graves after his resurrection, and went into the holy city, and appeared unto many." Not graves, but monumental tombs, are what the evangelist himself mentions. And the bodies which appeared unto many certainly were not resuscitated flesh and bones. That could never have been, concurrently, at least, with the doctrine of St. Paul. "But some man will say, How are the dead raised up? and with what body do they come? Thou fool, that which thou sowest is not quickened, except it die." And then, in continuation of his argument, the apostle explains that "there is a natural body, and there is a spiritual body." The world of nature on that morning, at Jerusalem, was powerfully interpenetrated by spirit, and so was very pliant, perhaps, to angelic agency. And it may be that angels opened the tombs of some well-known saints, in celebration of Christ's victory over death; and it may be, also, that the saints themselves were present at the time, because of there having been a door opened from Hades, by which for Christ to return into his natural body, in this world of nature, on his way to "the right hand of the Majesty on high." And these bodies of the saints, or these saints as spiritual bodies, were visible to many, but not to everybody. They were seen by those persons whose spiritual "eyes were opened," through that power of the Spirit which was abroad, and by which the time was characterized.

When the chief priests and Pharisees applied to Pilate, as the Roman governor, to have a guard set over the sepulchre, they said it was because "Sir, we remember that that deceiver said, while he was yet alive, After three days I will rise again." That prophecy was from the Spirit, just as afterwards the resurrection itself was. Peter argued that the resurrection of Jesus had been foretold by David in a psalm, which is called prophetic; and Peter, probably, had a much better knowledge of the Spirit, and its manner of uttering itself, than is possible at this dark, materialistic day. And, no doubt, that Spirit which was the resurrection of Jesus did flash with forethought of it, in the minds of some of the prophets. Rectified as to translation, these are the words which were cited by

Peter from David: "For thou wilt not leave my soul in Hades: neither wilt thou suffer thine Holy One to see corruption." The soul of Jesus was not to be left in the common world of spirits, the intermediate world, or waiting-place of spirits, though it was indeed to enter it, as certainly it did, when Jesus proceeded to preach to "the spirits in prison." Nor was the body of Jesus to see corruption. And it would seem like some security for the exact fulfilment of the prophecy, that for those hours during which the body was in the tomb it was partially embalmed. "Then took they the body of Jesus, and wound it in linen clothes with the spices, as the manner of the Jews is to bury. Now in the place where he was crucified, there was a garden; and in the garden a new sepulchre, wherein was never man yet laid. There laid they Jesus."

Moses and Elias had talked with Jesus, as to "his decease which he should accomplish at Jerusalem"; and not improbably they may have been present at the entombment of his mangled body, though invisibly; and it may be, too, that in Hades, somewhere, they may have heard Christ's announcement of himself to spirits in prison.

It was dark in the tomb, with its door shut and sealed; but suddenly and soon there was going to be "light from heaven, above the brightness of the sun," like the splendor, with which Paul, at his conversion, saw the risen Jesus invested.

At the resurrection of Jesus, "behold, there was a great earthquake; for the angel of the Lord descended from heaven, and came and rolled back the stone from the door, and sat upon it. His countenance was like lightning, and his raiment white as snow: and for fear of him, the keepers did shake, and became as dead men." It is not necessary to suppose that that earthquake was what might have been felt on the heights of Capernaum; for, no doubt, it was of the same local character, and from the same spiritual cause as when a little later "suddenly there came a sound from heaven as of a rushing mighty wind, and it filled all the house where they were sitting." It was an earthquake from spiritual power present, like what there was when "at midnight, Paul and Silas prayed, and sang praises unto God; and the prisoners heard them. And suddenly there was a great earthquake, so that the foundations of the prison were shaken; and immediately all the doors were opened, and every one's bands were loosed." Earth hangs on heaven by chains which grow so fine that they are what seraphs can handle, as they stand about the throne of God. And when angels approach material objects, it is with a touch more subtle and mighty than that of electricity. An angel with a countenance like lightning might well shake the earth by the sole of his foot. And because of such an one, at the door of the sepulchre, "the keepers did shake and became as dead men." And they were affected just as the companions of Paul were, at the time of his conversion; and they again were affected as those men were who were with Daniel when there was about him that power which disclosed itself in a vision, and on whom "a great quaking fell."

Behind the letter of the Scriptures, on these points, lies a broad field of what once was knowledge, but which now is a fog of materialism, for almost every reader. Peter the Apostle, had looked into the empty sepulchre on the morning of the resurrection, and afterwards had seen Jesus again and again, and talked with him; and what he wrote as to Jesus, about twenty-five years later than his last sight of his Master, is that he was "put to death in the flesh, but quickened by the Spirit."

But was that crucified body quickened? No; not altogether perhaps. Though there may probably have been a quickening, by which the mortal remains of Jesus may have been affected, on his recall from Hades. But was the heart that had been pierced healed again miraculously? Probably it was not.

The body of Jesus, as it lay in the tomb, was not the body of an ordinary man. Says St. Paul, "All flesh is not the same flesh," and that temple of the Holy Ghost which was the body of Jesus had probably been sublimed in such a manner as that on his return from the world of spirits into this realm of nature, his body, on its assumption, became but like that thin robe which justly availed for keeping him awhile within the sight of his disciples.

In the Book of Ecclesiasticus, it is said of Elisha, that "after his death his body prophesied," or was an outlet for spiritual power. A few months after the burial of Elisha there was war with the Moabites, "and it came to pass, as they were burying a man, that, behold, they spied a band of men; and they cast the man into the sepulchre of Elisha: and when the man was let down, and touched the bones of Elisha, he revived and stood upon his feet." Perhaps the body of Elisha, at the time of his death, was half ready for being translated, and it may be that after the body was dead there lingered in it something of that vitalized magnetism which, by its strength, may have been one of the conditions of that spiritual receptiveness, through which, at the will of the Lord, he was a prophet.

It is certain that there is a chemistry as to the connection between the soul and the body; and it is attested by a thousand wonderful facts, although so little is known, as yet, as to its laws.

Early in the Book of Genesis it is to be read, " And Enoch walked with God: and he was not; for God took him." According to the Epistle to the Hebrews, the translation of Enoch was connected with his faith. It is conceivable with his long life and walk with God, that the body of Enoch may have become so etherealized, as that his soul, on its passage from earth to heaven, may simply have parted from what dropped, in a moment, into a handful of common dust. And in some manner like this, probably, did the soul of Elijah clear itself of nature. For, certainly, it could not have been with an ordinary body that Elijah entered a chariot of fire, and went up to heaven in a whirlwind. And, no doubt, by some such path as that by which he vanished, Elijah was present at the transfiguration of Christ. But along with Elias, also, Moses "appeared in glory." And it is noticeable that, as to the mortal end of Moses, or what went with his body, there was a mystery. " So Moses the servant of the Lord died there in the land of Moab, according to the word of the Lord. And he buried him in a valley in the land of Moab, over against Beth-peor; but no man knoweth of his sepulchre unto this day."

On the morning of the resurrection, probably, the soul of Jesus entered his dead body, and then shook from itself the sublimated dust. And so Jesus retained about him only as much earthiness as would hold his wounds, and enable him to satisfy people as to his personal actuality and his identity.

At the door of the sepulchre, while angels in white were inside of it, suddenly Jesus was recognized by Mary, as he stood near her. "Jesus saith unto her, Touch me not; for I am not yet ascended to my Father." And yet only eight days later "saith he to Thomas, Reach hither thy finger, and behold my hands; and reach hither thy hand, and thrust it into my side: and be not faithless, but believing." These two incidents are worthy of notice, as being likely, some time, to suggest something as to the chemistry of the spiritual body.

The body which Thomas touched was that of Jesus while he was standing withinside of our earthly sphere; and perhaps it may have been capable of being hardened at will. But also it was the same body in which afterwards Jesus "ascended up far above all heavens." By his resurrection, Jesus was not merely an apparition, or a spirit; for he was thereby clothed with another nature than what a phantom wears. Said Jesus to the disciples, when they were frightened at his appearance among them, on the first evening after his resurrection: "Behold my hands and my feet, that it is I myself: handle me and see; for a spirit hath not flesh and bones, as ye see me have." And yet with that body he could appear suddenly in a room, the doors being shut.

On the morning of the resurrection, Jesus was not to be touched, as not having yet ascended to his Father; but within a few hours afterwards he was even to be handled. And thus, certainly, he had experienced some change further than that in the sepulchre, by the marvel of which he stood alive, and within the sight and hearing of Mary Magdalene. And some further change still than that would seem to have been experienced by him, when, after his last interview with his apostles, and his last words to them, on Olivet, "he was taken up and a cloud received him out of their sight." For, after this event, he was seen by Paul twice, at least; but not under the same conditions as before. For to Paul he was visible only through the Spirit, and in vision. And so, also, it was that he was visible to Stephen. When Stephen was put on his trial, "all that sat in the council, looking steadfastly on him, saw his face, as it had been the face of an angel." And, after his argument as to Christ, when his judges gnashed on him with their teeth, "he, being full of the Holy Ghost, looked up steadfastly into heaven, and saw the glory of God, and Jesus standing on the right hand of God." O wondrous fact, about which the more there is which is learned, the more certain and wonderful will it become! O, those triumphant words of Paul to Timothy, as to "the appearing of our Lord and Saviour Jesus Christ, who hath abolished death, and hath brought life and immortality to light through the good news"!

What, then, was the resurrection? It was the passage of Jesus from the world of spirits into heaven, through the realm of nature, and especially by the way of his mortal body. "O death, where is thy sting? O Hades, where is thy victory?"

But now there are persons who will say, "Why then did Jesus not walk into the judgment-hall, and speak to Caiaphas; and why did he not show himself in the market-place; and why did he not mount the steps of the altar, to the utter confusion of every enemy?" But why then does God not confute his blasphemers with thunder and lightning, every day? and why, under high heaven, are not the highest truths as to morals and philosophy borne in irresistibly upon all minds alike? And perhaps also Jesus would not have been able, and could not even have wished, to show himself to Caiaphas. Also affairs which involve the higher laws of the Spirit are not to be summoned for examination into the market-place. It is a precept which has wide and deep reasons behind it, spiritually, "Give not that which is holy unto the dogs, neither cast ye your pearls before swine." And the reasons even why Peter saw Jesus Christ, and those for which Caiaphas and Pilate did not see him, would be found, when spiritually considered, to corroborate one another. It is a general truth, "Draw nigh to God and he will draw nigh to you." And perhaps something psychologically being allowed for, only those who recognized Jesus as the Christ, or seeing him in his humiliation, were capable of being quickened, so as to see him, on his way through the earth to his glory.

As to the universe, Jesus, after his resurrection, was in a region intermediate between this world and the next, or rather he was in a state by which he was free of both worlds. He appeared among his friends suddenly, by some unearthly way, and then as suddenly he was gone. As affecting his visibility, there were two conditions, of which one was what may be called the fine earthiness, which he still held about him like a veil; and the other was the Spirit, and through the Spirit some persons were quickened as to their eyes and ears spiritually, so as that they not only saw and heard Jesus, but even also angels attendant on him.

The body of Jesus after the resurrection was the same body as before in the eye of an angel, perhaps, although it had ceased to be recognized by the law of gravitation, and perhaps might have stood before Pilate, and never have been seen. Essentially and germinally, the body which was taken up into heaven was the same body which was crucified on the cross, and the same body which the child Jesus had when he "increased in wisdom and stature, and in favor with God and man." In a grain of wheat, not as a possibility merely, but as an organized fact, there is latent "first the blade, then the ear, after that the full corn in the ear," not visibly to a human eye, but very curiously so, perhaps, to an angel by what may be called the spirit of science. From the cross to the sepulchre, there was carried the crucified body of Jesus; and a seal was set on the door against it, and a Roman guard. And that body as it was laid down in the grave-clothes was never seen again.

Jesus as he was seen outside of the sepulchre, talking with one and another and walking, and visible also to all the apostles together, and to five hundred persons at once, and to Paul also once and again, in vision, — Jesus crucified, dead, buried, and risen, is the original of that apostle's doctrine as to the resurrection, "It is sown a natural body, it is raised a spiritual body."

And why? Why at all should it be thought a thing incredible that God should raise the dead, and do so at that time especially? O fulness of the time! O extremity of human want, when the whole creation was groaning and travailing in pain together! O the earnestness of that expectation which everywhere was waiting in the truest souls, for the manifestation of the sons of God! And age after age, how many had prayed these words, in the faith of something great, "Lord, what is man, that thou takest knowledge of him? or the son of man, that thou makest account of him? Man is like to vanity: his days are as a shadow that passeth away. Bow thy heavens, O Lord, and come down: touch the mountains, and they shall smoke."

And towards that new tomb which was hewn out of the rock, truly the heavens were bowed down, in what was "the fulness of the time." And at that sepulchre, when radiant angels emerged withinside of it, it was because the way had been opened for them, from above, by the Spirit. The strength by which "was rolled back the stone from the door," the earthquake, and the quaking of the keepers simply were signs of there being present "power from on high."

Humanly speaking, the Father Everlasting was about to raise his Son from the dead, and to show him openly. But as under high heaven, the prophecies of the Spirit as to Jesus were then about to be made good, by the Spirit itself. The wrath of a nation had hurried on to a point, whence the highest praise as to

God was to begin. And the words of Peter are exact when he writes of Christ as having been "put to death in the flesh, but quickened by the Spirit."

But when Christ "ascended up on high," where did he go? For the firmament, scientifically, now is nowhere. Where then was it, that Christ Jesus went? "He was received up into heaven," just as it is written. But heaven has nothing to do with any firmament, whether phenomenal or real. And it is to be looked for, only in such a direction as that by which Christ with ascending "took captivity captive." Jesus said to Nicodemus, "If I have told you earthly things, and ye believe not, how shall ye believe if I tell you of heavenly things? And no man hath ascended up to heaven, but he that came down from heaven, even the Son of man, which is in heaven." Now, what does this mean, but that Jesus, as to his spirit and spiritual connections, was in heaven, while yet with his bodily tongue he was talking with Nicodemus in Jerusalem?

And there is nobody open to the Spirit but can feel how this may be. Because with myself, it is certain that my highest mood, spiritually, differs from my badness far more than any change which could happen for me, by the widest locomotion, or even by the death of my body. But it is said, "O, but heaven and earth are so different! For, as to our earthly lives, there are fixed points, by which to think; but as to heaven, who knows about it, any way, except by faith?" Now, that faith which is not an increment, spiritually of knowledge, is as worthless as ignorance itself. And this is true even as to the resurrection of Jesus. Faith is spiritual believing. It is the persuasion of a man as to things beyond his reach intellectually, because of what he is himself, or of what he knows, or otherwise feels. And this statement agrees with faith, as being possible, even as a gift of the Spirit. For the Spirit reaches persons only as they are open to it. The wicked Ahab could never have become St. Paul. But Saul the persecutor was in a ripe state of knowledge, theologically, when he was converted in a moment by a voice from heaven. And, no doubt, "the pricks" against which Paul was finding it hard to kick were the misgivings which he was having, as to its being possible, for many reasons, that Jesus of Nazareth might really be the Messiah, and the fulfilment of prophecy, and "the desire of all nations." And so, in a moment almost, he became another man than he had been, with hearing a voice from out of a blinding glory say, "I am Jesus of Nazareth, whom thou persecutest." And thenceforth with him, every age in the past, up to Abraham, was a witness for Christ, as also was the temple, and the veil of the temple too, and the order as to sacrifices, and the law as to clean and unclean, and the angel of the covenant, and every other angel that ever stooped on this earth for a visit. And on hearing the Master speaking from above, and from out of glory, at once Paul began to experience that change, a Hebrew of the Hebrews though he was, through which it seemed to him, with all the nations of the earth in full view, that "the law was our schoolmaster to bring us unto Christ, that we might be justified by faith."

Definite departments, those of nature and spirit as to man! For some purposes, at least, it is certain that the flowering of nature is what spirit begins from. And it is true, no doubt, as to the resurrection of Jesus, that even natural science, as an unbeliever, has got to yield its testimony, when the time shall have come. And that time will be when some person shall be wise with the wisdom of this present age, and childlike as towards the Spirit of the Universe, and God over all.

Notoriously, this earth hangs upon the sun; and should it then be an improbable thing, that there may be a "sun of righteousness" in the light of which, and dependent on which, for their best, our souls may have their being? Those planets, which are of the sisterhood of our earth, as to the sun, affect one another in their orbits; and is it then a thing too foreign for thought that, spiritually, we human beings may be rightly influenced as to our lives, by what, as to origin, is "far above all principality and power"? Every atom in this earth of ours, and in every human body, is sensitive as to the course of a comet; and should it then really be inconceivable that, with the Father of lights, there may be thoughts as to man, which may have their earthly expression at such times as those wherein, historically, and socially, and spiritually, mankind is as though it were reaching up towards heaven, in blind entreaty, at a great crisis? And is it, then, anything incredible? is it even a thing improbable? and is it not actually, as to heaven and earth, and as to all history, and as to science also, at its surest, a probability, which is almost like certainty itself, that the condescension of the Highest, as to human need at its uttermost, should have eventuated in Jesus and the resurrection?

Soul and body is what we human beings are. And bodily, there is nothing wonderful, which can be discovered for us, as to our connection with the sun or the moon or the stars, or with those laws of nature which concern this earth especially; but tenfold more than that, and a hundred-fold, we ought to be ready to believe as to our poor souls, struggling upwards out of sin and spiritual darkness. And, indeed, as countless almost as the rays of the sun which are called light, must be the connections which there are between heaven and earth, spiritually, because of God, "of whom the whole family in heaven and earth is named."

And now as to this earth, and all earthiness, "Thanks be to God, which giveth us the victory through our Lord Jesus Christ."

THE CHURCH AND THE SPIRIT.

THE resurrection of Jesus, or his quickening as to the body, was not a disconnected fact. It had been ordained from before Abraham; and spiritually, it had been intimated during many ages; and expressly it had been foretold in the utterances of Jesus himself. And it was the consummation of Judaism, as to its purpose, that, in connection with it, Christ should have been "put to death in the flesh, but quickened by the Spirit." On that evening of the first day, when Jesus suddenly appeared among the eleven, after his resurrection, he must have said much as to the Scriptures, which is quite outside of our ability even to conjecture about, for want of spiritual understanding. But to those eleven astonished apostles Jesus said, "These are the words which I spake unto you, while I was yet with you, that all things must be fulfilled which were written in the law of Moses, and in the prophets, and in the Psalms, concerning me. Then opened he their understanding that they might understand the Scriptures, and said unto them, Thus it is written, and thus it behoved Christ to suffer, and to rise from the dead the third day. And that repentance and remission of sins should be preached in his name among all nations, beginning at Jerusalem. And ye are witnesses of these things." And afterwards Jesus said, "Behold, I send the promise of my Father upon you: but tarry ye in the city of Jerusalem, until ye be endued with power from on high."

That promise of the Father, which was revealed to the world through the consciousness of Jesus Christ; that prophesying of the Spirit, as to its course, and which indeed is characteristic of it, was what was verified, at the day of Pentecost. But not to Jesus only had that wonderful event been foreshown, for also as to its certainty there had been indications from the Spirit, through the prophets, from long ages before. And so it was that Peter said to an assemblage of the Jews on the day of Pentecost, "Therefore let all the house of Israel know assuredly, that God hath made that same Jesus, whom ye have crucified, both Lord and Christ." And his particular citation as to prophecy is, "that which was spoken by the prophet Joel; and it shall come to pass in the last days, saith God, I will pour out of my Spirit upon all flesh: and your sons and your daughters shall prophesy, and your young men shall see visions, and your old men shall dream dreams; and on my servants and on my handmaidens I will pour out in those days of my Spirit; and they shall prophesy." And of this prophecy thus cited by St. Peter, the grandest instances are the Apostle to the Gentiles, and Ananias by whom he was cured of his blindness, and Peter himself along with Cornelius, that centurion of the Italian band. And indeed, it was through these four men, and what they experienced in vision, or during entrancement by the Spirit, that the Gospel got itself extended as an offer to the Gentiles, and to people everywhere, who were neither Pharisees nor

Sadducees, nor even Galileans. Religiously, and still more ecclesiastically, this is what has never perhaps been sufficiently considered. And for persons of competent understanding, it would seem to imply what might be the death of theological dogmatism.

Paul was journeying to Damascus, with letters from the high-priest, for persecuting the disciples of Jesus, when "suddenly there shined round about him a light from heaven: and he fell to the earth, and heard a voice saying unto him, Saul, Saul, why persecutest thou me? And he said, Who art thou, Lord? And the Lord said, I am Jesus, whom thou persecutest: it is hard for thee to kick against the pricks. And he, trembling and astonished, said, Lord, what wilt thou have me to do? And the Lord said unto him, Arise, and go into the city, and it shall be told thee what thou must do." And at Damascus there was a man called Ananias, and in a vision, just as Paul had heard the Lord, he also heard him directing him as to Paul, and where he was to be found, and saying, "Go thy way: for he is a chosen vessel unto me, to bear my name before the Gentiles, and kings, and the children of Israel. For I will show him how great things he must suffer for my name's sake. And Ananias went his way, and entered into the house; and putting his hands on him, said, Brother Saul, the Lord, even Jesus, that appeared unto thee in the way as thou camest, hath sent me, that thou mightest receive thy sight, and be filled with the Holy Ghost. And immediately there fell from his eyes as it had been scales; and he received sight forthwith, and arose, and was baptized."

Simultaneously with the events just narrated, would

seem to have been the experiences of Paul and Cornelius. In Cæsarea, Cornelius was an officer in a Roman legion; but yet he was a Gentile believer in the God of Abraham; and he had a vision, in which an angel directed him to send to Peter, and told him also of the town and the house where the Apostle was to be found. And on this angelic impulse, three persons were sent with a message from a quarter, which, for a Jew, was unclean. How, then, was it possibly to be received by Peter? But to Peter also, against the arrival of the messengers, there was a vision vouchsafed, wherein he saw what was curiously significant; and wherein also thrice it was said, "What God hath cleansed, that call not thou common." O wonderful history of that time when, through the Spirit, heaven was so close to this earth! For when Peter and Cornelius met, the Jews in the company were astonished, "because that on the Gentiles also was poured out the gift of the Holy Ghost. For they heard them speak with tongues, and magnify God."

What is time on this earth, except as man is concerned with it? And so it was well because of the coming of Christ, that time as to men should have begun to count the years afresh. "Power from on high," was the promise of Christ as to this earth, as he left it, by rising. And when it arrived it was power, adapted as to man, by the fatherhood of God. For, indeed, it was power of the same origin as that, with the movement of which, a world without form and void began to take shape, and grow, and bring forth, and become this surrounding nature. But it is said, "O, angels and visions are so different from stages of development, or from the path of nature, as she feels her way upwards!" Is man then properly to be catalogued along with the whale or the elephant? Also if ever we men are to be spirits, why should we not be spiritually met to-day? And not the Gospel only, nor yet along with it, the philosophy also of history, but even material science itself, by the way of analogy, would demand of men, a state of expectancy as to the Highest, and as to "power from on high."

And as mediator between God and mankind, and as foretold by prophets, and as trusted in to-day, what is Jesus Christ, but an advance in the human race, a later Adam, who was made "a quickening spirit"?

In spiritual darkness, what bewilderment there has been as to the day of Pentecost! And as to that day, very strangely, some time, on reading, will many things seem, which have been written by persons zealous as to the letter of the Scripture, and by others, also, who have thought as to human nature, that the limitation as to experience, of any man, anywhere and in any age, should be accounted as the exact measure of human susceptibility, as to the Sun of righteousness, during all time. For that outpouring of the Spirit was simply the quickening of men as to their immortal faculties and connections, and as to some ways, which are latent mostly, by which human beings are "members one of another," whether in the flesh, or out of it. And that "manifestation of the Spirit" was "power from on high" reaching earth, through the "one Mediator between God and men, the man Christ Jesus."

But say some persons, "How was that, and how possibly could it have been? O that we could heartily think it!" And is this present a day for such a difficulty as that? In a few years, it will be possible for any common man to send his word round the earth in a moment almost, and even almost to converse simultaneously with all the chief cities of the world. Surely, for a person of ordinary intelligence, a telegraph-office ought to be a humble but sufficient hint as to the manner in which, through the Spirit, all souls, everywhere, lie open to God and his angels.

Under high heaven, everywhere, there is the Spirit of God; but rocks and graven images are not as susceptible of it as human beings; nor yet is a cannibal open to it, in the same degree, as an ascetic. And what Christianity means is that a man living in the spirit of Jesus Christ, on this earth may hope and be sure, that in some way his soul will be reached by "the Comforter which is the Holy Ghost." And the book of Acts, as the history of the Spirit, in its connection with the first age of the Christian Church, is what any man may trust to, as manifesting the condescension and love with which he himself is regarded as he goes to church as a Christian, or collects himself for meditation in his closet.

At the conversion of the Apostle to the Gentiles, I myself was contemplated in the foreknowledge of God, as much as Saul, "a Jew of Tarsus, a city in Cilicia, a citizen of no mean city." And it was by the same way as that by which the promise looked when it said, as to Abraham, "In thee shall all families of the earth be blessed." And the vision, which Peter had on the seaside, at Joppa, was vouchsafed for me, just as certainly as it was in favor of a Roman centurion, at Cæsarea. And at Athens, on the hill of Mars, when Paul addressed the philosophers, Epicureans, and Stoics, as to God and the resurrection, I myself was preached unto, by the Spirit. Indeed, every miracle which is recorded in the book of Acts is connected with that Gospel, which is the life of my life, and which has been like a light shining in darkness, these many hundreds of years. And just as being of faith, I am "blessed with faithful Abraham," so also was it a matter of as great concern for me as it was for any Roman, when Paul, at Rome, "dwelt two whole years in his own hired house, and received all that came in unto him, preaching the kingdom of God, and teaching those things which concern the Lord Jesus Christ." Jew and Gentile became one in Christ. "For through him we both have access by one Spirit unto the Father. Now, therefore, ye are no more strangers and foreigners, but fellow-citizens with the saints, and of the household of God; and are built upon the foundation of the apostles and prophets, Jesus Christ himself being the chief corner-stone; in whom all the building fitly framed together groweth unto a holy temple in the Lord: in whom ye also are builded together for a habitation of God through the Spirit."

The preceding statement concerns the origin of Christianity; for the Church did not grow, as a sect grows to-day. It was not a human undertaking, and its leadership was unearthly and strange, for it chose as its instruments "the foolish things of the world." What an outburst of soul those words of Paul are! A Jew of Tarsus, and a few men in Judæa, fishermen mostly, and calling themselves apostles, were opposed to Jerusalem and the temple and the priesthood, and to the Roman Empire, and to Paganism, everywhere with its thousands of temples. "And base things of the world, and things which are despised, hath God chosen, yea, and things which are not, to bring to naught things that are; that no flesh should glory in his presence." It would seem, tone and style being considered, and time and place, that never possibly could those words have been written by Paul unless by inspiration from that Spirit, which is from everlasting to everlasting, and which can choose an earthen vessel, wherewith to demolish a kingdom. The early Church was quickened in the world by the Spirit: and visions, angels, and prophets were agencies through which it was acted upon. The Holy Ghost was advice, and courage, and inspiration; and it was waited for implicitly.

Just before Jesus was taken up, he commanded the Apostles not to leave Jerusalem, but to wait, and said, "Ye shall receive power, after that the Holy Ghost is come upon you: and ye shall be witnesses unto me both in Jerusalem, and in all Judæa, and in Samaria, and unto the uttermost part of the earth." And while they were all waiting together in one place, "suddenly there came a sound from heaven as of a rushing mighty wind, and it filled all the house where they were sitting. And there were seen tongues flashing about, like as of fire, and it rested upon every one of them, and they were all filled with the Holy Ghost, and began to speak with other tongues, as the Spirit gave them utterance." And so the Apostles and others became "lively oracles" and instruments of the Spirit. Because of a miracle at the gate of the temple, which was called Beautiful, Peter and James were placed as criminals before the high-priest. And then what Christ had said came true, "But when they shall lead you, and deliver you up, take no thought beforehand what ye shall speak, neither do ye premeditate: but whatsoever shall be given you in that hour, that speak ye: for it is not ye that speak, but the Holy Ghost." "And when they had set them in the midst, they asked, By what power or by what name have ye done this?" and, just as had been foretold, the answer which came was from "Peter, filled with the Holy Ghost." On being discharged, Peter and John joined their friends immediately. "And when they had prayed, the place was shaken where they were assembled together; and they were all filled with the Holy Ghost, and they spake the word of God with boldness." Ten years after this last incident, Peter lay in prison, between two keepers; and unceasing prayer was made for him by the Church. "And behold, the angel of the Lord came upon him, and a light shined in the prison: and he smote Peter on the side, and raised him up, saying, Arise, go quickly, and his chains fell off from his hands."

What happened to Philip was a curious instance of the manner in which men were actuated by the Spirit. He was at the city of Samaria. "And the angel of the Lord spake unto Philip, saying, Arise, and go toward the south unto the way that goeth down from Jerusalem unto Gaza." And as he went, he met a man who had been at Jerusalem to worship; and who proved to be "of great authority under Candace, queen of the Ethiopians." He "was returning, and, sitting in his chariot, read Esaias the prophet. Then the Spirit said unto Philip, Go near, and join thyself to this chariot." At the end of the conference, the Ethiopian "answered and said, I believe that Jesus Christ is the Son of God. And he commanded the chariot to stand still: and they went down both into the water, both Philip and the eunuch; and he baptized him. And when they were come up out of the water, the Spirit of the Lord caught away Philip, that the eunuch saw him no more: and he went on his way rejoicing. But Philip was found at Azotus." This was an interposition by the Holy Ghost, with which, probably, a kingdom was concerned. And it was an amazing discovery made, as to Ethiopia, in these latter times, by adventurous travellers, that it was a country which was Christian, and which, also, had churches.

But we modern Christians, ecclesiastically derive from St. Paul, the Apostle to the Gentiles, and it was with a view to us all that Paul was such a manifestation of the Spirit as he was, and that he was also himself such a wonderful interpreter, as to the Spirit. Peter, James, and Jude, and almost even John, with the rest of the apostles, are like nothing, in comparison with Paul, as to the philosophy of revelation, although he called himself, as perhaps he may have been, in some ways, "the least of the Apostles."

As to Christianity, Paul wrote to the Galatians, "It pleased God, who separated me from my mother's womb, and called me by his grace, to reveal his Son in me." And his start as an Apostle was thus. At Antioch, in the church, there were prophets; and "as they ministered to the Lord, and fasted, the Holy Ghost said, Separate me Barnabas and Saul for the work whereunto I have called them." It should be noticed, that it was by the speech of these prophets, in the church, that the Holy Ghost had its utterance. And so it was, that Paul was started as an Apostle to the Gentiles. And always afterwards, there was an opening over him, from heaven. He went through Phrygia and about Galatia, but was "forbidden of the Holy Ghost to preach the word in Asia"; and when he wished to go into Bithynia, it was not what "the Spirit suffered." Soon afterwards "a vision appeared to Paul in the night; there stood a man of Macedonia, and prayed him, saying, Come over into Macedonia, and help us. And after he had seen the vision, immediately we endeavored to go into Macedonia, assuredly gathering that the Lord had called us for to preach the gospel unto them." A year after this, Paul was at Athens, and by a few words of his on the hill of Mars, Plato and Epicurus were surpassed. From Athens he went to Corinth, where he was rejected by most of the Jews. And in that city, he lodged with a man whose house was close to the synagogue. "Then spake the Lord to Paul in the night by a vision, Be not afraid, but speak, and hold not thy peace; for I am with thee, and no man shall set on thee to hurt thee: for I have much people in this city." In connection with this vision, it is well to remember how famous the name of Corinth has been ever since, because of the "manifestation of the Spirit" in the church there, and as to which Paul wrote. After some five or six years, Paul was at Miletus, whence he sent for the elders of the church at Ephesus; because he was feeling himself hedged in upon a road, from which he could not hold back, and because of which "they should see his face no more." He reviewed his life amongst them; and he exhorted them; and he prayed with them. And a very affecting time it was. "And now, behold, I go bound in the spirit unto Jerusalem, not knowing the things that shall befall me there: save that the Holy Ghost witnesseth in every city, saying that bonds and afflictions abide me." At Jerusalem, the high-priest Ananias was awaiting him; and also the Lord, in a vision; and at Malta, a shipwreck was about to be his experience.

Paul had advanced to Cæsarea, when there happened a curious incident, as to the manner in which the Holy Ghost would sometimes express itself. "And as we tarried there many days, there came down from Judæa a certain prophet, named Agabus. And when he was come unto us, he took Paul's girdle, and bound his own hands and feet, and said, Thus saith the Holy Ghost, so shall the Jews at Jerusalem bind the man that owneth this girdle, and shall deliver him into the hands of the Gentiles." On the stairs of the castle, at Jerusalem, Paul though in custody, had leave to speak, which he did in Hebrew. And he told of the manner of his conversion at Damascus, and of his hearing Jesus speak, and also of his return afterwards to Jerusalem, where he both saw Christ and heard him. "And it came to pass, that, when I was come again to Jerusalem, even while I prayed in the temple, I was in a trance; and saw him saying unto me, Make haste, and get thee quickly out of Jerusalem: for they will not receive thy testimony concerning me. And I said, Lord, they know that I imprisoned and beat in every synagogue them that believed on thee: and when the blood of thy martyr Stephen was shed, I also was standing by, and consenting unto his death, and kept the raiment of them that slew him. And he said unto me, Depart; for I will send thee far hence unto the Gentiles." By these words, then and on the next day, the Jews were greatly enraged. "And when there arose a great dissension, the chief captain, fearing lest Paul should have been pulled in pieces of them, commanded the soldiers to go down, and to take him by force from among them, and to bring him into the castle. And the night following the Lord stood by him, and said, Be of good cheer, Paul; for as thou hast testified of me in Jerusalem, so must thou bear witness also at Rome." On the voyage to Italy, the vessel in which he was embarked, was in great danger for a long time. But said Paul, "There stood by me this night the angel of God, whose I am, and whom I serve, saying, Fear not, Paul; thou must be brought before Cæsar: and, lo, God hath given thee all them that sail with thee."

The preceding two or three pages, not one person in ten will read intelligently, without being much surprised. Such talk as there has been, and such folly also as to the Fathers of the Church, and the Founders! Not Augustine, great, good man as he was, nor anybody between him and St. Clement, nor yet St. Clement himself, ought ever to have been accounted as a Father. And were James and John and Peter and Paul truly founders of the Church, though so often they have been so called? No founders at all were they; for they were but "earthen vessels," as Paul himself would have said. Precisely, they were mere earthen vessels, through which the Spirit could speak among men, and act.

The true Church is the Church of the Spirit. And it is not anything, either as to place or state of intelligence, wherein one believer can say, "I am of Paul; and another, I am of Apollos." O the grandeur, spiritually, of those words of Paul himself! They are the words of an Apostle, who was so great, as to the Spirit, because, partly, of his ability for self-humiliation. And these are the words, "Who then is Paul, and who is Apollos, but ministers by whom ye believed, even as the Lord gave to every man? I have planted, Apollos watered, but God gave the increase. So, then, neither is he that planteth anything, neither he that watereth, but God that giveth the increase."

But there is something more yet to be learned from the history of Paul. He was converted in a moment. And what happened to Saul the persecutor, is what is possible, in some degree, for everybody, at this present day. For though Jesus does not now appear in vision, yet "because ye are sons, God hath sent forth the Spirit of his Son into your hearts."

It was, as they were taught by the Comforter, and as they had things brought to their remembrance by the Holy Ghost, that the Apostles came at last to understand what their Master had been and was become. It was by the Spirit that they were endowed and sent and guided as Apostles.

The discipleship of Paul began very differently from that of the other Apostles. Perhaps, personally, he had never "known Christ after the flesh," and it is certain that he assisted at the martyrdom of Stephen. Paul was the convert of Christ in glory. And in Paul, Judaism itself was converted, and became luminous with the Spirit, and a witness for Christ. It was in spirit that Paul saw and heard Jesus; and even the gospel, which he preached, he had by the Spirit. He speaks of there being to be a judgment of "the secrets of men by Jesus Christ according to my gospel." He tells of a meeting at Jerusalem, with which even Peter was concerned, and says, "But of these who seemed to be somewhat, (whatsoever they were, it maketh no matter to me: God accepteth no man's person:) for they who seemed to be somewhat in conference added nothing to me." And what even he told the Corinthians, as to the Lord's Supper, was what Jesus Christ had told him. "For I have received of the Lord that which also I delivered unto you, That the Lord Jesus the same night in which he was betrayed took bread: and when he had given thanks, he brake it, and said, Take, eat: this is my body, which is broken for you: this do in remembrance of me."

That last evening of the earthly life of Jesus was the subject of a revelation to Paul. Does that seem to be a strange, inconceivable thing? Yet it is incredible, altogether, only because of inconsideration. In common life, there are things which might hint psychologically, as to its possibility. And an electric telegram is no mean argument as to its probability.

When "suddenly there shone from heaven a great light round about"; and when a voice was heard saying, "I am Jesus of Nazareth whom thou persecutest," it may well have been that electrically, magnetically, spiritually, Jesus was revealed in the mind of Paul, with all the suddenness of a flash, and the fulness of a gospel. For that voice which was heard was the voice of Jesus himself, and therefore of all that ever Jesus had been, or thought, or done, or endured.

Twenty-four years after his conversion, Paul wrote his Epistle to the Galatians, in which he tells of what his zeal and knowledge had been as a Jew; and of its having pleased God to reveal his Son in him; and of the little intercourse which he had ever had with the other Apostles. "But I certify you, brethren, that the gospel which was preached of me is not after man. For I neither received it of man, neither was I taught it, but by the revelation of Jesus Christ."

Perhaps it was because of his state theologically as well as fervently, that Paul was approachable, for conversion, in the way through which he was, by Christ in glory. And in the history of Christianity, and as concerning its development, it is certainly a very significant fact, that the Spirit should have obtained its broadest, deepest, and highest interpretation through a man who was not even one of the twelve.

It would seem to be of the essence of Christianity, that "Christ is the head of the Church," and that "the head of Christ is God." Times and seasons may not always be the same for the Church, any more than they are for the world, which changes from day to day, with the course of time and the discoveries of science. And Jesus, at "the head of all principality and power," and with many millions of souls calling themselves by his name, in regard to interest and administration, may be as certainly "the Shepherd and Bishop of your souls" as when he came within sight of Stephen, when he was about to be martyred, or as when he showed himself on a plane, so near to this earth, as that Paul could hear him speak. Miracles are not for every age perhaps, and certainly not for every day and hour, or else they would soon cease to be " signs and wonders."

Says St. Paul, " No man can say that Jesus is the Lord but by the Holy Ghost." No doubt this sentiment is in accordance with the manner of his own conversion. But yet what person is there to-day, who has that knowledge as to the Spirit, for which, reasonably, Paul ought to be credited? And it is plain, that we live by our affinities spiritually, as surely as our bodies last on, by those affinities, which they have for air and food, through the lungs and the stomach. An earnest aspiration is the opening of a channel between man and God: and an act in the spirit of Christ is affinity with him, wherever he may be. And there are ways which psychology knows of, and as to which even the science of nature has its corroborations, by which it would seem that the recognition of Jesus as " the head over all things to the church," might be as simple as the way by which the eye finds the place of the sun at noonday. It is true, that every day is not clear at noon; and it is true, also, that many a man is living by the Holy Ghost, who cannot think himself that he is living so, because of his humility, or because of his " philosophy falsely so called."

There must be spiritual affinity in some way, however humble, before a person can be reached by the Holy Ghost; for a statue of stone has never yet been quickened. And Jerusalem, which is from above, has many ways which reach down towards this earth, but they do not open in every age, and over all places, alike.

The philosophy of the whole material universe is involved in my body, and in its various organs and faculties, — in my eyes, ears, lungs, heart, and ability for action. In the atmosphere of the sun, there can be no great disturbance, but it reports itself in me. And myself, I could not go to New York, probably, but the planet Uranus would have some sense of my journey. And now is it not strange that my body, my old coat of clay, should be so wonderful; and yet that it should be so hard for me to believe in my spiritual relations, and even in the mere possibility of there being either help for me, or detriment in the invisible? And yet there is nothing more simple and natural, if only I could think so, than that with believing in the God and the Father of our Lord Jesus Christ, I should have the Spirit of His Son come in upon my soul.

Before a man can see, he must open his eyes and look. As to God, it is written that " without faith it is impossible to please him," — faith enough, that is to say, for making a man open his eyes and consider. " For he that cometh to God must believe that he is, and that he is a rewarder of them that diligently seek him." Widely different as to spiritual results are even these two states, — that of denial as to spiritual influences, and that of expectant dependence on heaven, even when doubtful as to whether it has itself ever been met. But, indeed, probably there is not a thought which I have of any weight, but is the weightier because of some personage or law of the spiritual world. It was a glorious utterance of Christ, which concerned me, personally, when arguing from parental love as to its readiness with children, he exclaimed, "How much more shall your heavenly Father give the Holy Spirit to them that ask him?" As a Christian, I am cautioned against incidentally incurring a condition, wherein Satan might tempt me. On my repentance of evil, I am told that there is joy among the angels of God. And I know that in my true prayers, "the Spirit itself maketh intercession" for me. All round my spiritual sphere, I am open; and it is at my own choice, whether or not I will be divinely connected. And just as I was "blest with faithful Abraham," so also was I involved spiritually in the history of the Jewish Church. And every miracle which is recorded in the New Testament happened on my behalf. The messengers who went to Peter, at Joppa, were a deputation on my behalf, because of a vision, which a centurion had. And when Paul was converted, it was partly because I was one of the Gentiles, for whom he was to be started as an Apostle. And those miracles, and all the other miracles of the Scriptures are signs, or sign-posts, by which it was intended that we Christians should be aided in placing ourselves aright as to mental attitude before Heaven, and conformably also with those forces, invisible and occult, which sweep round the world, and which sometimes aid in shaping the souls of men, and sometimes also in confounding them.

What then! are we to be expecting the age of the Apostles over again, and those manifestations of the

Spirit, by which it was accompanied? No! for never does time go backward: and also the administration, which is from above always is providential and ongoing. And truly, many of the gifts, by which the Spirit manifested itself in the earliest days of the Church, ought to-day to be accounted but like food for "babes in Christ." But yet not improbably, they may all reappear, in the Church, for a time, when people shall begin to be doubtful about the rationalism and ritualism, and the mere way of tradition, by which, respectively, to a great degree, they have been living "in a vain show" of Christianity. And indeed it is possible, that the Spirit may be more ready with its minor manifestations than many Christians can easily suppose.

The gifts of the Spirit are not all of them of the same significance: just as the faculties, by which man is better than dogs, are not of uniform excellence. The mere working of miracles does not argue as much power mentally, as the discerning of spirits. The faculty of speaking in divers kinds of tongues might be worthless almost, unless a person were present with a gift for the interpretation of tongues. And even the two gifts conjointly, would apparently, by St. Paul, have been accounted inferior to "the word of wisdom." Also a man might have the Spirit manifest itself through him, without his being, himself, in the least degree, the better for it; for by "the word of wisdom" a man might be the mouthpiece of power from above, and yet himself remain unenlightened, though a wonder all the while, and a spectacle to angels and men. The Spirit can do better than quicken the nature of man superficially, even though thereby, for the time, it may be made to flash with wonders.

The Spirit, as to manifestation, finds and takes us human beings, as its instruments, according to its own wisdom. And, therefore, among the twelve, there was a Judas, in order that the other eleven might plainly seem to be "earthen vessels." The manifestation of the Spirit, through individuals, by signs and wonders, is but an indication, on the surface, of those powers by which men are all influenced, as being the offspring of God. And Paul, and Peter, and Ananias of Damascus, and Cornelius, a centurion of the Italian band, are instances of the manner in which men are divinely dealt with, as individuals and as nations both.

And at this present time, the Spirit may be trusted for some other manifestations than what were made through Jews and Gentiles eighteen centuries ago. Age after age, more and more susceptible of the fashioning power of the Spirit, did this earth become as it slowly grew into shape, and supported the creatures that swarmed and raced about it. Progress is recognized as being a law as to human beings, even though the way of it may be through darkness often, and with convulsions for its footsteps. And in the Christian Church it cannot be otherwise, than that with ripening under heaven, one generation after another, souls on earth should generally have become susceptible through the Spirit to some diviner issues than could well have been manifested while Nero was emperor of the world, or than even at the time when Constantine became a Christian, and the first Christian emperor of Rome. And if only a little something more were developed as to its state, or supplied, never would the world have been as open to the Spirit as it is at this time, by predispositions accruing from politics, and from science, and from good-will among men towards one another.

In that region, whence we mortals are acted upon spiritually, it is written "that one day is with the Lord as a thousand years, and a thousand years as one day." Probably it is far off as yet, still, as St. Paul would say, it is nearer than when we Christians first believed, — that New Jerusalem, which St. John saw in vision, and as to which he said, "I John saw the holy city, New Jerusalem, coming down from God out of heaven, prepared as a bride adorned for her husband." And latterly men prophetic, in one way and another, have had sight of that New Jerusalem as an ideal, without well knowing what it was, and have thereby become reformers as to the ways of this world. And poets, in the quiet of meditation, have felt their souls strangely attuned, without suspecting, perhaps, that it was by the music which is made by heaven as it draws nearer to earth.

The agonizing doubts which many Christians are having, are but the throes of souls in bondage to creeds, who are struggling, unconsciously, for "the glorious liberty of the children of God." At this time every sect almost, and even the Papal, is more sharply divided against itself than it is against its neighbors. And this is because of that quickening of the Spirit, which mere traditionary belief cannot endure, and always resists. What was said to the disciples, by Jesus Christ, as to the end of the world, involves the philosophy of the universe, intellectually, as to its grander periods. And wars and rumors of wars, of which there have latterly been so many, and earthquakes and pestilences in different places, and the rise of false prophets are signs of the times, and of the pressure downwards of power from on high. Jesus said to the disciples, "I came not to send peace but a sword," and this was because even of his being the Prince of Peace; for there is nothing which so exasperates evil as the presence of goodness. Also, of the nature of the times, wherein we are living, Spiritualism is evidence, for it finds that the veil is grown thin, which separates between us denizens of nature and some of the dwellers in the sphere of spirit; and it shows also that civilized people are, psychically, more sensitive, at the present moment, than probably they ever have been before. The heavens are being bowed towards the earth; and there are signs of the nearer coming of the Son of Man, even though from a quarter where indeed a thousand years are as one day. It may be a long while, before the kingdoms of this world will become the suburbs of the New Jerusalem; but yet of that city of God as archetypal there is more thought in the minds of men to-day, than ever there has been before; and slowly but surely the ways of this world, politically, are being drawn out, in a manner, by which they can be met, by those streets which reach down, spiritually, from above.

Already there is about us the atmosphere of "that great city, the holy Jerusalem, descending out of heaven." And happy are they who have any sense of it! For thereby they have become kings and priests unto God and the Father, and are clear of this earth as to priestcraft and darkness.

Let those who are "taught of the Lord" teach what they learn. Let those who have "joy in the Holy Ghost" not fear to show it. Let those who are quickened from within as to righteousness, they know not how, trust that perhaps they are prophets of the Spirit. And let every one who catches a strain, like the song which John heard in the Spirit, repeat it as best he can for his fellow-creatures.

"Great and marvellous are thy works, Lord God Almighty; just and true are thy ways, thou King of saints."

INDEXES.

INDEX TO TEXTS QUOTED.

INDEX OF SUBJECTS.

THE END.

Cambridge: Electrotyped and Printed by Welch, Bigelow, & Co.

www.ingramcontent.com/pod-product-compliance
Lightning Source LLC
LaVergne TN
LVHW021313110826
845150LV00003B/554

* 9 7 8 1 4 2 5 5 5 8 1 8 5 *